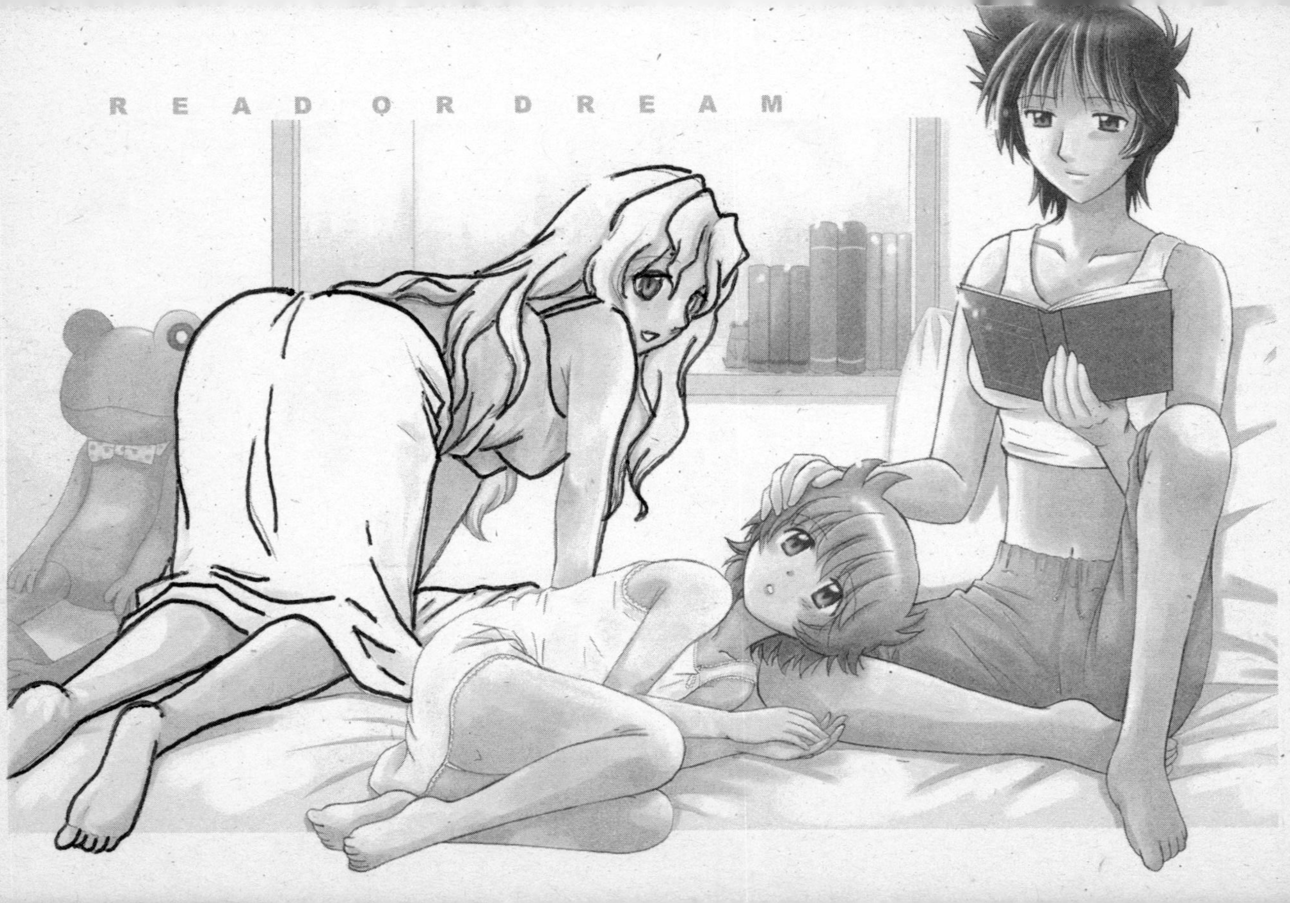
READ OR DREAM

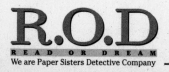

R.O.D
READ OR DREAM
We are Paper Sisters Detective Company

R.O.D
READ OR DREAM

We are Paper Sisters Detective Company

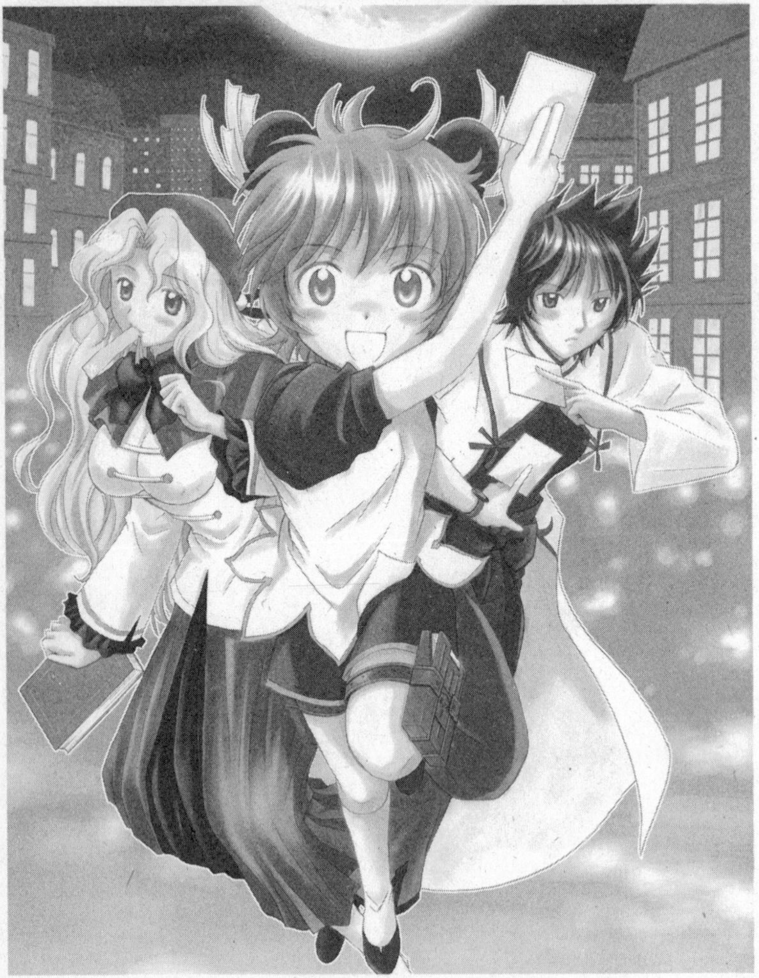

Story by Hideyuki Kurata
Art by Ran Ayanaga

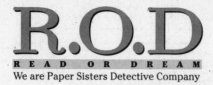

R.O.D
READ OR DREAM
We are Paper Sisters Detective Company

C O N T E N T S

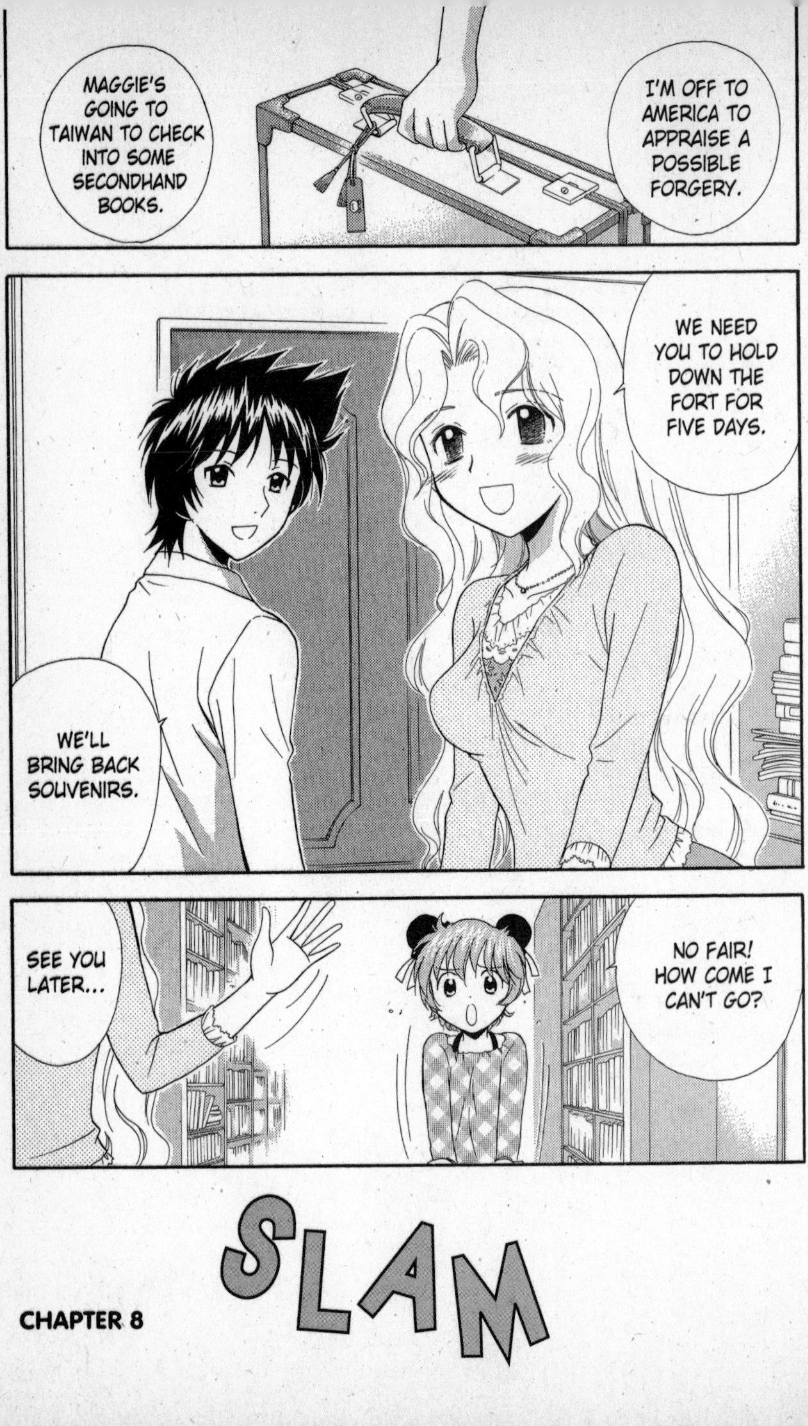
I'M OFF TO AMERICA TO APPRAISE A POSSIBLE FORGERY.
MAGGIE'S GOING TO TAIWAN TO CHECK INTO SOME SECONDHAND BOOKS.
WE NEED YOU TO HOLD DOWN THE FORT FOR FIVE DAYS.
WE'LL BRING BACK SOUVENIRS.
NO FAIR! HOW COME I CAN'T GO?
SEE YOU LATER...
SLAM

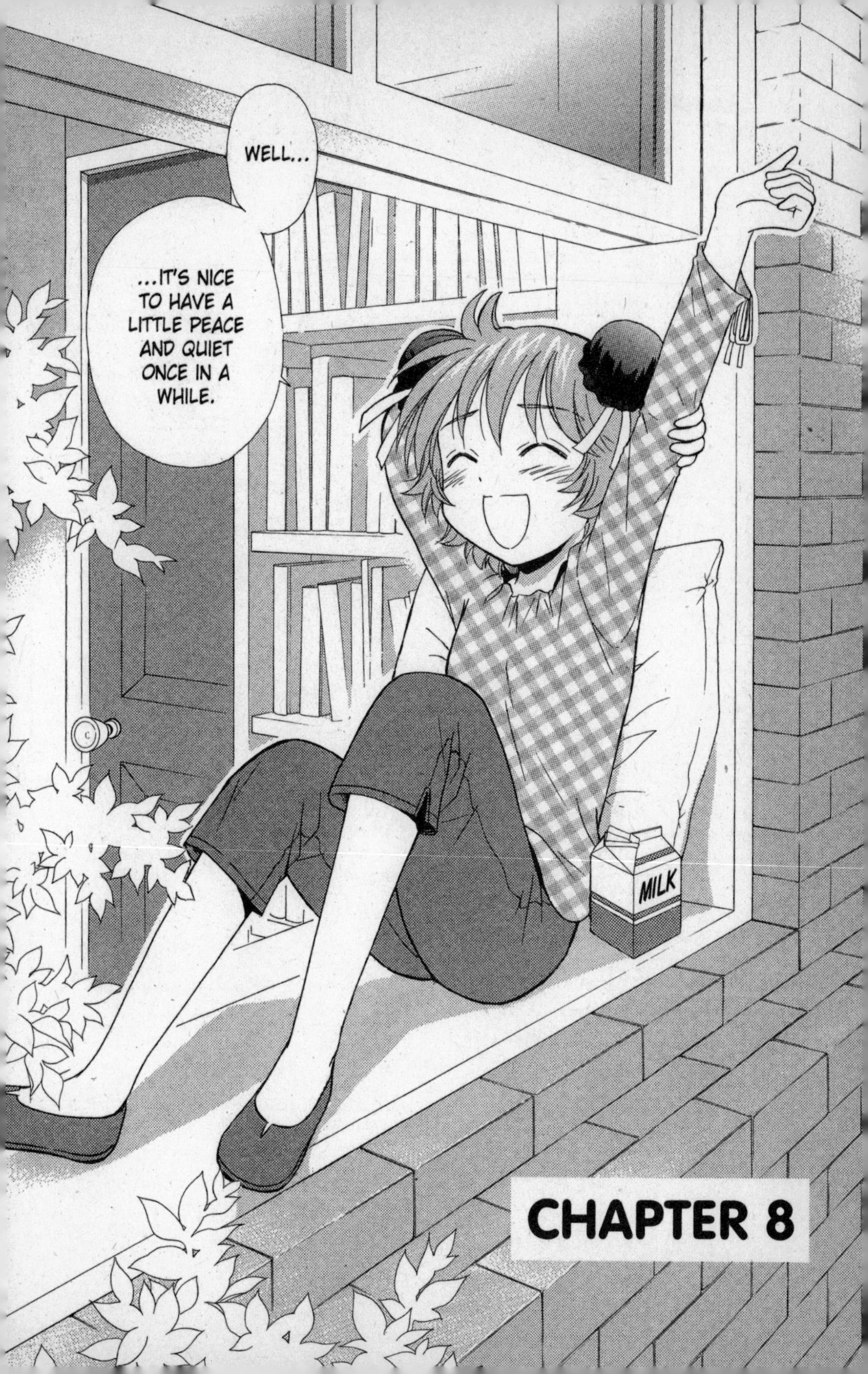
WELL...
...IT'S NICE TO HAVE A LITTLE PEACE AND QUIET ONCE IN A WHILE.
MILK
CHAPTER 8

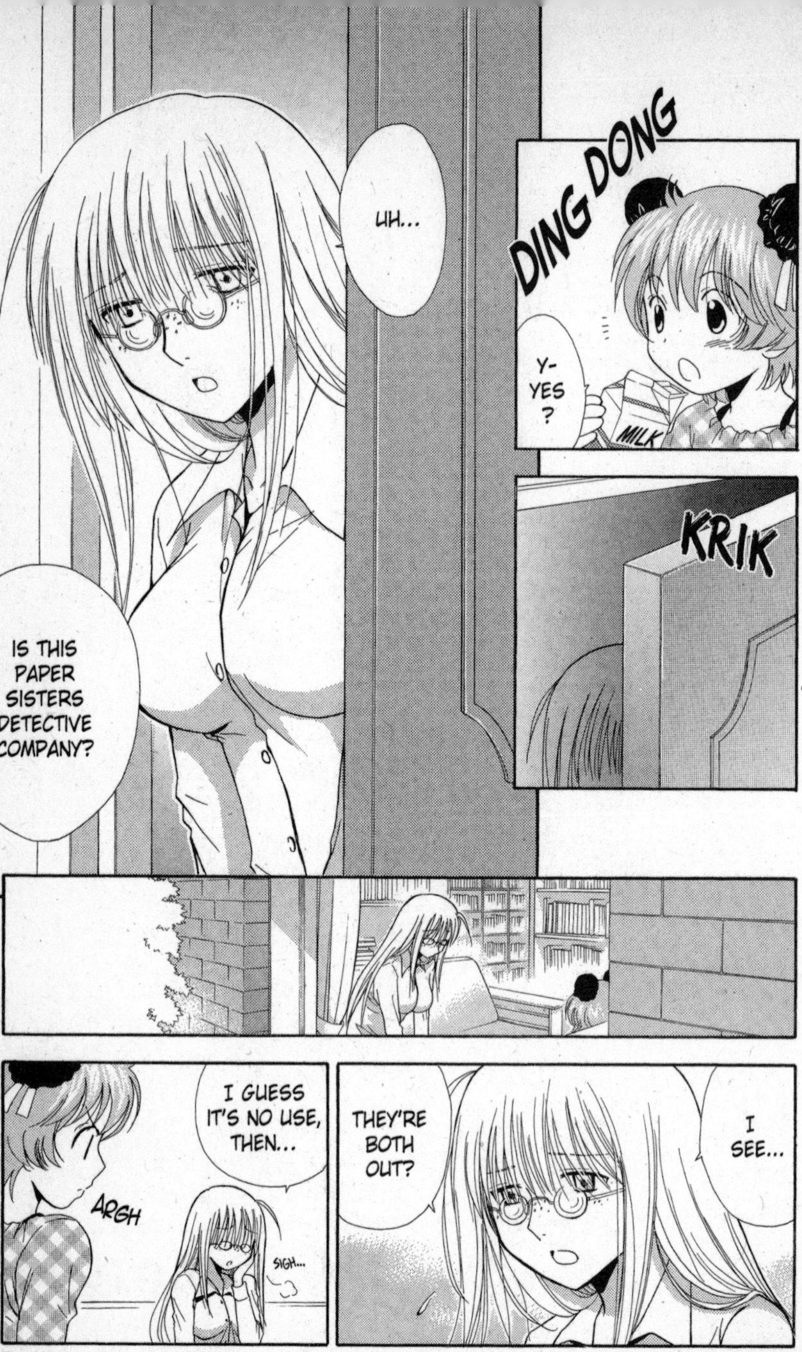
DING DONG
Y-YES?
MILK
KRIK
UH...
IS THIS PAPER SISTERS DETECTIVE COMPANY?
I SEE...
THEY'RE BOTH OUT?
I GUESS IT'S NO USE, THEN...
ARGH
SIGH...

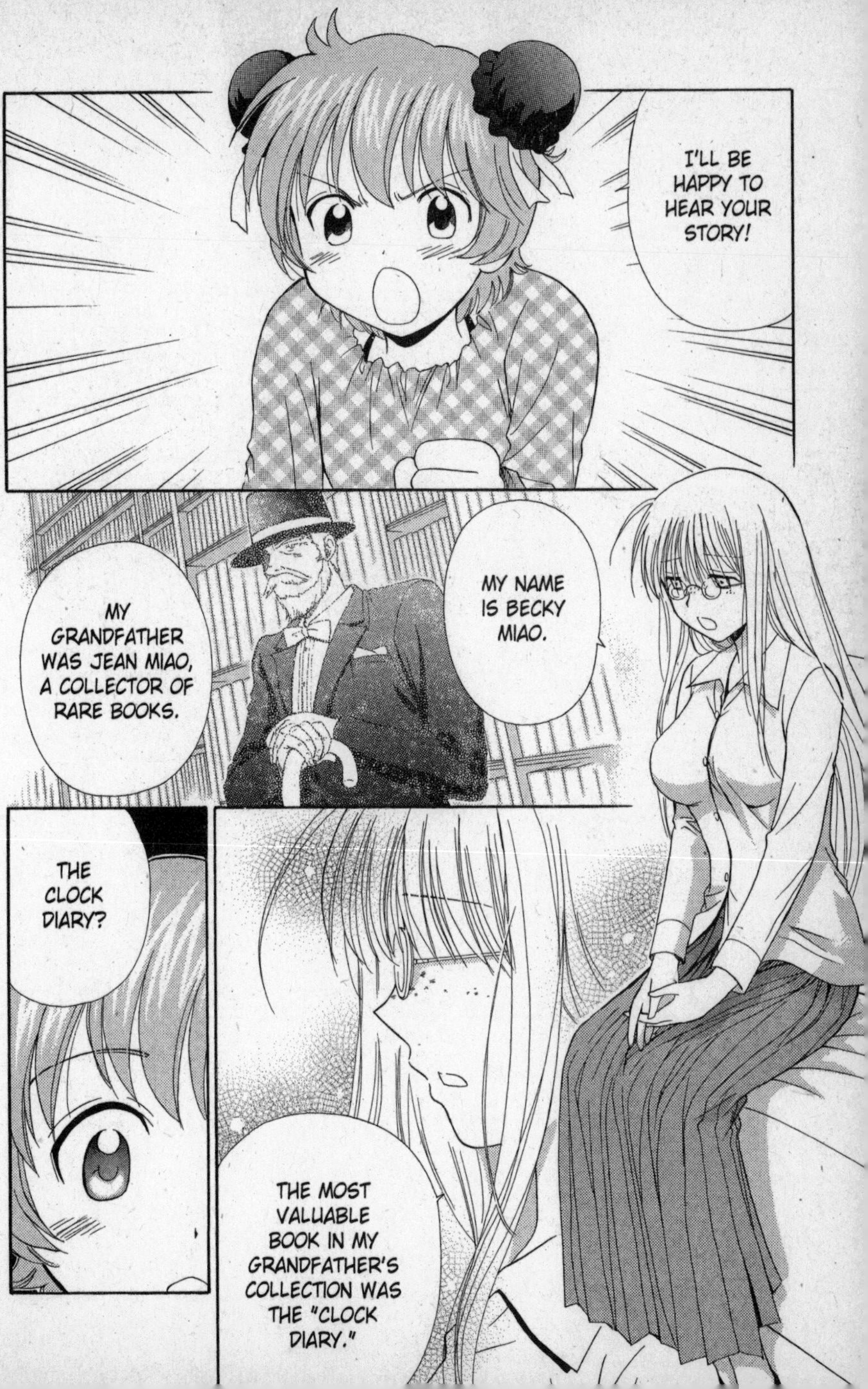
I'LL BE HAPPY TO HEAR YOUR STORY!
MY NAME IS BECKY MIAO.
MY GRANDFATHER WAS JEAN MIAO, A COLLECTOR OF RARE BOOKS.
THE MOST VALUABLE BOOK IN MY GRANDFATHER'S COLLECTION WAS THE "CLOCK DIARY."
THE CLOCK DIARY?

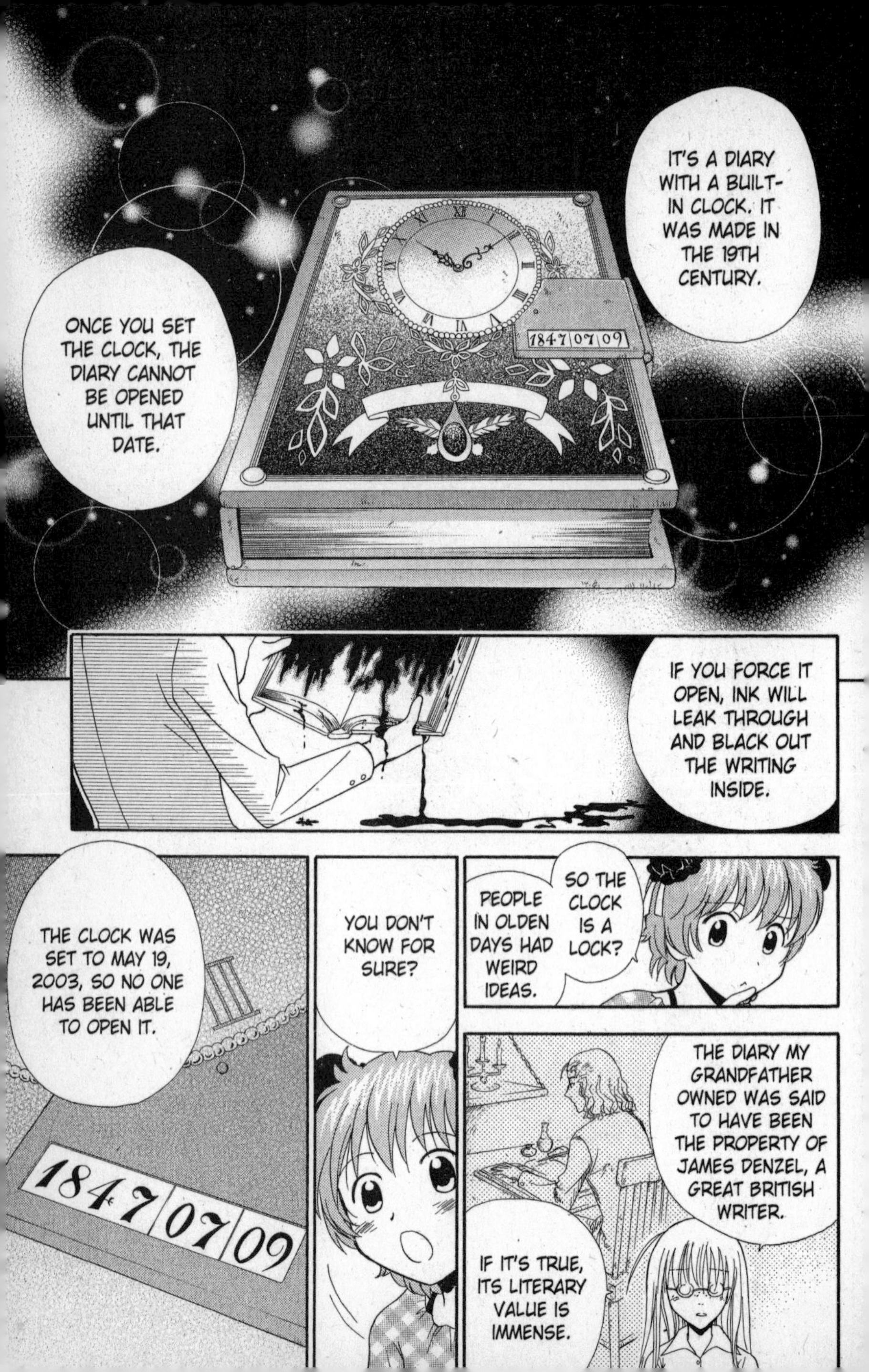
IT'S A DIARY WITH A BUILT-IN CLOCK. IT WAS MADE IN THE 19TH CENTURY.
1847 07 09
ONCE YOU SET THE CLOCK, THE DIARY CANNOT BE OPENED UNTIL THAT DATE.
IF YOU FORCE IT OPEN, INK WILL LEAK THROUGH AND BLACK OUT THE WRITING INSIDE.
SO THE CLOCK IS A LOCK?
PEOPLE IN OLDEN DAYS HAD WEIRD IDEAS.
THE DIARY MY GRANDFATHER OWNED WAS SAID TO HAVE BEEN THE PROPERTY OF JAMES DENZEL, A GREAT BRITISH WRITER.
IF IT'S TRUE, ITS LITERARY VALUE IS IMMENSE.
YOU DON'T KNOW FOR SURE?
THE CLOCK WAS SET TO MAY 19, 2003, SO NO ONE HAS BEEN ABLE TO OPEN IT.
1847 07 09

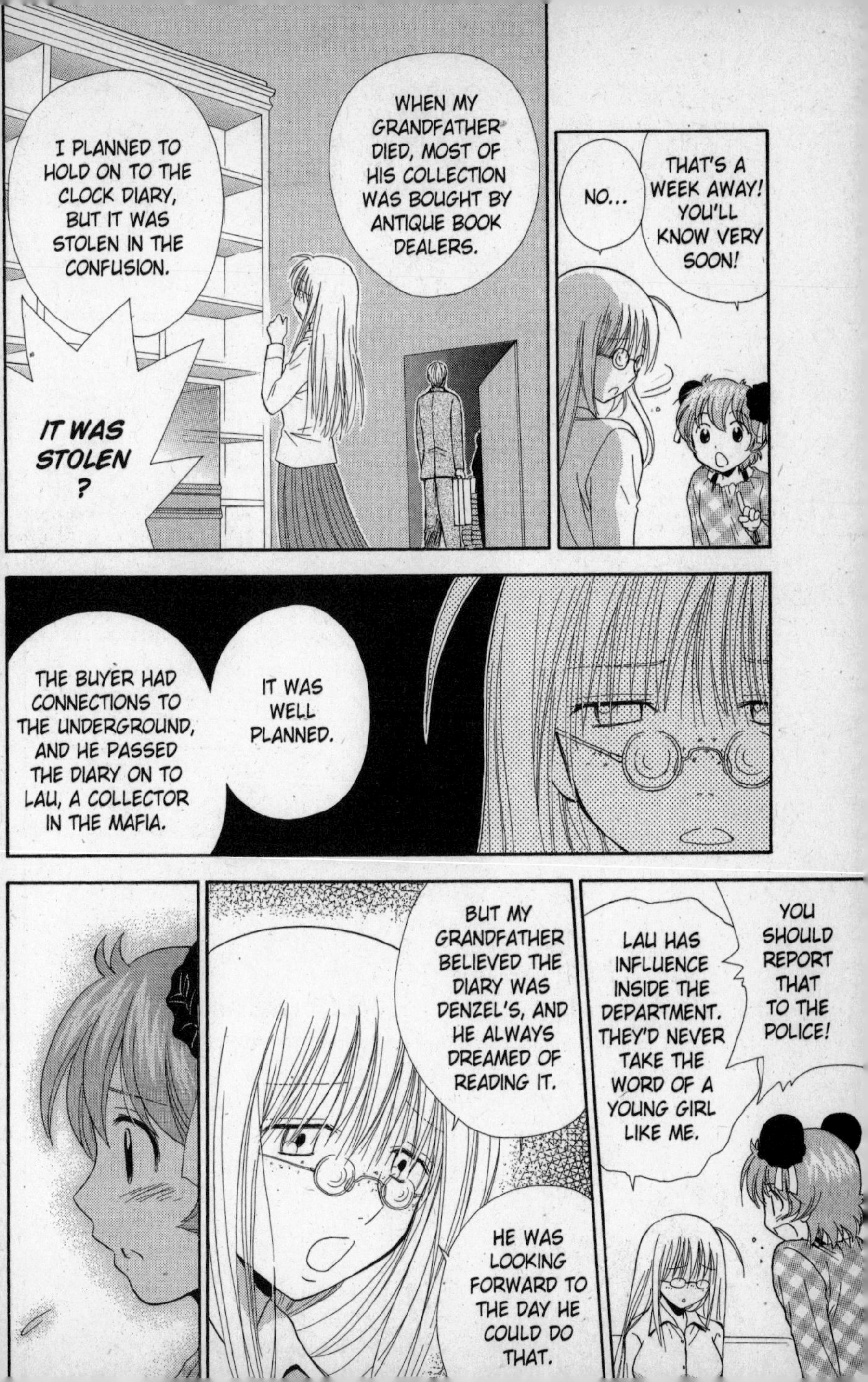
THAT'S A WEEK AWAY! YOU'LL KNOW VERY SOON!
NO...
WHEN MY GRANDFATHER DIED, MOST OF HIS COLLECTION WAS BOUGHT BY ANTIQUE BOOK DEALERS.
I PLANNED TO HOLD ON TO THE CLOCK DIARY, BUT IT WAS STOLEN IN THE CONFUSION.
IT WAS STOLEN?
IT WAS WELL PLANNED.
THE BUYER HAD CONNECTIONS TO THE UNDERGROUND, AND HE PASSED THE DIARY ON TO LAU, A COLLECTOR IN THE MAFIA.
YOU SHOULD REPORT THAT TO THE POLICE!
LAU HAS INFLUENCE INSIDE THE DEPARTMENT. THEY'D NEVER TAKE THE WORD OF A YOUNG GIRL LIKE ME.
BUT MY GRANDFATHER BELIEVED THE DIARY WAS DENZEL'S, AND HE ALWAYS DREAMED OF READING IT.
HE WAS LOOKING FORWARD TO THE DAY HE COULD DO THAT.

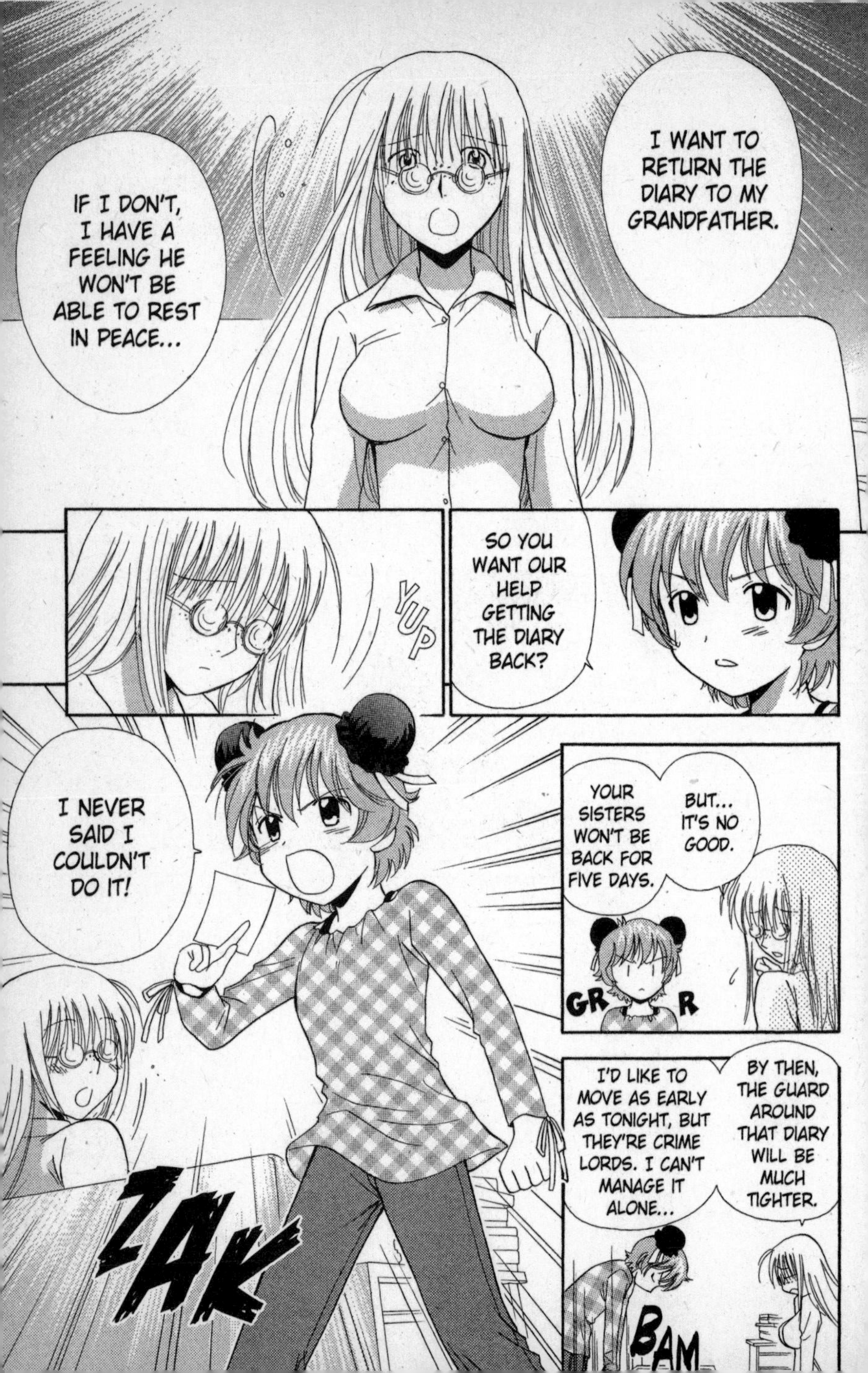
I WANT TO RETURN THE DIARY TO MY GRANDFATHER.
IF I DON'T, I HAVE A FEELING HE WON'T BE ABLE TO REST IN PEACE...
SO YOU WANT OUR HELP GETTING THE DIARY BACK?
YUP
BUT... IT'S NO GOOD.
YOUR SISTERS WON'T BE BACK FOR FIVE DAYS.
GR R
BY THEN, THE GUARD AROUND THAT DIARY WILL BE MUCH TIGHTER.
I'D LIKE TO MOVE AS EARLY AS TONIGHT, BUT THEY'RE CRIME LORDS. I CAN'T MANAGE IT ALONE...
BAM
I NEVER SAID I COULDN'T DO IT!
ZAK

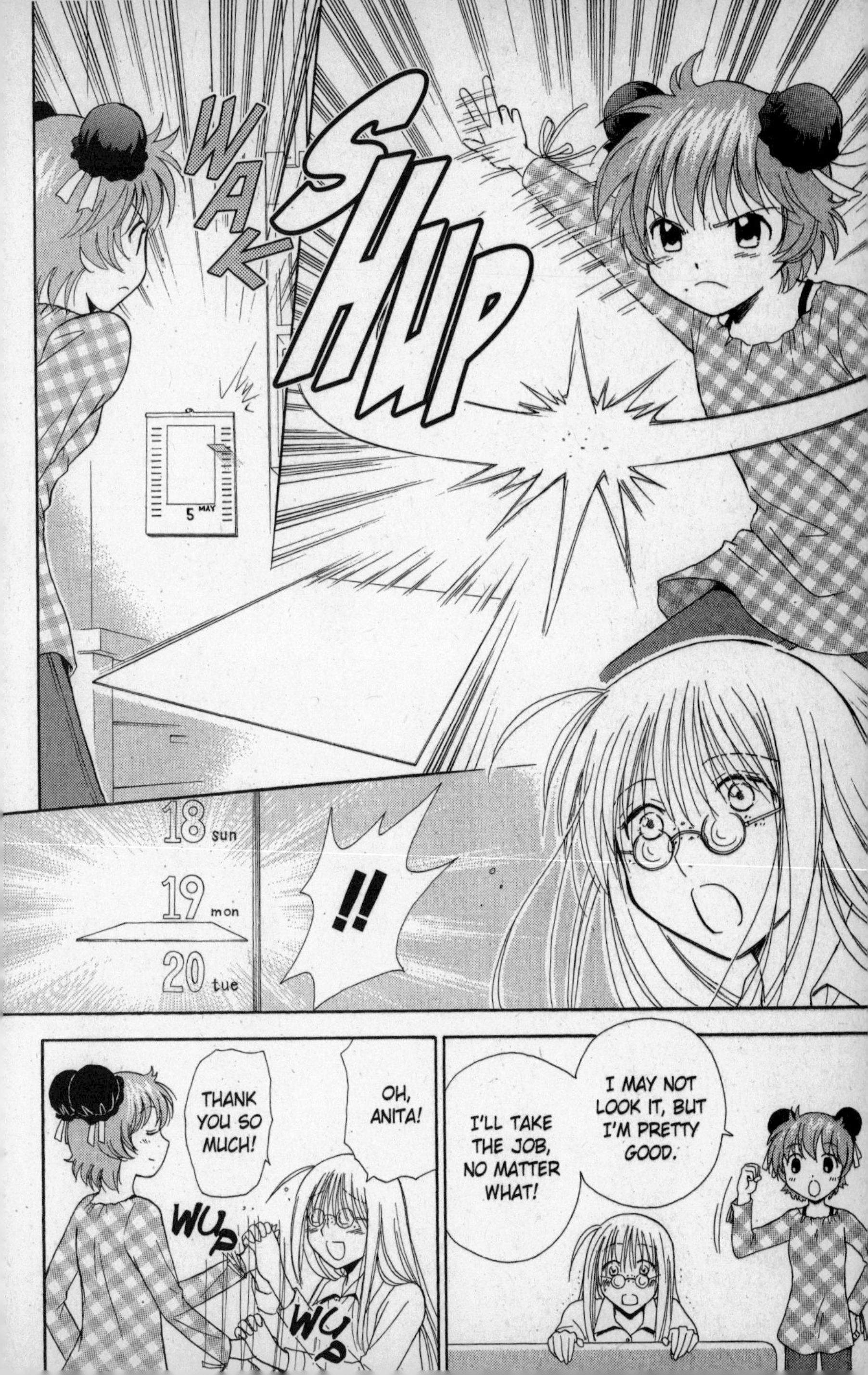
SHUP
WAK
5 MAY
18 sun
19 mon
20 tue
!!
I MAY NOT LOOK IT, BUT I'M PRETTY GOOD.
I'LL TAKE THE JOB, NO MATTER WHAT!
OH, ANITA!
THANK YOU SO MUCH!
WUP
WUP

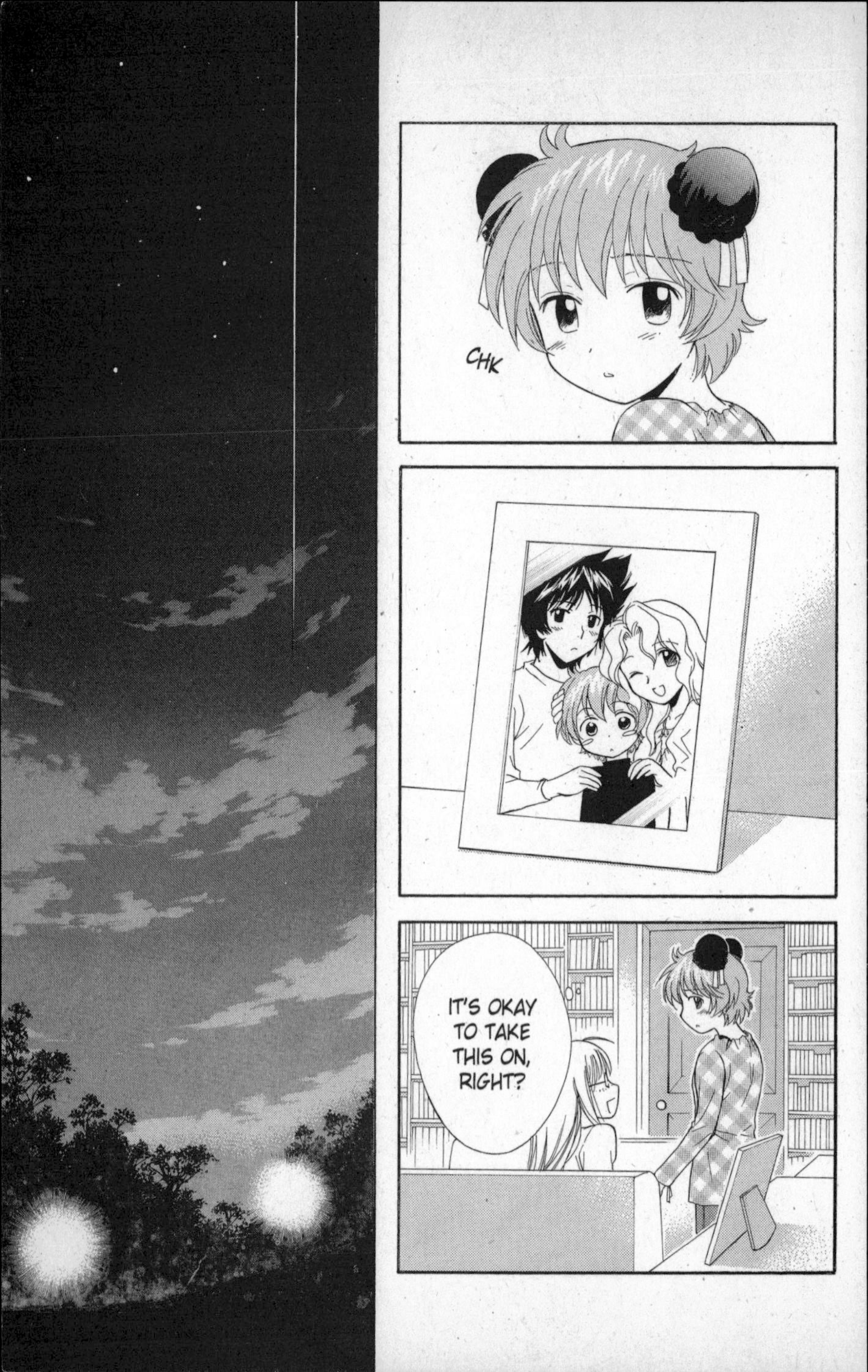
CHK
IT'S OKAY TO TAKE THIS ON, RIGHT?

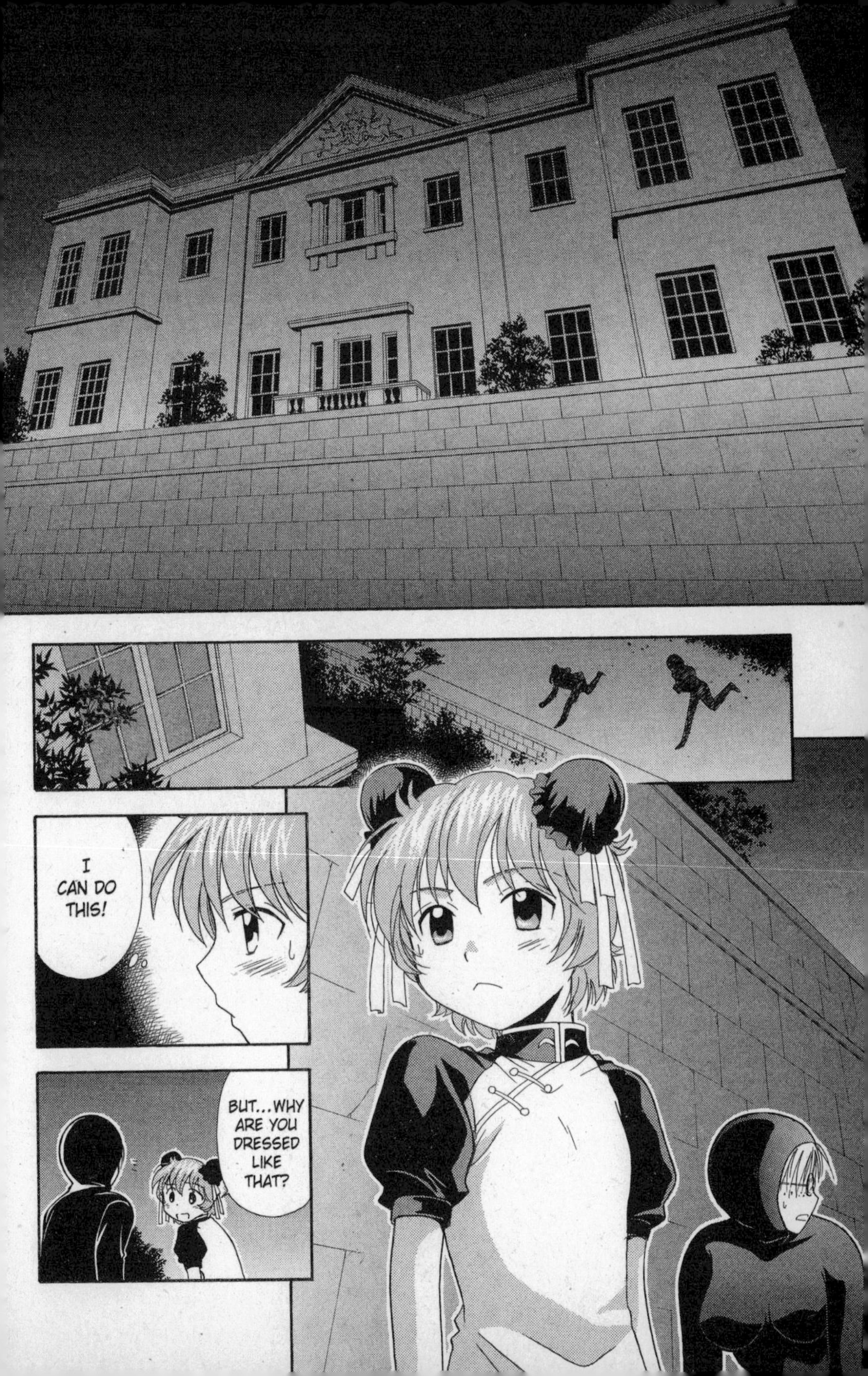
I CAN DO THIS!
BUT...WHY ARE YOU DRESSED LIKE THAT?

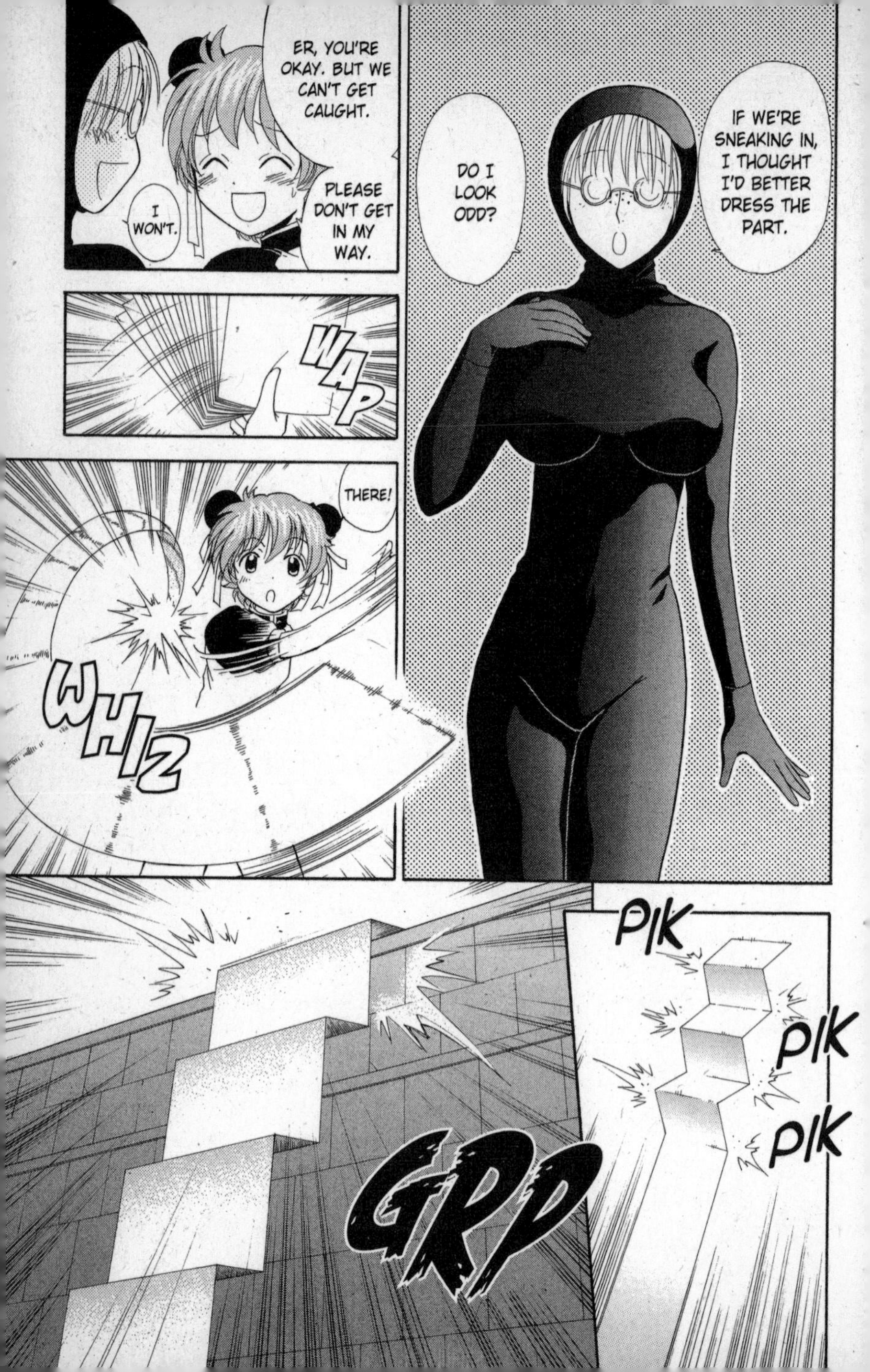
IF WE'RE SNEAKING IN, I THOUGHT I'D BETTER DRESS THE PART.
DO I LOOK ODD?
ER, YOU'RE OKAY. BUT WE CAN'T GET CAUGHT.
PLEASE DON'T GET IN MY WAY.
I WON'T.
WAP
THERE!
WHIZ
PIK
PIK
PIK
GRP

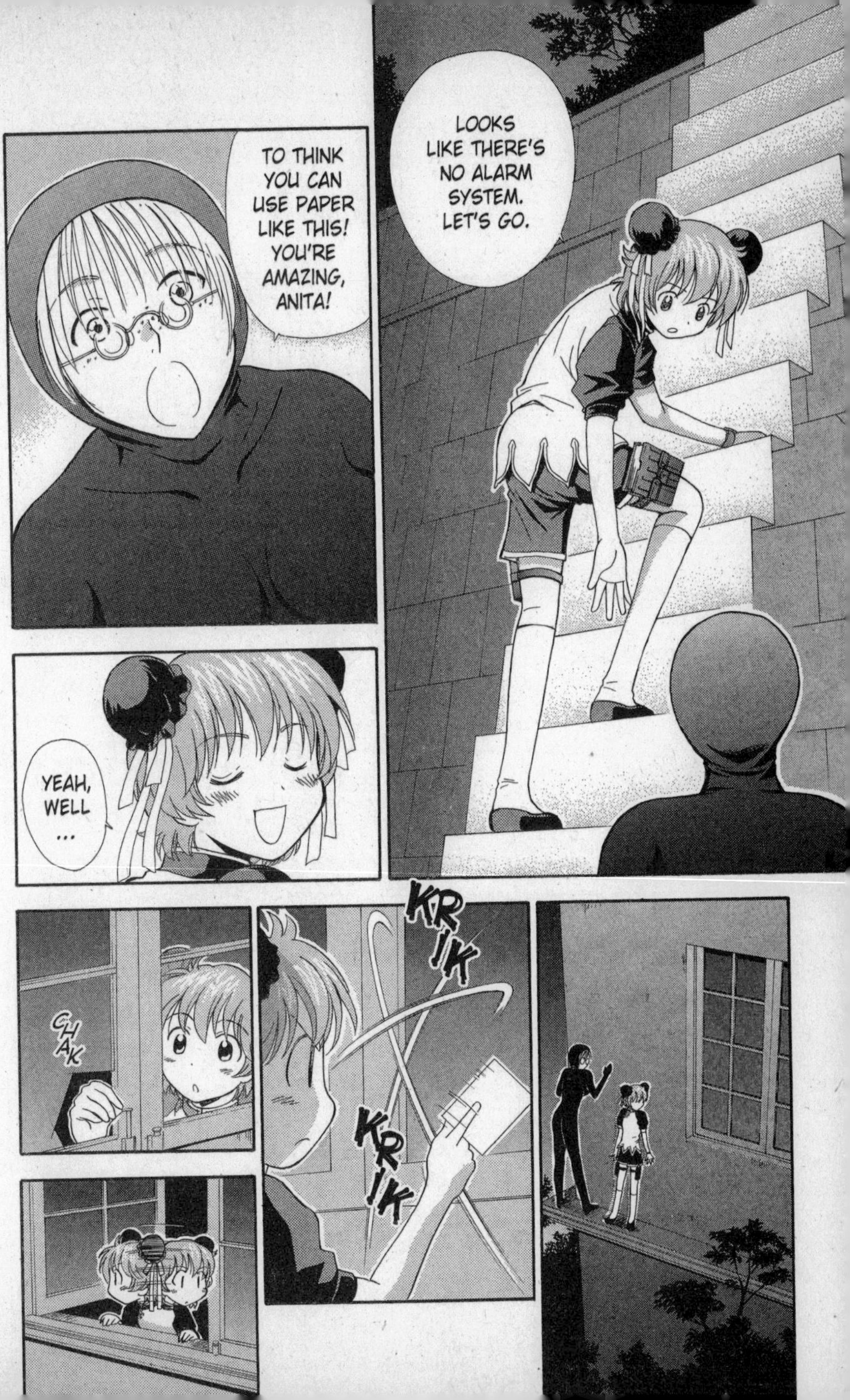
LOOKS LIKE THERE'S NO ALARM SYSTEM. LET'S GO.
TO THINK YOU CAN USE PAPER LIKE THIS! YOU'RE AMAZING, ANITA!
YEAH, WELL ...
KRIK
KRIK
CHAK

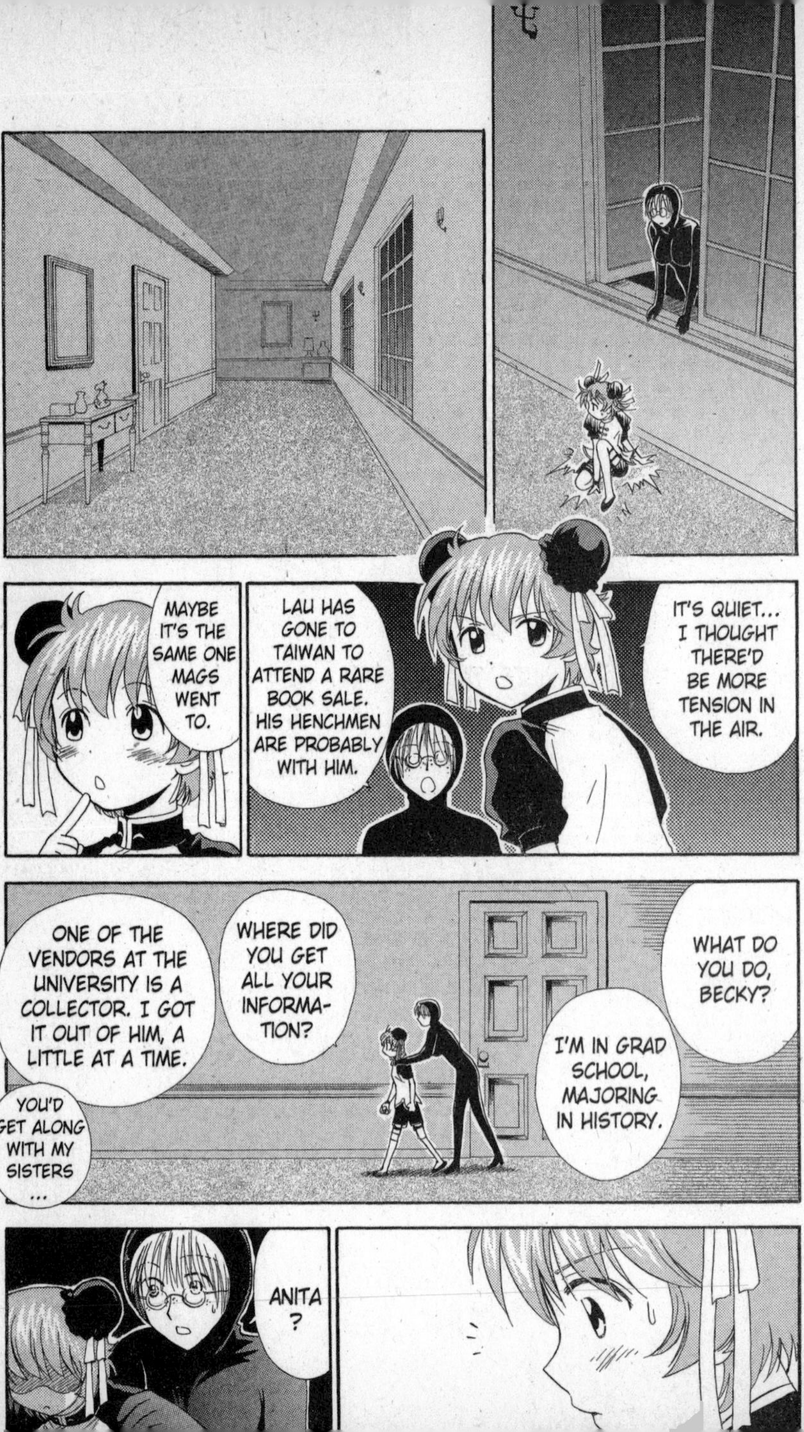
IT'S QUIET... I THOUGHT THERE'D BE MORE TENSION IN THE AIR.
LAU HAS GONE TO TAIWAN TO ATTEND A RARE BOOK SALE. HIS HENCHMEN ARE PROBABLY WITH HIM.
MAYBE IT'S THE SAME ONE MAGS WENT TO.
WHAT DO YOU DO, BECKY?
I'M IN GRAD SCHOOL, MAJORING IN HISTORY.
WHERE DID YOU GET ALL YOUR INFORMATION?
ONE OF THE VENDORS AT THE UNIVERSITY IS A COLLECTOR. I GOT IT OUT OF HIM, A LITTLE AT A TIME.
YOU'D GET ALONG WITH MY SISTERS...
ANITA?

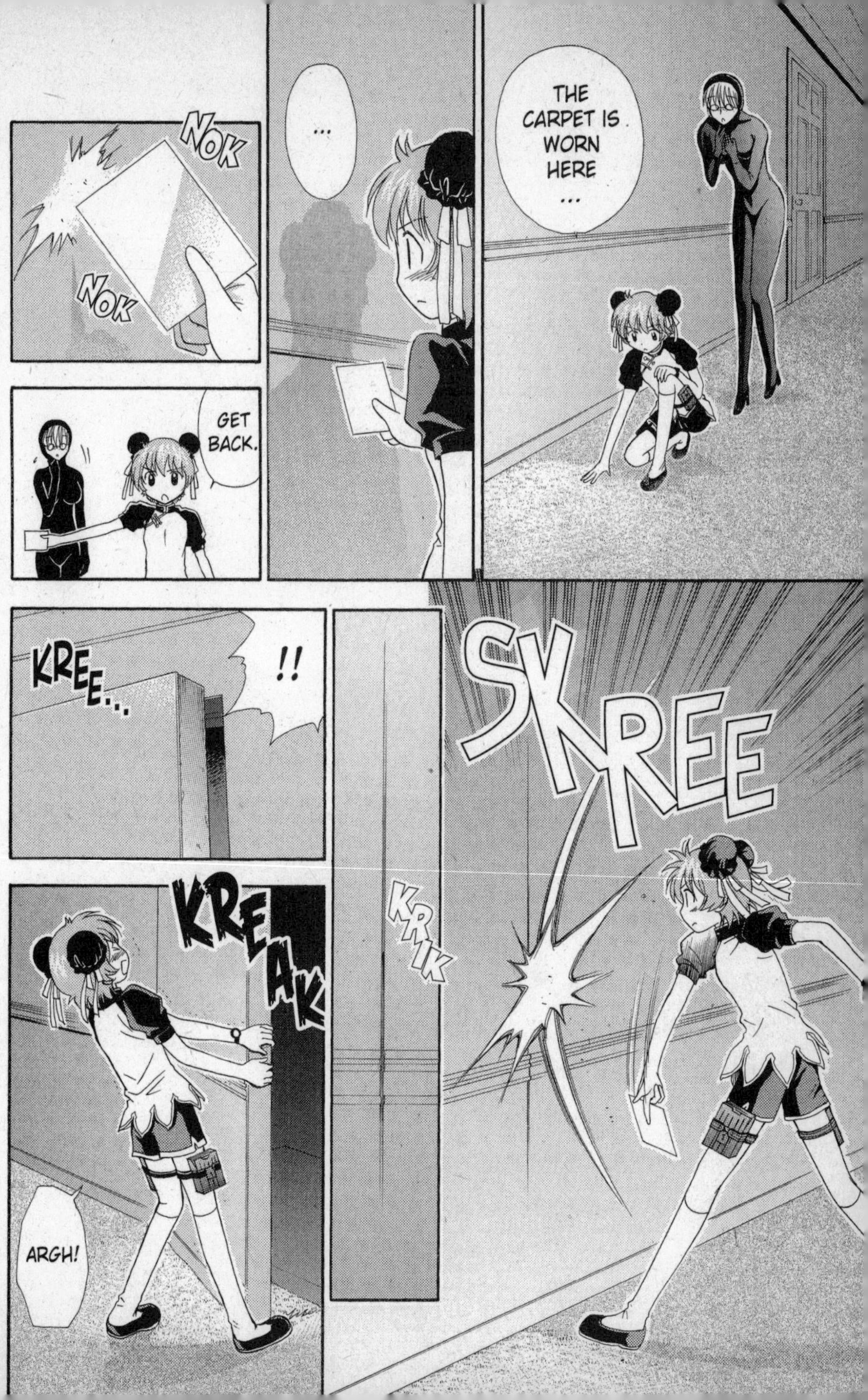
THE CARPET IS WORN HERE ...
...
NOK
NOK
GET BACK.
SKREE
KRIK
KREE...
!!
KREAK
ARGH!

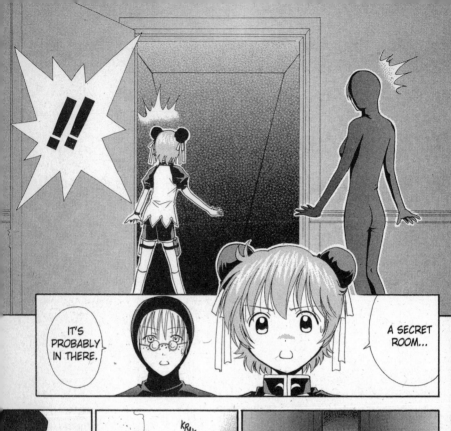

!!

IT'S
PROBABLY
IN THERE.

A SECRET
ROOM...

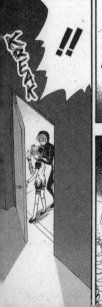

KREAK

!!

KRAK

KRAK

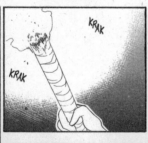

TAK

TAK

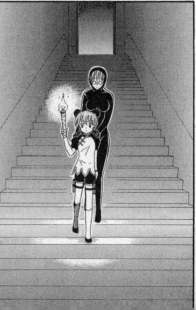

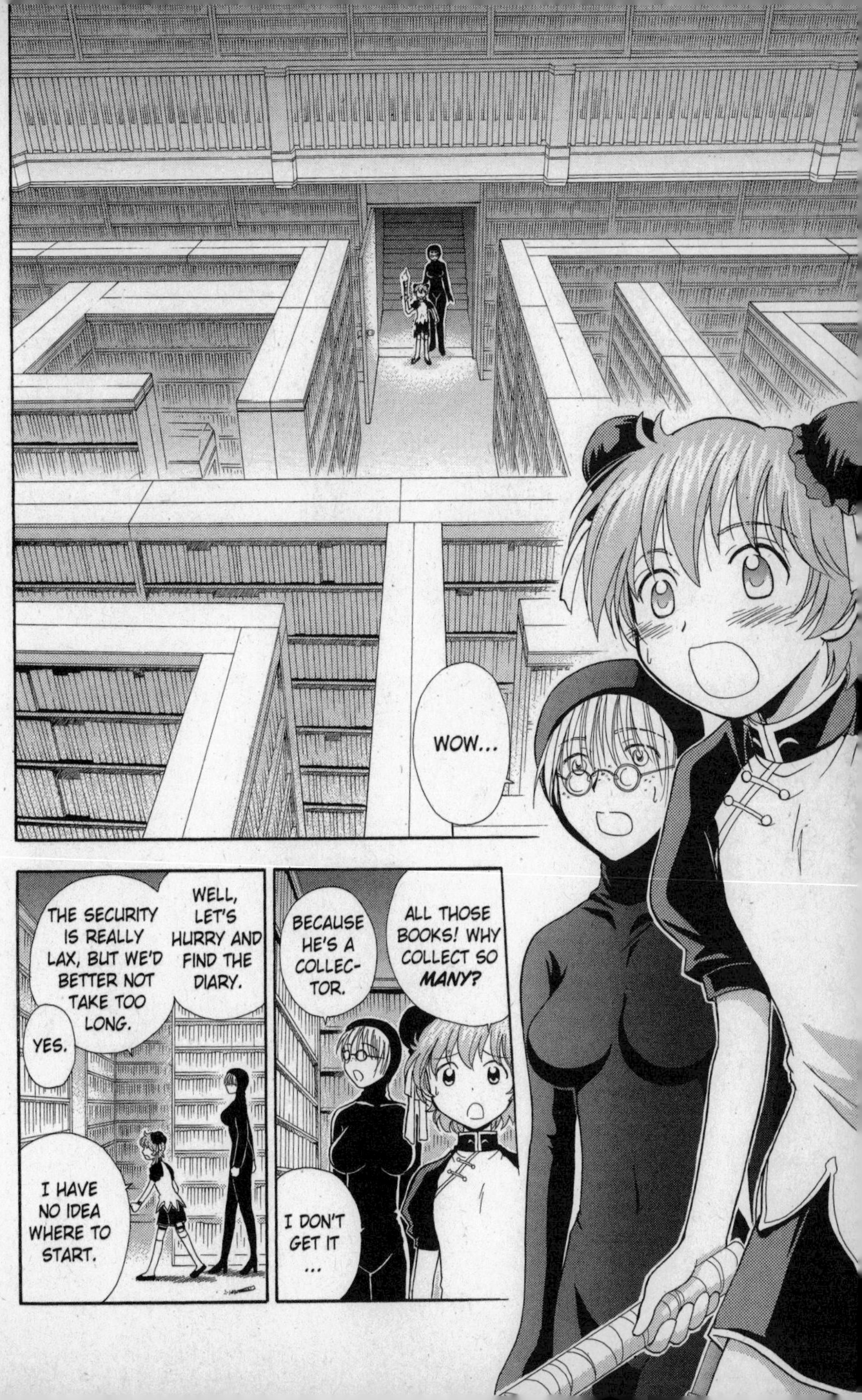
WOW...
ALL THOSE BOOKS! WHY COLLECT SO *MANY?*
BECAUSE HE'S A COLLEC-TOR.
I DON'T GET IT ...
WELL, LET'S HURRY AND FIND THE DIARY.
THE SECURITY IS REALLY LAX, BUT WE'D BETTER NOT TAKE TOO LONG.
YES.
I HAVE NO IDEA WHERE TO START.

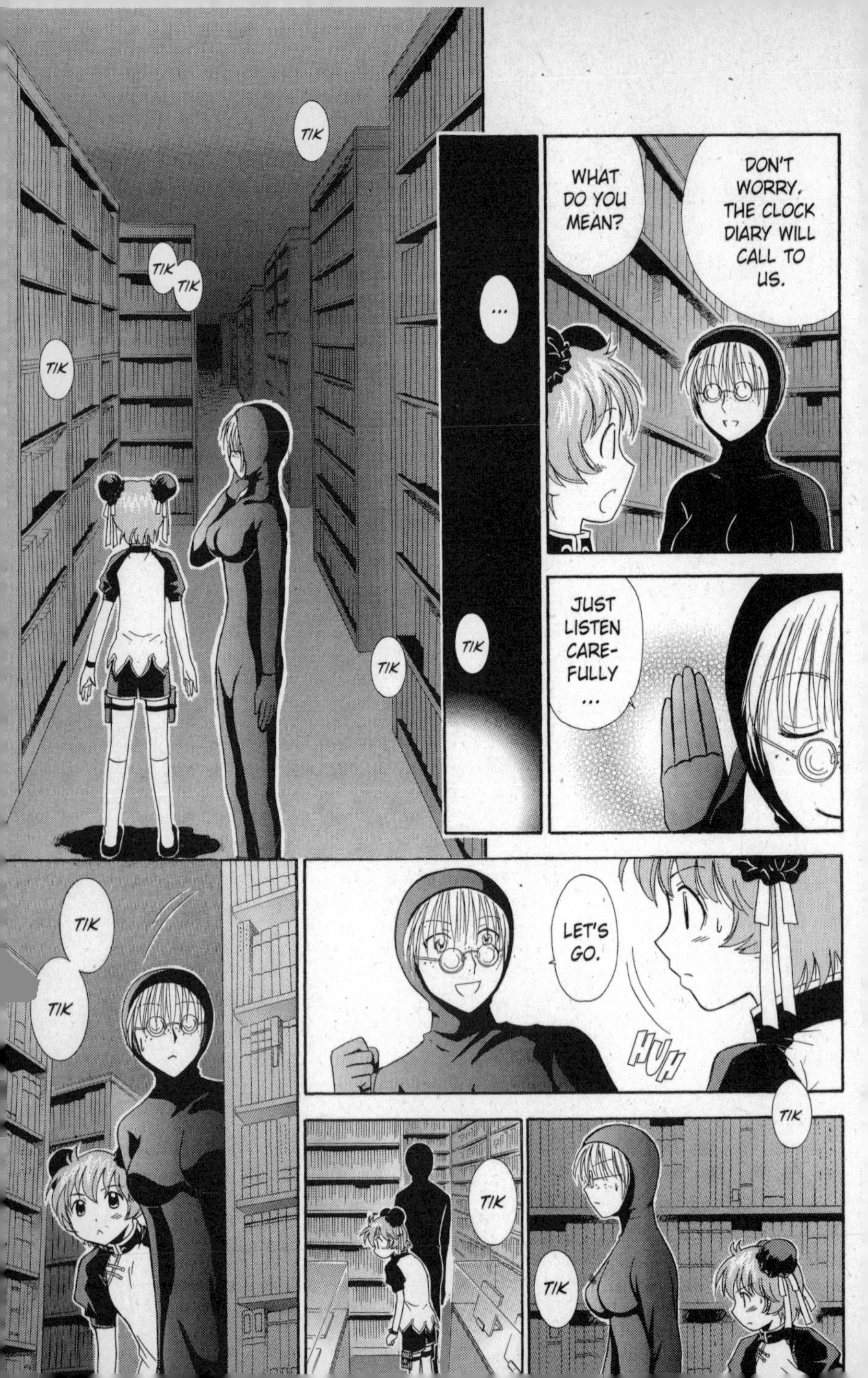
DON'T WORRY. THE CLOCK DIARY WILL CALL TO US.
WHAT DO YOU MEAN?
JUST LISTEN CARE-FULLY ...
...
TIK
TIK
TIK
TIK
TIK
TIK
TIK
LET'S GO.
HUH
TIK
TIK
TIK
TIK
TIK

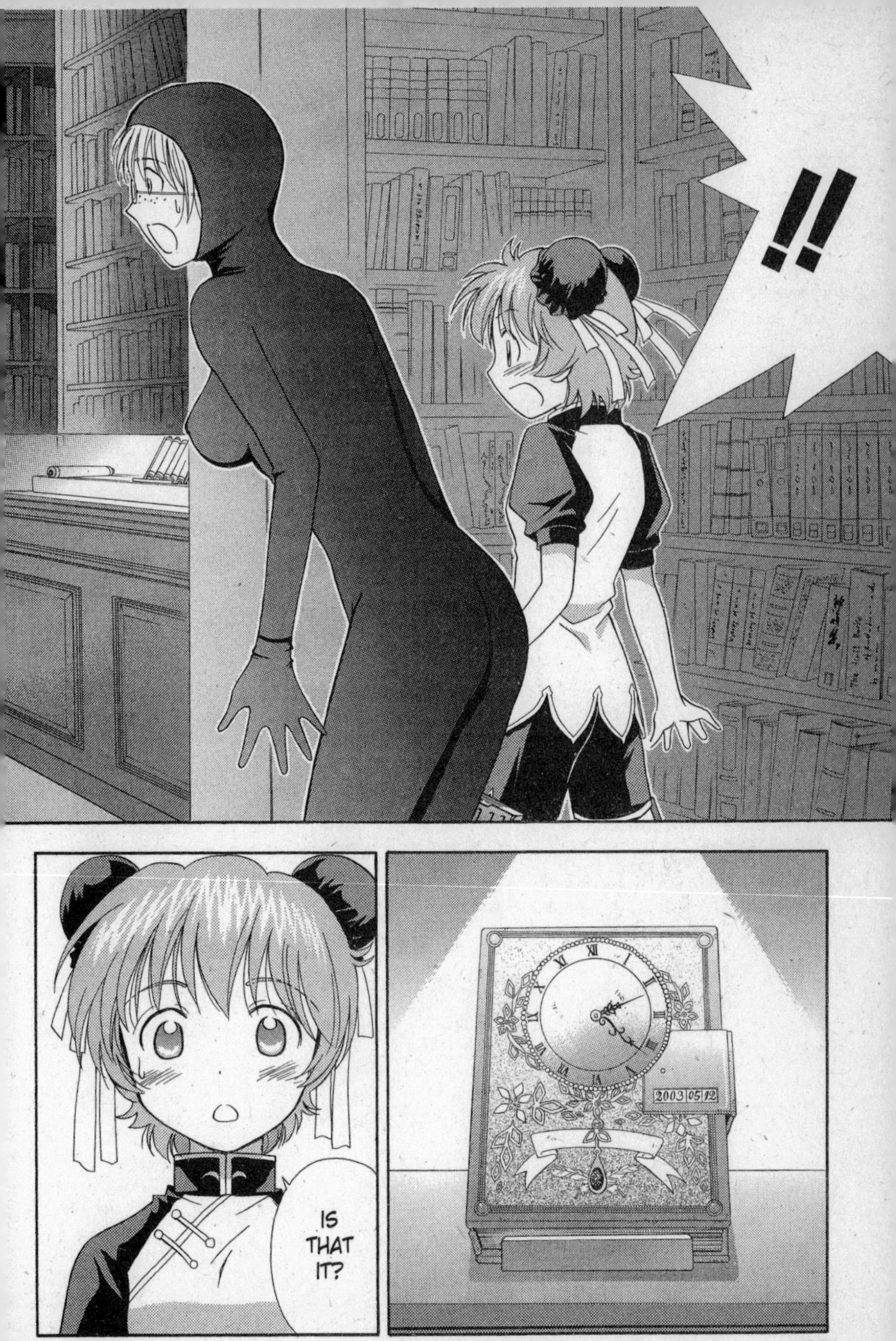
!!
2003 05 12
IS THAT IT?

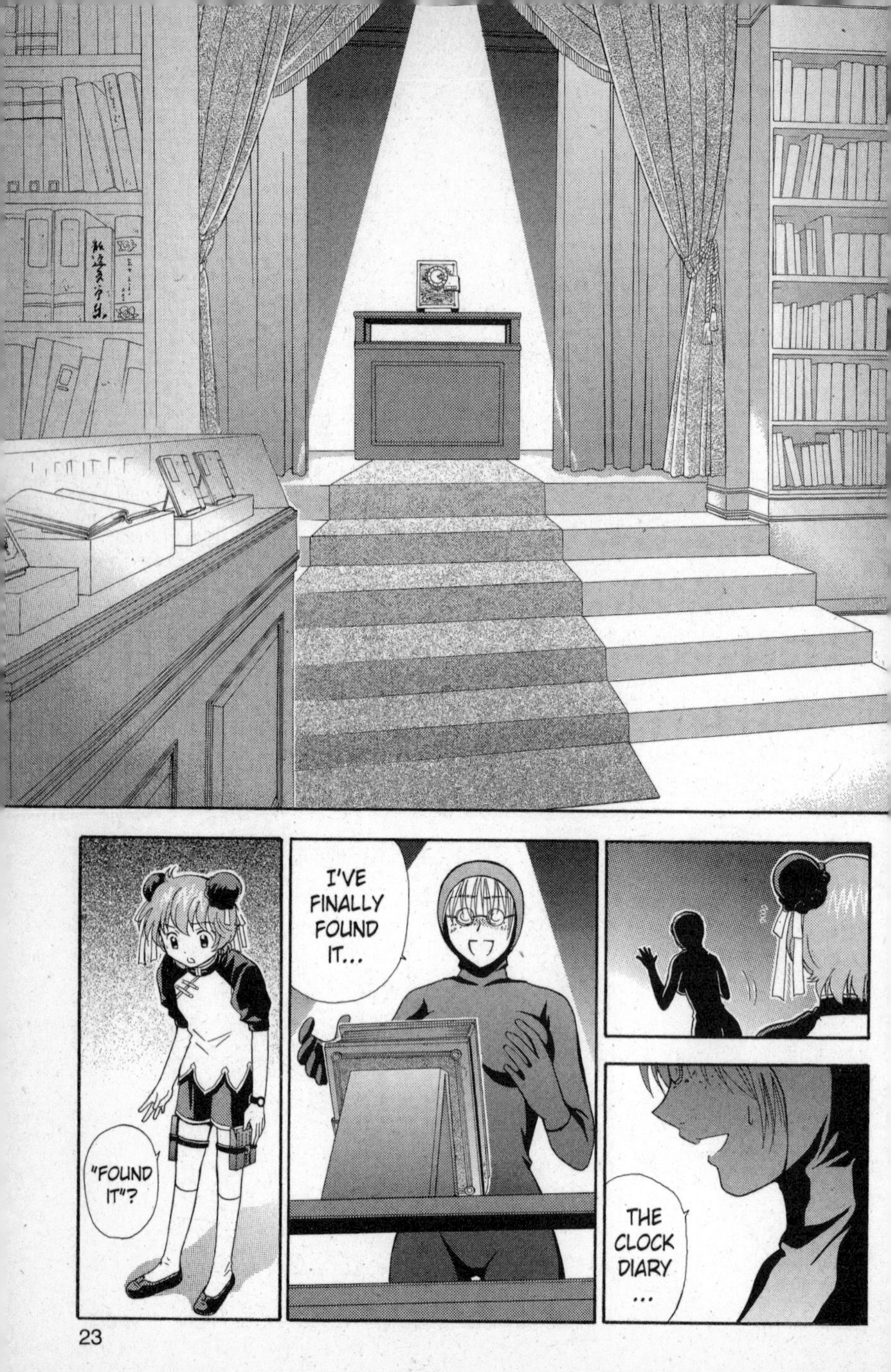
THE CLOCK DIARY ...
I'VE FINALLY FOUND IT...
"FOUND IT"?

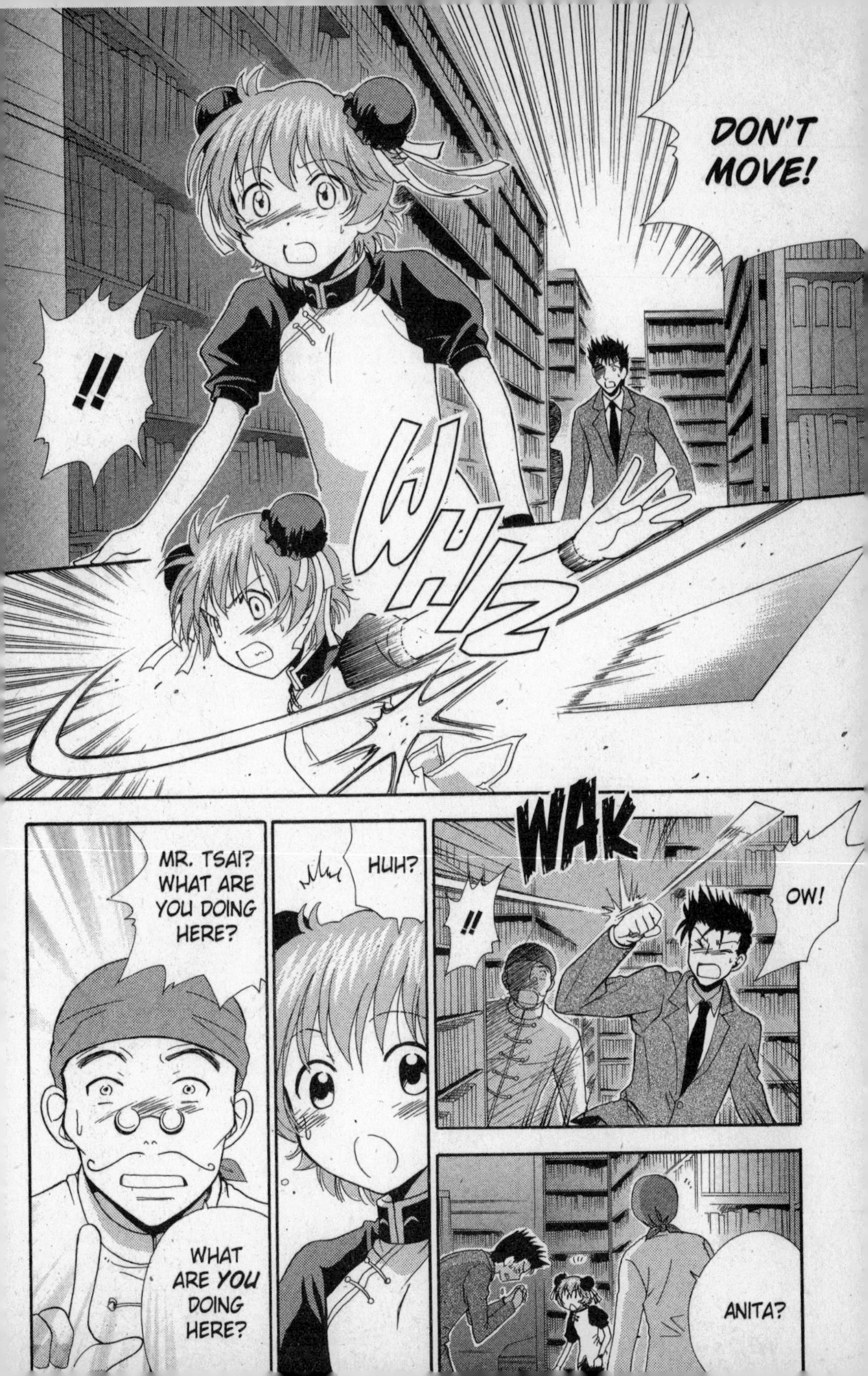
DON'T MOVE!
!!
WHIZ
WAK
OW!
!!
ANITA?
HUH?
MR. TSAI? WHAT ARE YOU DOING HERE?
WHAT ARE YOU DOING HERE?

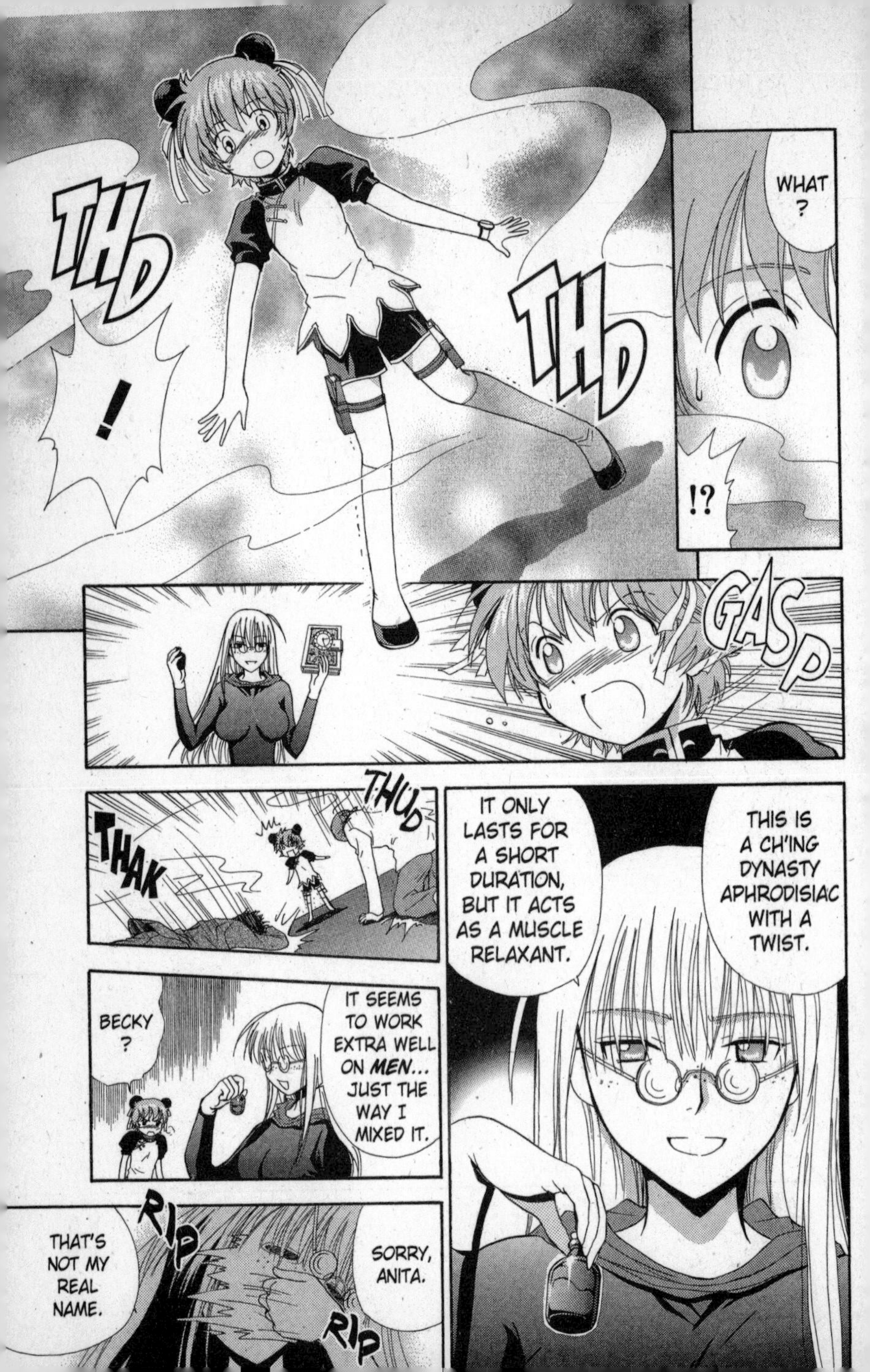
WHAT?
!?
THD
THD
!
GASP
THIS IS A CH'ING DYNASTY APHRODISIAC WITH A TWIST.
IT ONLY LASTS FOR A SHORT DURATION, BUT IT ACTS AS A MUSCLE RELAXANT.
THUD
THAK
IT SEEMS TO WORK EXTRA WELL ON MEN... JUST THE WAY I MIXED IT.
BECKY?
SORRY, ANITA.
RIP
THAT'S NOT MY REAL NAME.
RIP

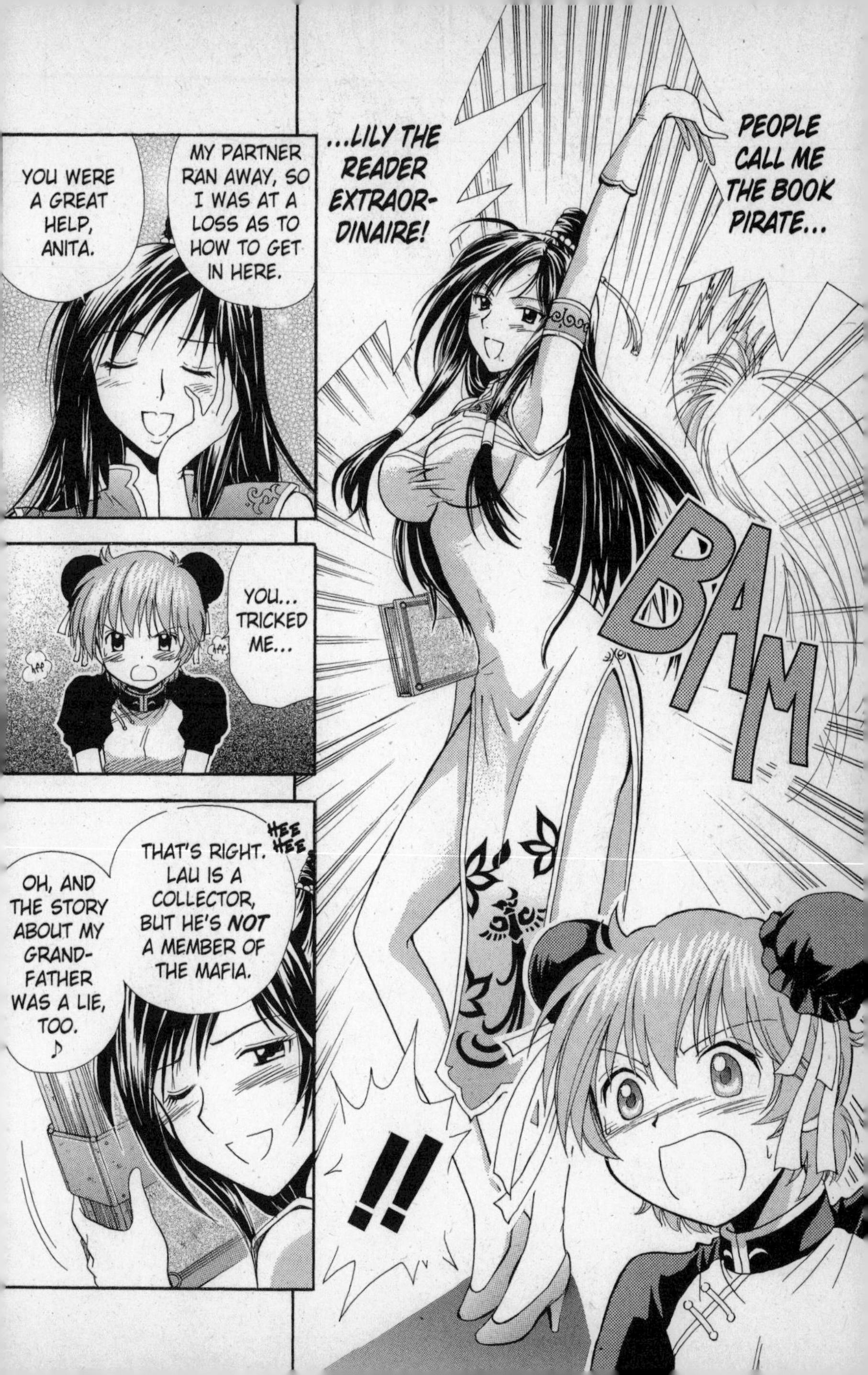
PEOPLE CALL ME THE BOOK PIRATE...
...LILY THE READER EXTRAOR-DINAIRE!
BAM
!!
MY PARTNER RAN AWAY, SO I WAS AT A LOSS AS TO HOW TO GET IN HERE.
YOU WERE A GREAT HELP, ANITA.
hff
YOU... TRICKED ME...
hff
HEE HEE
THAT'S RIGHT. LAU IS A COLLECTOR, BUT HE'S *NOT* A MEMBER OF THE MAFIA.
OH, AND THE STORY ABOUT MY GRAND-FATHER WAS A LIE, TOO. ♪

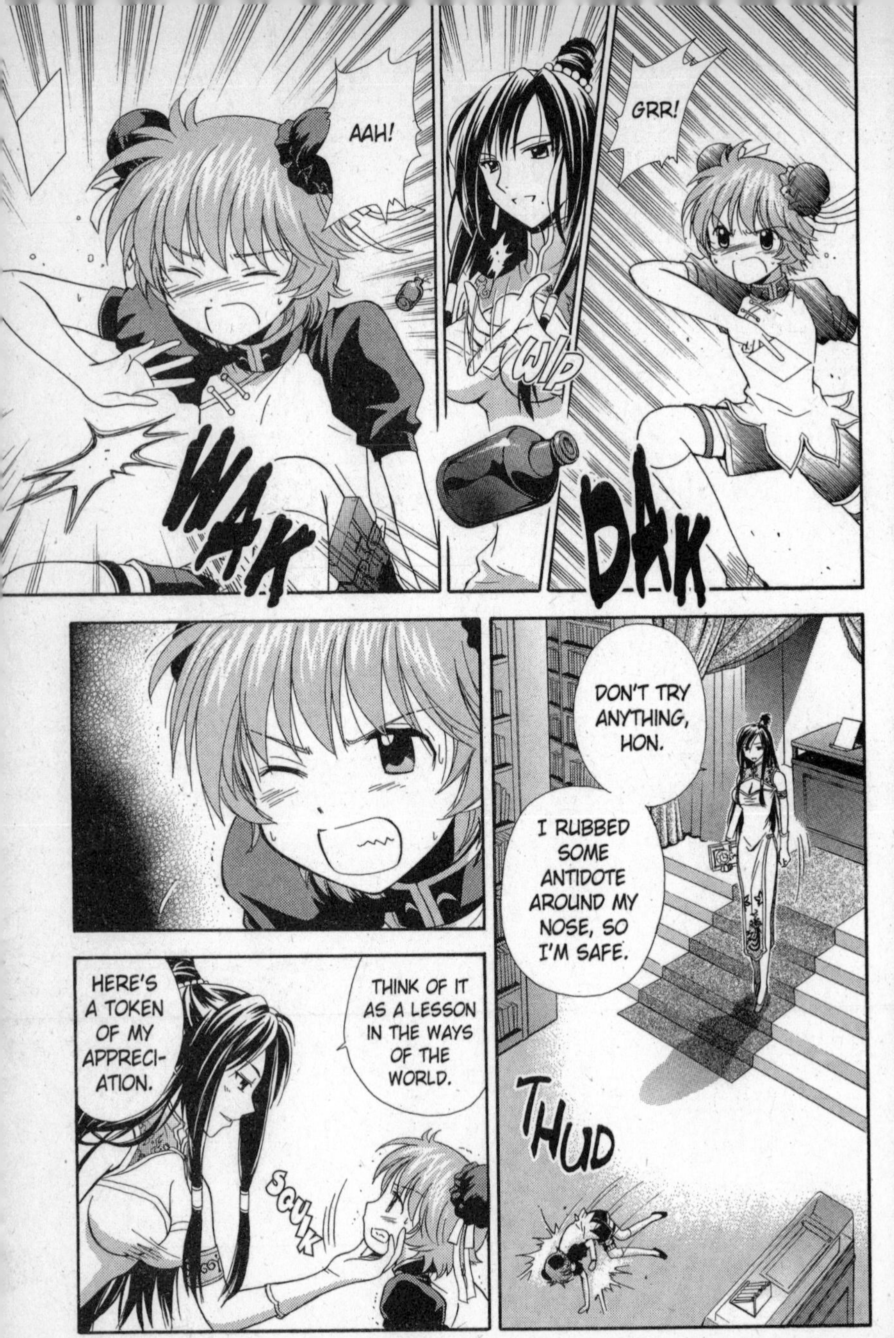
GRR!
DAK
WIP
AAH!
WAK
DON'T TRY ANYTHING, HON.
I RUBBED SOME ANTIDOTE AROUND MY NOSE, SO I'M SAFE.
THUD
THINK OF IT AS A LESSON IN THE WAYS OF THE WORLD.
HERE'S A TOKEN OF MY APPRECI-ATION.
SCUK

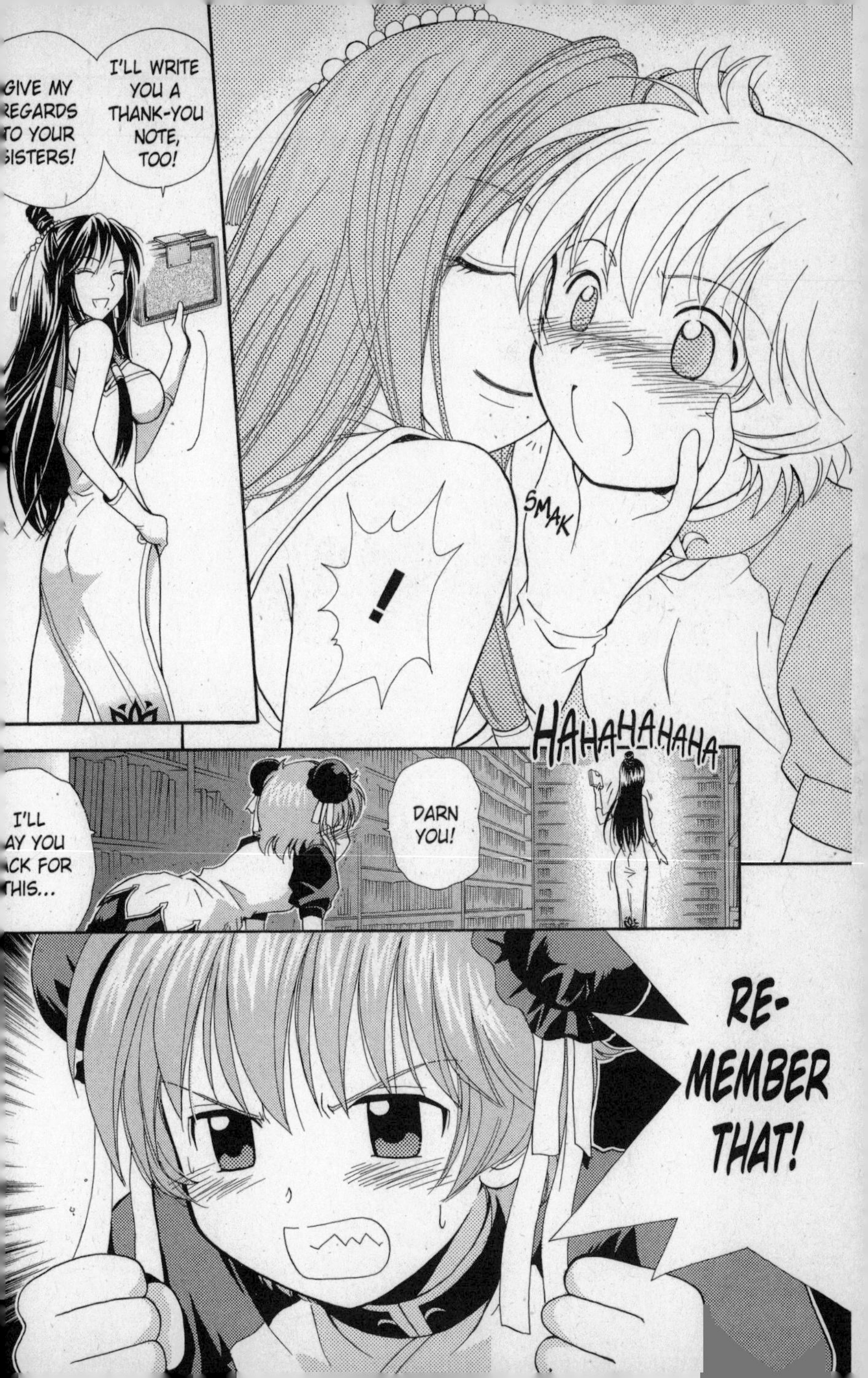
SMAK
!
I'LL WRITE YOU A THANK-YOU NOTE, TOO!
GIVE MY REGARDS TO YOUR SISTERS!
HAHAHAHAHA
DARN YOU!
I'LL AY YOU CK FOR THIS...
RE-MEMBER THAT!

CHAPTER 9

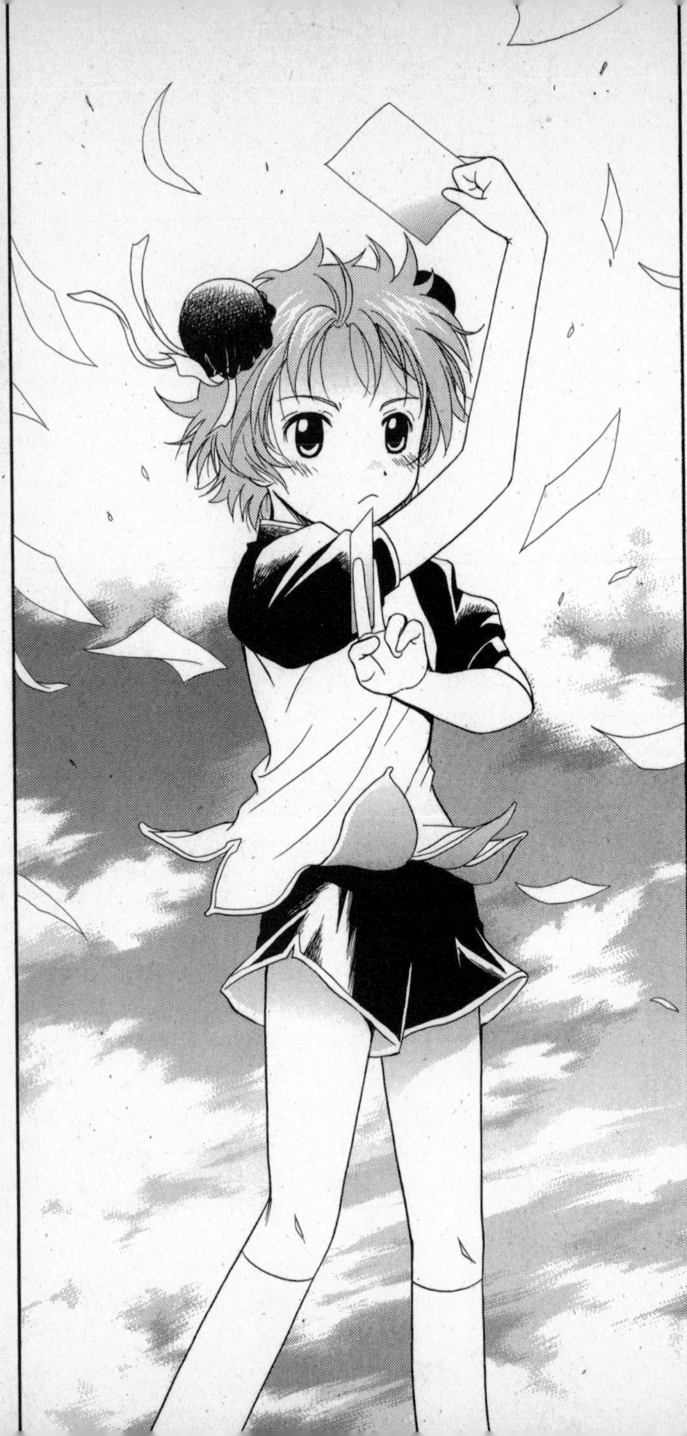

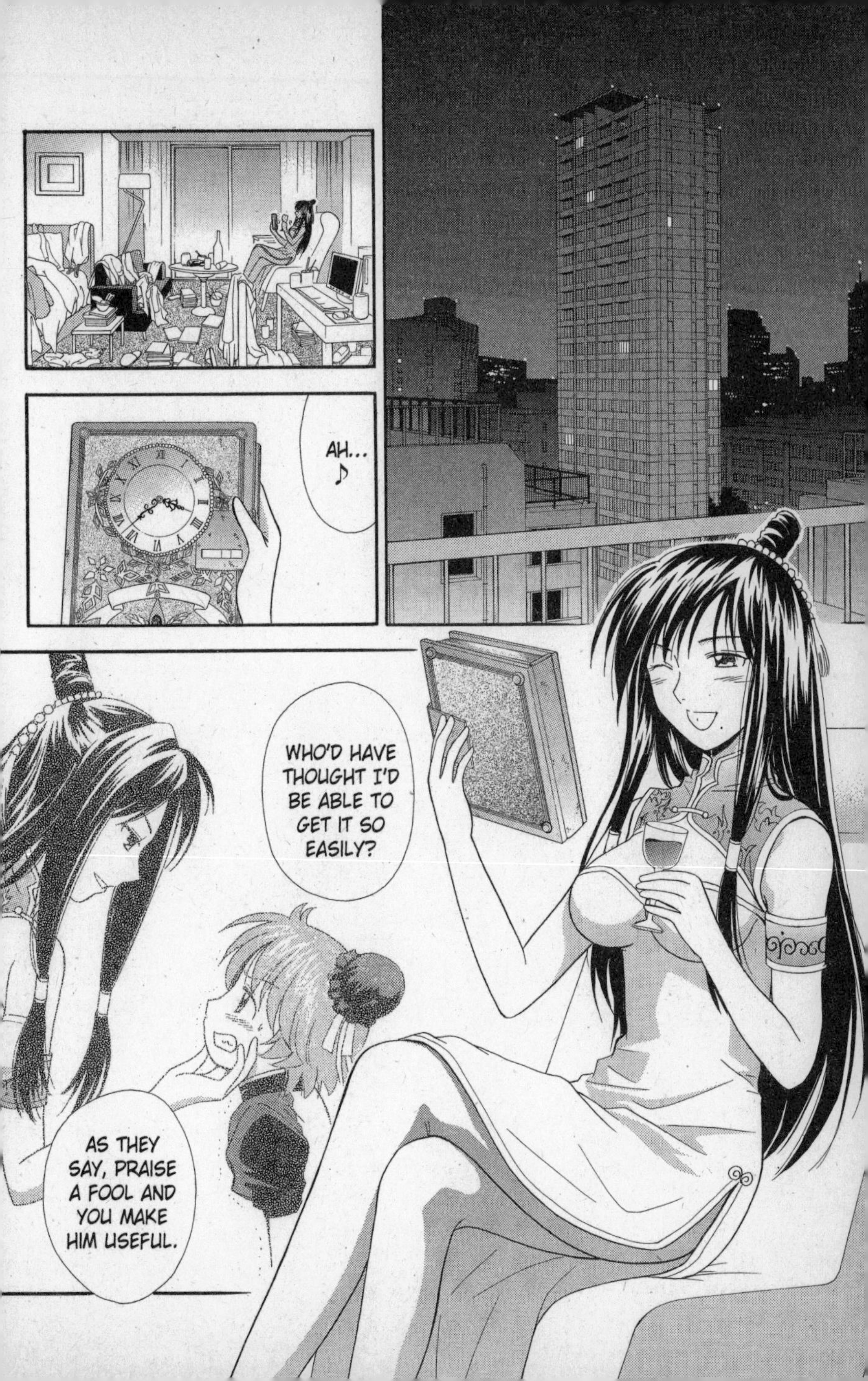
AH... ♪
WHO'D HAVE THOUGHT I'D BE ABLE TO GET IT SO EASILY?
AS THEY SAY, PRAISE A FOOL AND YOU MAKE HIM USEFUL.

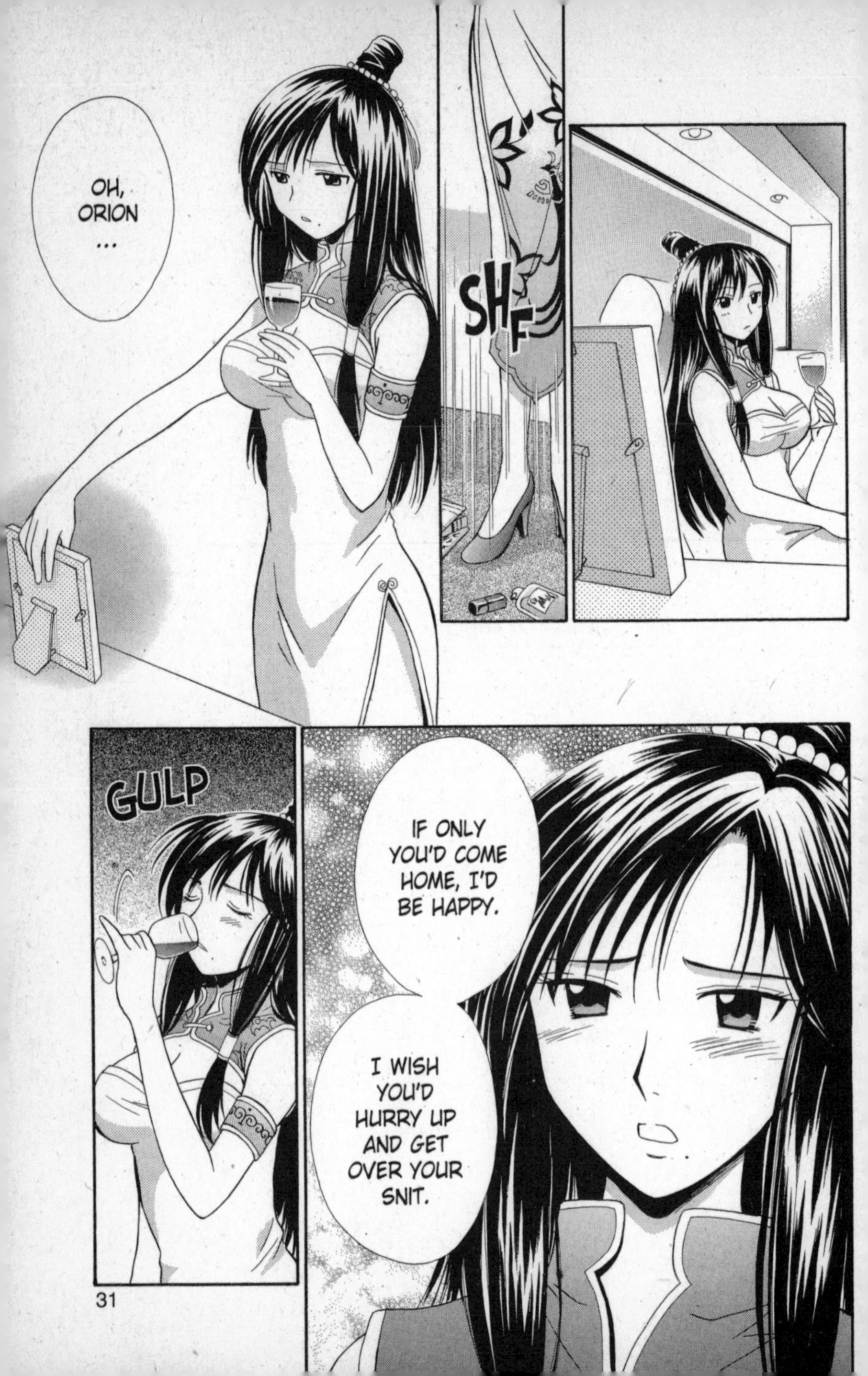
SHF
OH, ORION ...
IF ONLY YOU'D COME HOME, I'D BE HAPPY.
I WISH YOU'D HURRY UP AND GET OVER YOUR SNIT.
GULP

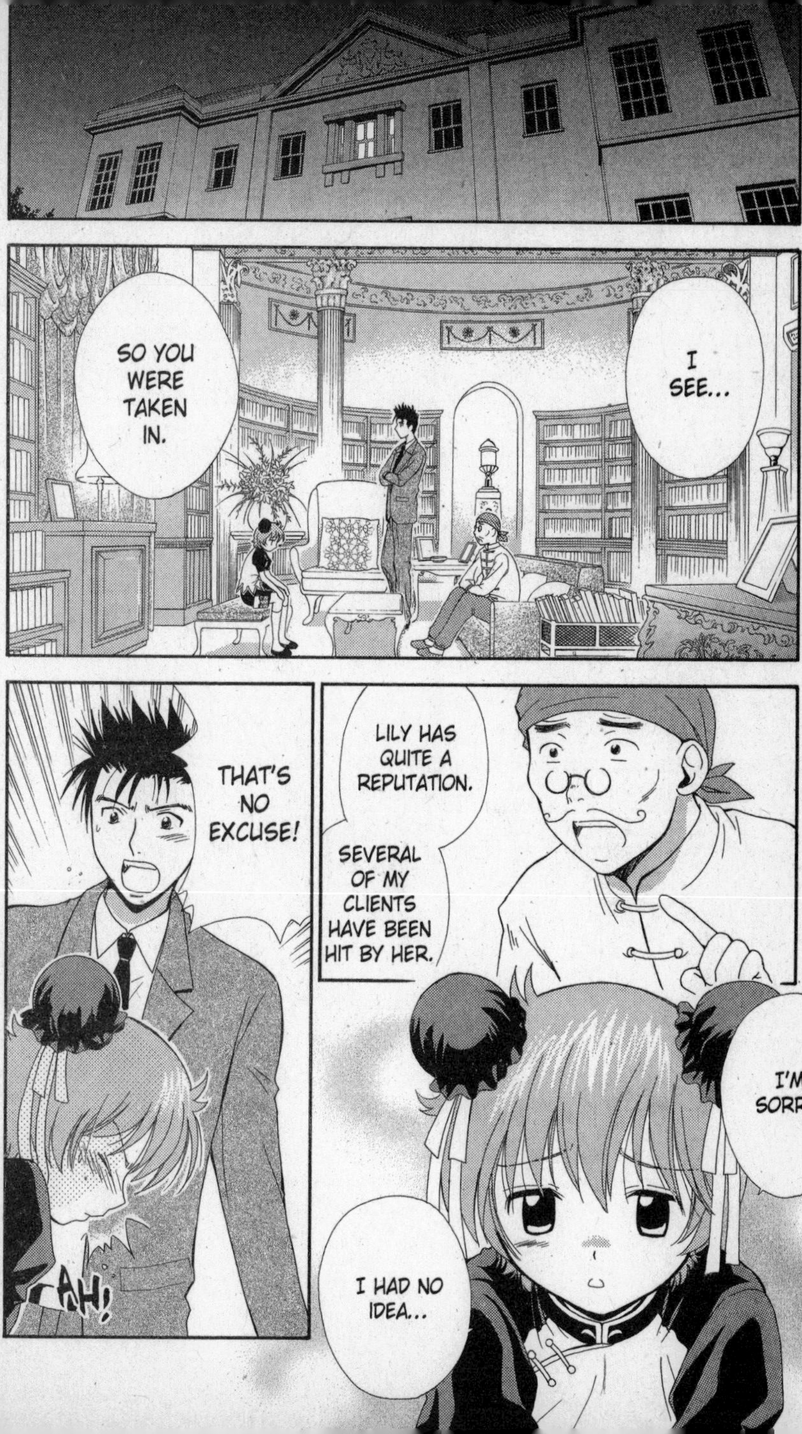
I SEE...
SO YOU WERE TAKEN IN.
LILY HAS QUITE A REPUTATION.
SEVERAL OF MY CLIENTS HAVE BEEN HIT BY HER.
I'M SORRY...
I HAD NO IDEA...
THAT'S NO EXCUSE!
AH!

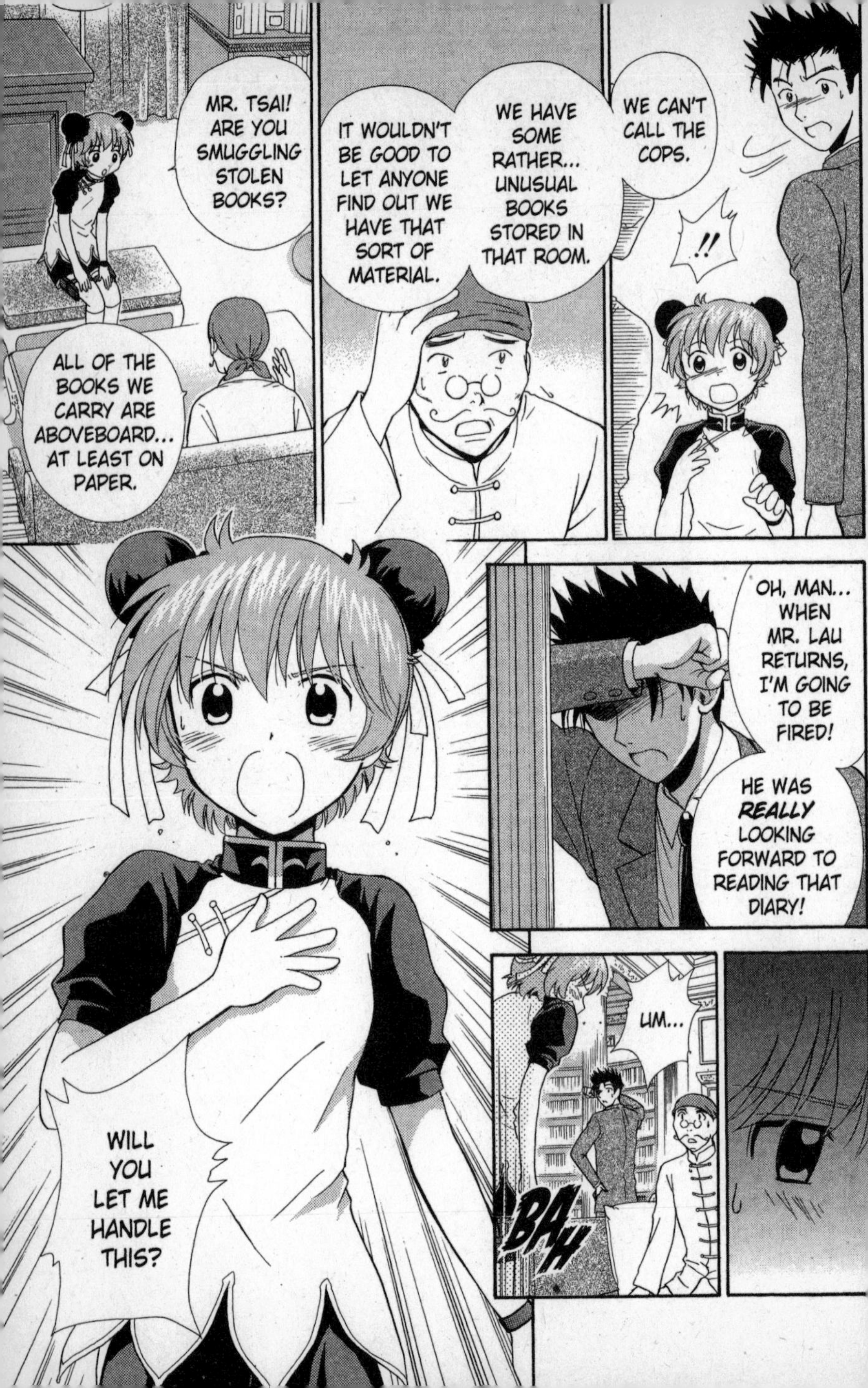
WE CAN'T CALL THE COPS.
!!
WE HAVE SOME RATHER... UNUSUAL BOOKS STORED IN THAT ROOM.
IT WOULDN'T BE GOOD TO LET ANYONE FIND OUT WE HAVE THAT SORT OF MATERIAL.
MR. TSAI! ARE YOU SMUGGLING STOLEN BOOKS?
ALL OF THE BOOKS WE CARRY ARE ABOVEBOARD... AT LEAST ON PAPER.
OH, MAN... WHEN MR. LAU RETURNS, I'M GOING TO BE FIRED!
HE WAS REALLY LOOKING FORWARD TO READING THAT DIARY!
UM...
BAH
WILL YOU LET ME HANDLE THIS?

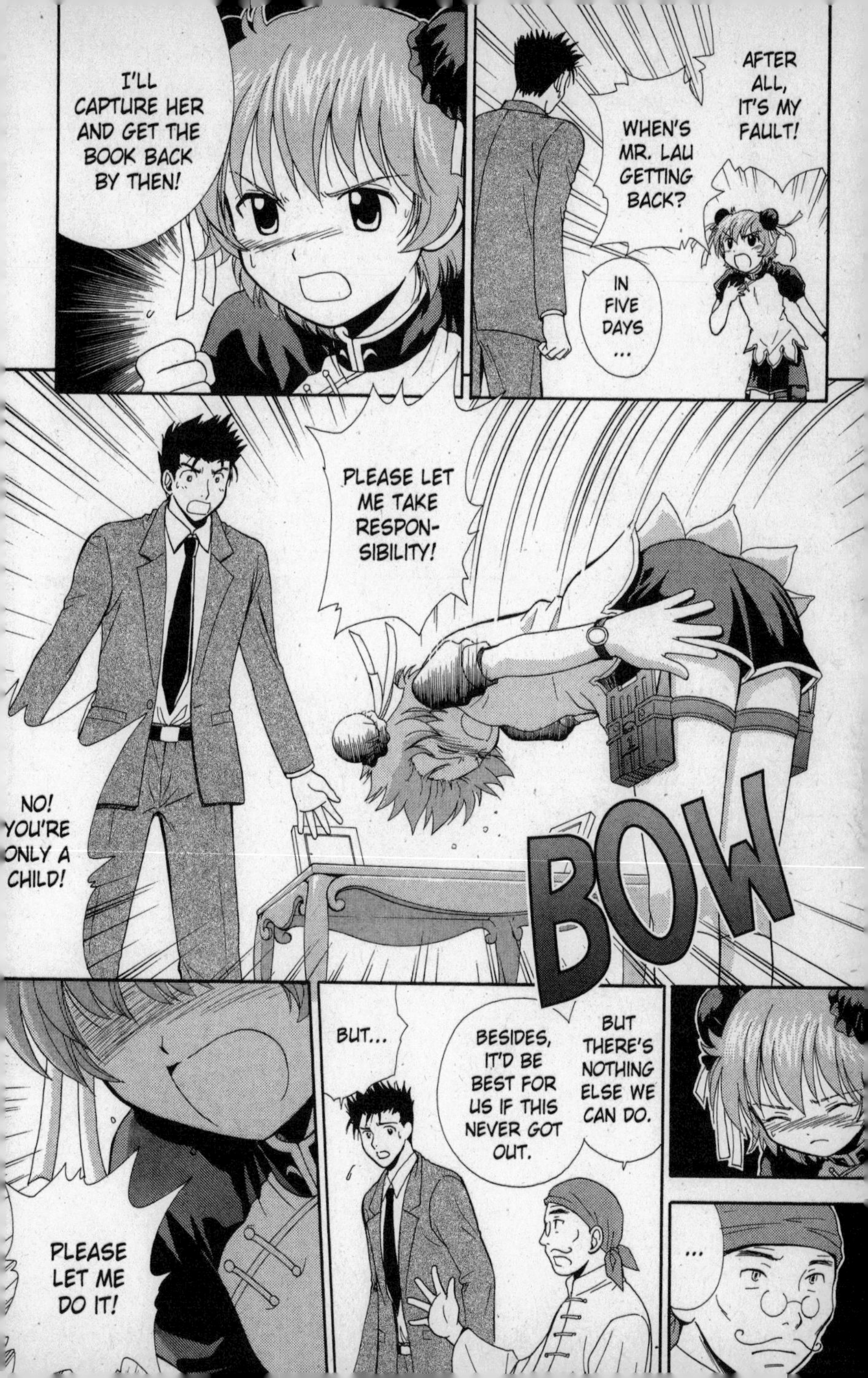
AFTER ALL, IT'S MY FAULT!
WHEN'S MR. LAU GETTING BACK?
IN FIVE DAYS ...
I'LL CAPTURE HER AND GET THE BOOK BACK BY THEN!
PLEASE LET ME TAKE RESPONSIBILITY!
BOW
NO! YOU'RE ONLY A CHILD!
...
BUT THERE'S NOTHING ELSE WE CAN DO.
BESIDES, IT'D BE BEST FOR US IF THIS NEVER GOT OUT.
BUT...
PLEASE LET ME DO IT!

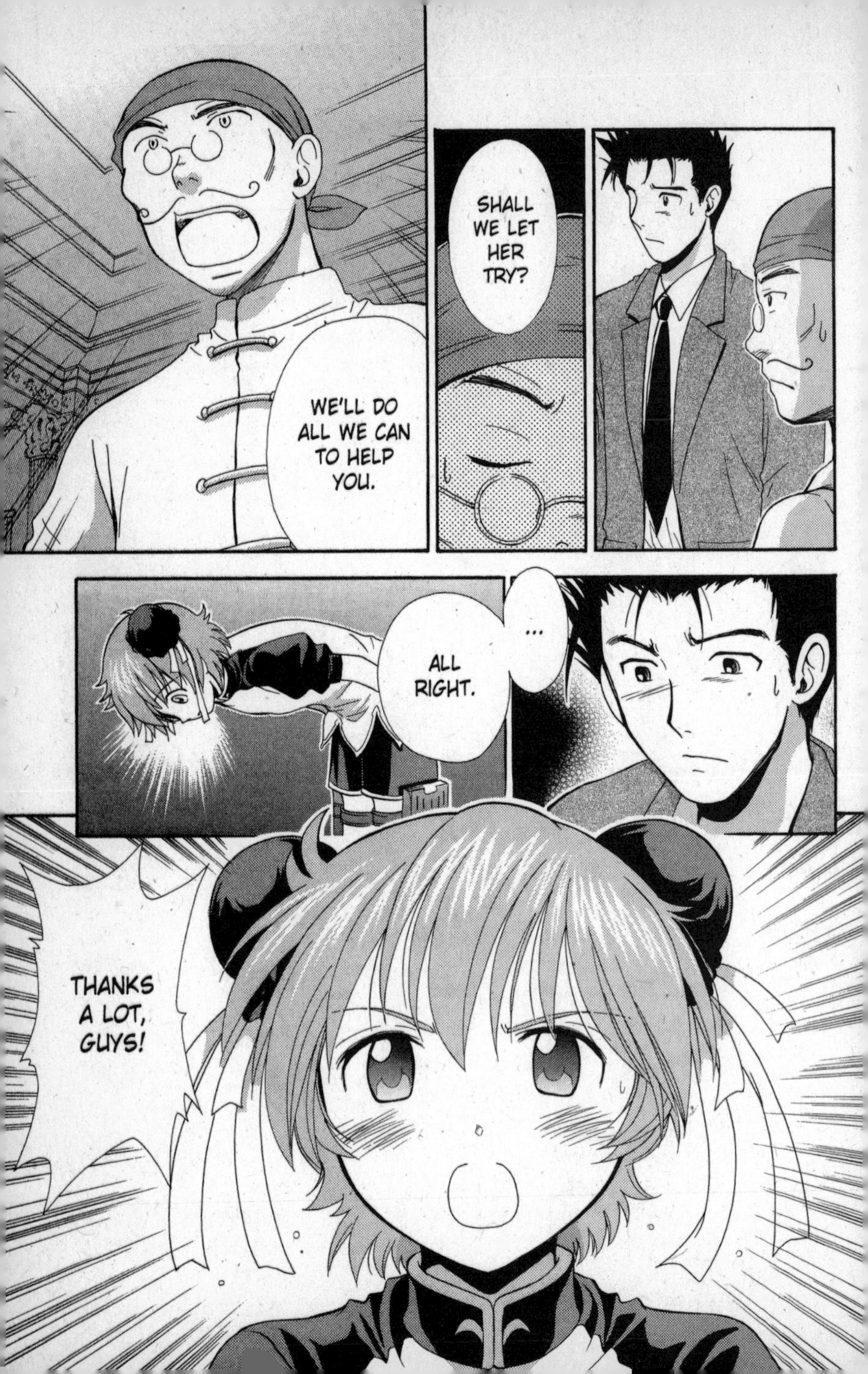
SHALL WE LET HER TRY?
WE'LL DO ALL WE CAN TO HELP YOU.
...
ALL RIGHT.
THANKS A LOT, GUYS!

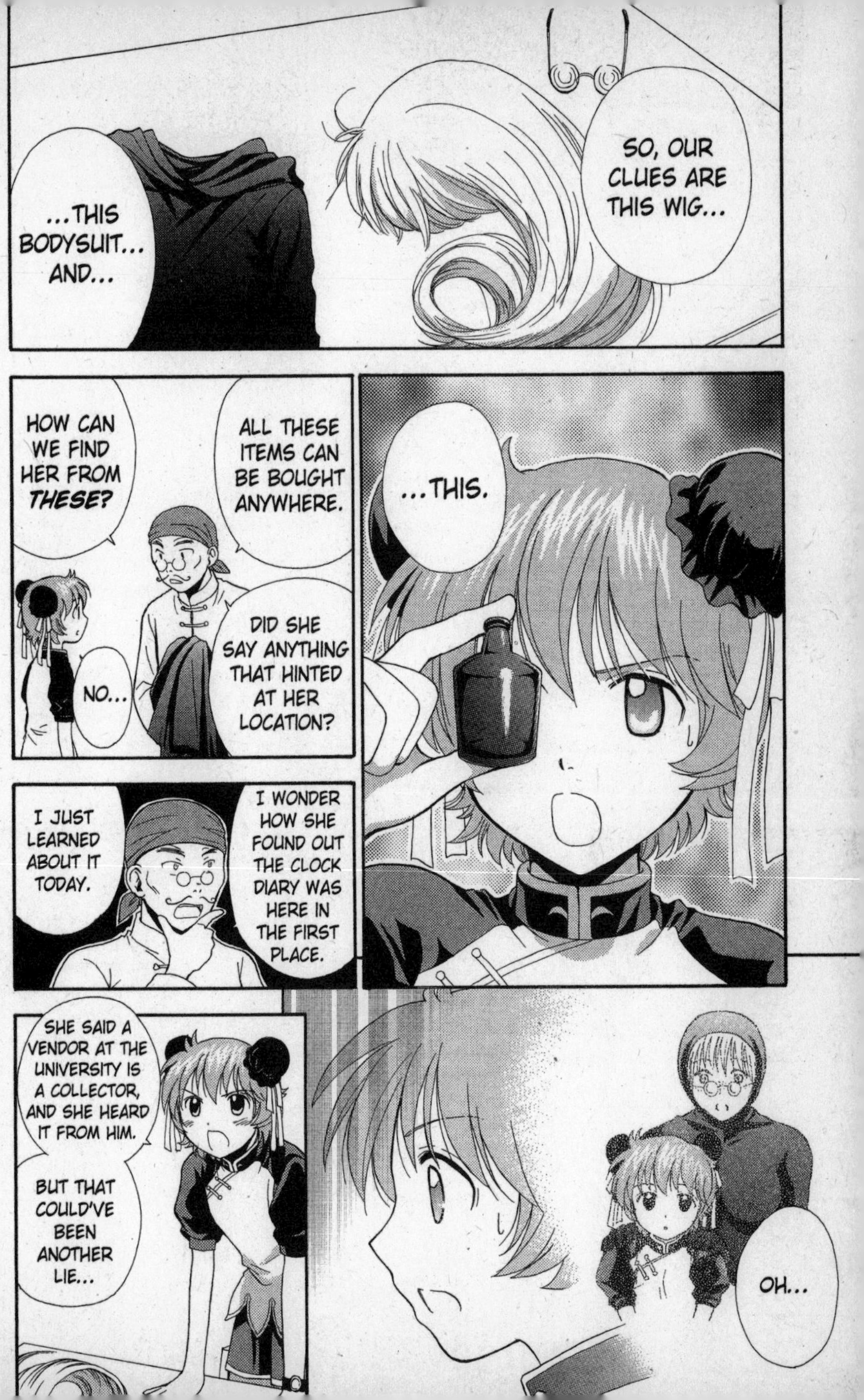
SO, OUR CLUES ARE THIS WIG...
...THIS BODYSUIT... AND...
...THIS.
ALL THESE ITEMS CAN BE BOUGHT ANYWHERE.
HOW CAN WE FIND HER FROM *THESE?*
DID SHE SAY ANYTHING THAT HINTED AT HER LOCATION?
NO...
I WONDER HOW SHE FOUND OUT THE CLOCK DIARY WAS HERE IN THE FIRST PLACE.
I JUST LEARNED ABOUT IT TODAY.
OH...
SHE SAID A VENDOR AT THE UNIVERSITY IS A COLLECTOR, AND SHE HEARD IT FROM HIM.
BUT THAT COULD'VE BEEN ANOTHER LIE...

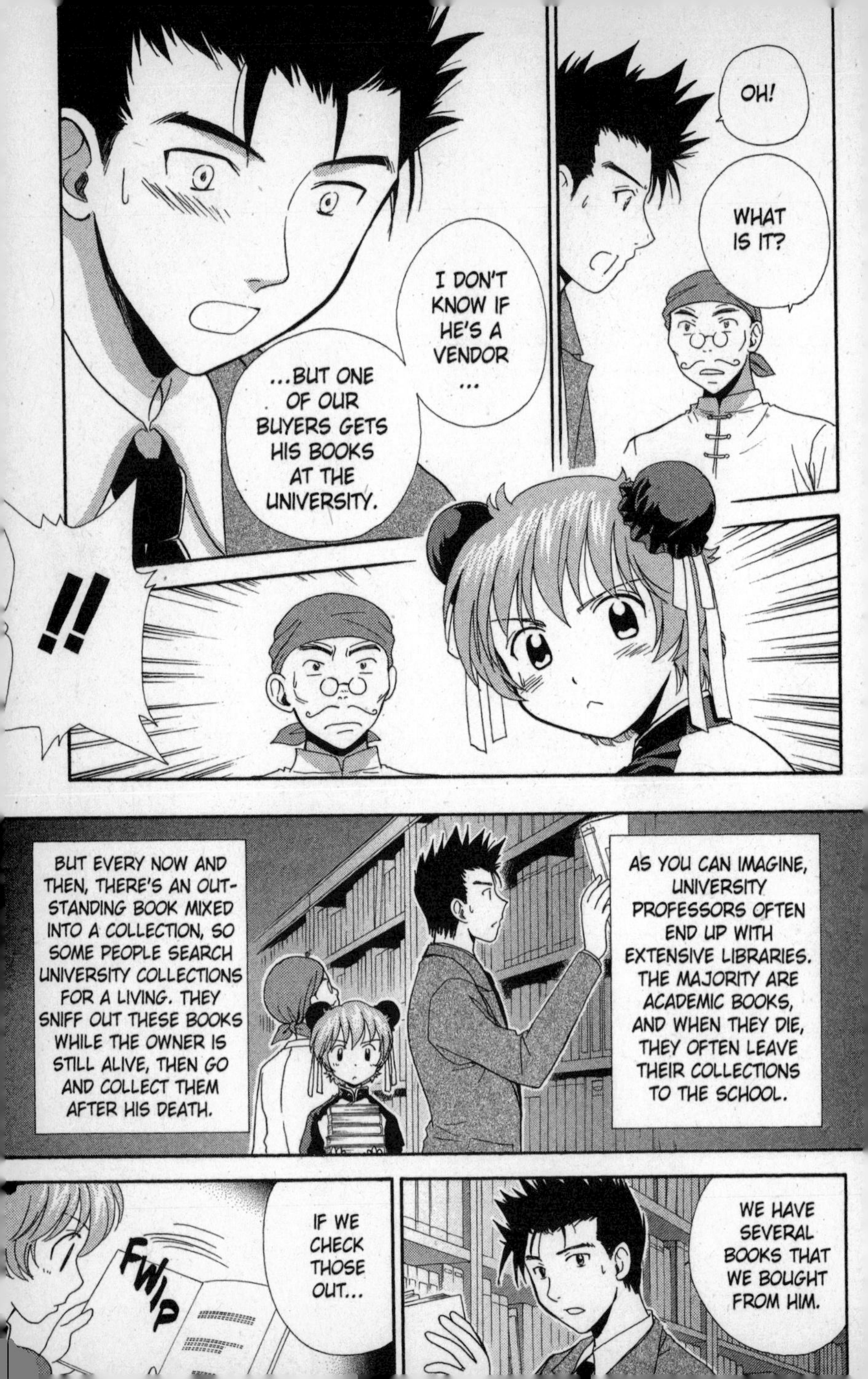
OH!
WHAT IS IT?
I DON'T KNOW IF HE'S A VENDOR ...
...BUT ONE OF OUR BUYERS GETS HIS BOOKS AT THE UNIVERSITY.
!!
AS YOU CAN IMAGINE, UNIVERSITY PROFESSORS OFTEN END UP WITH EXTENSIVE LIBRARIES. THE MAJORITY ARE ACADEMIC BOOKS, AND WHEN THEY DIE, THEY OFTEN LEAVE THEIR COLLECTIONS TO THE SCHOOL.
BUT EVERY NOW AND THEN, THERE'S AN OUT-STANDING BOOK MIXED INTO A COLLECTION, SO SOME PEOPLE SEARCH UNIVERSITY COLLECTIONS FOR A LIVING. THEY SNIFF OUT THESE BOOKS WHILE THE OWNER IS STILL ALIVE, THEN GO AND COLLECT THEM AFTER HIS DEATH.
WE HAVE SEVERAL BOOKS THAT WE BOUGHT FROM HIM.
IF WE CHECK THOSE OUT...
FWIP

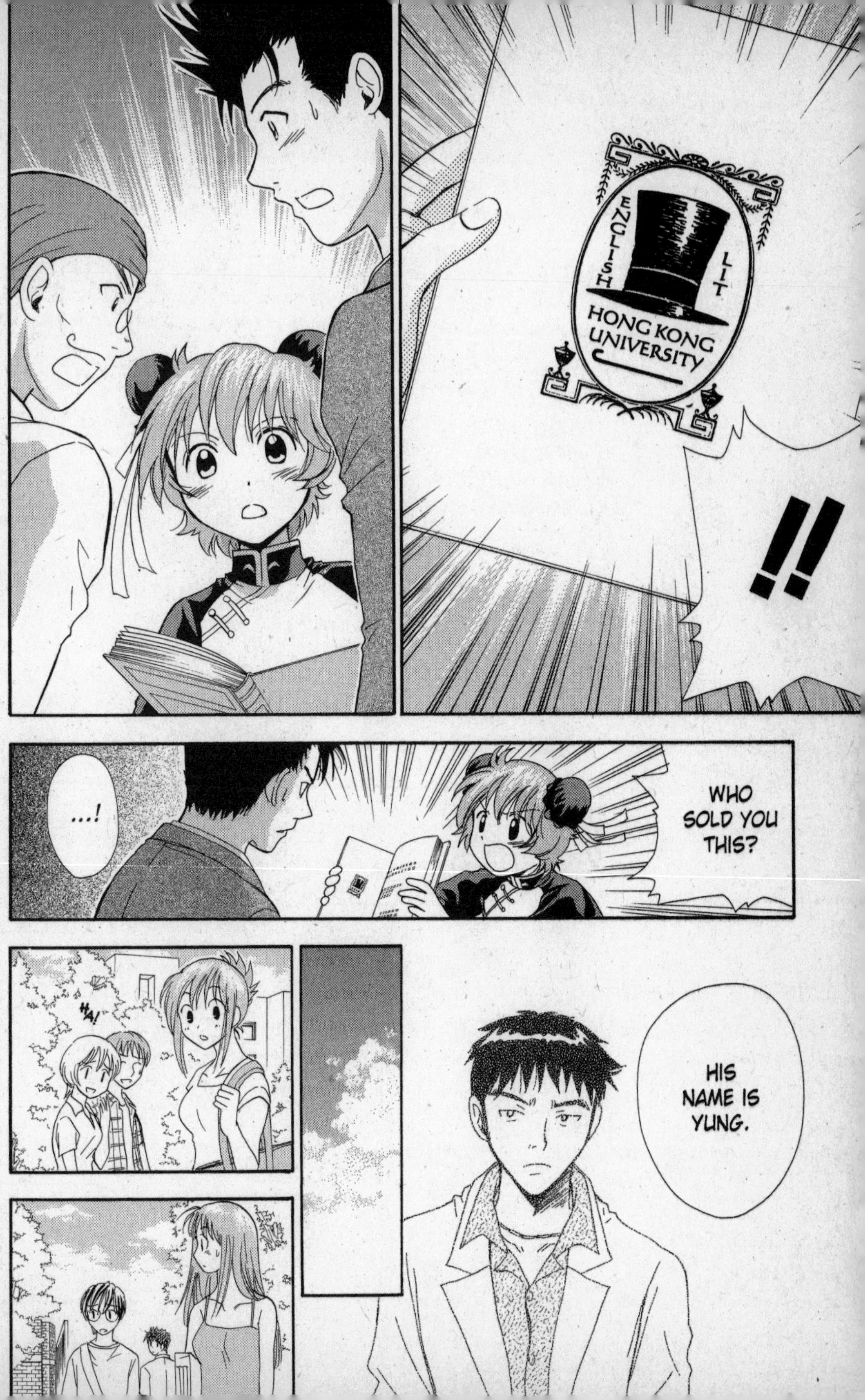
ENGLISH
LIT
HONG KONG UNIVERSITY
!!
WHO SOLD YOU THIS?
...!
HIS NAME IS YUNG.
HA!

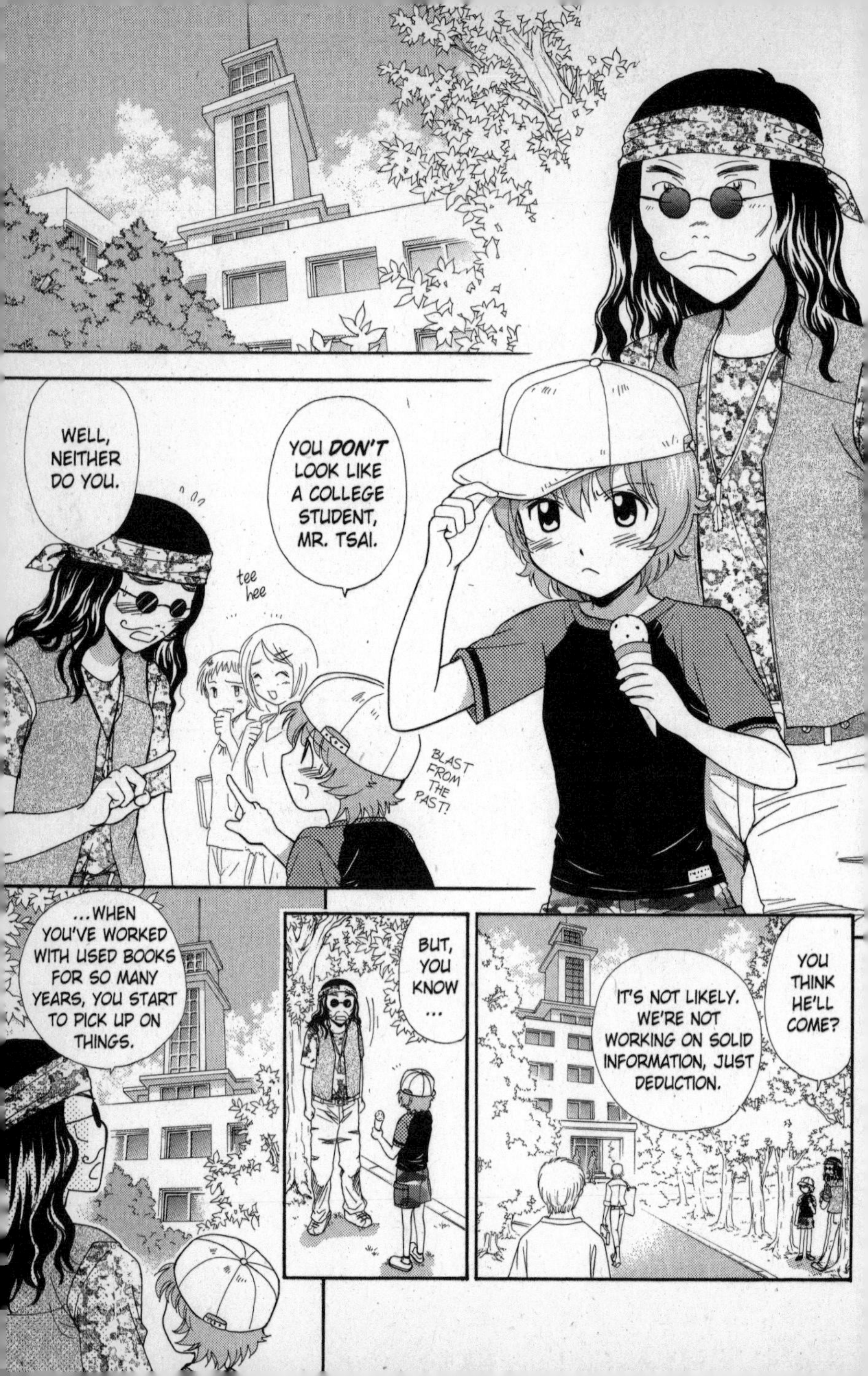
YOU **DON'T** LOOK LIKE A COLLEGE STUDENT, MR. TSAI.
WELL, NEITHER DO YOU.
tee hee
BLAST FROM THE PAST!
YOU THINK HE'LL COME?
IT'S NOT LIKELY. WE'RE NOT WORKING ON SOLID INFORMATION, JUST DEDUCTION.
BUT, YOU KNOW ...
...WHEN YOU'VE WORKED WITH USED BOOKS FOR SO MANY YEARS, YOU START TO PICK UP ON THINGS.

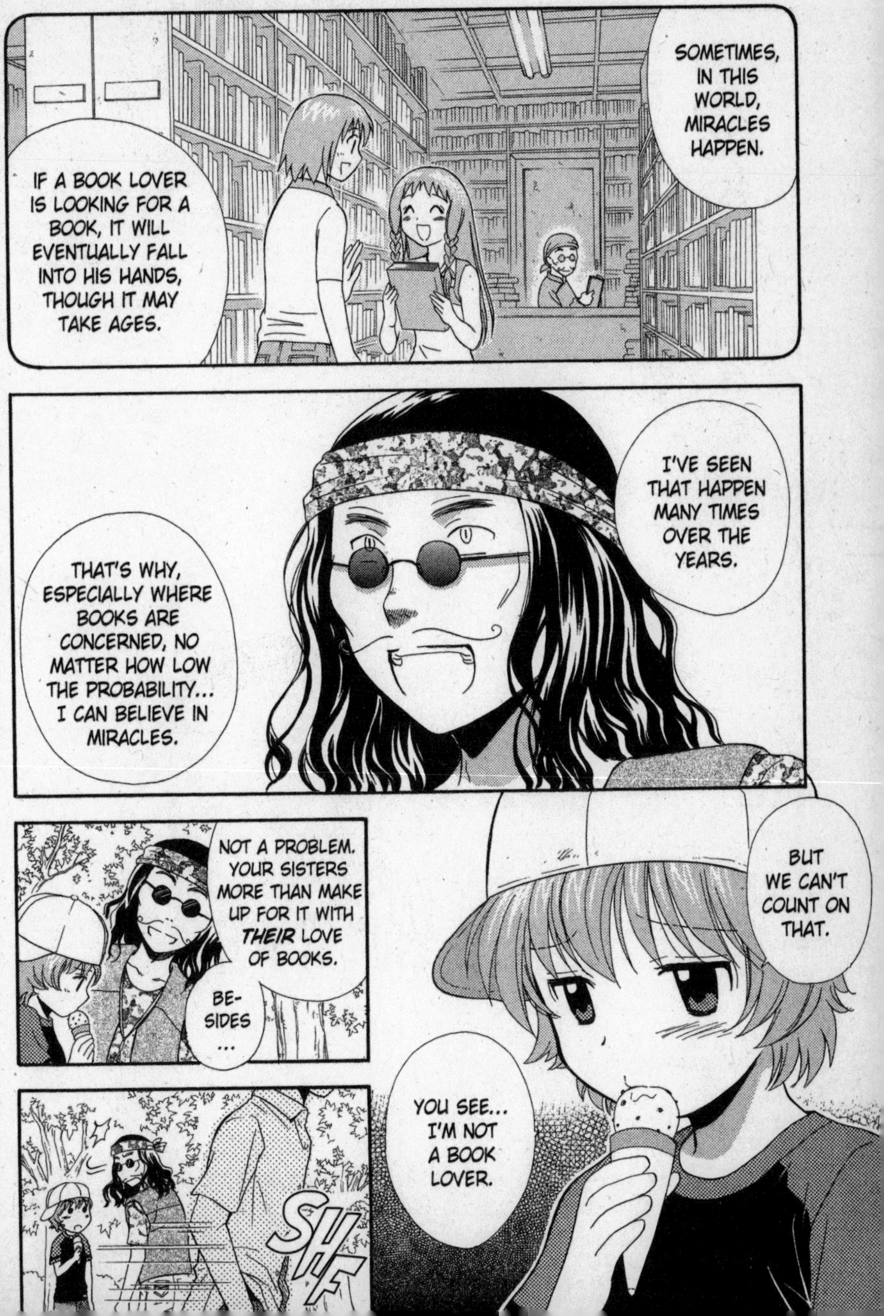
SOMETIMES, IN THIS WORLD, MIRACLES HAPPEN.
IF A BOOK LOVER IS LOOKING FOR A BOOK, IT WILL EVENTUALLY FALL INTO HIS HANDS, THOUGH IT MAY TAKE AGES.
I'VE SEEN THAT HAPPEN MANY TIMES OVER THE YEARS.
THAT'S WHY, ESPECIALLY WHERE BOOKS ARE CONCERNED, NO MATTER HOW LOW THE PROBABILITY... I CAN BELIEVE IN MIRACLES.
BUT WE CAN'T COUNT ON THAT.
YOU SEE... I'M NOT A BOOK LOVER.
NOT A PROBLEM. YOUR SISTERS MORE THAN MAKE UP FOR IT WITH *THEIR* LOVE OF BOOKS.
BE-SIDES ...
SHF

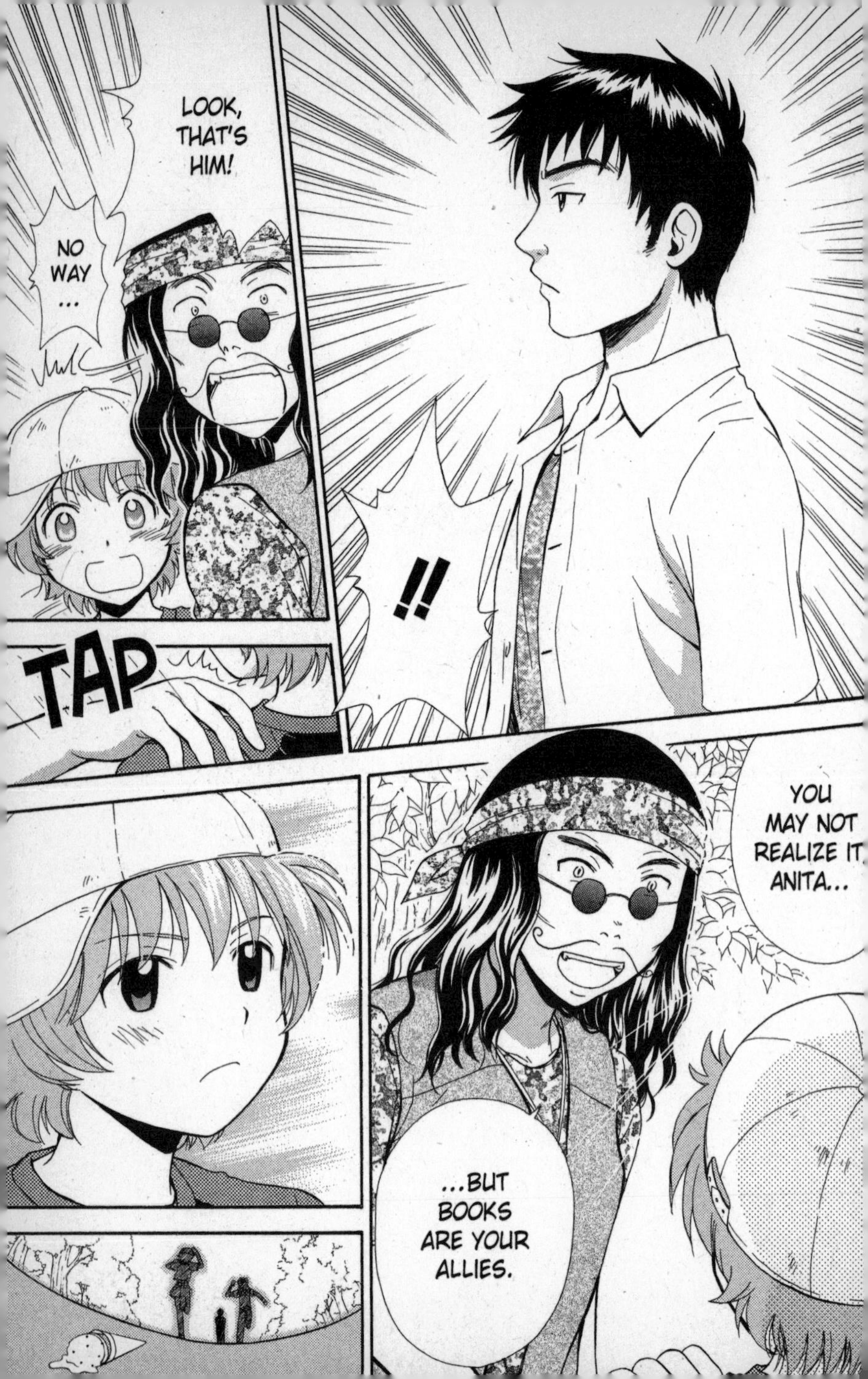
!!
LOOK, THAT'S HIM!
NO WAY ...
TAP
YOU MAY NOT REALIZE IT, ANITA...
...BUT BOOKS ARE YOUR ALLIES.

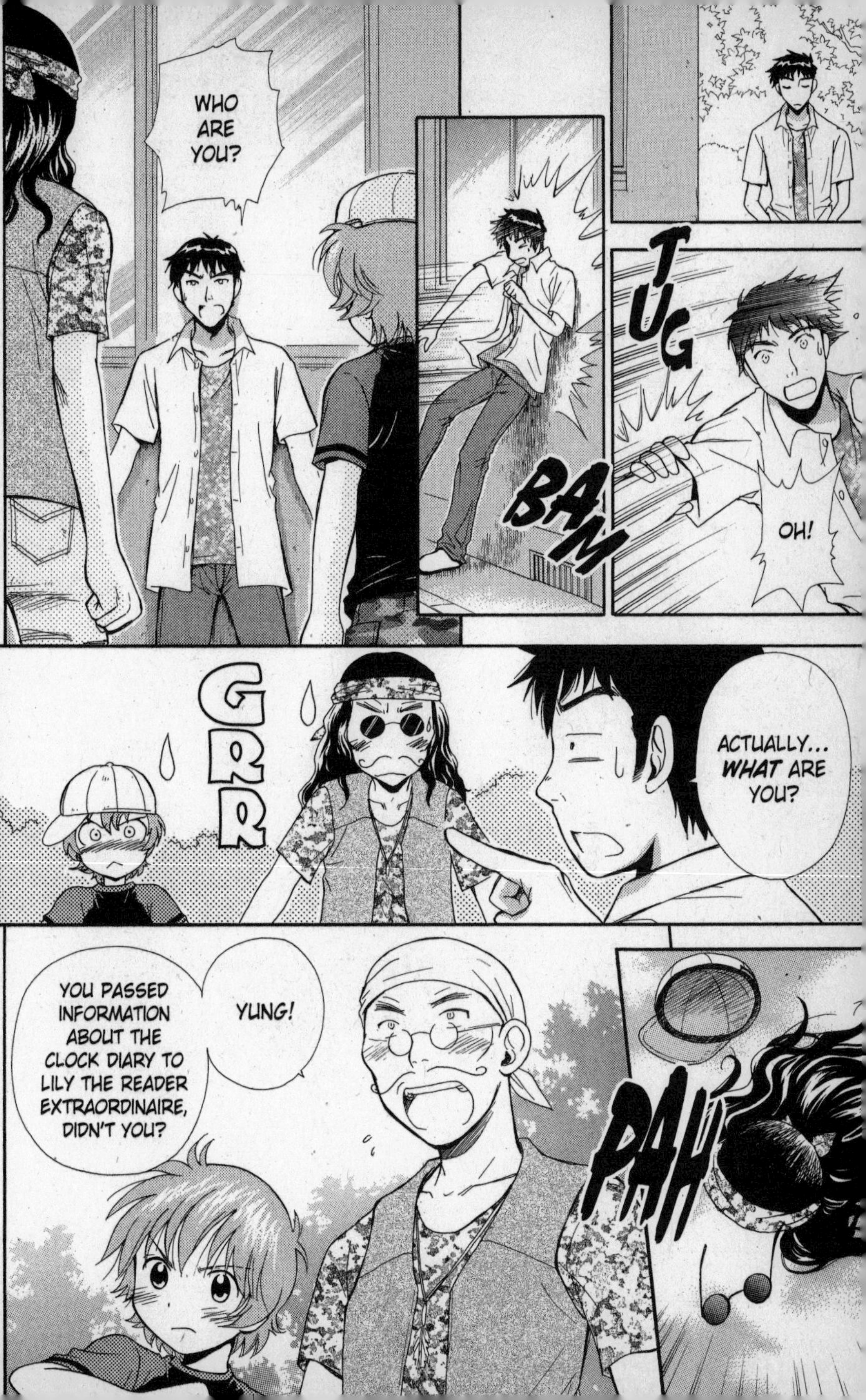
TUG
OH!
BAM
WHO ARE YOU?
ACTUALLY... WHAT ARE YOU?
GRR
PAH
YUNG!
YOU PASSED INFORMATION ABOUT THE CLOCK DIARY TO LILY THE READER EXTRAORDINAIRE, DIDN'T YOU?

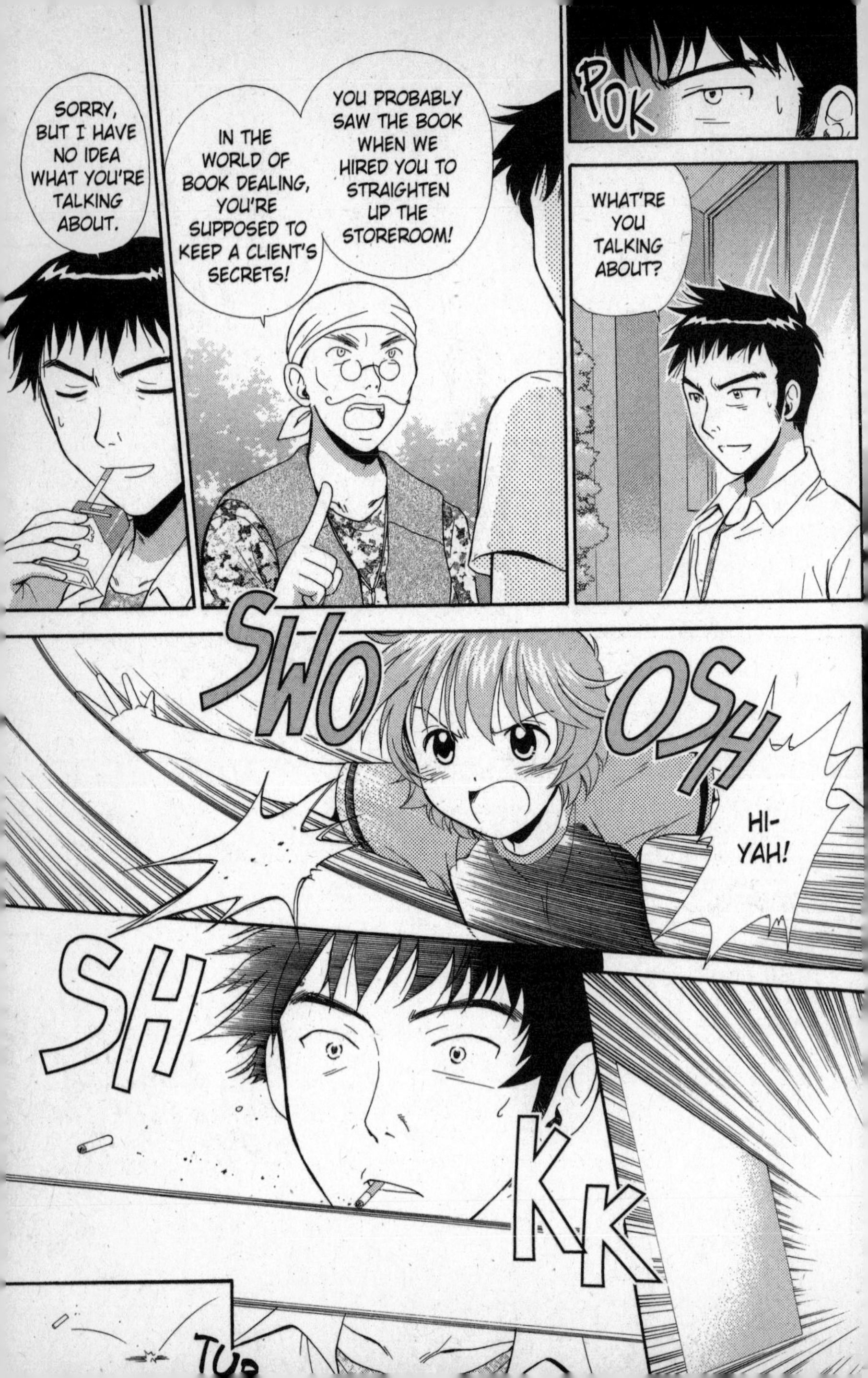
POK
WHAT'RE YOU TALKING ABOUT?
YOU PROBABLY SAW THE BOOK WHEN WE HIRED YOU TO STRAIGHTEN UP THE STOREROOM!
IN THE WORLD OF BOOK DEALING, YOU'RE SUPPOSED TO KEEP A CLIENT'S SECRETS!
SORRY, BUT I HAVE NO IDEA WHAT YOU'RE TALKING ABOUT.
SWOOSH
HI-YAH!
SHKK

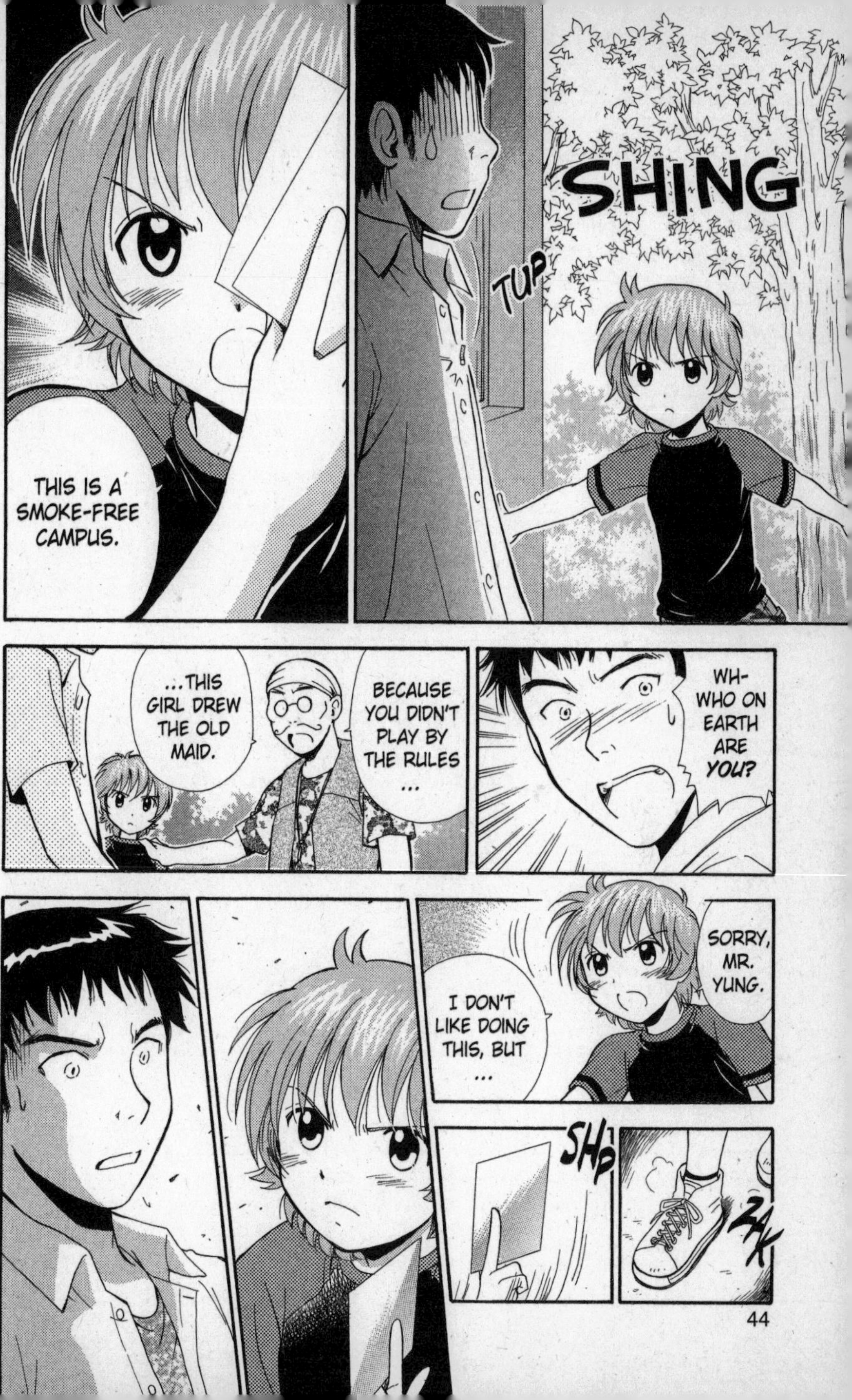
SHING
TUP
THIS IS A SMOKE-FREE CAMPUS.
WH- WHO ON EARTH ARE YOU?
BECAUSE YOU DIDN'T PLAY BY THE RULES ...
...THIS GIRL DREW THE OLD MAID.
SORRY, MR. YUNG.
I DON'T LIKE DOING THIS, BUT ...
ZAK
SHP

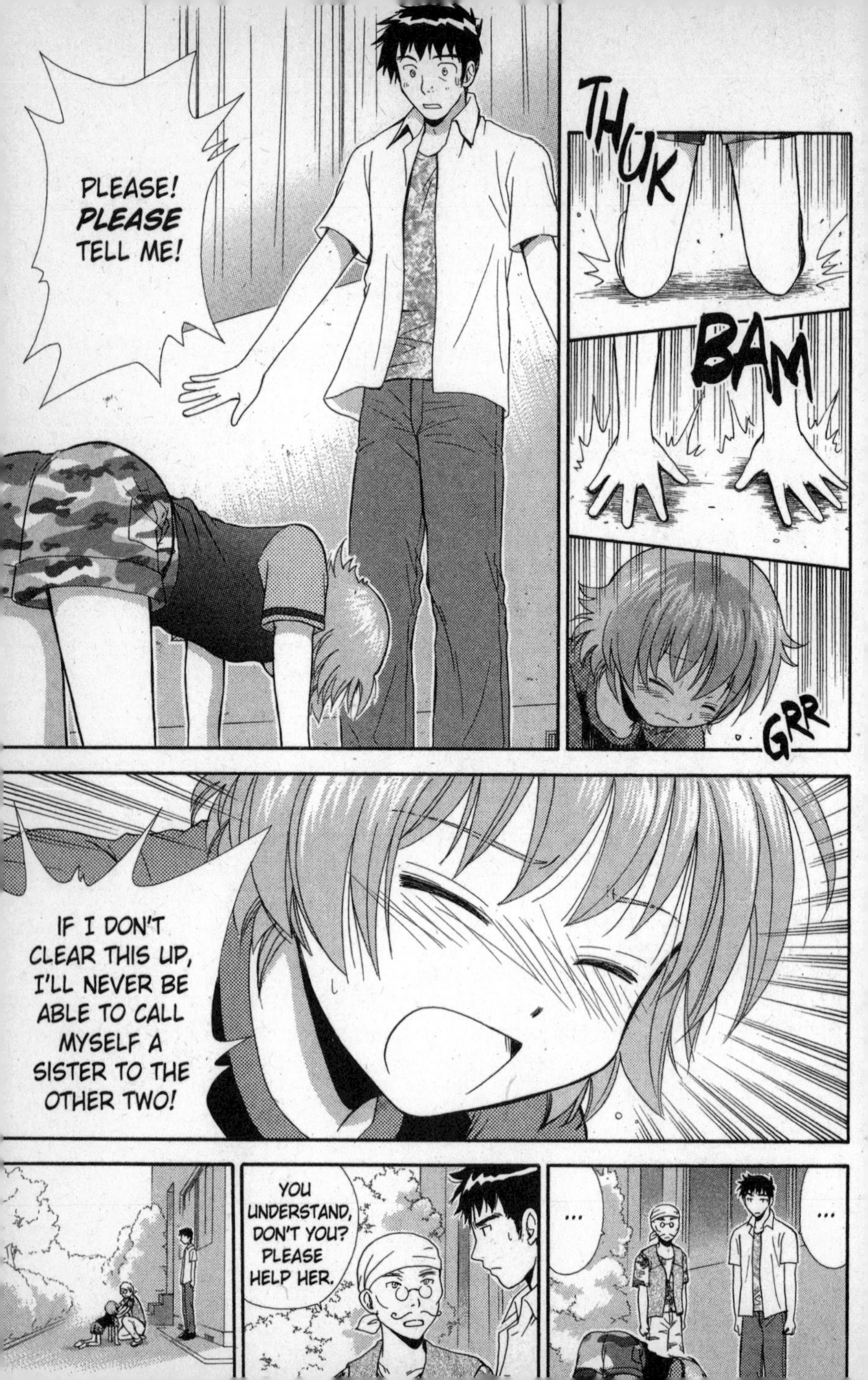
THUK
BAM
GRR
PLEASE! *PLEASE* TELL ME!
IF I DON'T CLEAR THIS UP, I'LL NEVER BE ABLE TO CALL MYSELF A SISTER TO THE OTHER TWO!
...
...
YOU UNDERSTAND, DON'T YOU? PLEASE HELP HER.

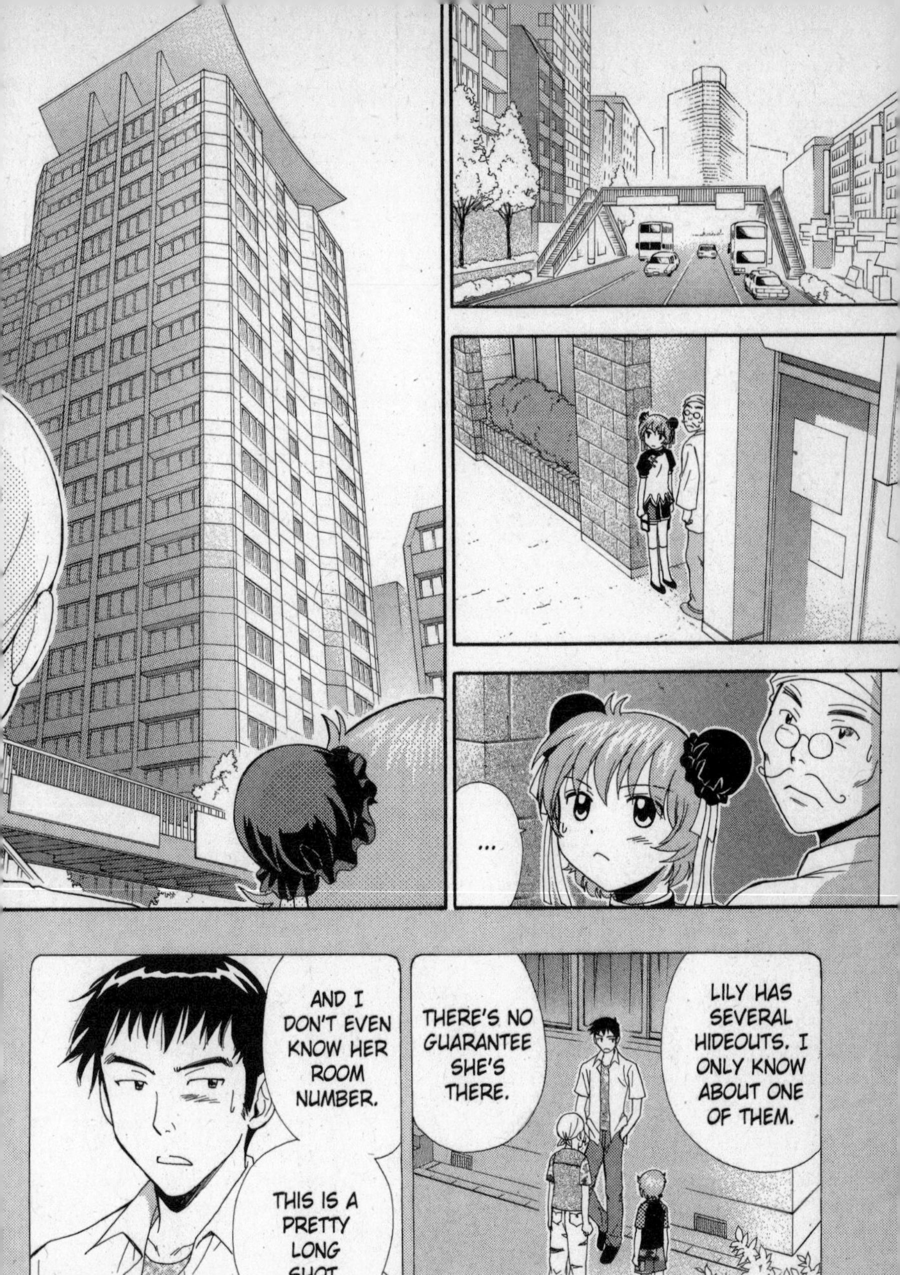
...
LILY HAS SEVERAL HIDEOUTS. I ONLY KNOW ABOUT ONE OF THEM.
THERE'S NO GUARANTEE SHE'S THERE.
AND I DON'T EVEN KNOW HER ROOM NUMBER.
THIS IS A PRETTY LONG SHOT.

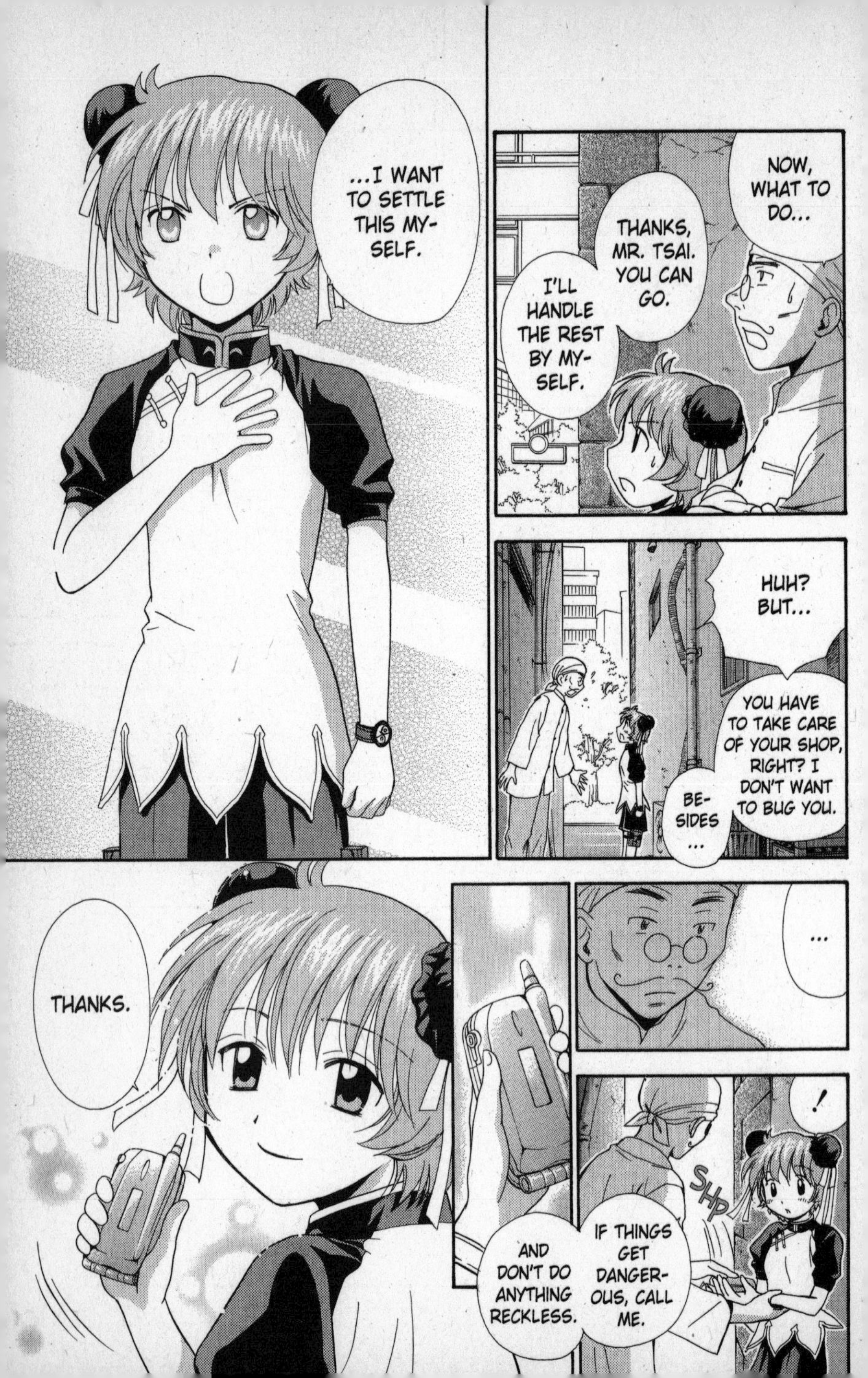
NOW, WHAT TO DO...
THANKS, MR. TSAI. YOU CAN GO.
I'LL HANDLE THE REST BY MYSELF.
HUH? BUT...
YOU HAVE TO TAKE CARE OF YOUR SHOP, RIGHT? I DON'T WANT TO BUG YOU.
BESIDES...
...I WANT TO SETTLE THIS MYSELF.
...
!
SHP
IF THINGS GET DANGEROUS, CALL ME.
AND DON'T DO ANYTHING RECKLESS.
THANKS.

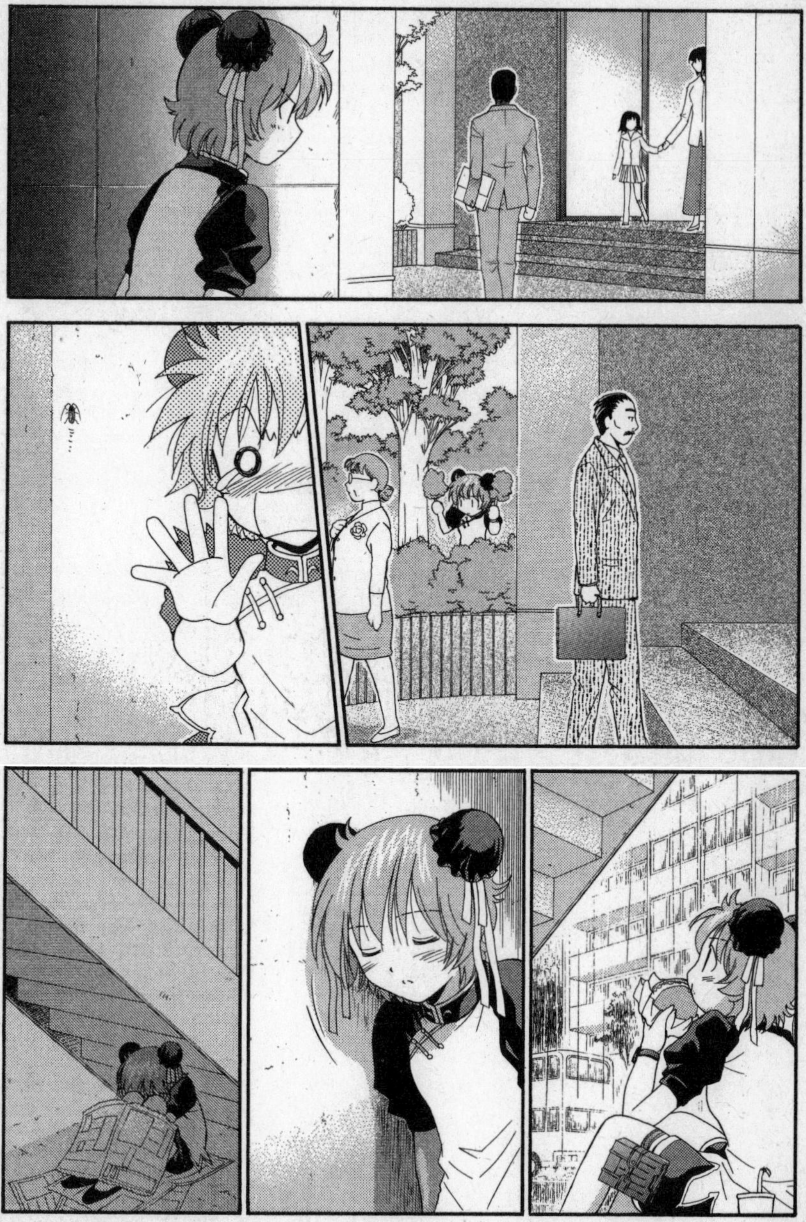

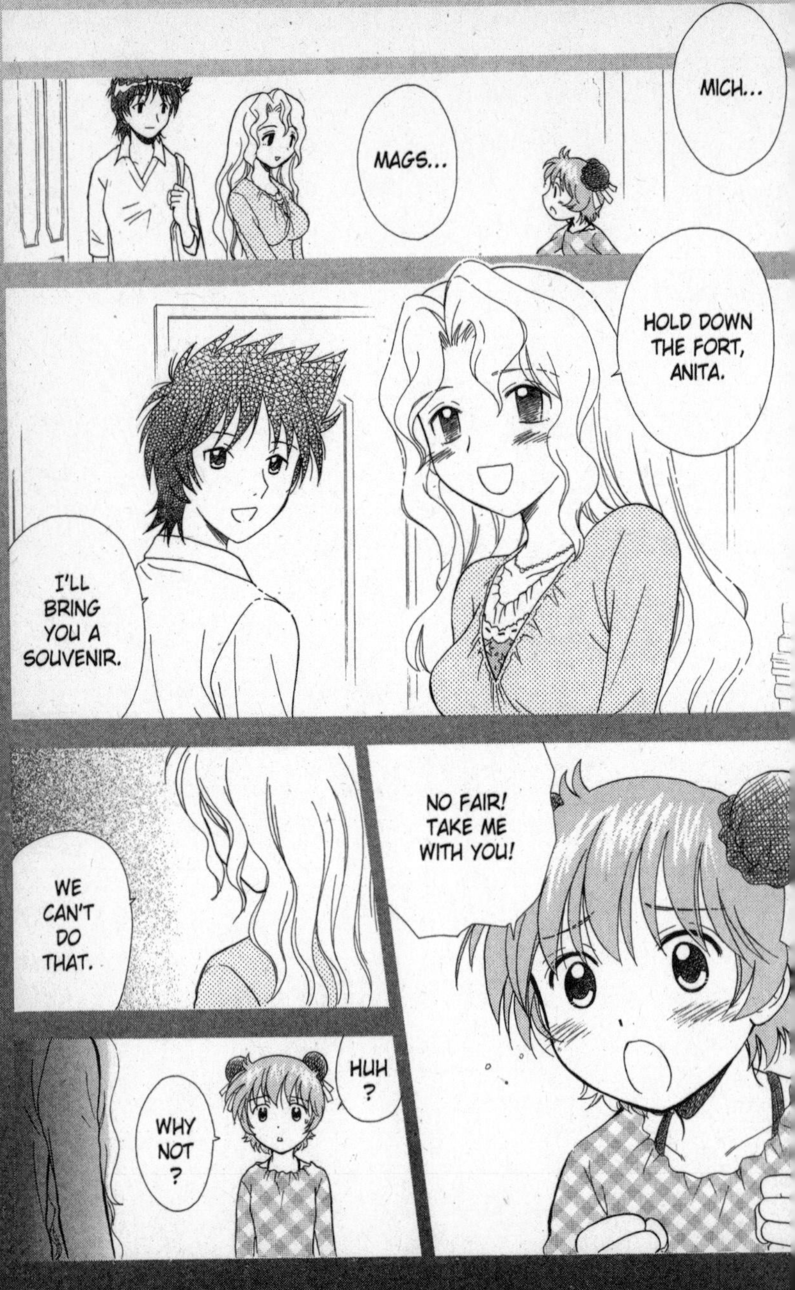
MICH...
MAGS...
HOLD DOWN THE FORT, ANITA.
I'LL BRING YOU A SOUVENIR.
NO FAIR! TAKE ME WITH YOU!
WE CAN'T DO THAT.
HUH ?
WHY NOT ?

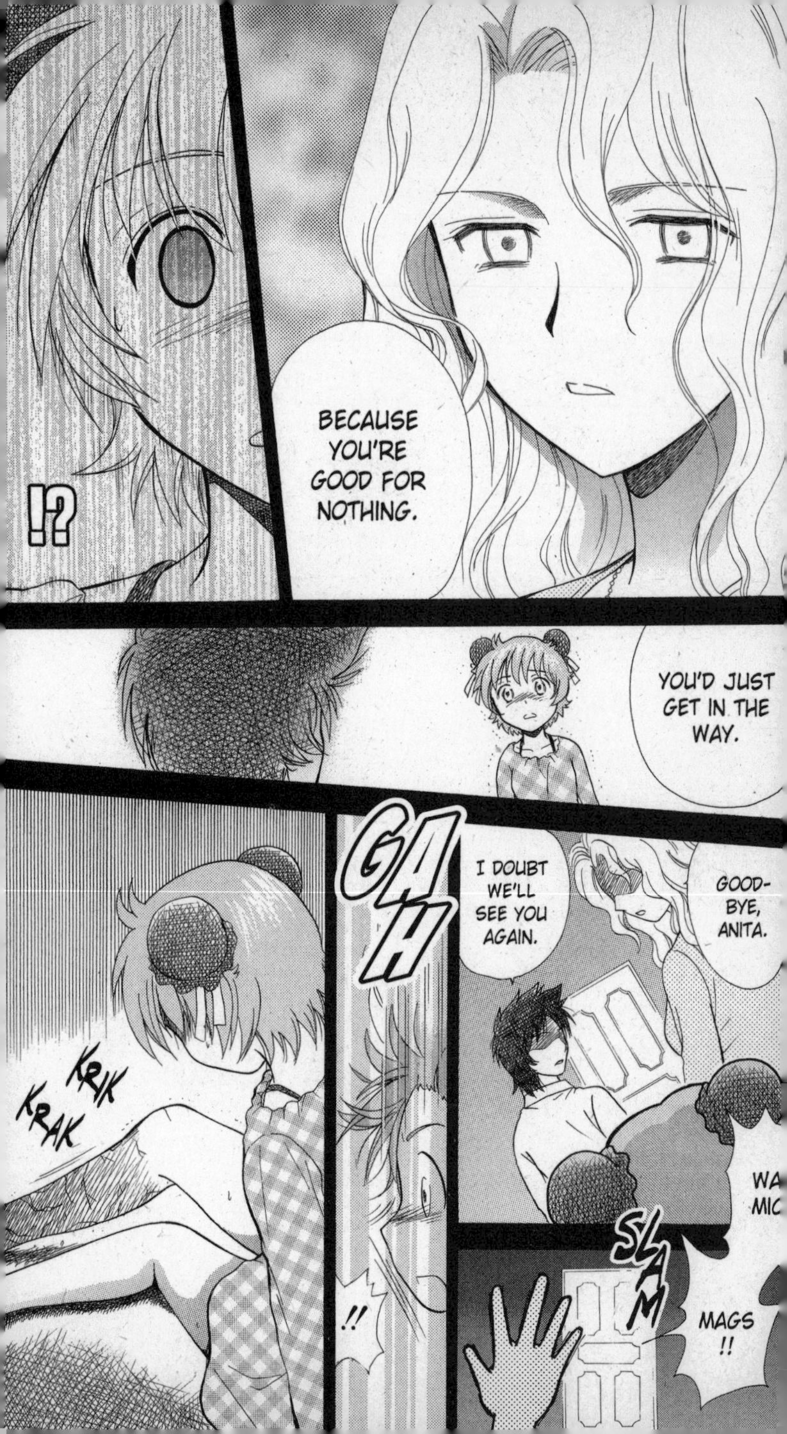
BECAUSE YOU'RE GOOD FOR NOTHING.
!?
YOU'D JUST GET IN THE WAY.
GOOD-BYE, ANITA.
I DOUBT WE'LL SEE YOU AGAIN.
MAGS!!
SLAM
GAH
!!
KRIK KRAK

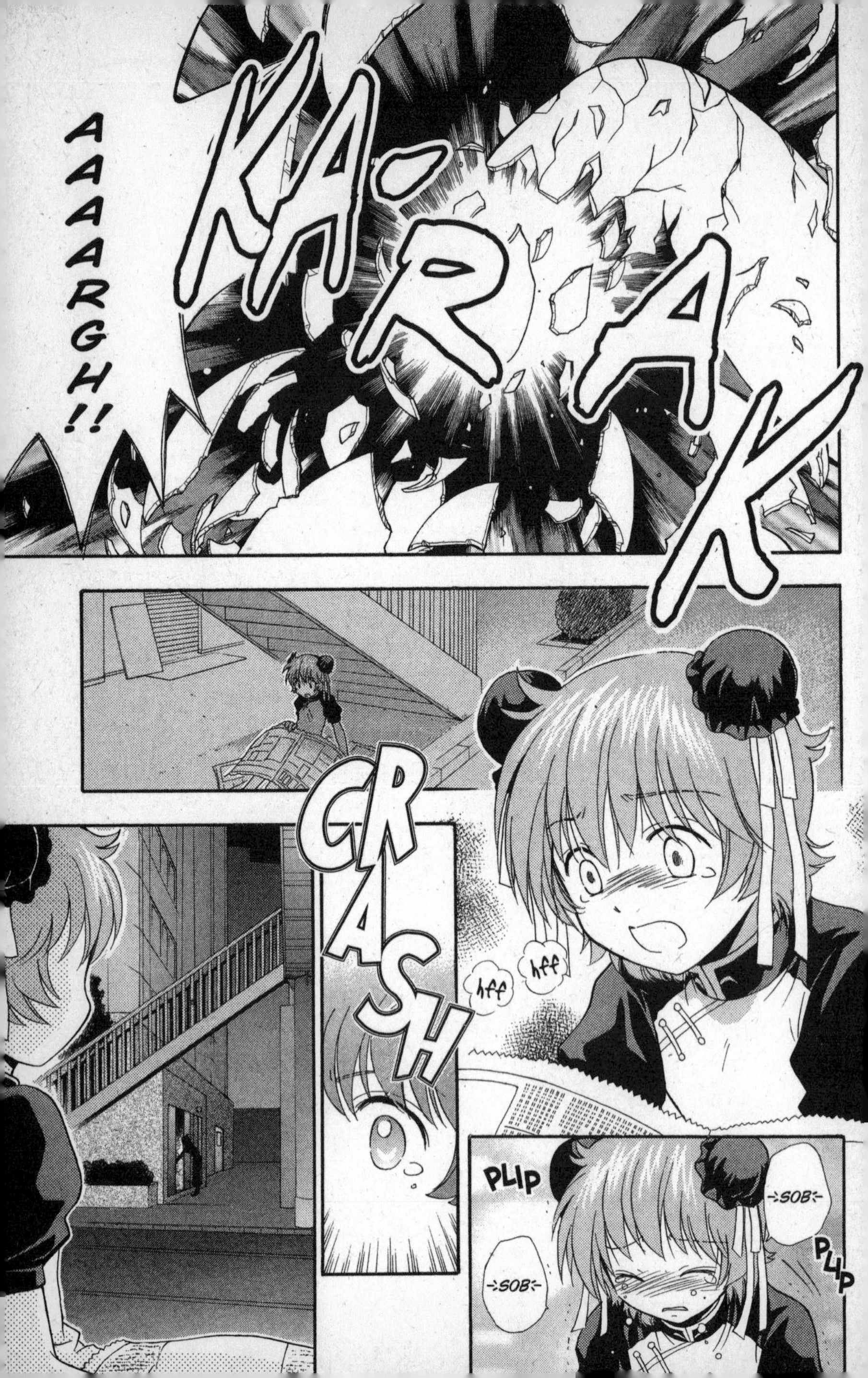
KA-RA-K
AAAARGH!!
hff
hff
CRASH
-SOB-
PLIP
-SOB-
PLIP

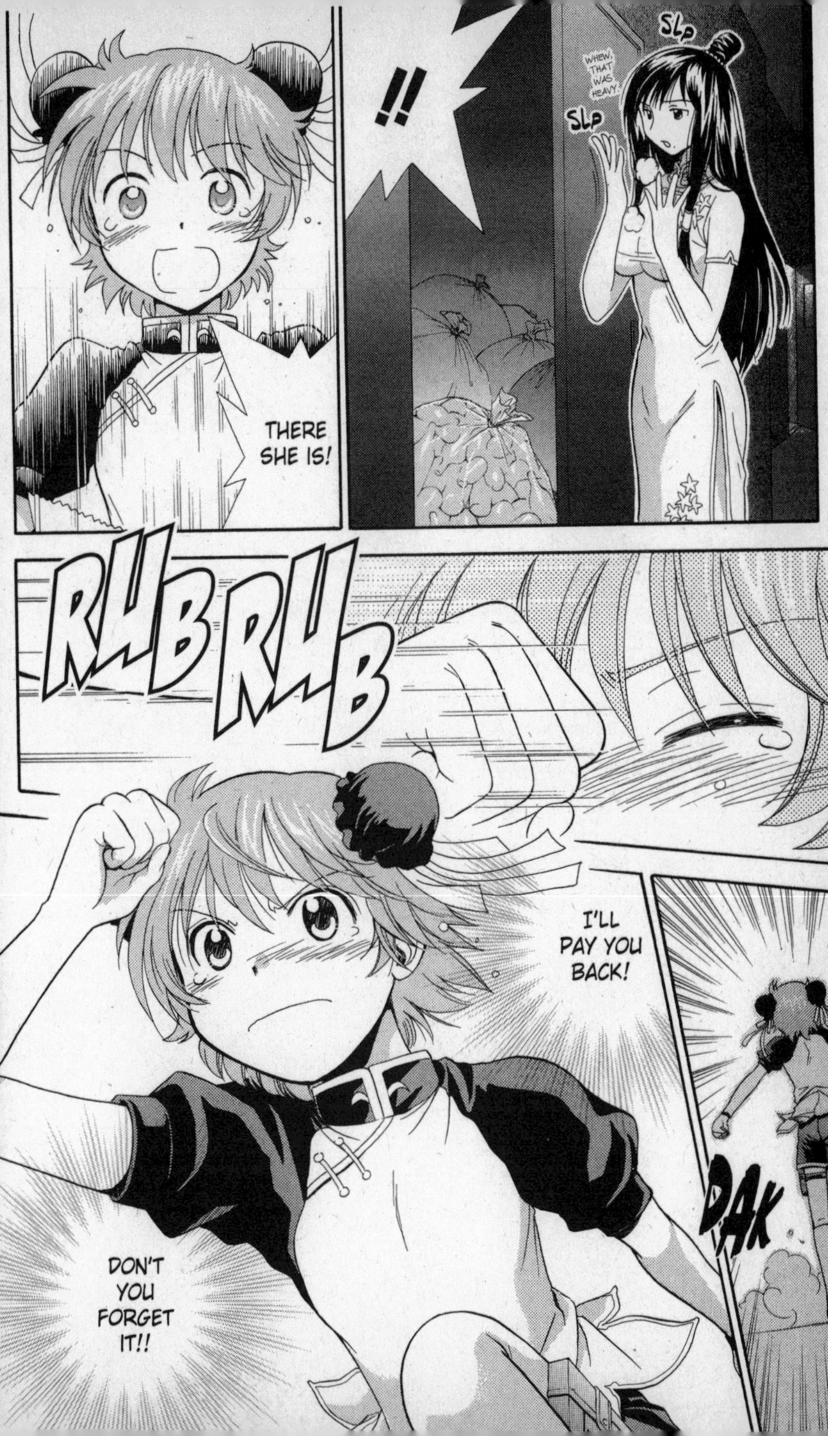
SLP
WHEW, THAT WAS HEAVY.
SLP
!!
THERE SHE IS!
RUB RUB
DAK
I'LL PAY YOU BACK!
DON'T YOU FORGET IT!!

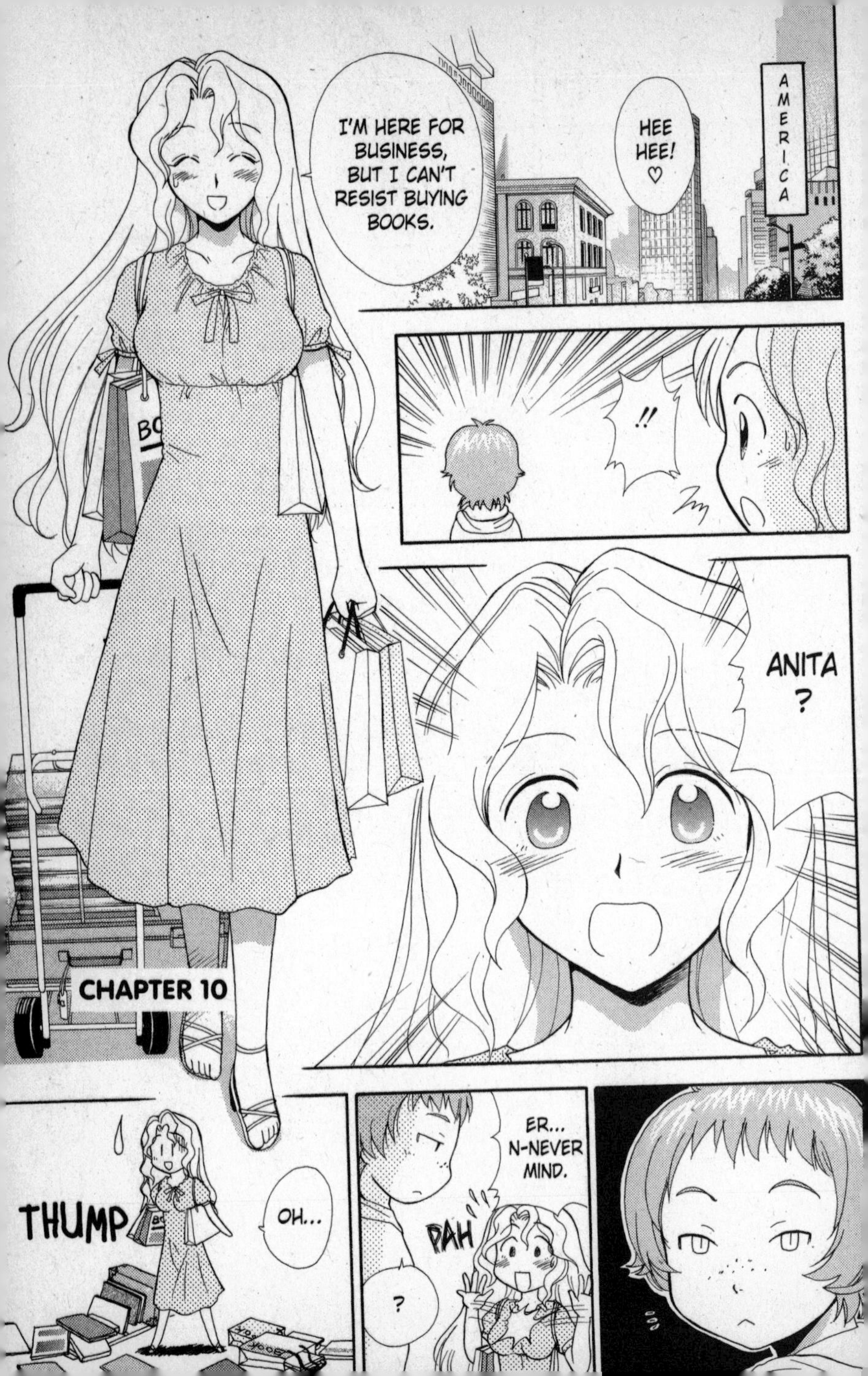
AMERICA
HEE HEE! ♡
I'M HERE FOR BUSINESS, BUT I CAN'T RESIST BUYING BOOKS.
CHAPTER 10
!!
ANITA ?
ER... N-NEVER MIND.
PAH
?
OH...
THUMP

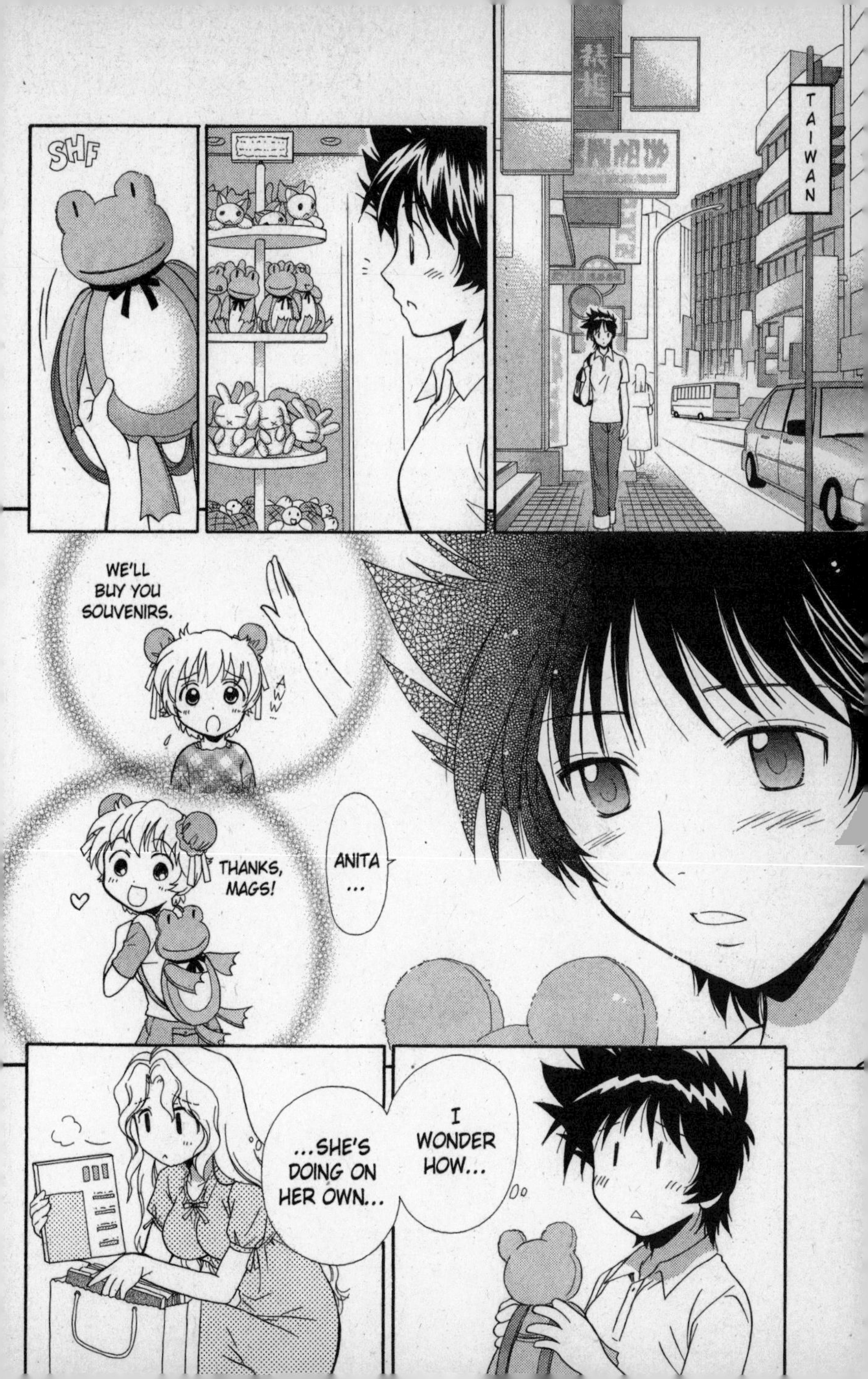
TAIWAN
SHF
WE'LL BUY YOU SOUVENIRS.
THANKS, MAGS!
ANITA ...
I WONDER HOW...
...SHE'S DOING ON HER OWN...

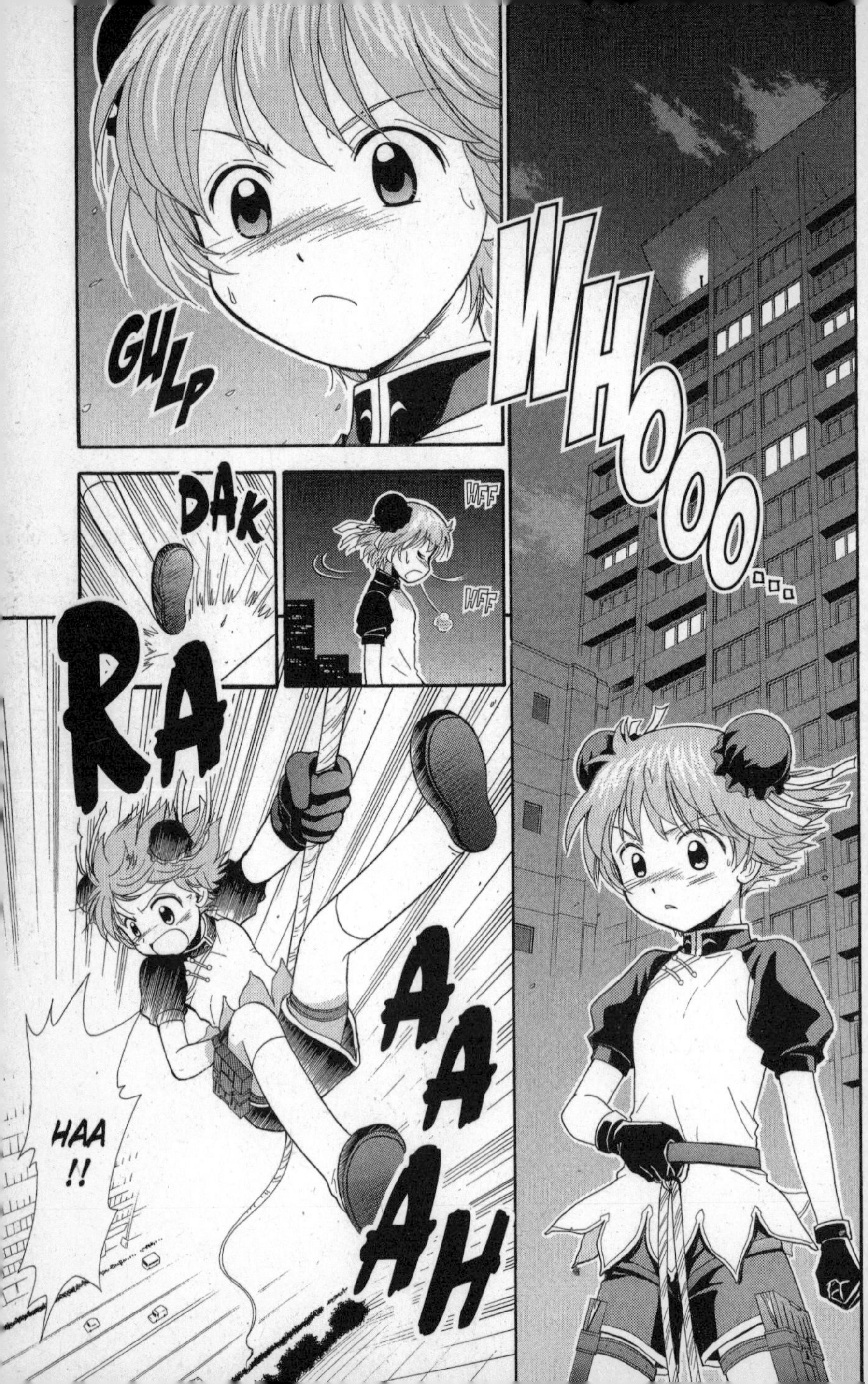
WHOOOO...
GULP
HFF
HFF
DAK
RAAAAH
HAA !!

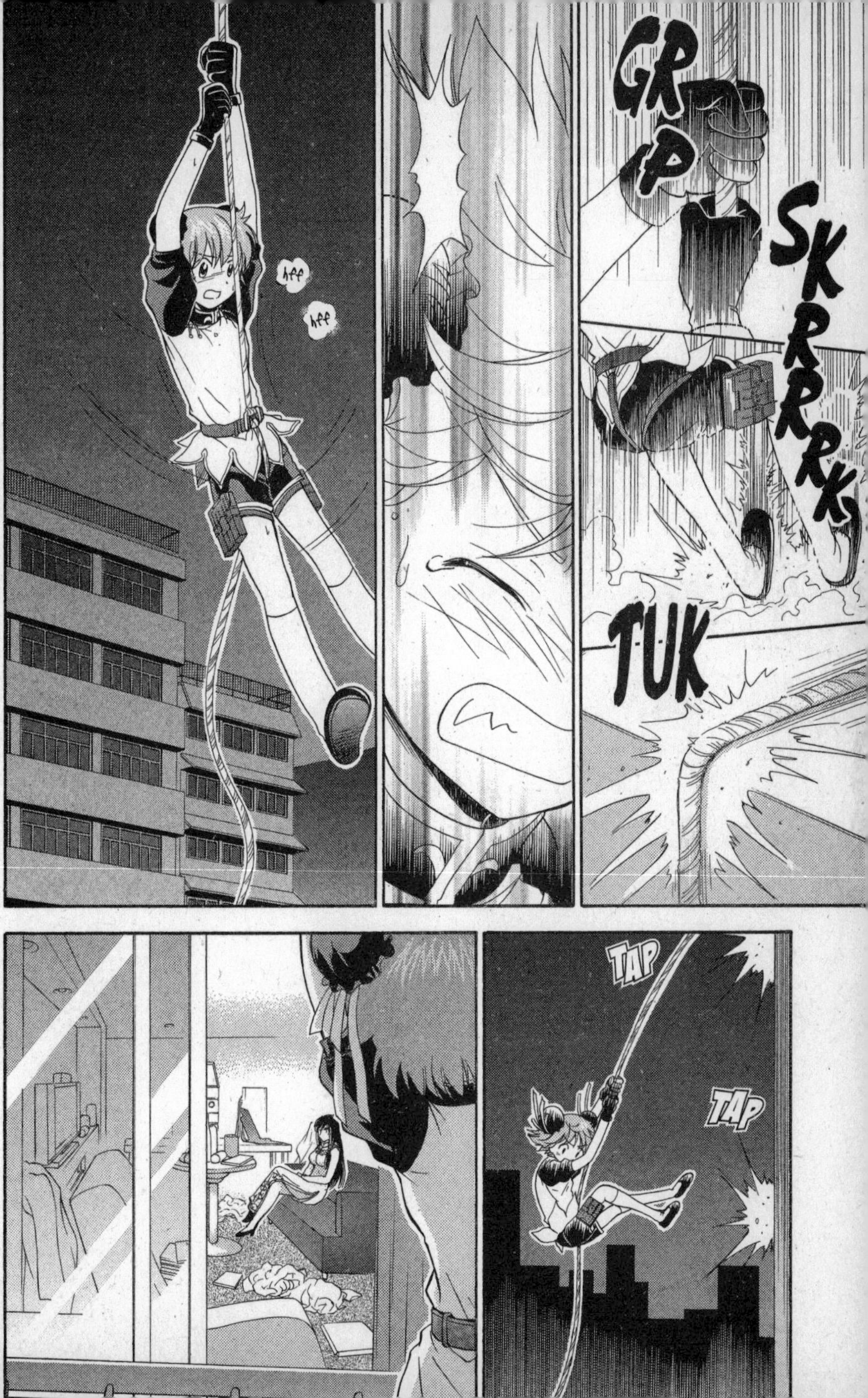
GRIP
SKRRRK
TUK
hff
hff
TAP
TAP

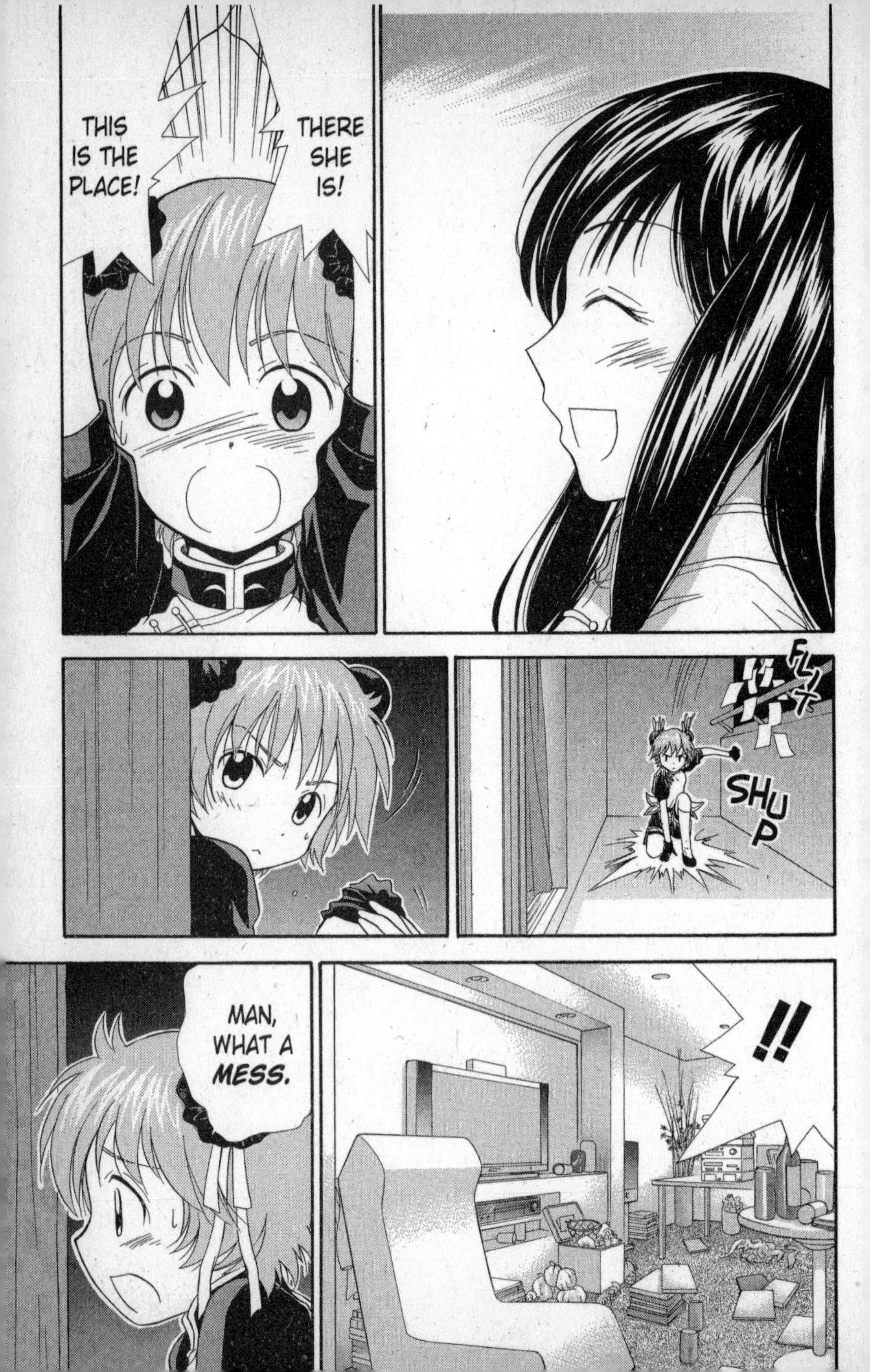
THERE SHE IS!
THIS IS THE PLACE!
FLIT
SHUP
!!
MAN, WHAT A MESS.

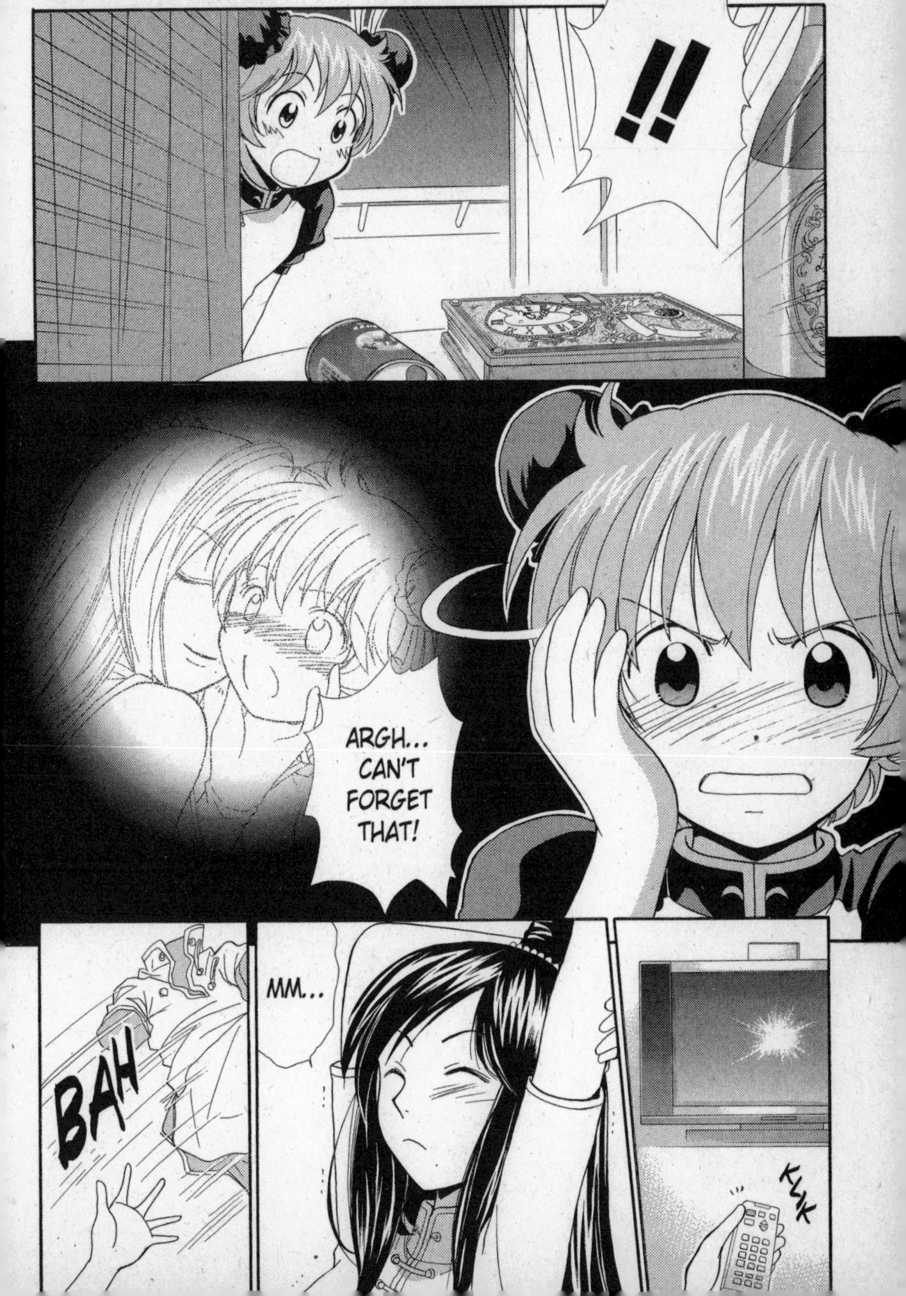
!!
ARGH... CAN'T FORGET THAT!
KLIK
MM...
BAH

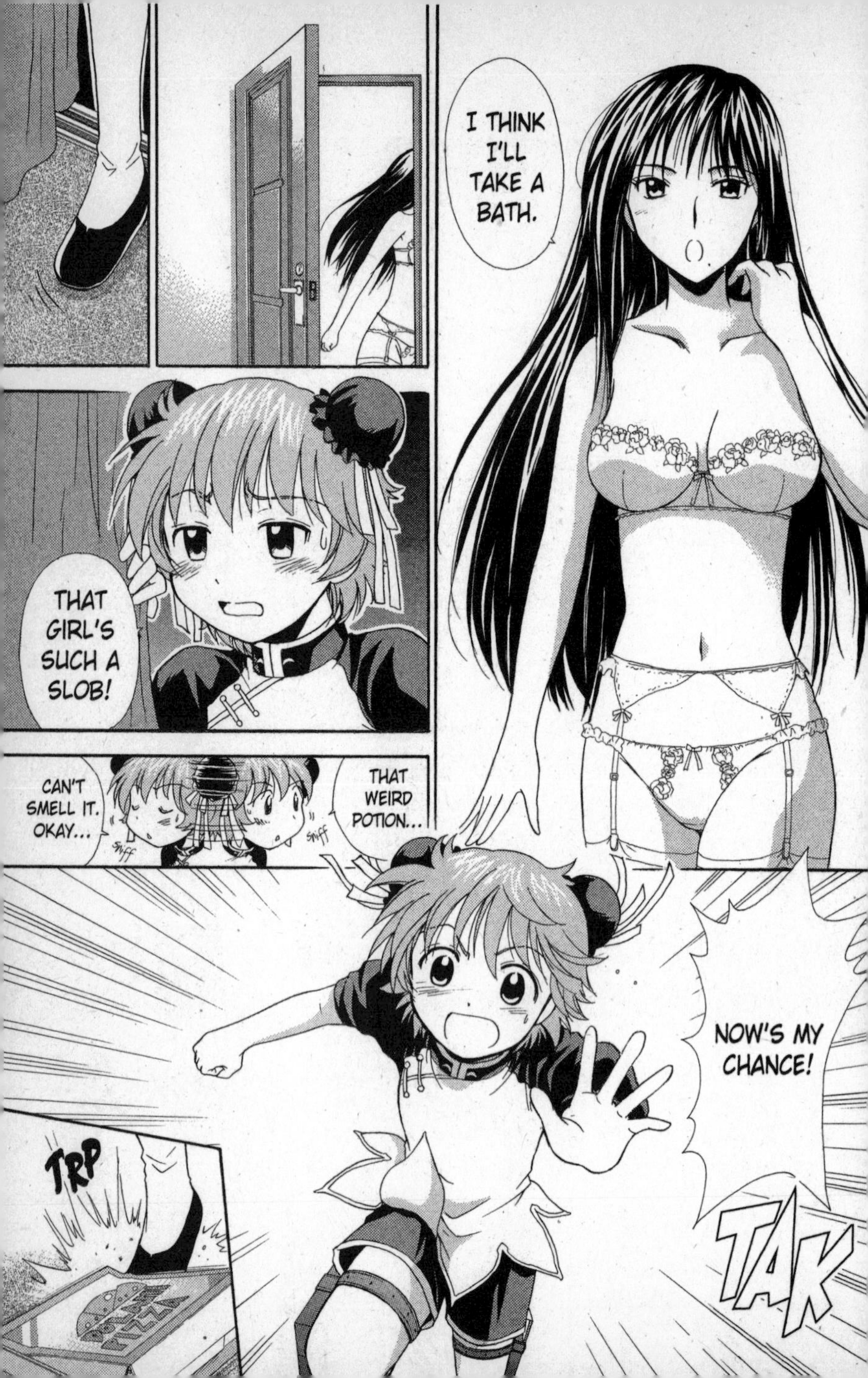
I THINK I'LL TAKE A BATH.
THAT GIRL'S SUCH A SLOB!
THAT WEIRD POTION...
Sniff
Sniff
CAN'T SMELL IT. OKAY...
NOW'S MY CHANCE!
TAK
TRP

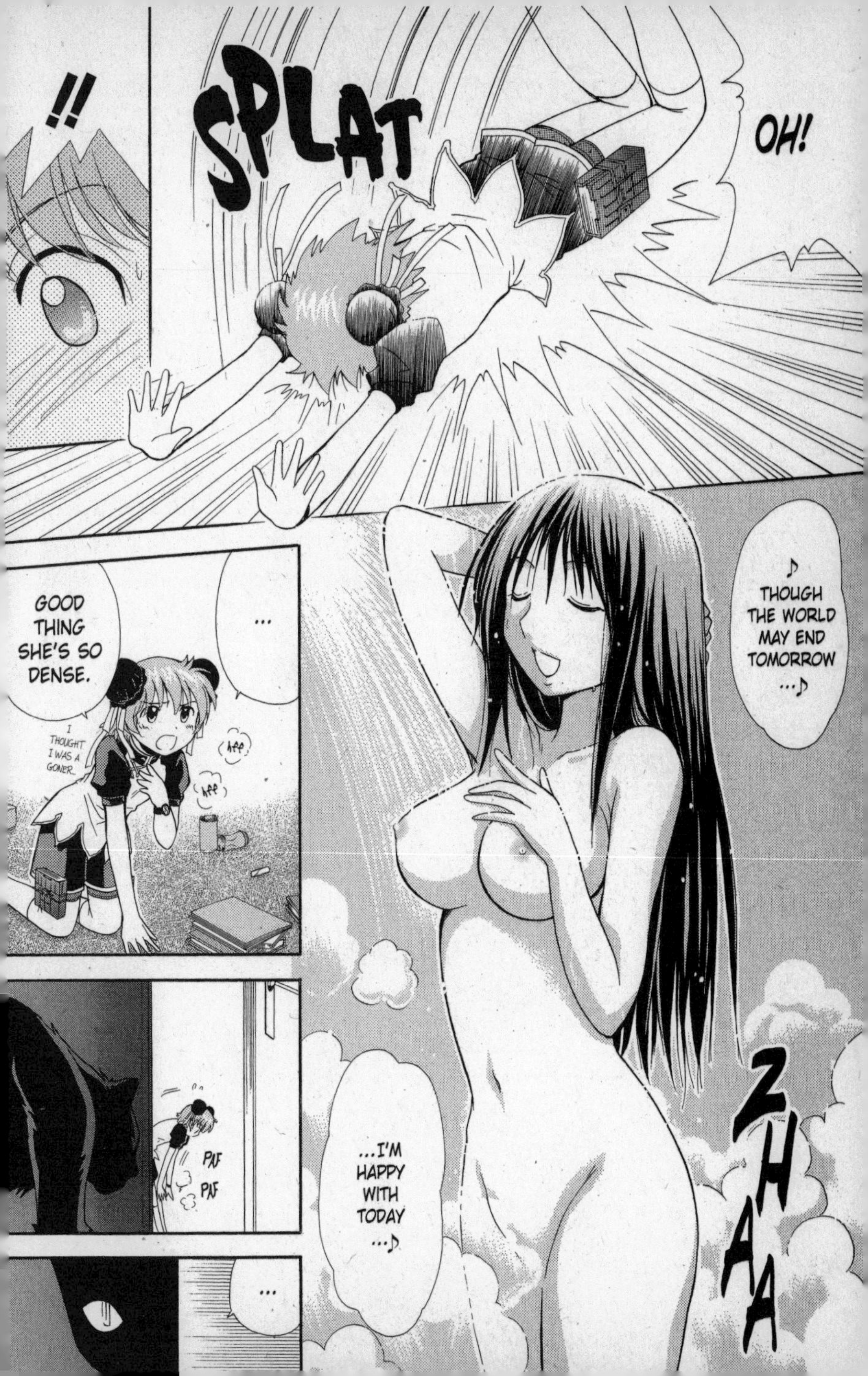
OH!
SPLAT
!!
♪ THOUGH THE WORLD MAY END TOMORROW ...♪
...I'M HAPPY WITH TODAY ...♪
ZHAAA
...
GOOD THING SHE'S SO DENSE.
I THOUGHT I WAS A GONER...
hff
hff
PAF
PAF
...

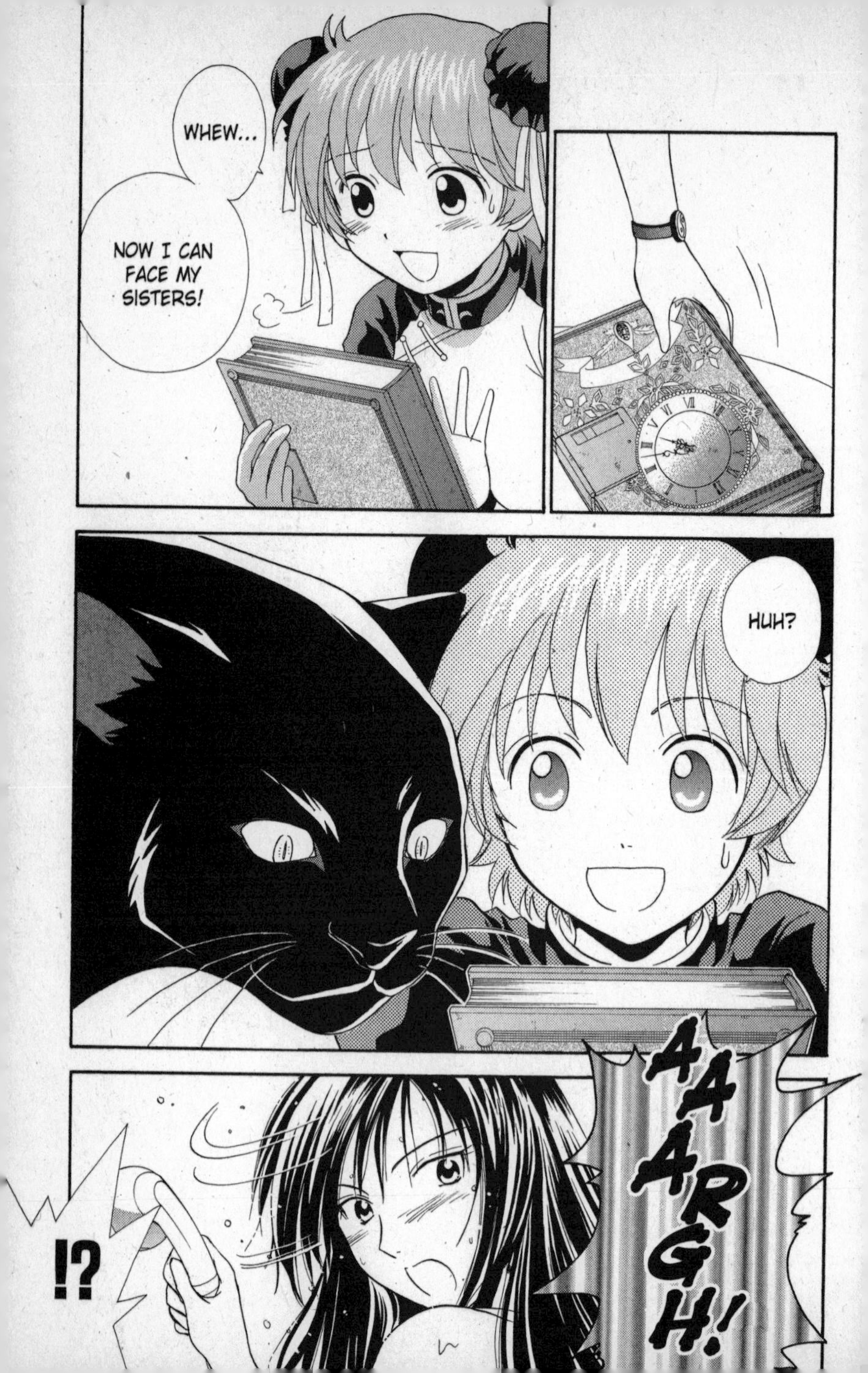
WHEW...
NOW I CAN FACE MY SISTERS!
HUH?
AAARGH!
!?

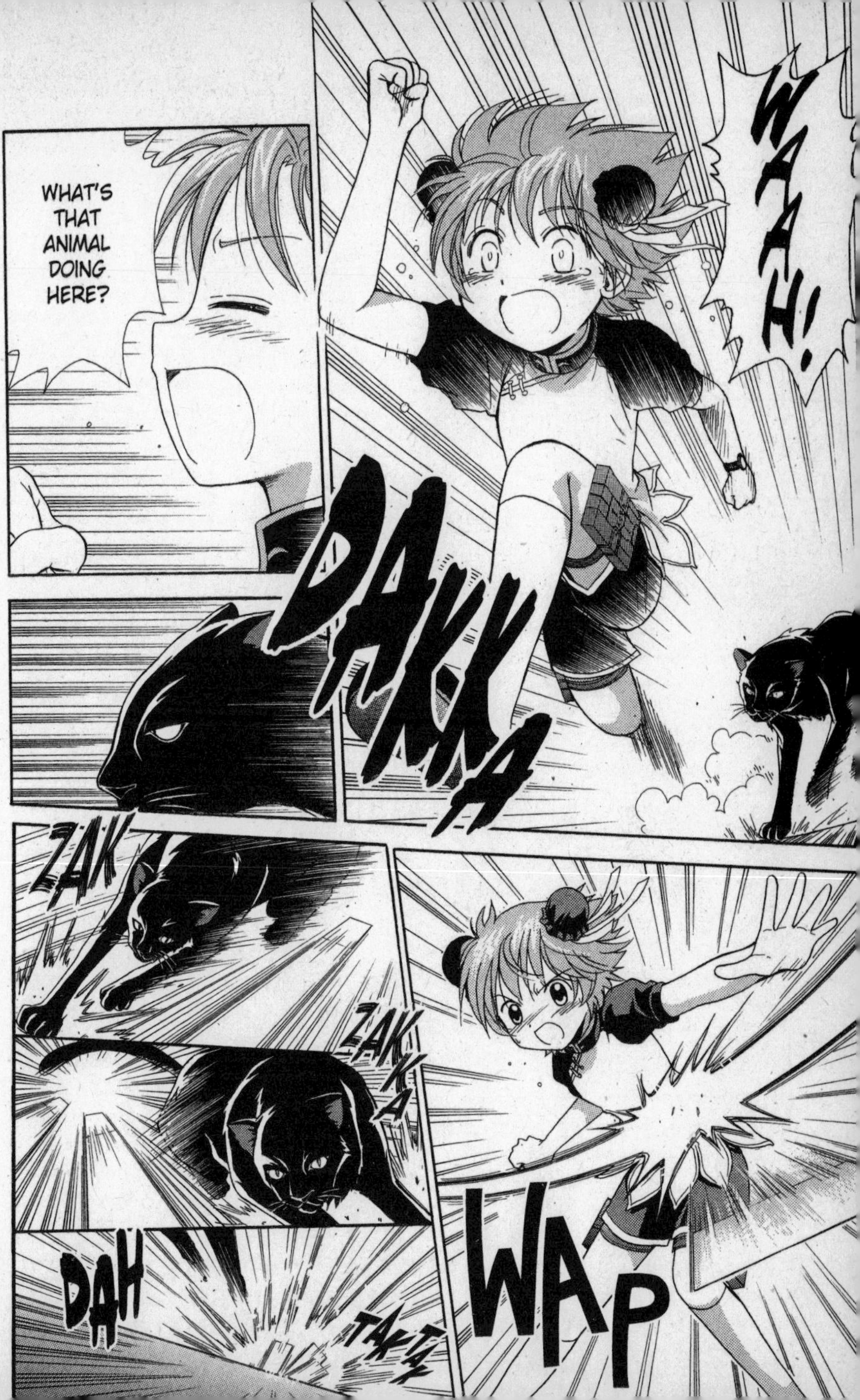
WAAH!
DAKKAA
WHAT'S THAT ANIMAL DOING HERE?
WAP
ZAK
ZAKKA
DAH
TAKTAK

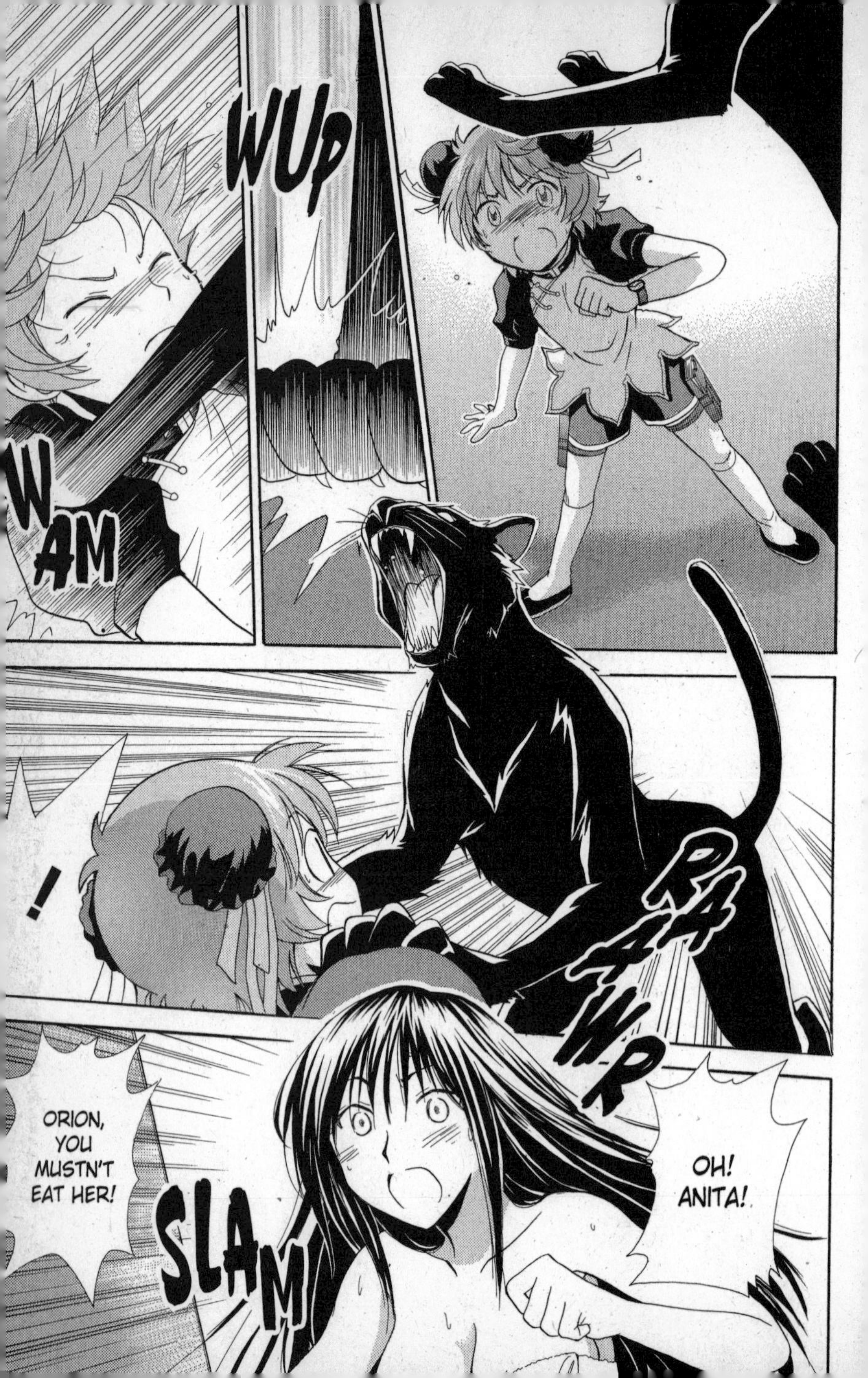
WUP
WAM
RAAWR
!
OH! ANITA!
SLAM
ORION, YOU MUSTN'T EAT HER!

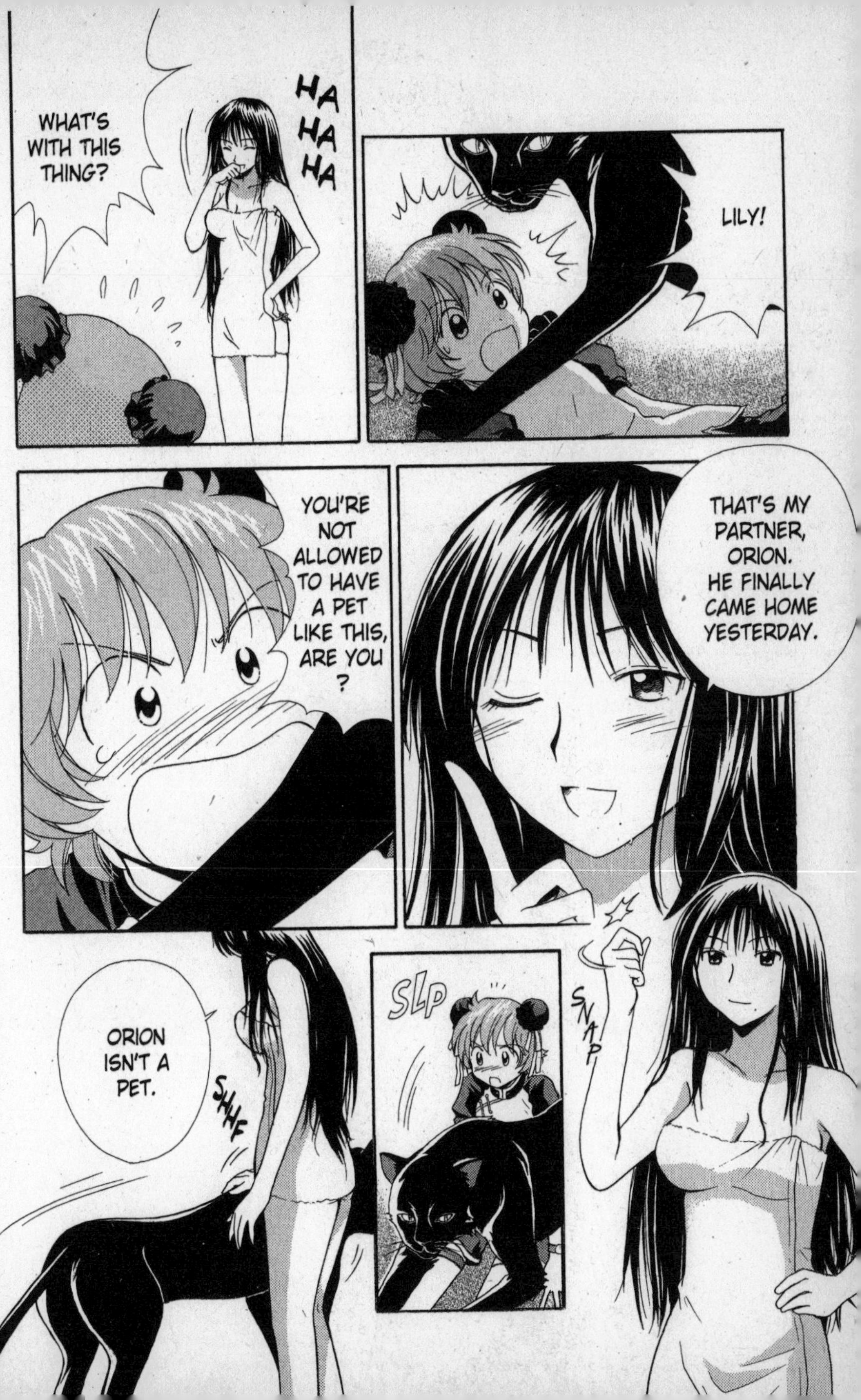
LILY!
HA HA HA
WHAT'S WITH THIS THING?
THAT'S MY PARTNER, ORION. HE FINALLY CAME HOME YESTERDAY.
YOU'RE NOT ALLOWED TO HAVE A PET LIKE THIS, ARE YOU?
SNAP
SLP
ORION ISN'T A PET.
SHHF

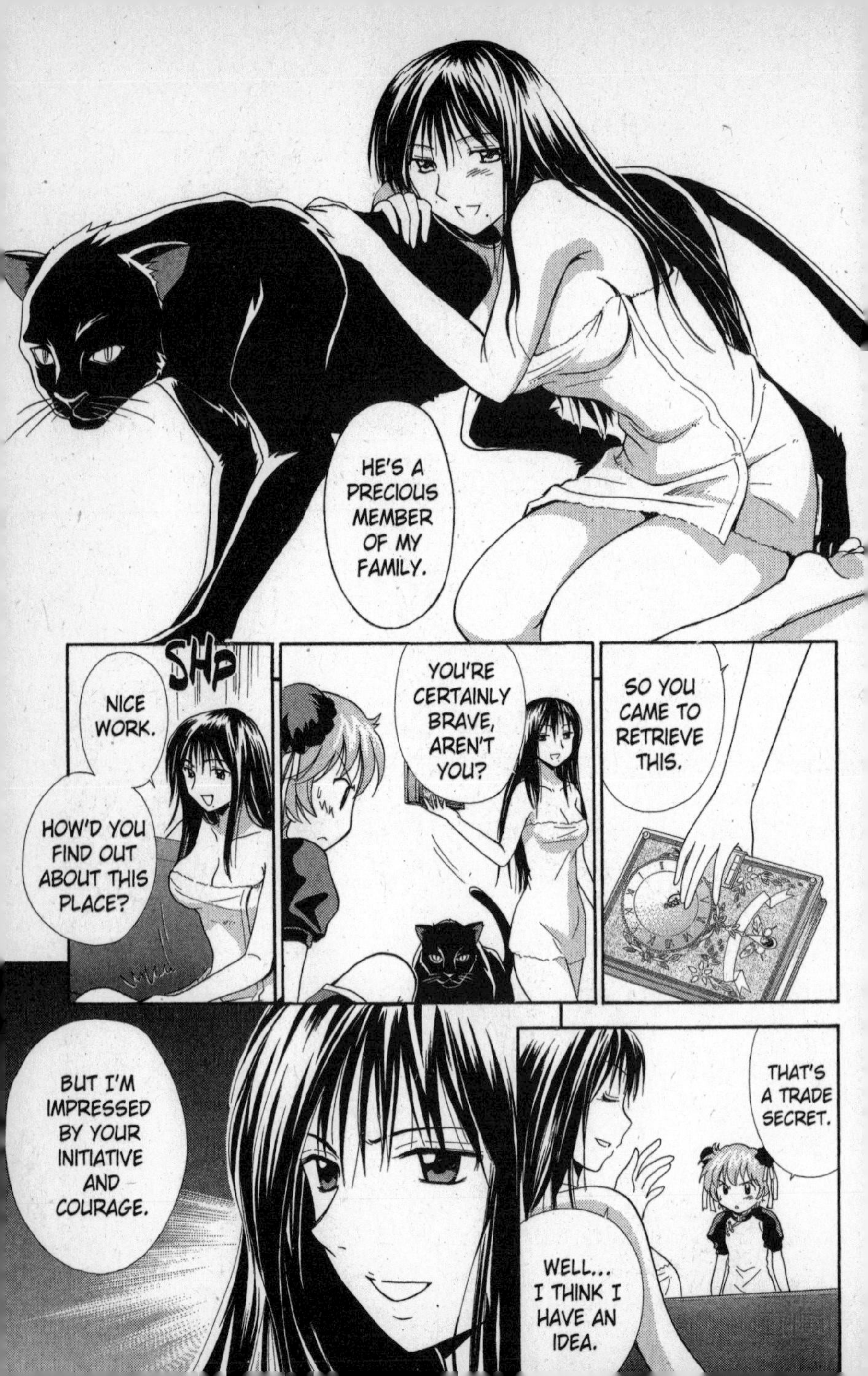
HE'S A PRECIOUS MEMBER OF MY FAMILY.
SO YOU CAME TO RETRIEVE THIS.
YOU'RE CERTAINLY BRAVE, AREN'T YOU?
SHP
NICE WORK.
HOW'D YOU FIND OUT ABOUT THIS PLACE?
THAT'S A TRADE SECRET.
WELL... I THINK I HAVE AN IDEA.
BUT I'M IMPRESSED BY YOUR INITIATIVE AND COURAGE.

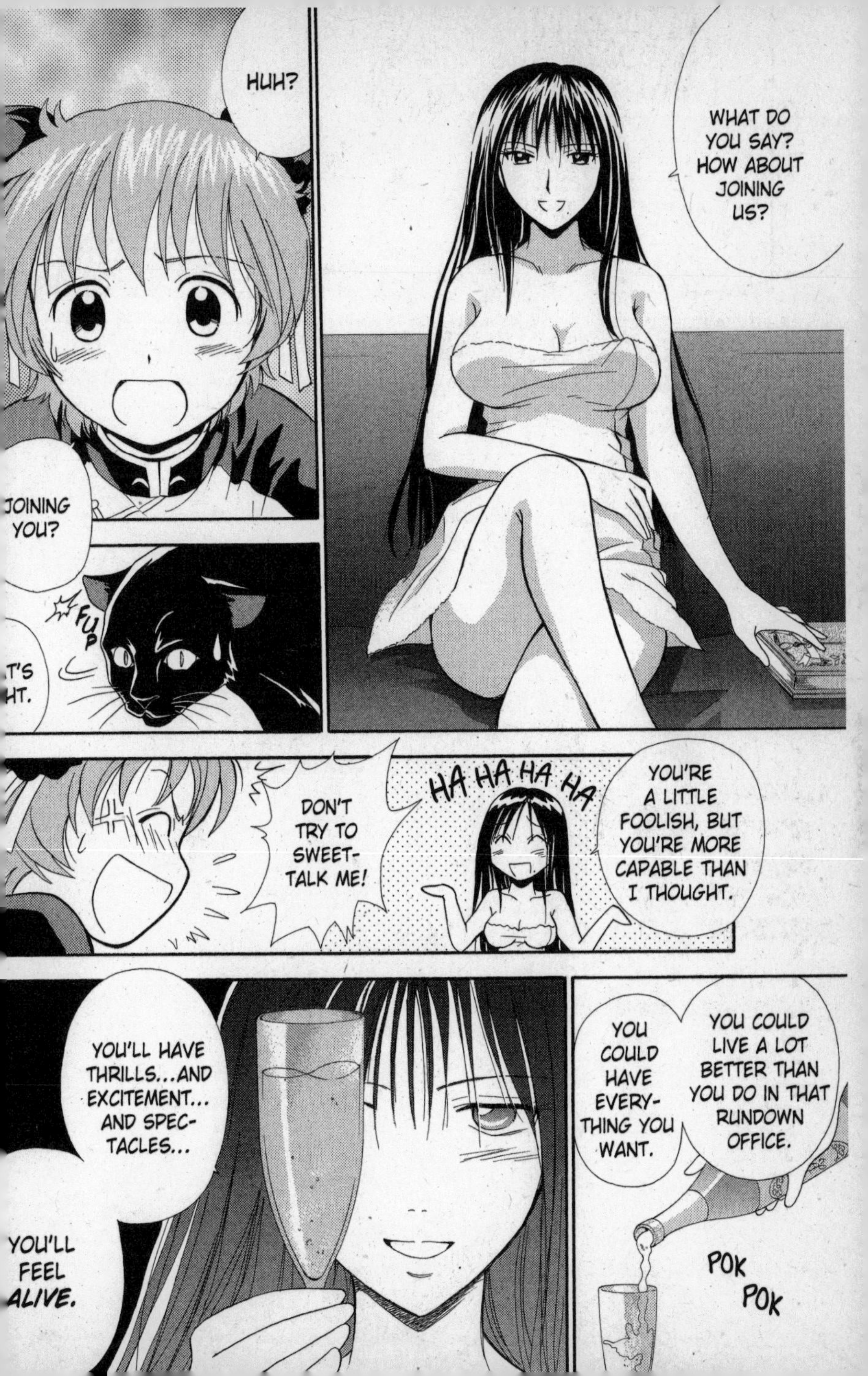
WHAT DO YOU SAY? HOW ABOUT JOINING US?
HUH?
JOINING YOU?
FUP
HA HA HA HA
YOU'RE A LITTLE FOOLISH, BUT YOU'RE MORE CAPABLE THAN I THOUGHT.
DON'T TRY TO SWEET-TALK ME!
YOU COULD LIVE A LOT BETTER THAN YOU DO IN THAT RUNDOWN OFFICE.
YOU COULD HAVE EVERY-THING YOU WANT.
POK POK
YOU'LL HAVE THRILLS...AND EXCITEMENT... AND SPEC-TACLES...
YOU'LL FEEL ALIVE.

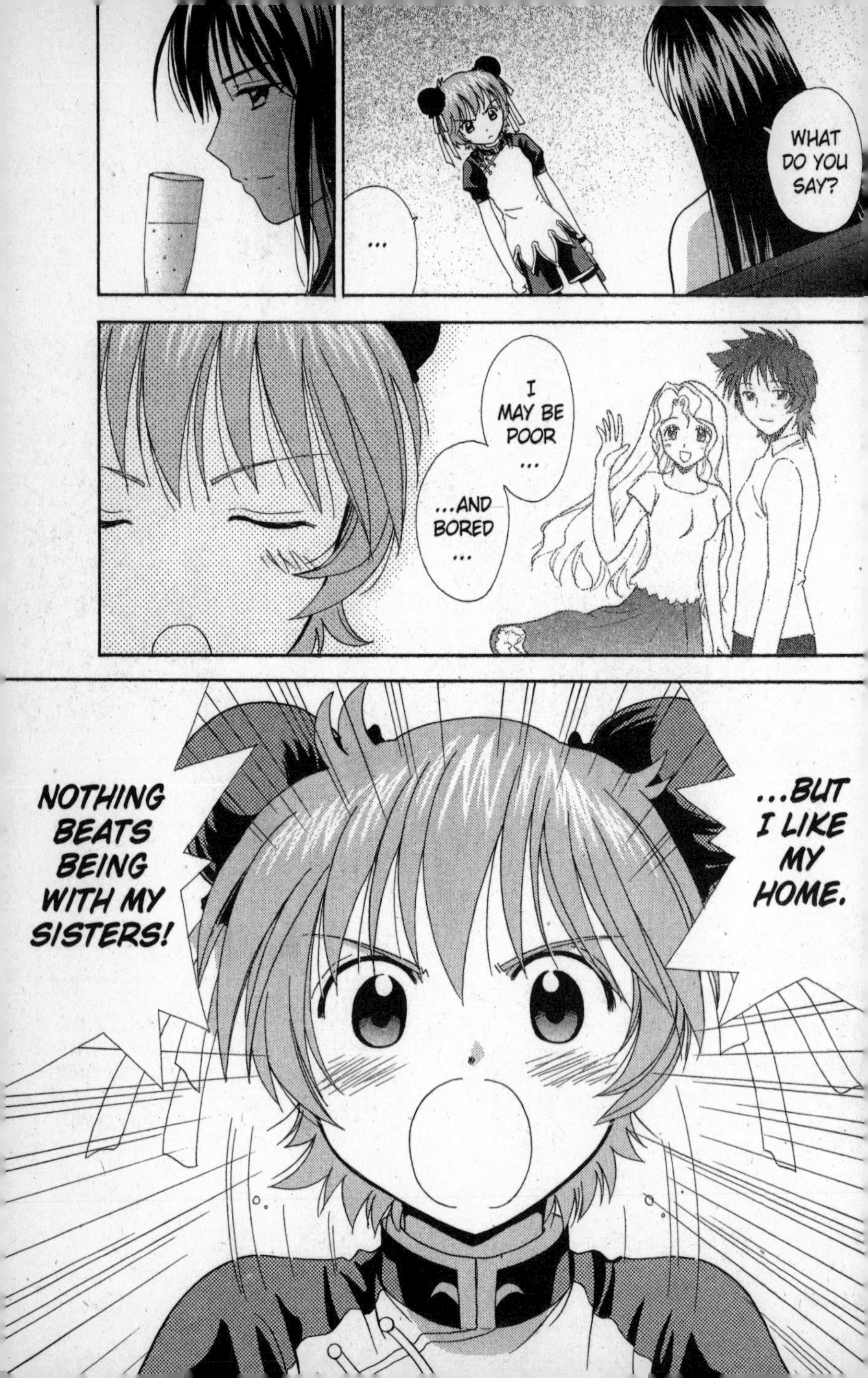
WHAT DO YOU SAY?
...
I MAY BE POOR ...
...AND BORED ...
...BUT I LIKE MY HOME.
NOTHING BEATS BEING WITH MY SISTERS!

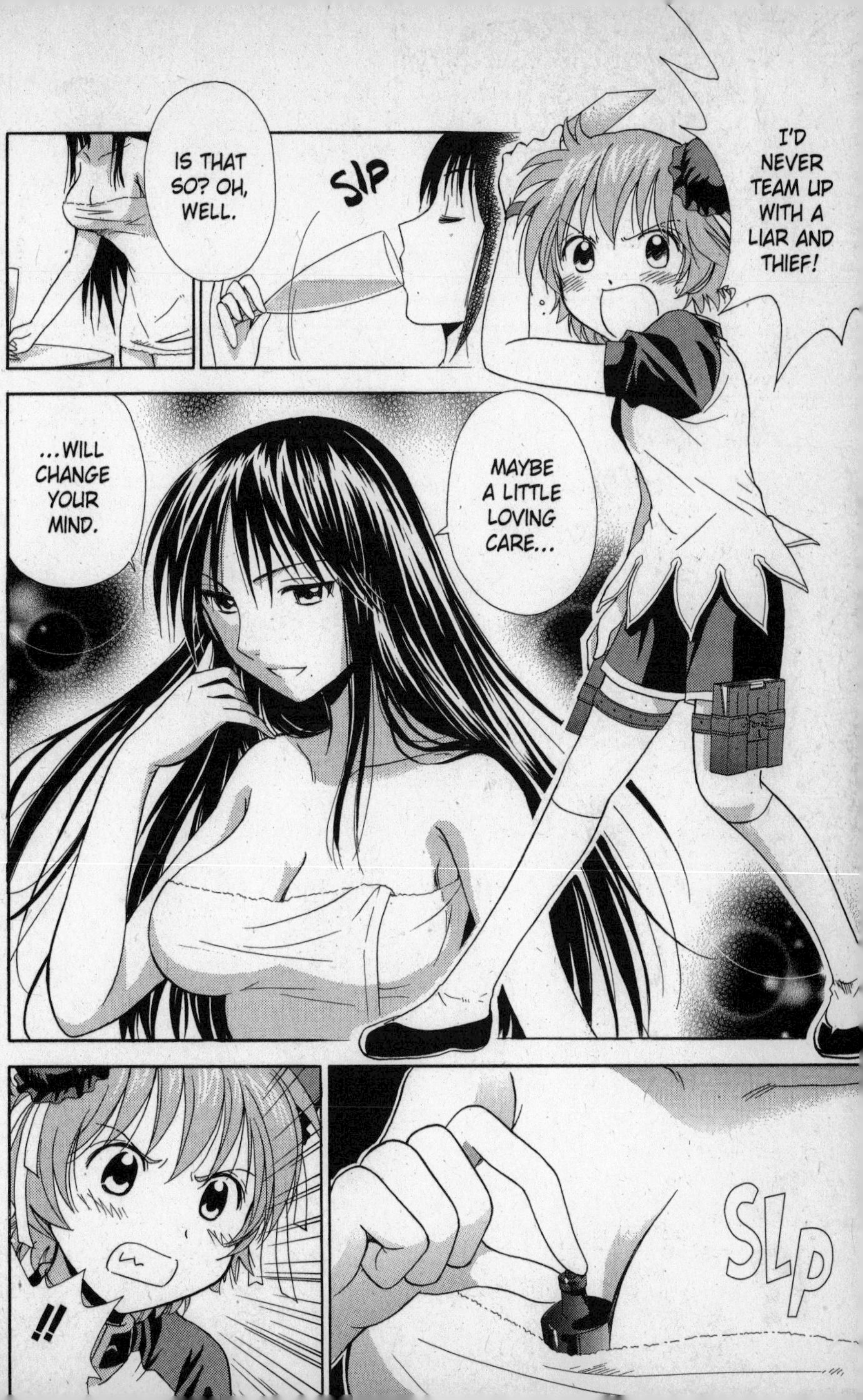
I'D NEVER TEAM UP WITH A LIAR AND THIEF!
SLIP
IS THAT SO? OH, WELL.
MAYBE A LITTLE LOVING CARE...
...WILL CHANGE YOUR MIND.
SLP
!!

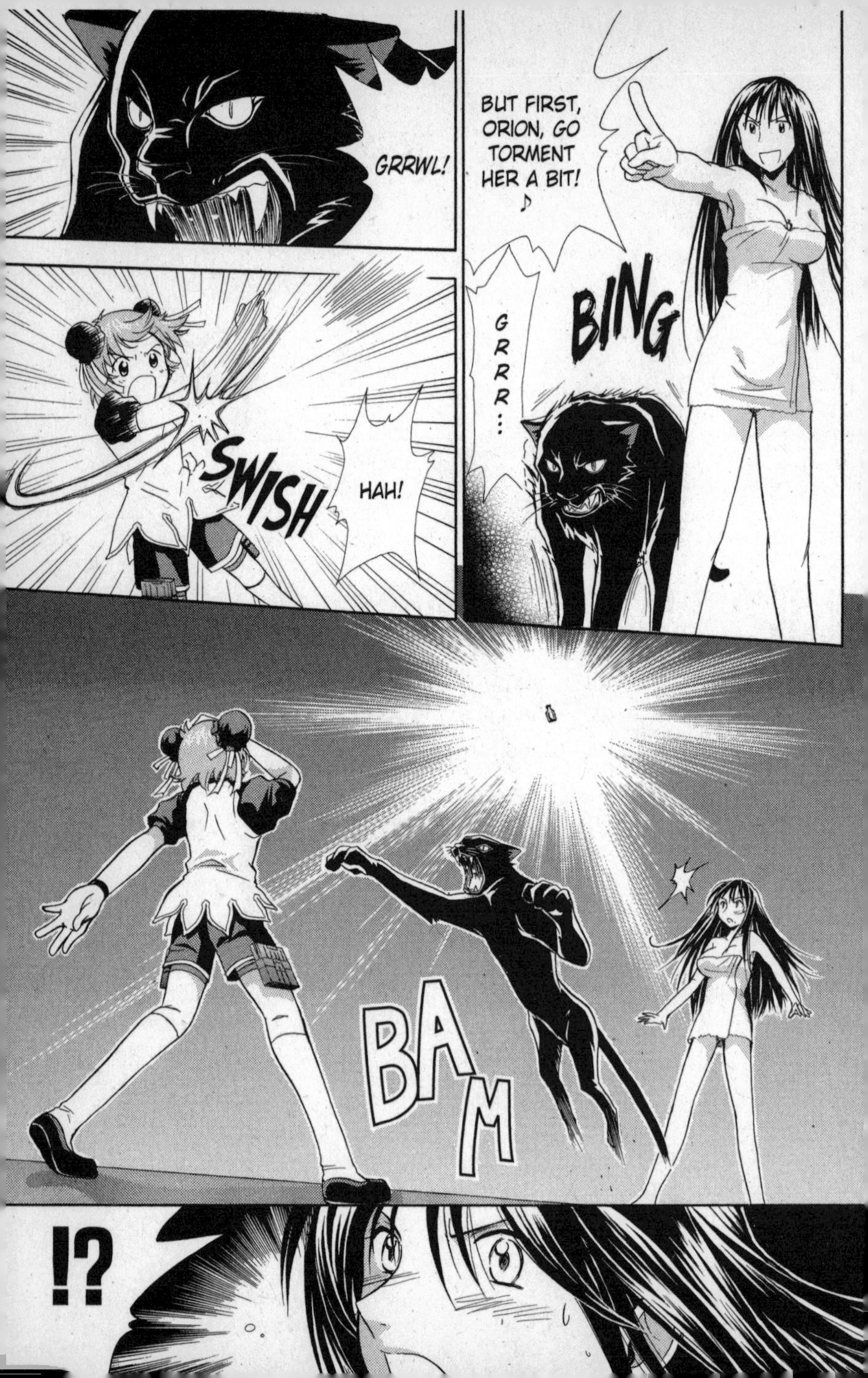
BUT FIRST, ORION, GO TORMENT HER A BIT! ♪
BING
GRRR...
GRRWL!
SWISH
HAH!
BAM
!?

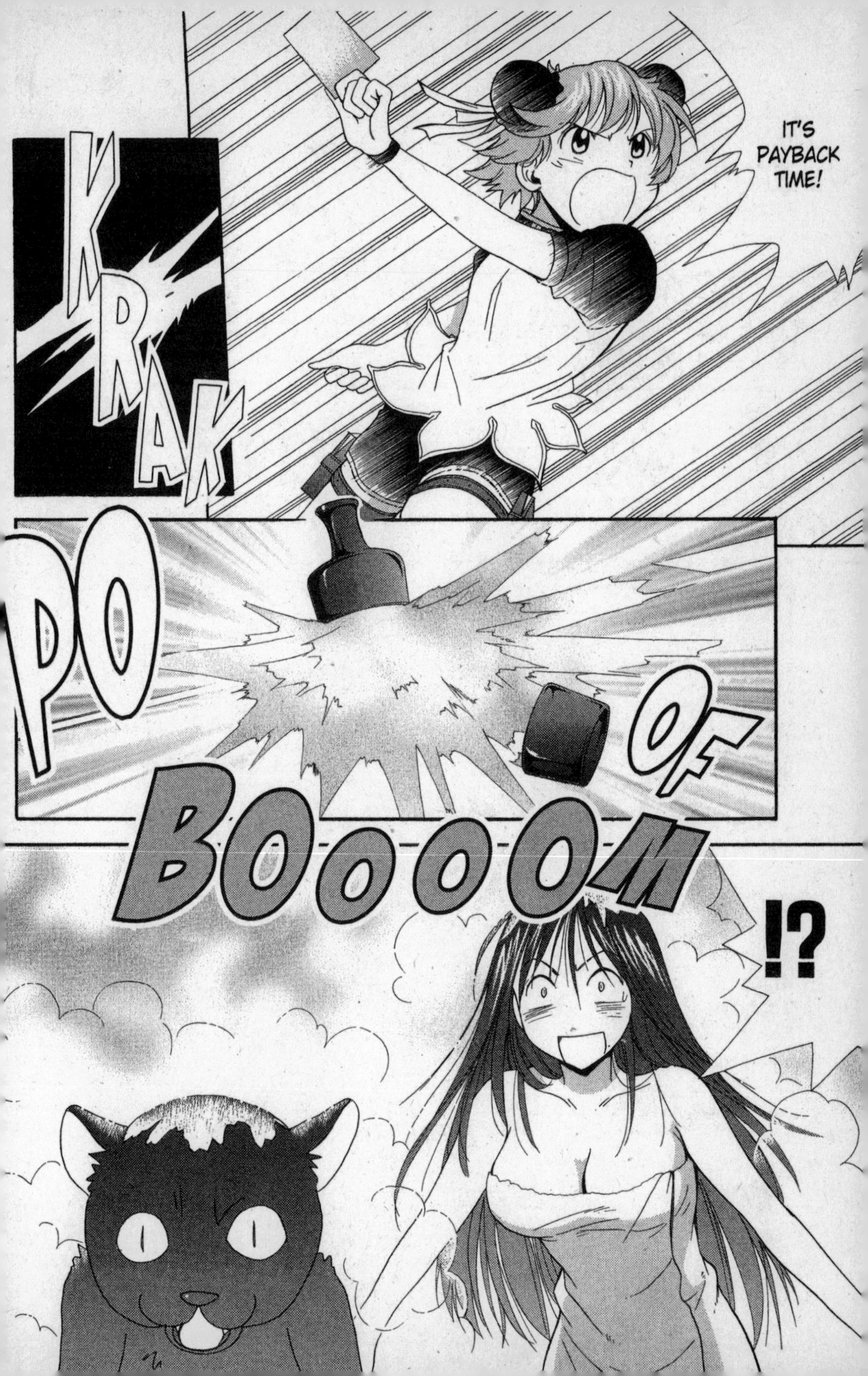
IT'S PAYBACK TIME!
KRAK
POOF
BOOOOOM
!?

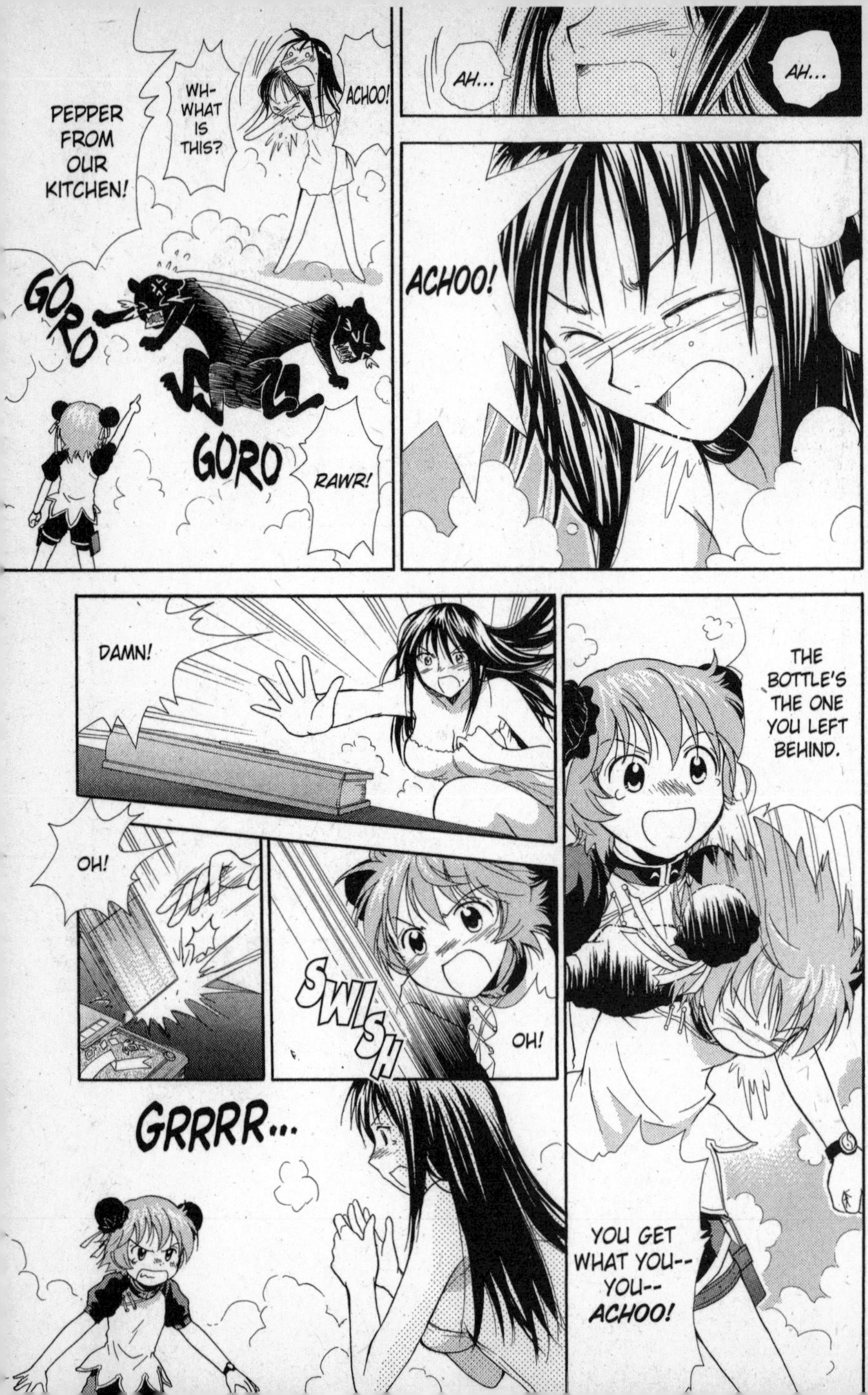
AH...
AH...
ACHOO!
ACHOO!
WH- WHAT IS THIS?
PEPPER FROM OUR KITCHEN!
GORO
GORO
RAWR!
THE BOTTLE'S THE ONE YOU LEFT BEHIND.
DAMN!
SWISH
OH!
OH!
YOU GET WHAT YOU-- YOU-- ACHOO!
GRRRR...

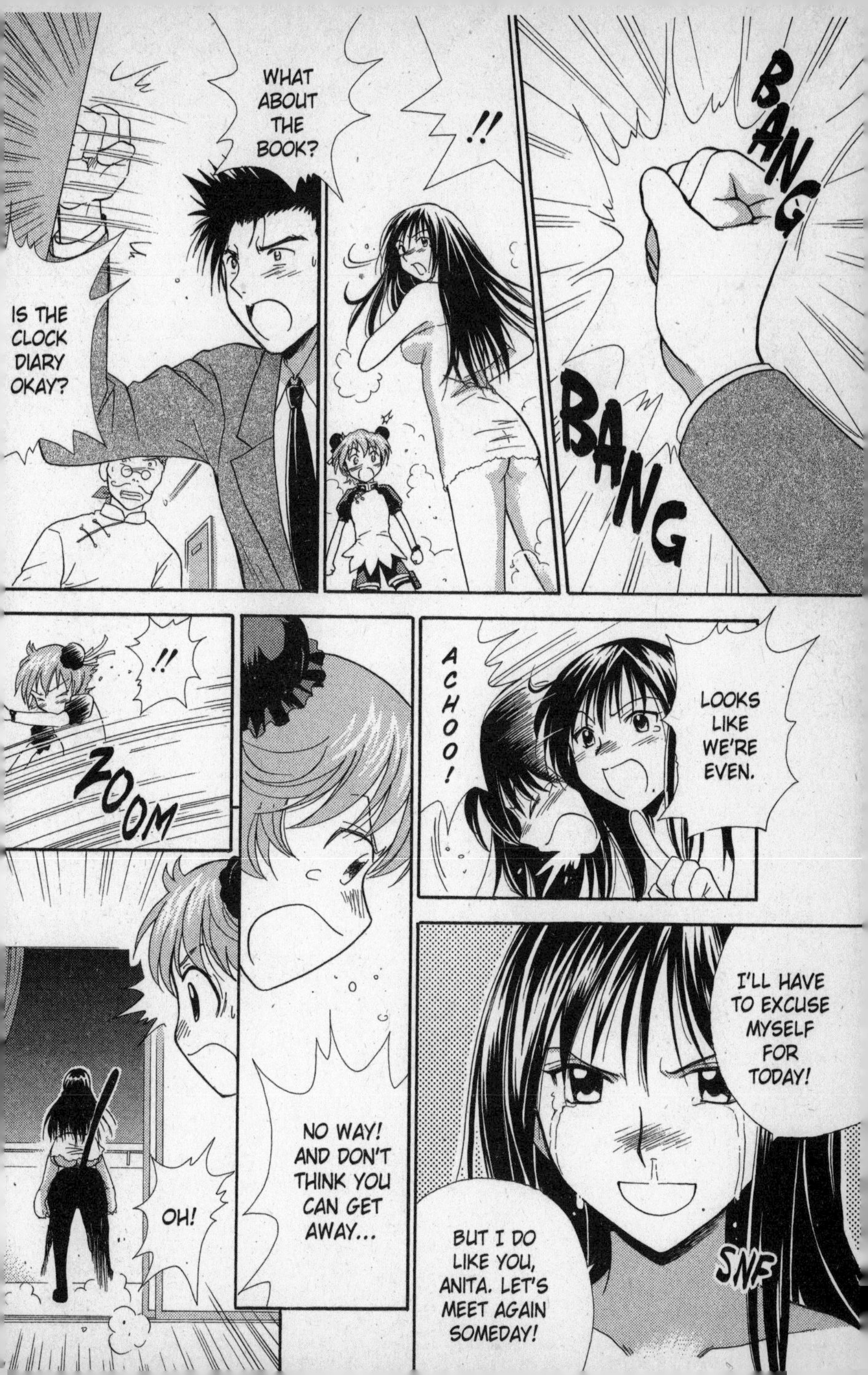
BANG
BANG
BANG
!!
WHAT ABOUT THE BOOK?
IS THE CLOCK DIARY OKAY?
ACHOO!
LOOKS LIKE WE'RE EVEN.
I'LL HAVE TO EXCUSE MYSELF FOR TODAY!
SNF
BUT I DO LIKE YOU, ANITA. LET'S MEET AGAIN SOMEDAY!
NO WAY! AND DON'T THINK YOU CAN GET AWAY...
!!
ZOOM
OH!

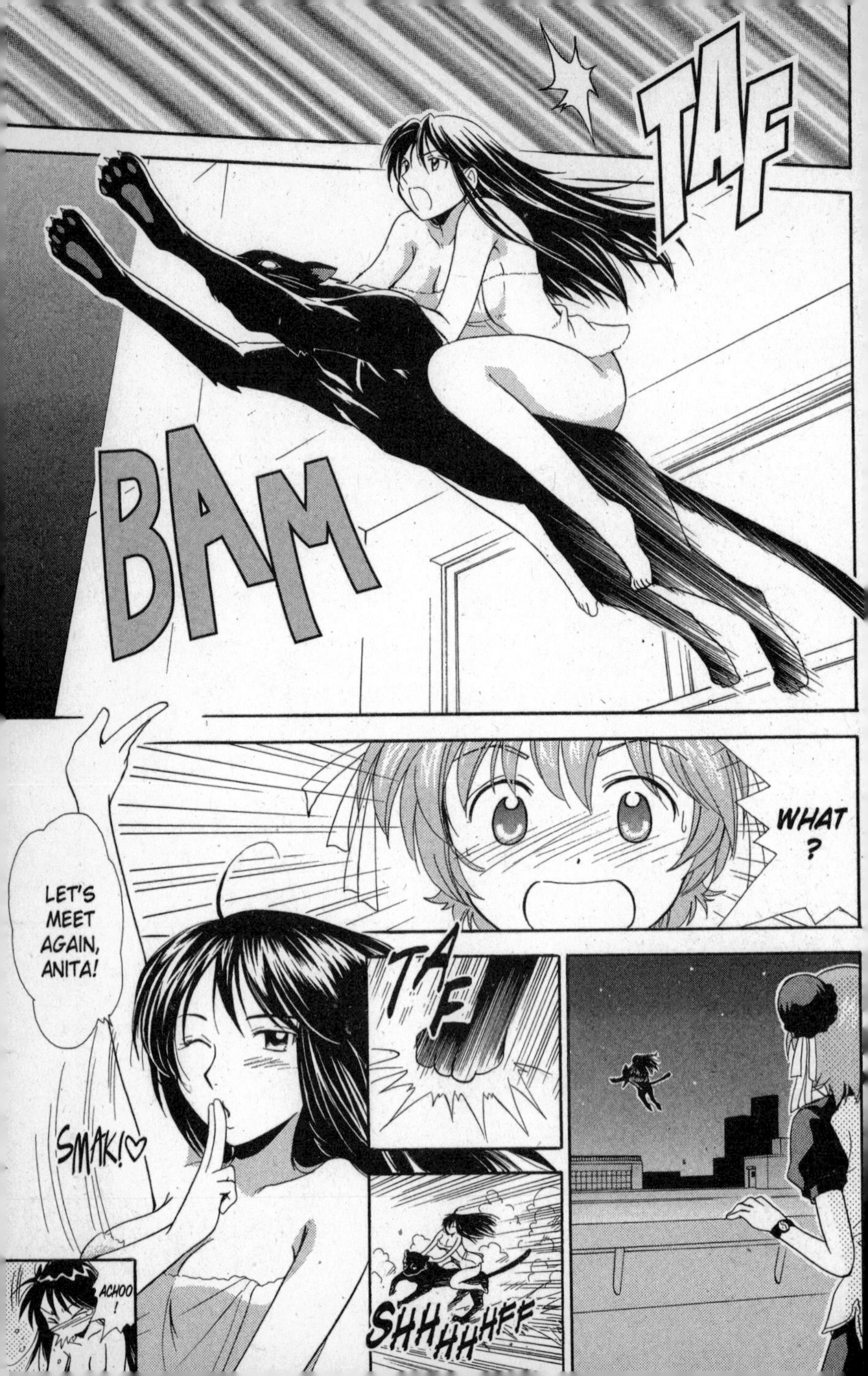
TAF
BAM
WHAT ?
LET'S MEET AGAIN, ANITA!
SMAK!♡
TAF
SHHHHHFF
ACHOO !

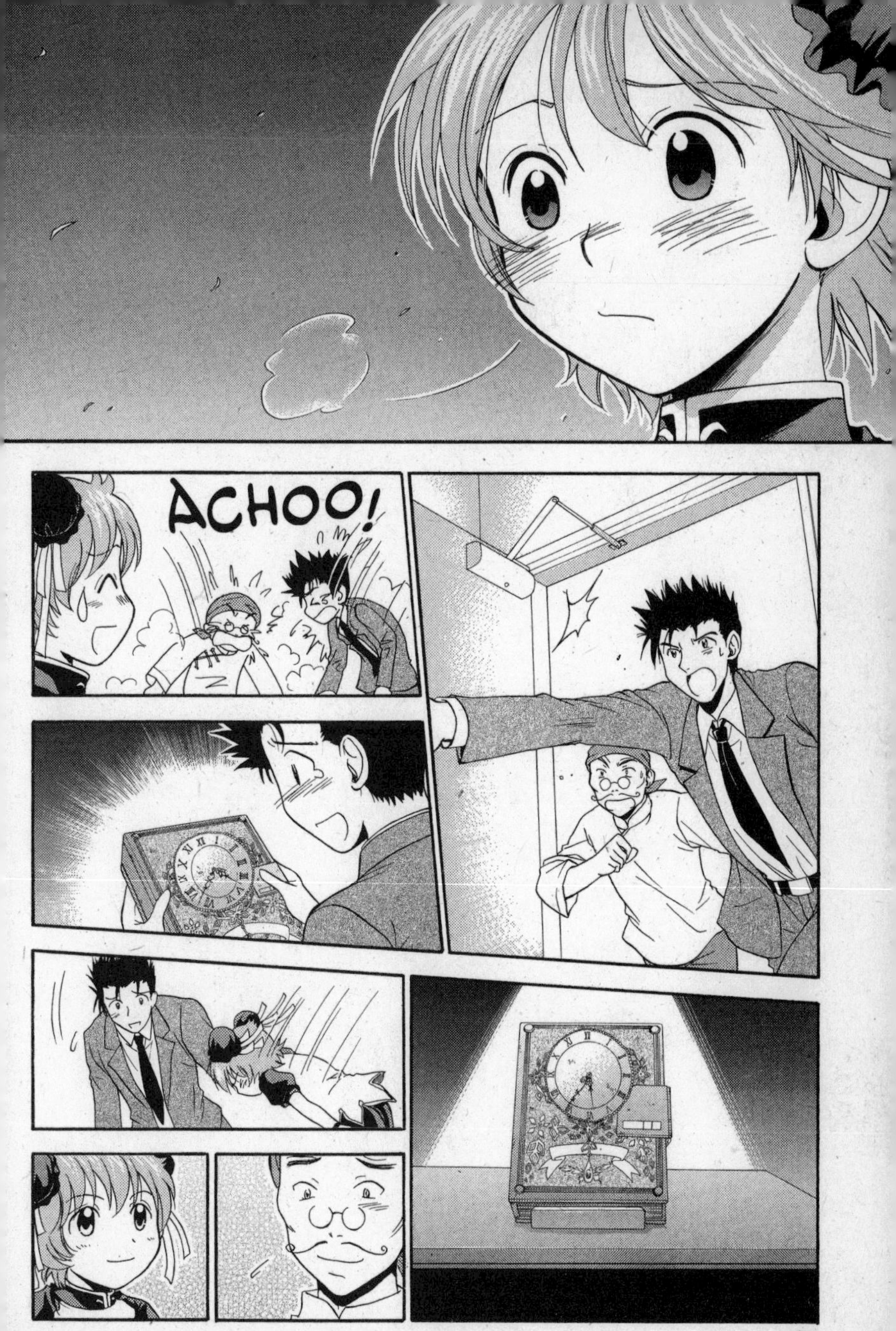
ACHOO!

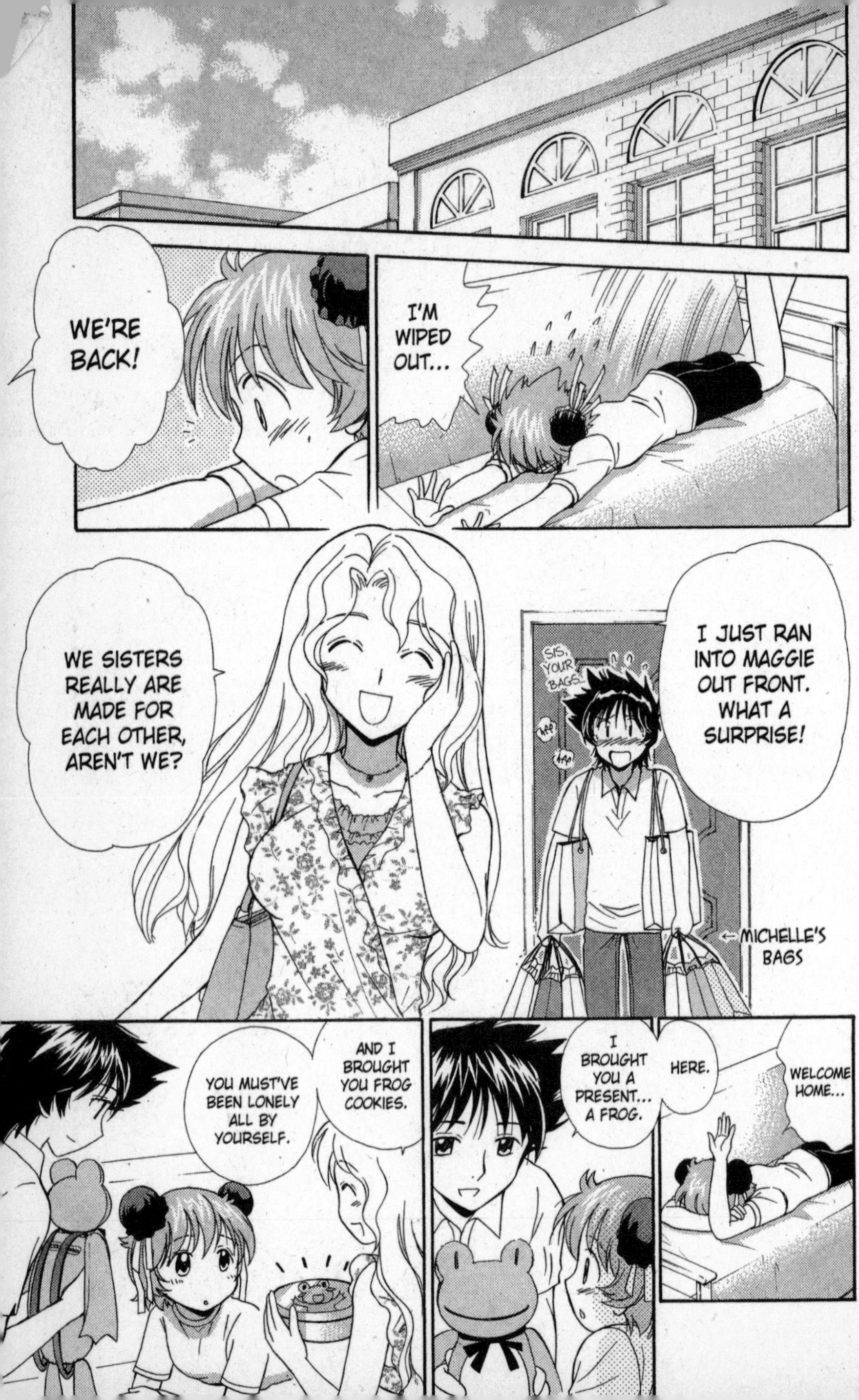
I'M WIPED OUT...
WE'RE BACK!
I JUST RAN INTO MAGGIE OUT FRONT. WHAT A SURPRISE!
SIS, YOUR BAGS.
HAP
HAP
MICHELLE'S BAGS
WE SISTERS REALLY ARE MADE FOR EACH OTHER, AREN'T WE?
WELCOME HOME...
HERE.
I BROUGHT YOU A PRESENT... A FROG.
AND I BROUGHT YOU FROG COOKIES.
YOU MUST'VE BEEN LONELY ALL BY YOURSELF.

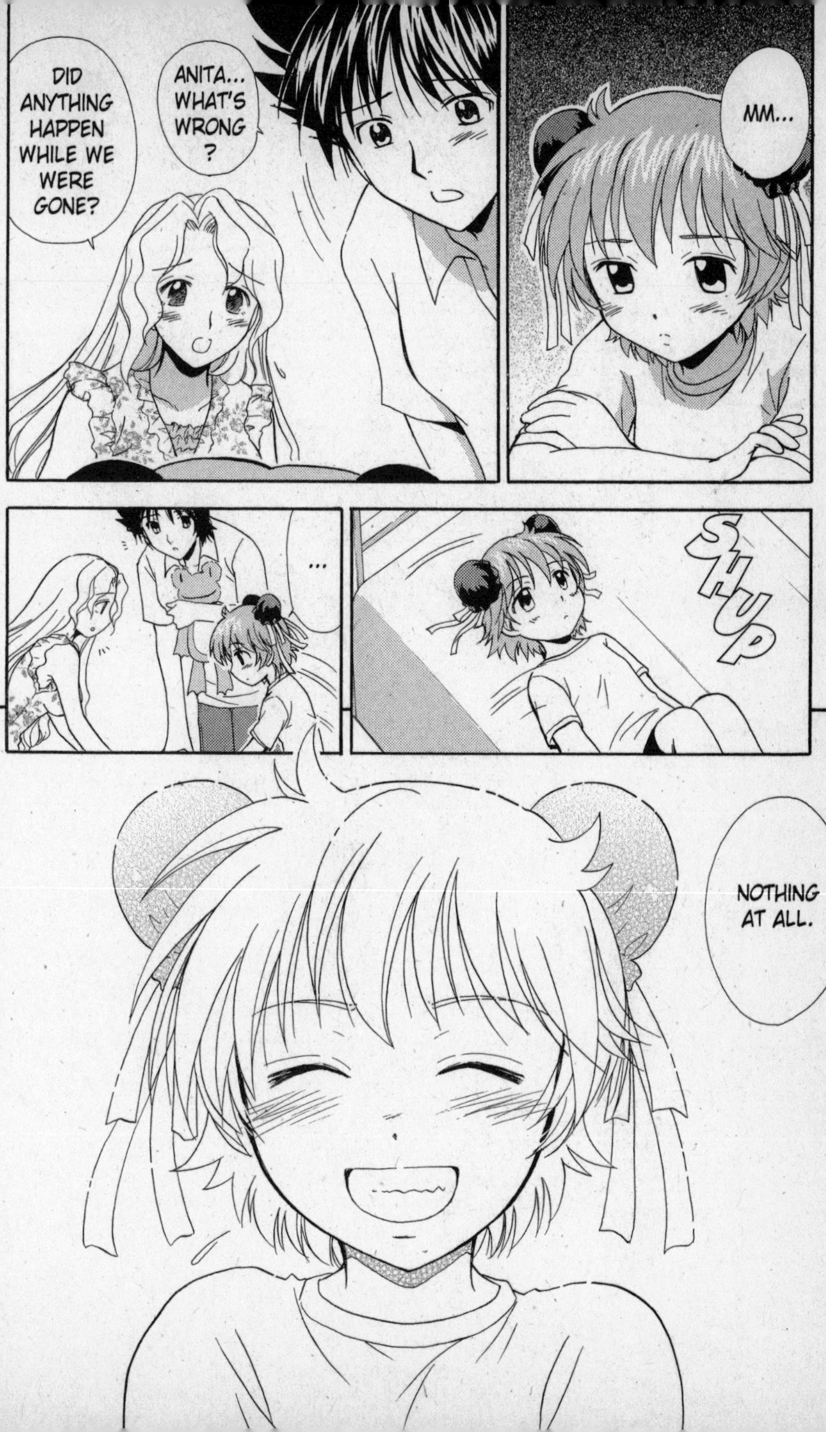
MM...
ANITA... WHAT'S WRONG?
DID ANYTHING HAPPEN WHILE WE WERE GONE?
SHUP
...
NOTHING AT ALL.

CHAPTER 11

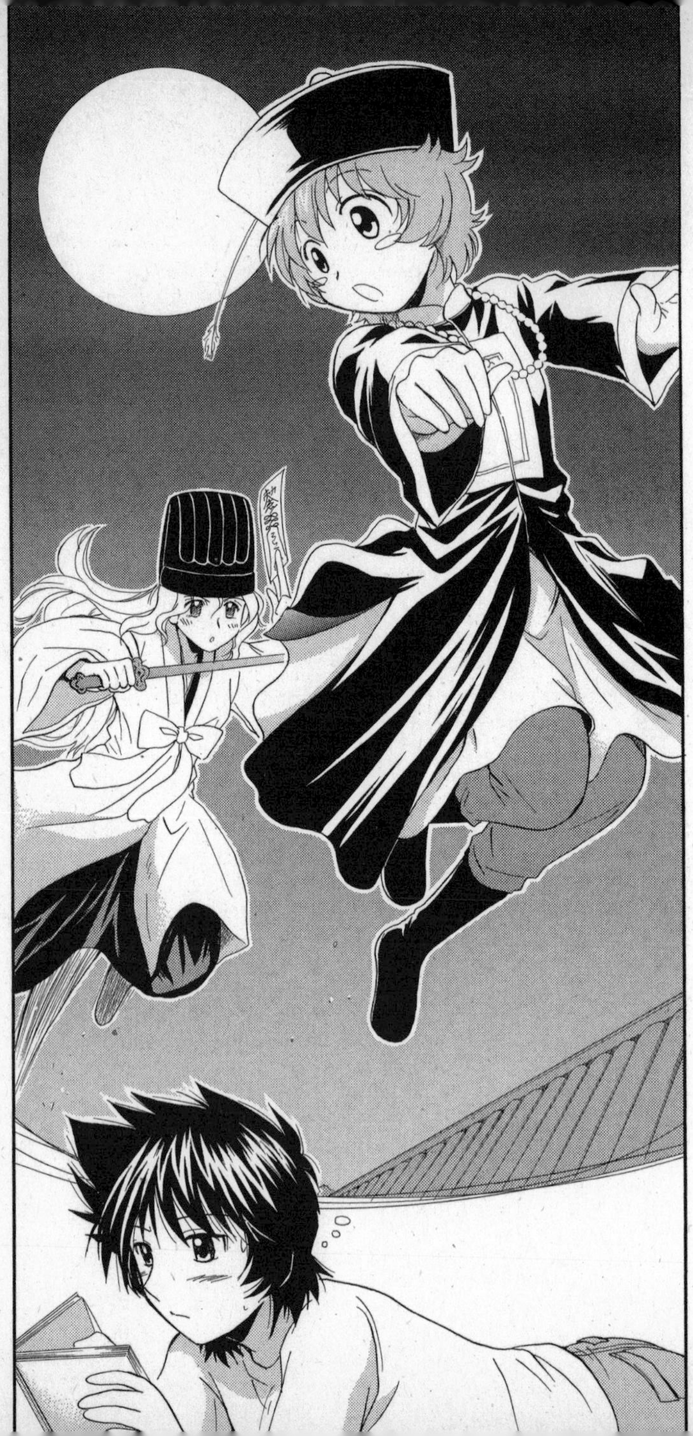

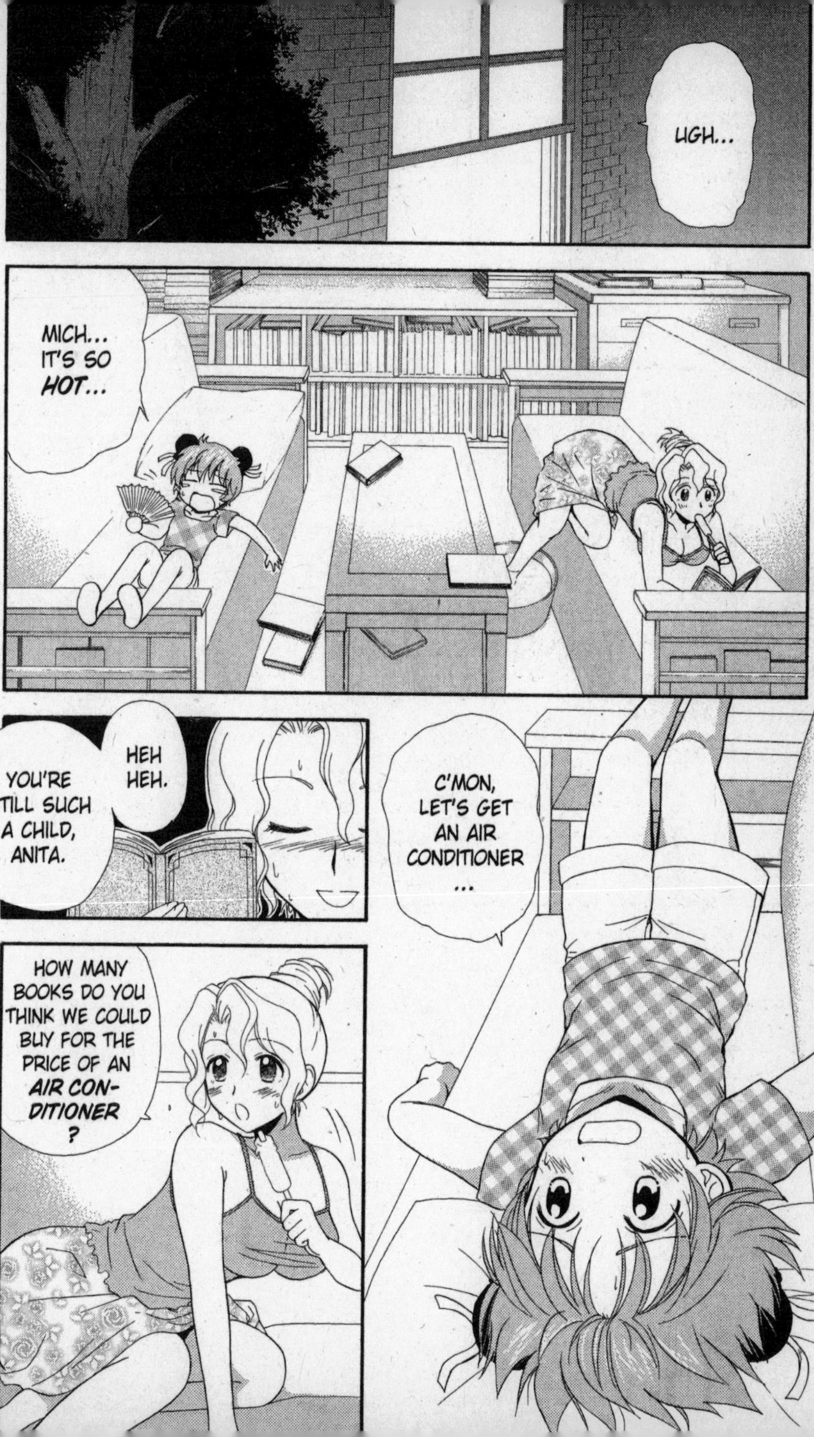
UGH...
MICH... IT'S SO *HOT*...
C'MON, LET'S GET AN AIR CONDITIONER ...
HEH HEH.
YOU'RE STILL SUCH A CHILD, ANITA.
HOW MANY BOOKS DO YOU THINK WE COULD BUY FOR THE PRICE OF AN *AIR CONDITIONER*?

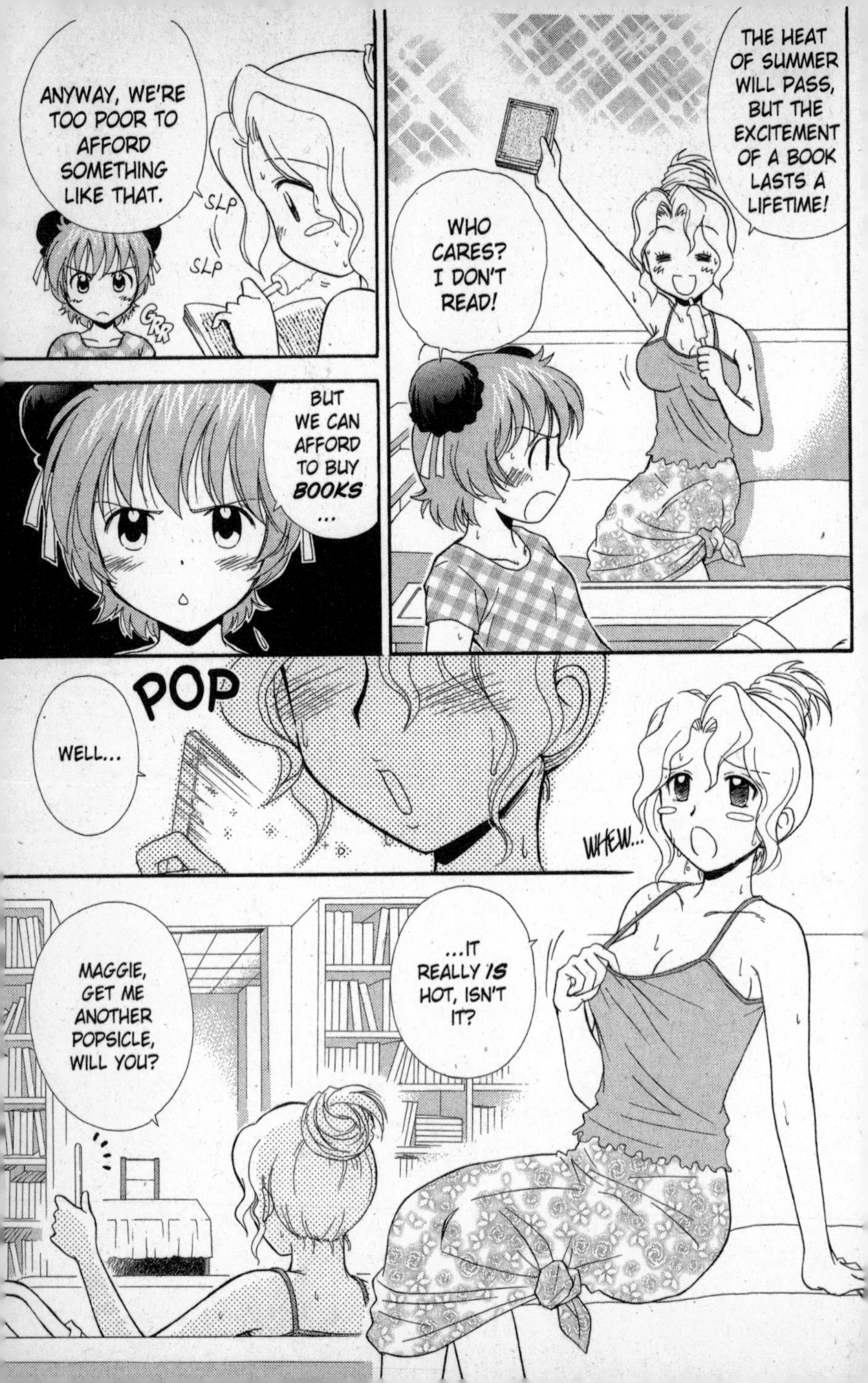
THE HEAT OF SUMMER WILL PASS, BUT THE EXCITEMENT OF A BOOK LASTS A LIFETIME!
WHO CARES? I DON'T READ!
ANYWAY, WE'RE TOO POOR TO AFFORD SOMETHING LIKE THAT.
SLP
SLP
GRR
BUT WE CAN AFFORD TO BUY BOOKS ...
WHEW...
POP
WELL...
...IT REALLY IS HOT, ISN'T IT?
MAGGIE, GET ME ANOTHER POPSICLE, WILL YOU?

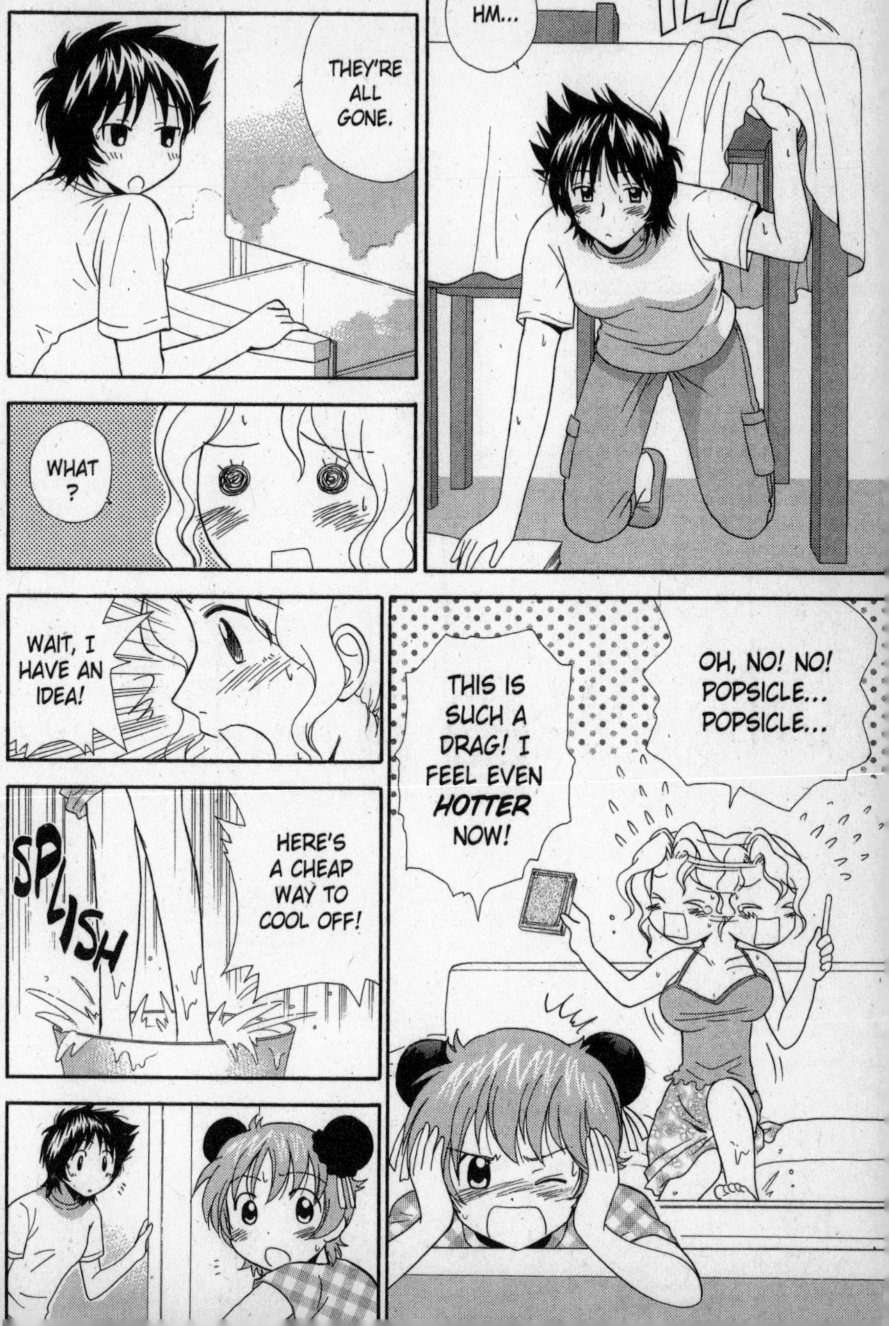
TUP
HM...
THEY'RE ALL GONE.
WHAT ?
OH, NO! NO! POPSICLE... POPSICLE...
THIS IS SUCH A DRAG! I FEEL EVEN *HOTTER* NOW!
WAIT, I HAVE AN IDEA!
HERE'S A CHEAP WAY TO COOL OFF!
SPLISH

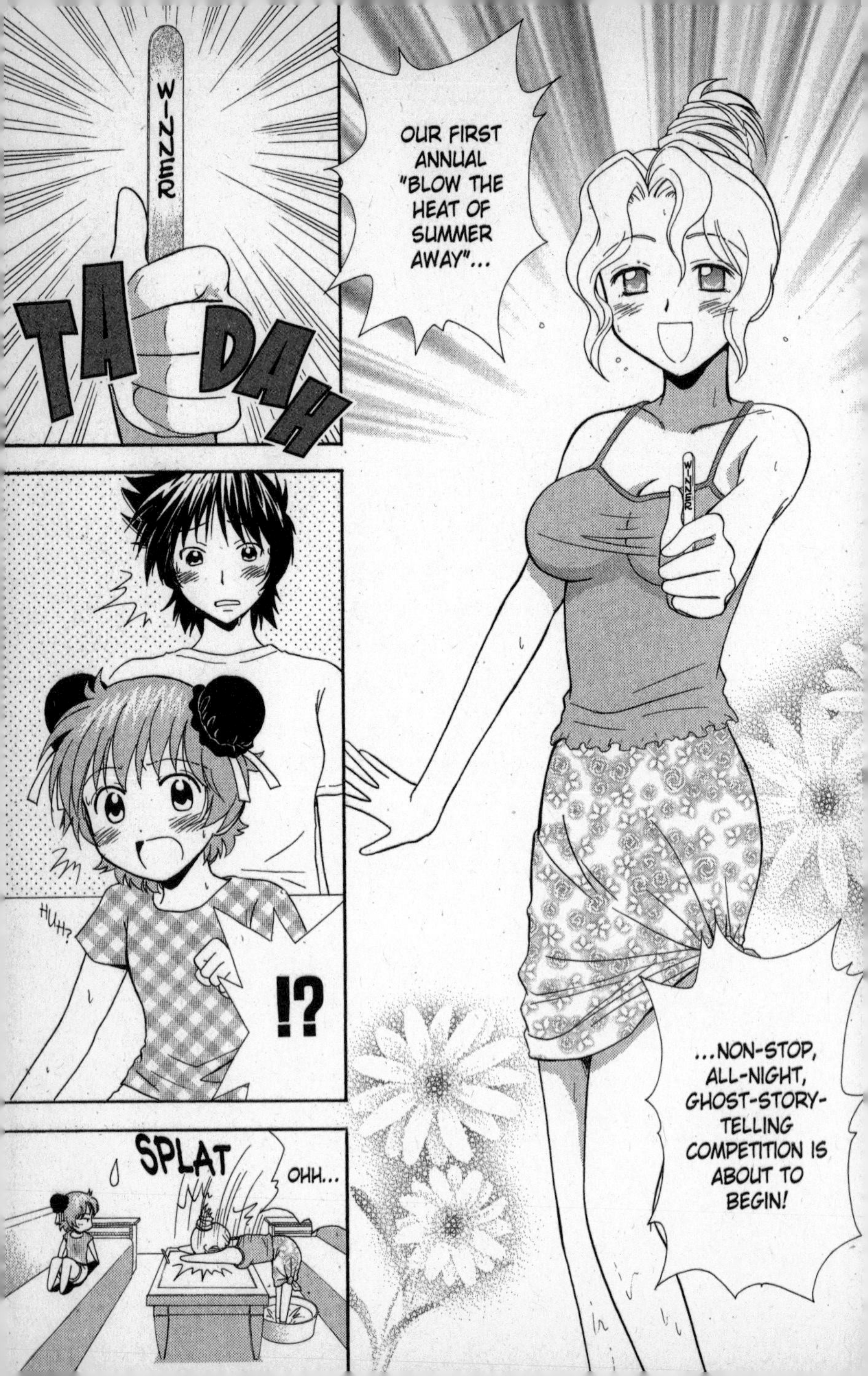
OUR FIRST ANNUAL "BLOW THE HEAT OF SUMMER AWAY"...
...NON-STOP, ALL-NIGHT, GHOST-STORY-TELLING COMPETITION IS ABOUT TO BEGIN!
WINNER
TA DAH
HUH?
!?
SPLAT
OHH...

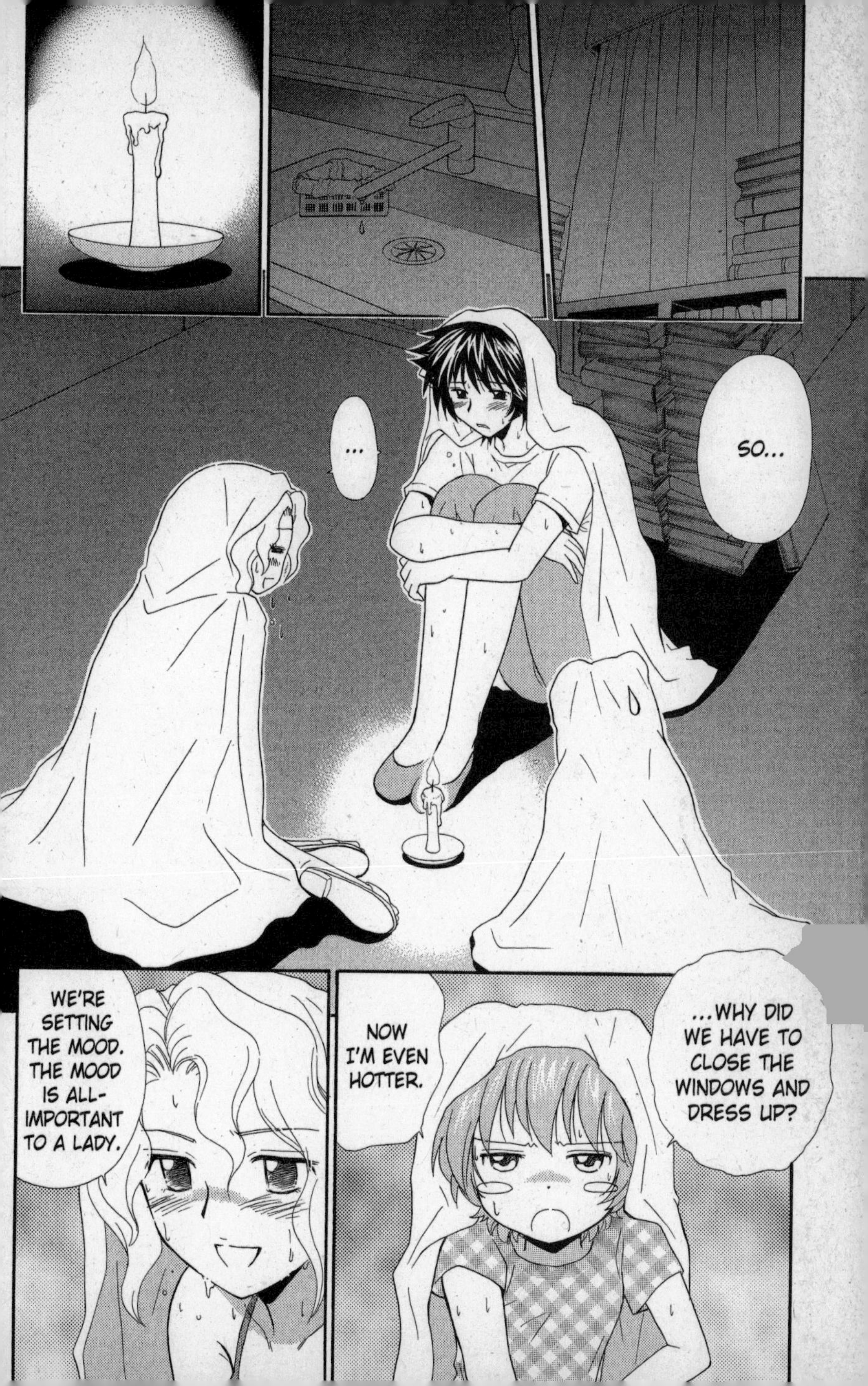
SO...
...
...WHY DID WE HAVE TO CLOSE THE WINDOWS AND DRESS UP?
NOW I'M EVEN HOTTER.
WE'RE SETTING THE MOOD. THE MOOD IS ALL-IMPORTANT TO A LADY.

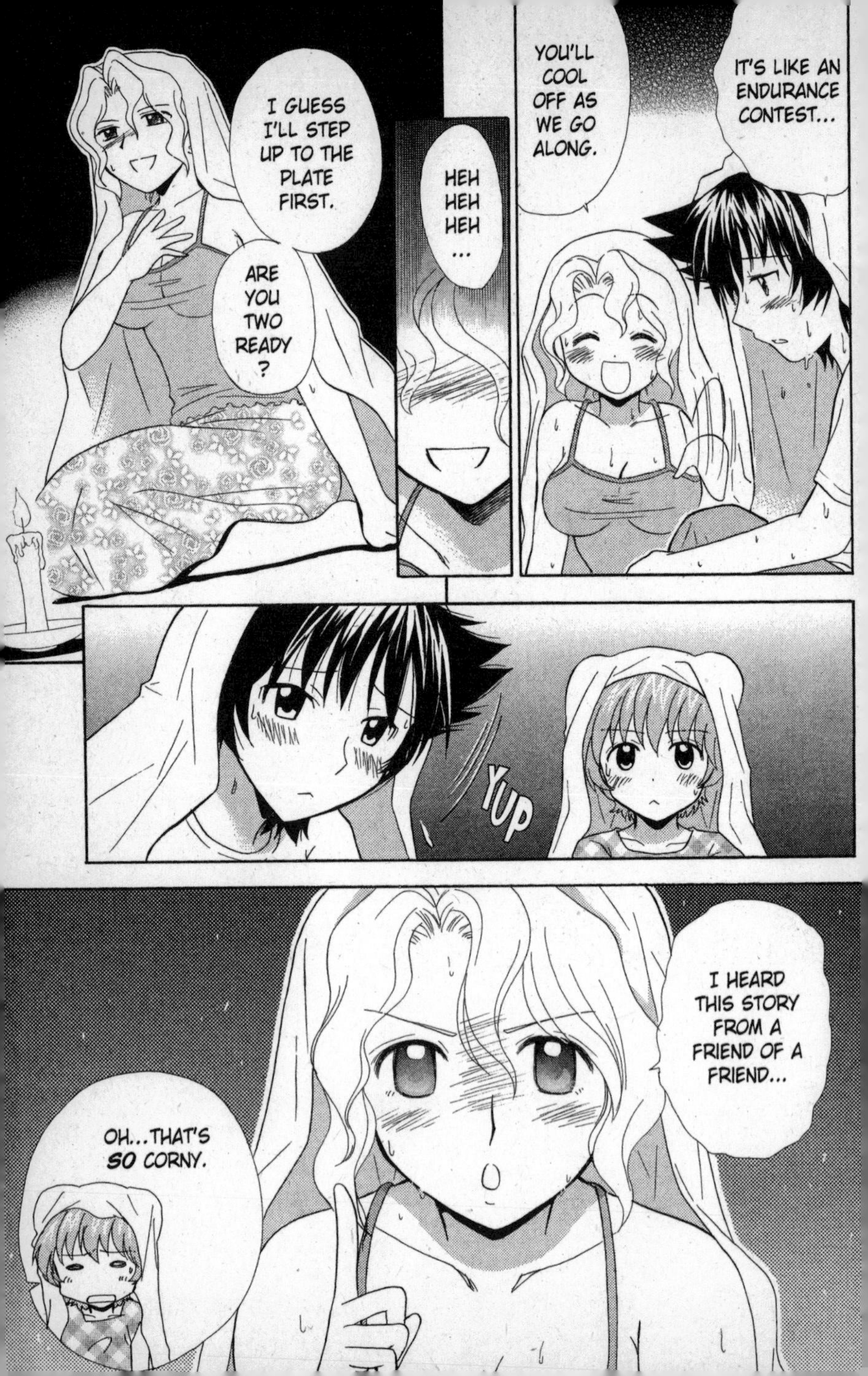
IT'S LIKE AN ENDURANCE CONTEST...
YOU'LL COOL OFF AS WE GO ALONG.
HEH HEH HEH ...
I GUESS I'LL STEP UP TO THE PLATE FIRST.
ARE YOU TWO READY ?
YUP
I HEARD THIS STORY FROM A FRIEND OF A FRIEND...
OH...THAT'S SO CORNY.

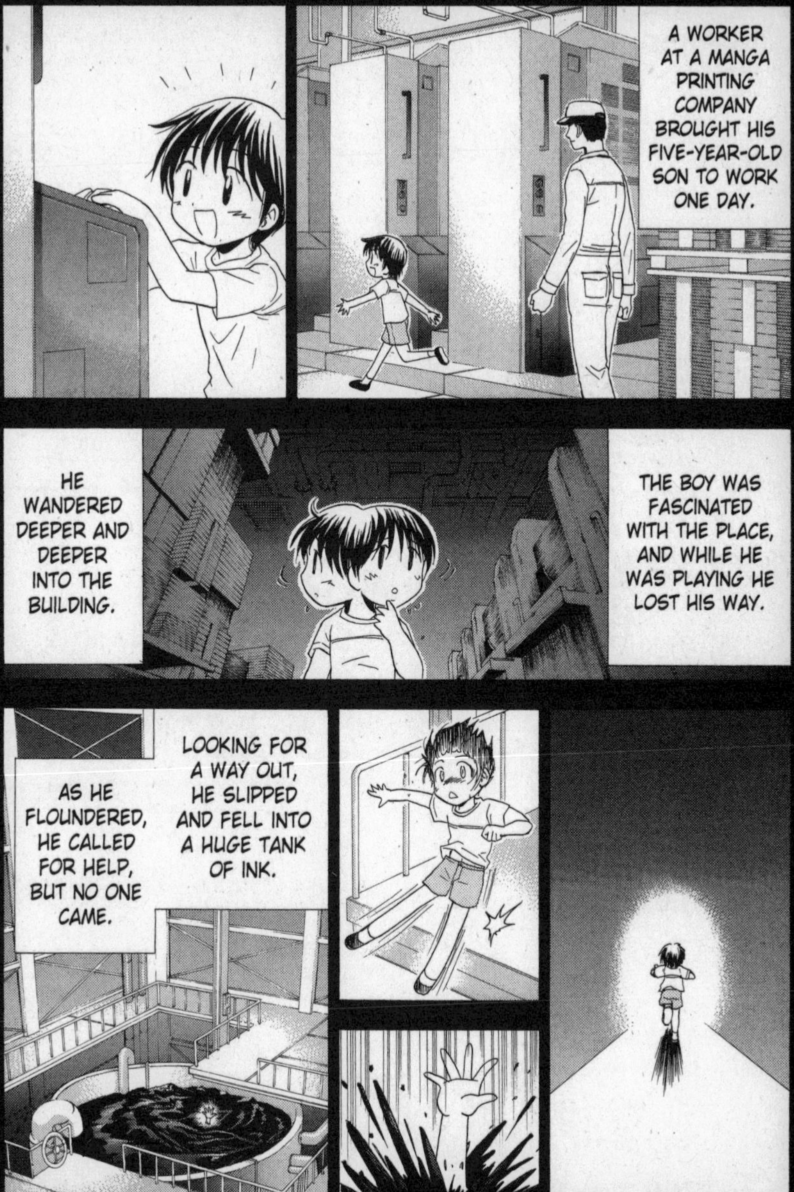
A WORKER AT A MANGA PRINTING COMPANY BROUGHT HIS FIVE-YEAR-OLD SON TO WORK ONE DAY.
THE BOY WAS FASCINATED WITH THE PLACE, AND WHILE HE WAS PLAYING HE LOST HIS WAY.
HE WANDERED DEEPER AND DEEPER INTO THE BUILDING.
LOOKING FOR A WAY OUT, HE SLIPPED AND FELL INTO A HUGE TANK OF INK.
AS HE FLOUNDERED, HE CALLED FOR HELP, BUT NO ONE CAME.

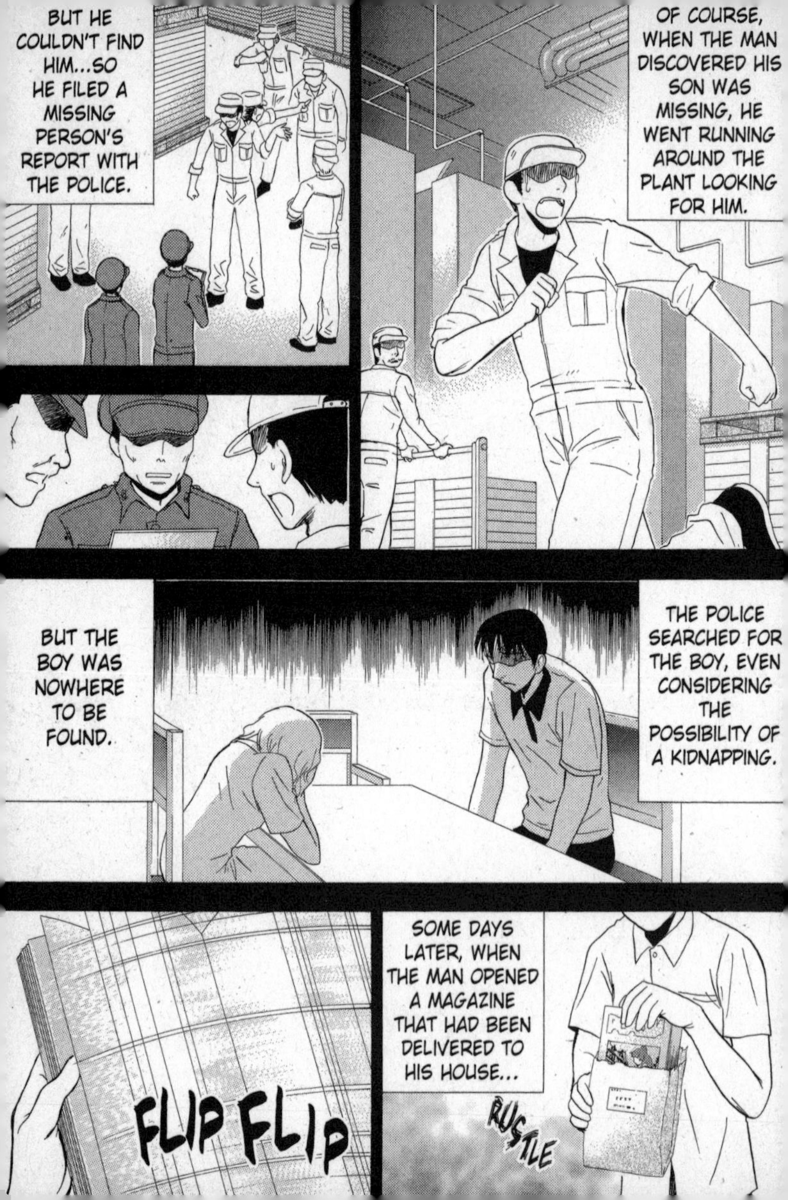
OF COURSE, WHEN THE MAN DISCOVERED HIS SON WAS MISSING, HE WENT RUNNING AROUND THE PLANT LOOKING FOR HIM.
BUT HE COULDN'T FIND HIM...SO HE FILED A MISSING PERSON'S REPORT WITH THE POLICE.
THE POLICE SEARCHED FOR THE BOY, EVEN CONSIDERING THE POSSIBILITY OF A KIDNAPPING.
BUT THE BOY WAS NOWHERE TO BE FOUND.
SOME DAYS LATER, WHEN THE MAN OPENED A MAGAZINE THAT HAD BEEN DELIVERED TO HIS HOUSE...
RUSTLE
FLIP FLIP

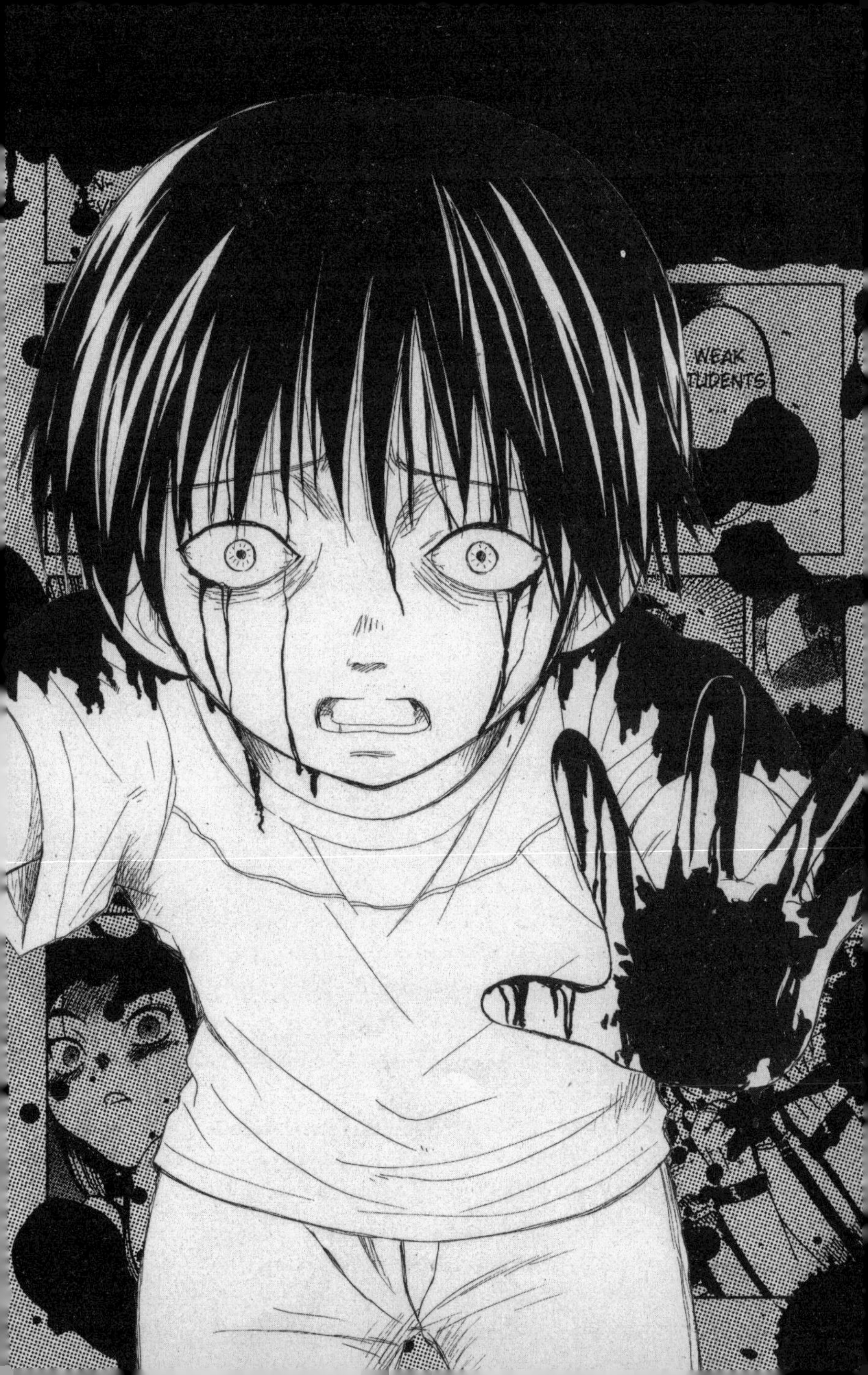
WEAK TUDENTS...

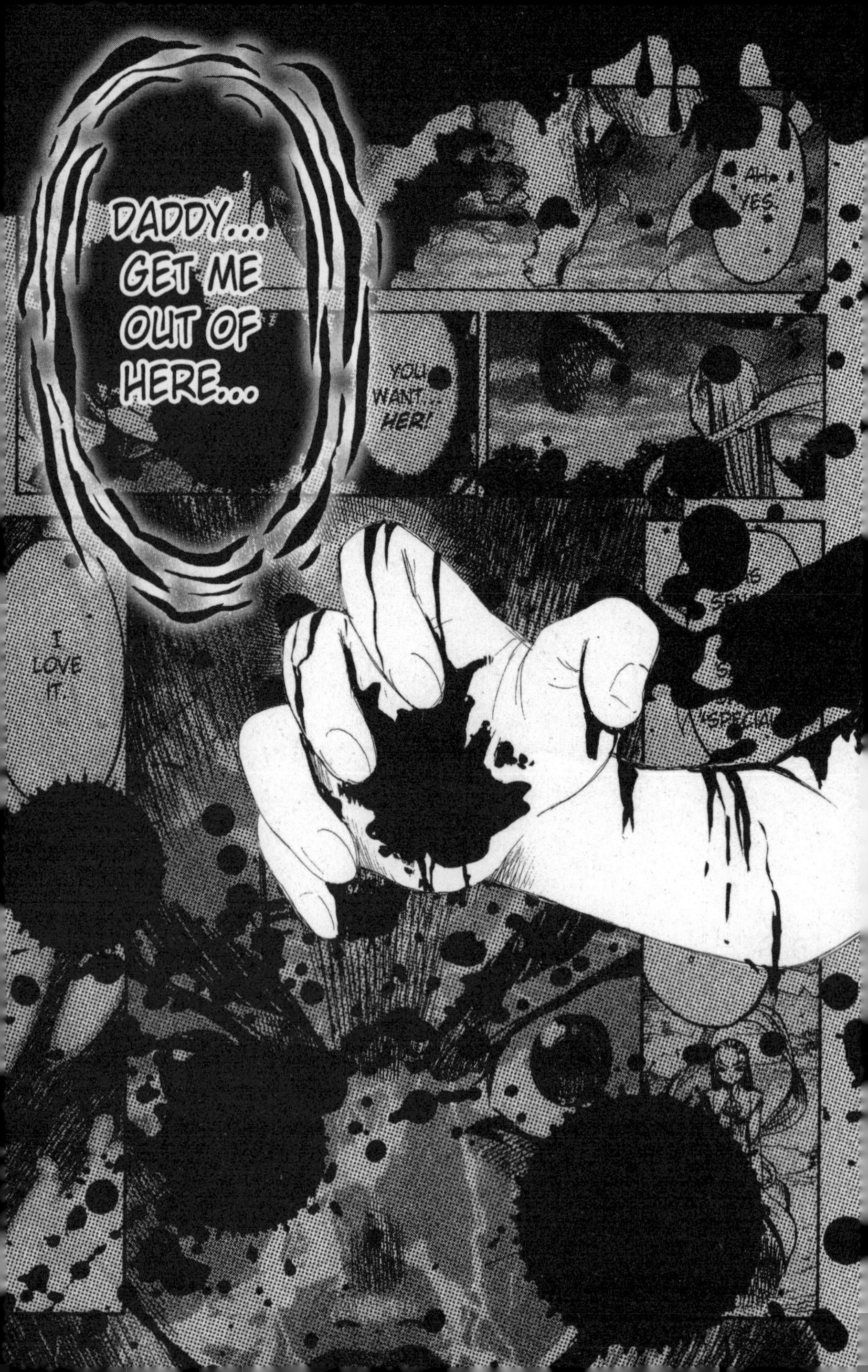
AH... YES.
DADDY... GET ME OUT OF HERE...
YOU... WANT... HER!
I LOVE IT...

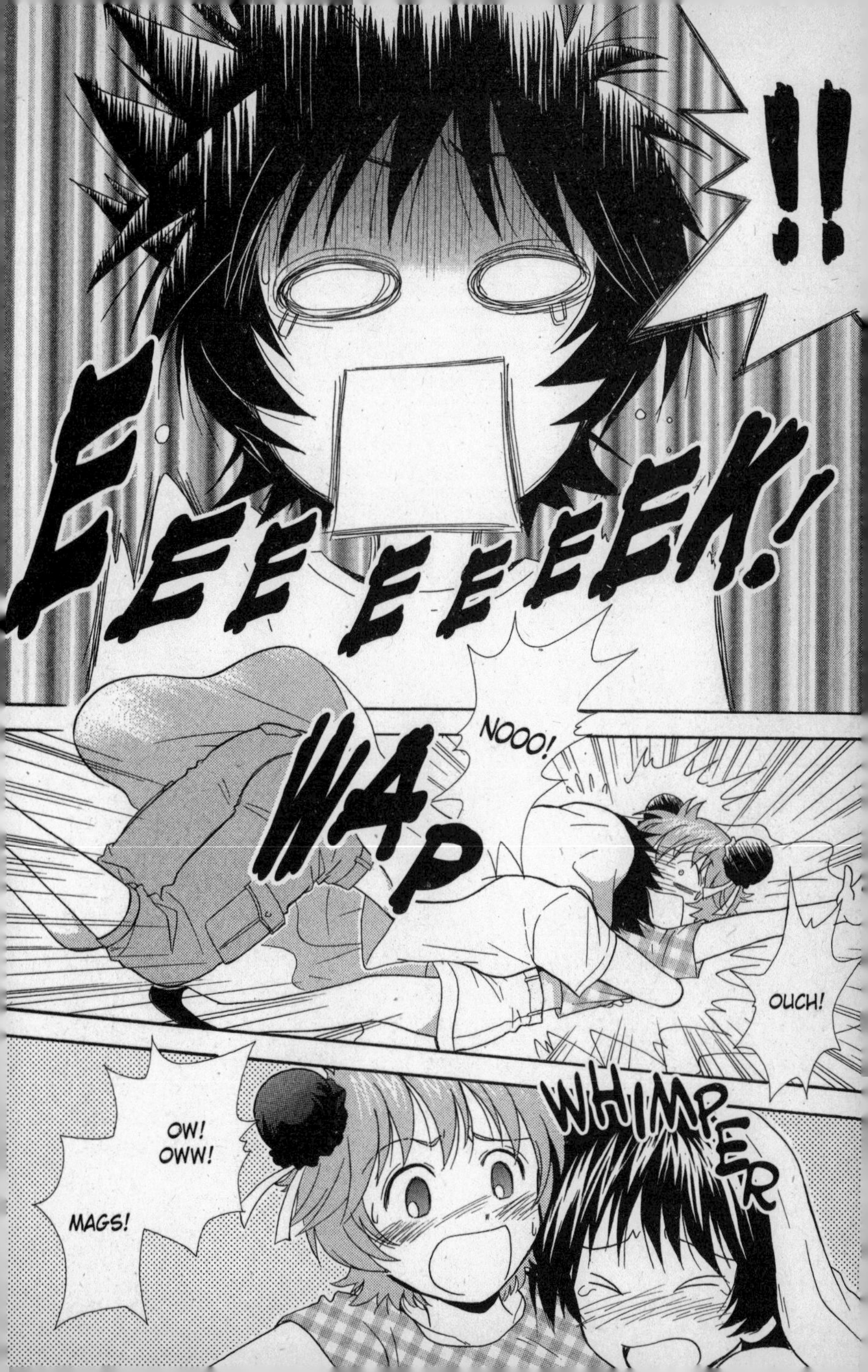

EEEEEEEEK!!
NOOO!
OUCH!
WAP
WHIMPER
OW! OWW!
MAGS!

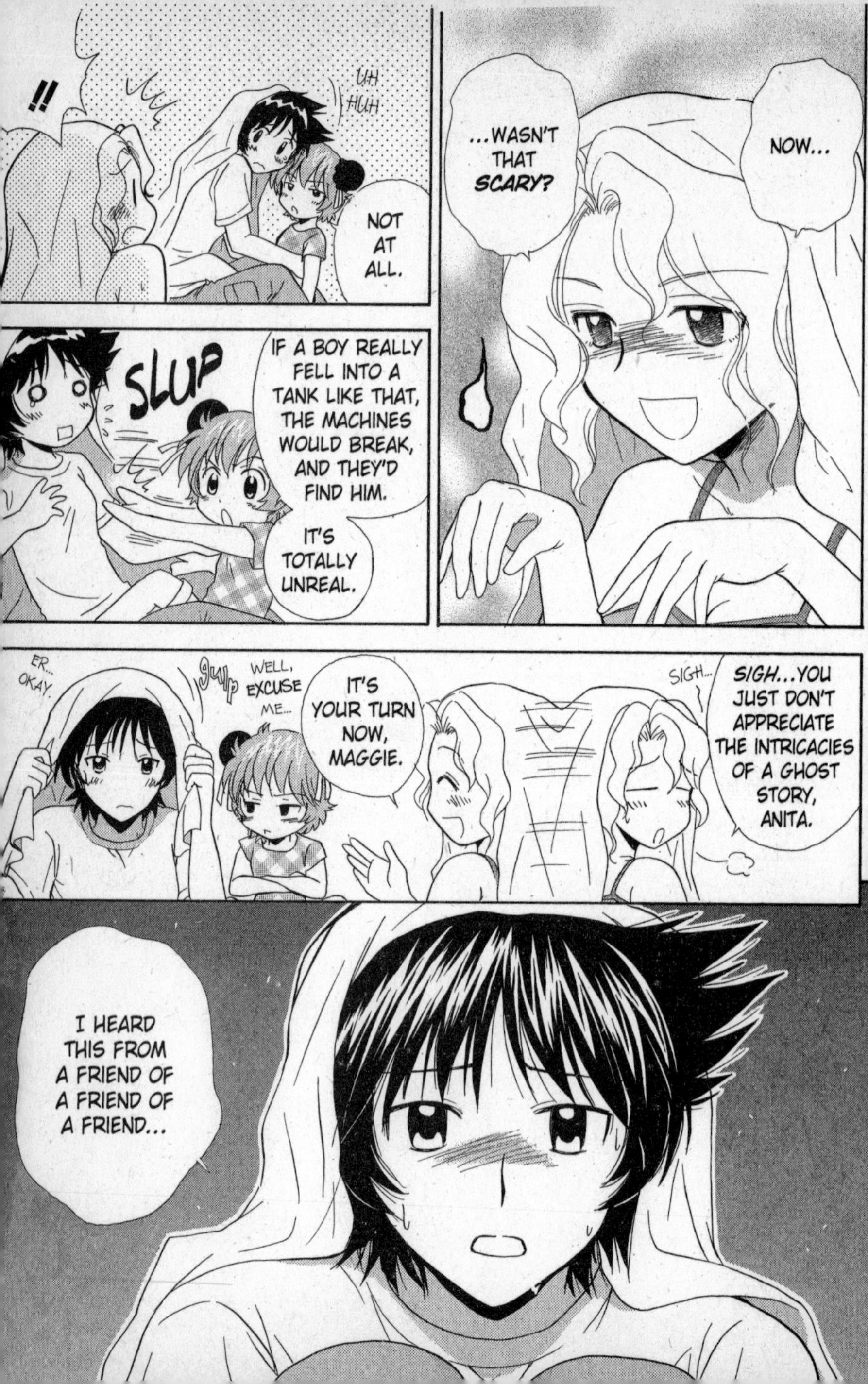
NOW...
...WASN'T THAT SCARY?
!!
UH HUH
NOT AT ALL.
SLUP
IF A BOY REALLY FELL INTO A TANK LIKE THAT, THE MACHINES WOULD BREAK, AND THEY'D FIND HIM.
IT'S TOTALLY UNREAL.
SIGH...YOU JUST DON'T APPRECIATE THE INTRICACIES OF A GHOST STORY, ANITA.
SIGH...
IT'S YOUR TURN NOW, MAGGIE.
WELL, EXCUSE ME...
gulp
ER... OKAY.
I HEARD THIS FROM A FRIEND OF A FRIEND OF A FRIEND...

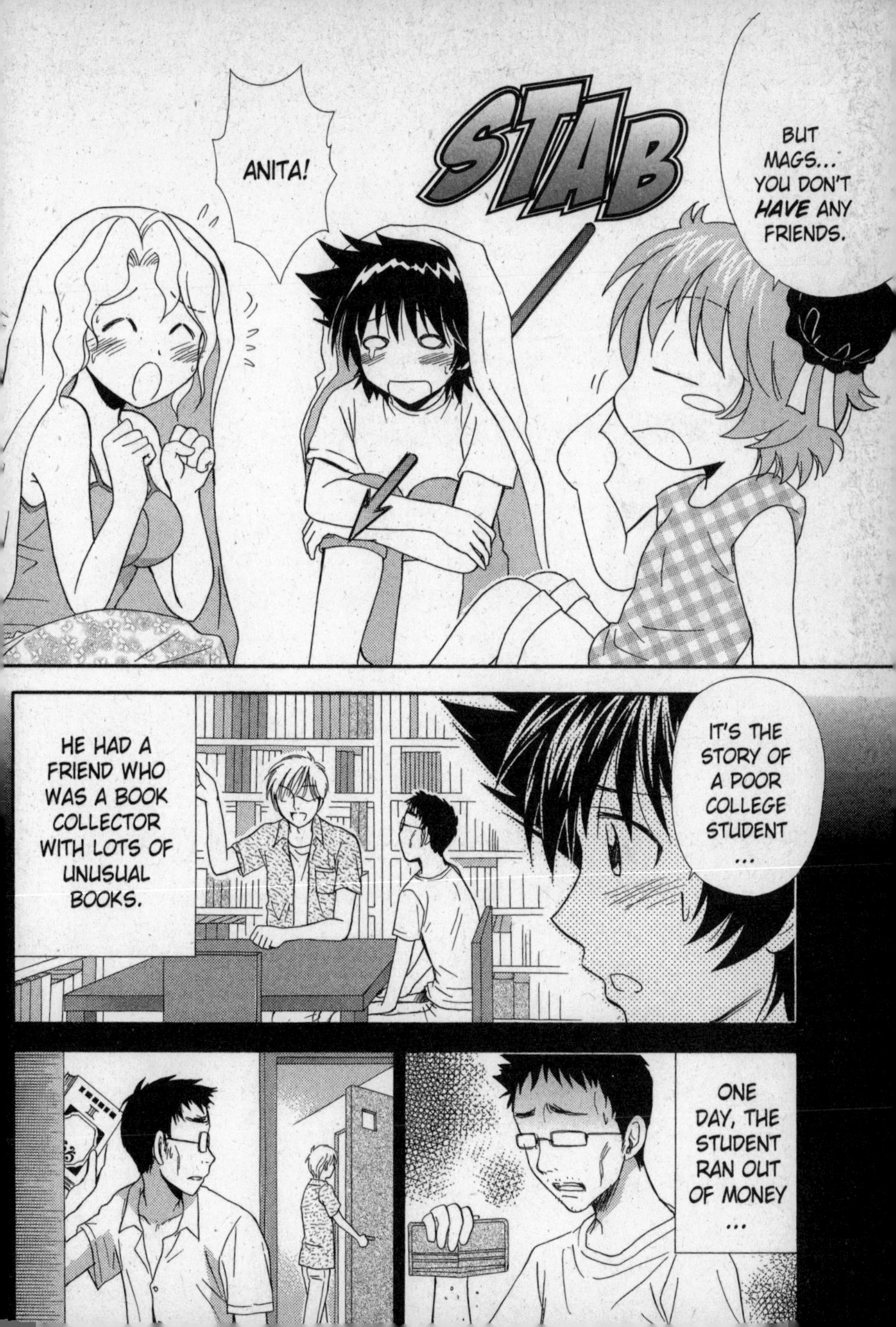
BUT MAGS... YOU DON'T *HAVE* ANY FRIENDS.
STAB
ANITA!
IT'S THE STORY OF A POOR COLLEGE STUDENT ...
HE HAD A FRIEND WHO WAS A BOOK COLLECTOR WITH LOTS OF UNUSUAL BOOKS.
ONE DAY, THE STUDENT RAN OUT OF MONEY ...

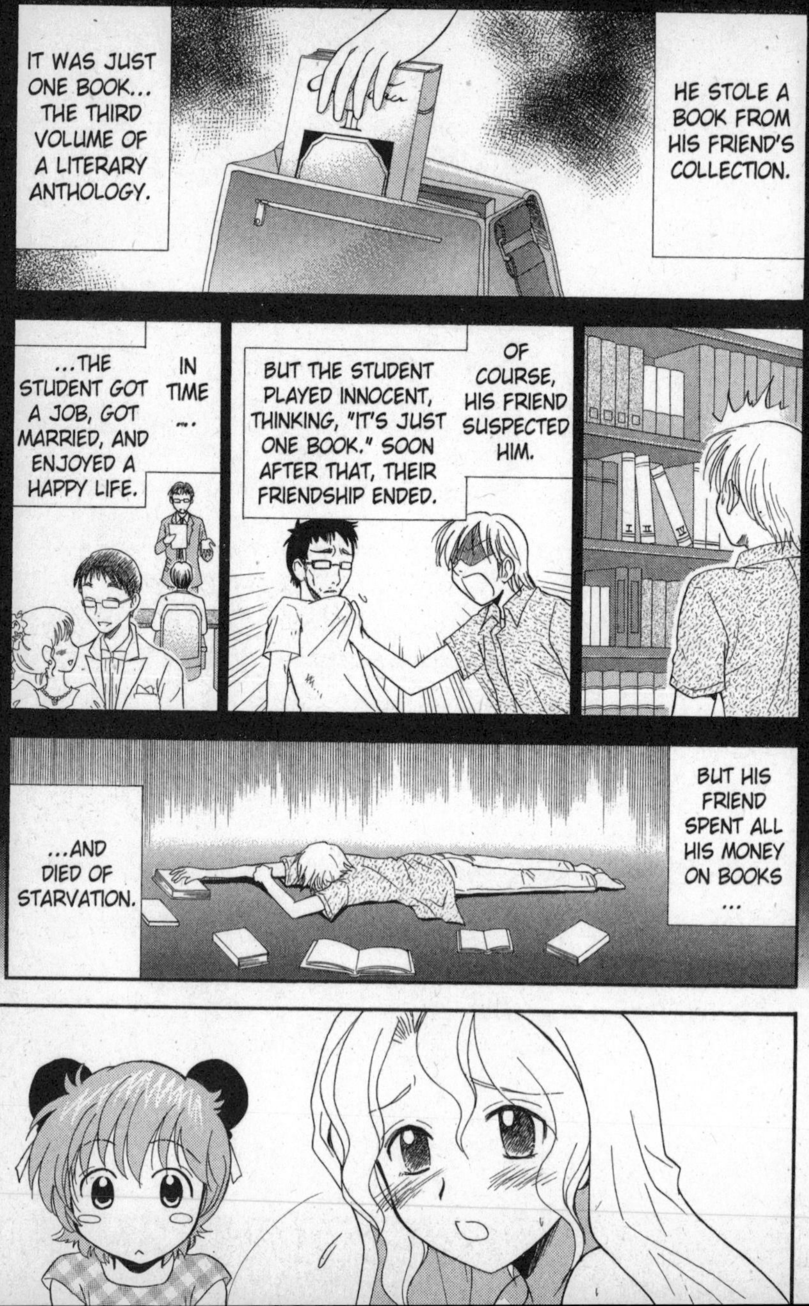
HE STOLE A BOOK FROM HIS FRIEND'S COLLECTION.
IT WAS JUST ONE BOOK... THE THIRD VOLUME OF A LITERARY ANTHOLOGY.
OF COURSE, HIS FRIEND SUSPECTED HIM.
BUT THE STUDENT PLAYED INNOCENT, THINKING, "IT'S JUST ONE BOOK." SOON AFTER THAT, THEIR FRIENDSHIP ENDED.
IN TIME ...
...THE STUDENT GOT A JOB, GOT MARRIED, AND ENJOYED A HAPPY LIFE.
BUT HIS FRIEND SPENT ALL HIS MONEY ON BOOKS ...
...AND DIED OF STARVATION.

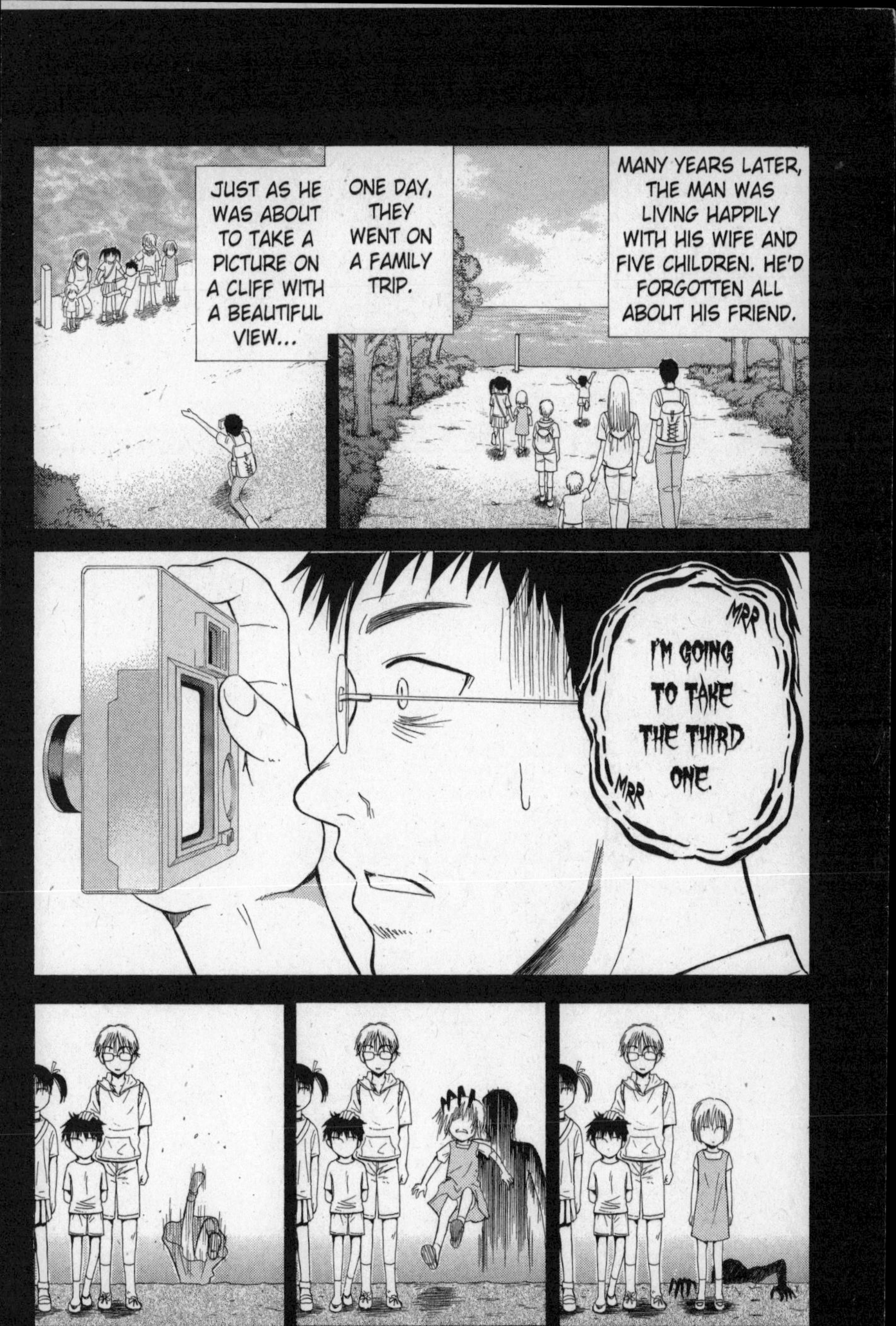
MANY YEARS LATER, THE MAN WAS LIVING HAPPILY WITH HIS WIFE AND FIVE CHILDREN. HE'D FORGOTTEN ALL ABOUT HIS FRIEND.
ONE DAY, THEY WENT ON A FAMILY TRIP.
JUST AS HE WAS ABOUT TO TAKE A PICTURE ON A CLIFF WITH A BEAUTIFUL VIEW...
MRR
I'M GOING TO TAKE THE THIRD ONE.
MRR

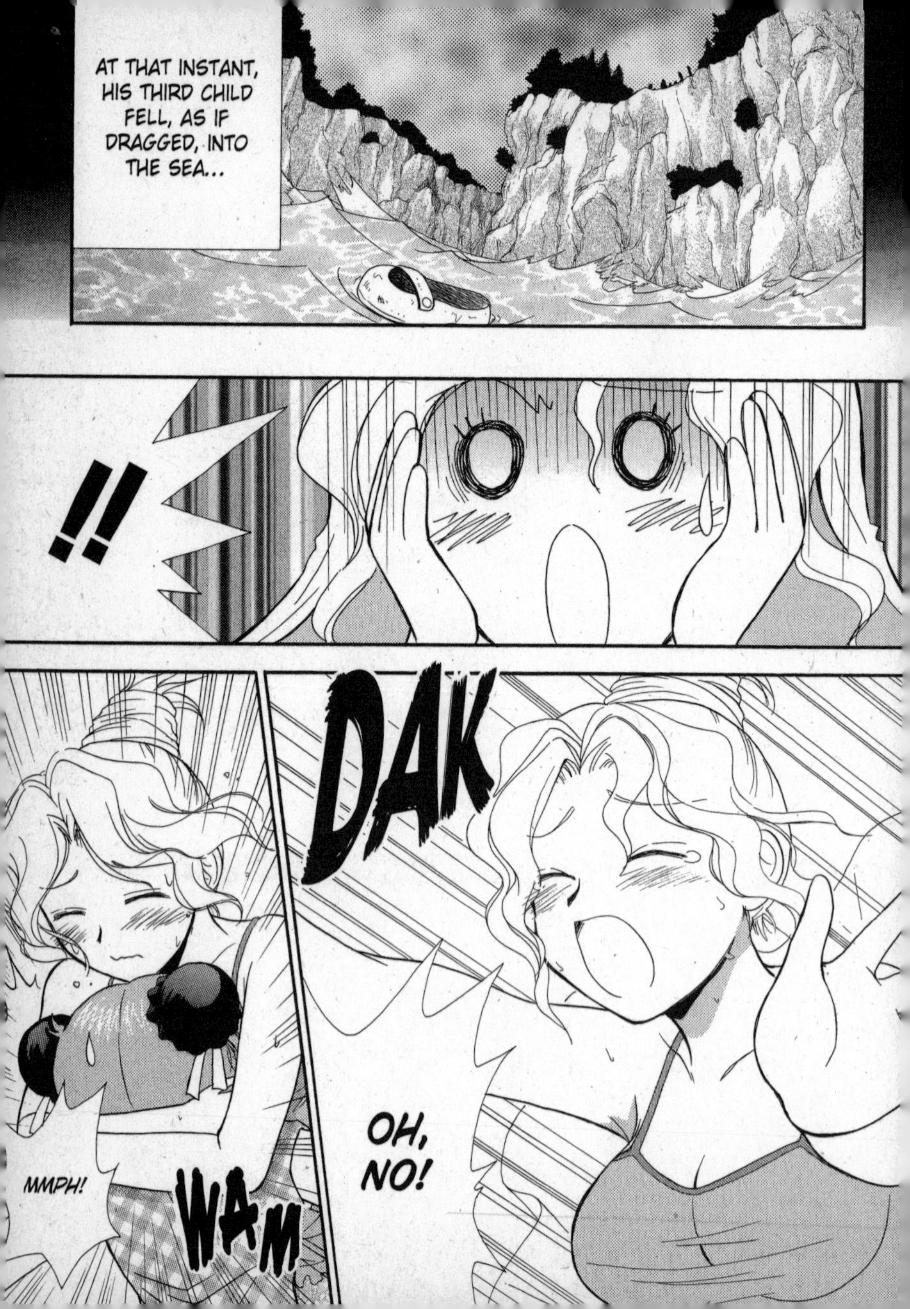
AT THAT INSTANT, HIS THIRD CHILD FELL, AS IF DRAGGED, INTO THE SEA...
!!
DAK
OH, NO!
MMPH!
WAM

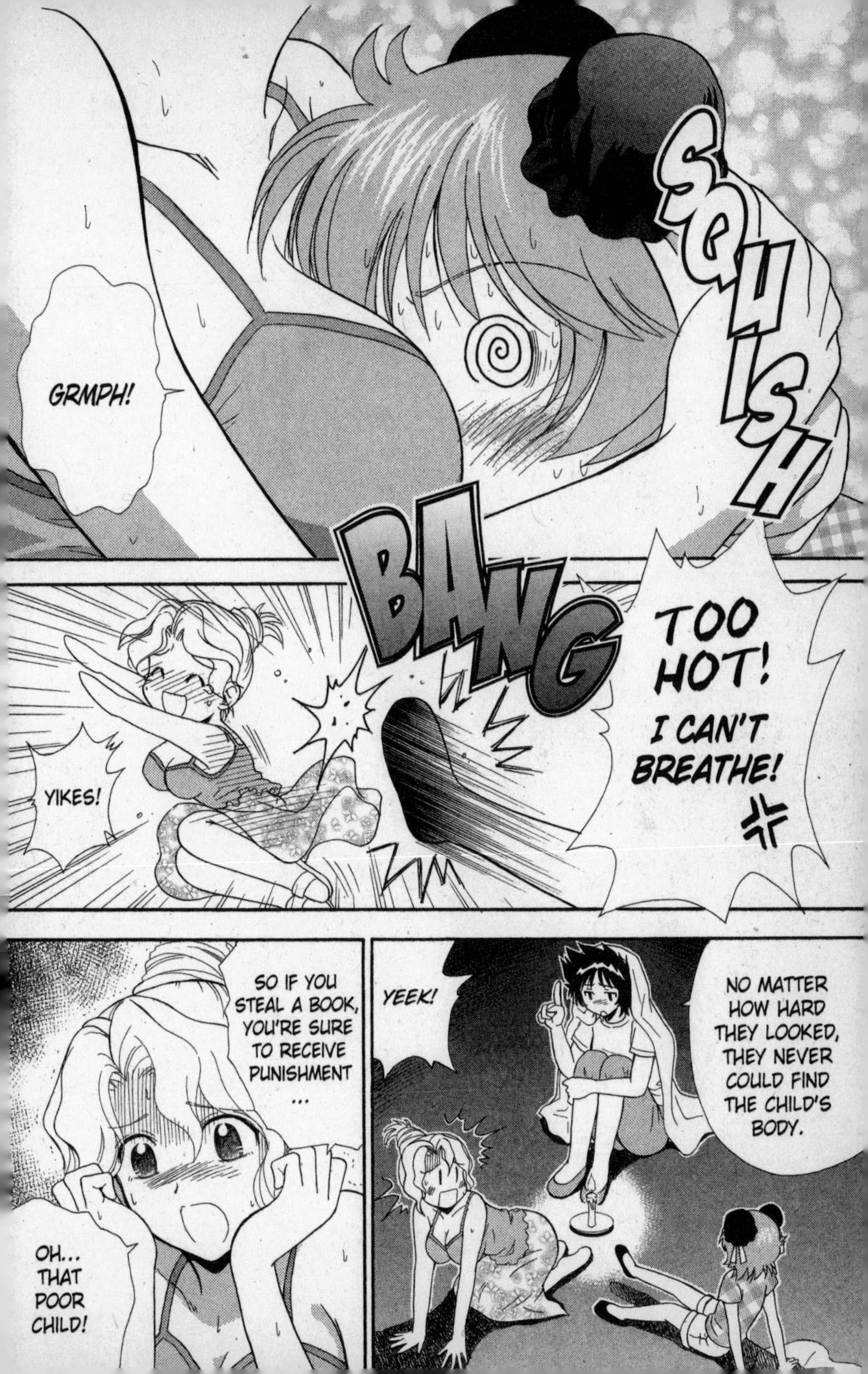
SQUISH
GRMPH!
BANG
TOO HOT! I CAN'T BREATHE!
YIKES!
NO MATTER HOW HARD THEY LOOKED, THEY NEVER COULD FIND THE CHILD'S BODY.
YEEK!
SO IF YOU STEAL A BOOK, YOU'RE SURE TO RECEIVE PUNISHMENT ...
OH... THAT POOR CHILD!

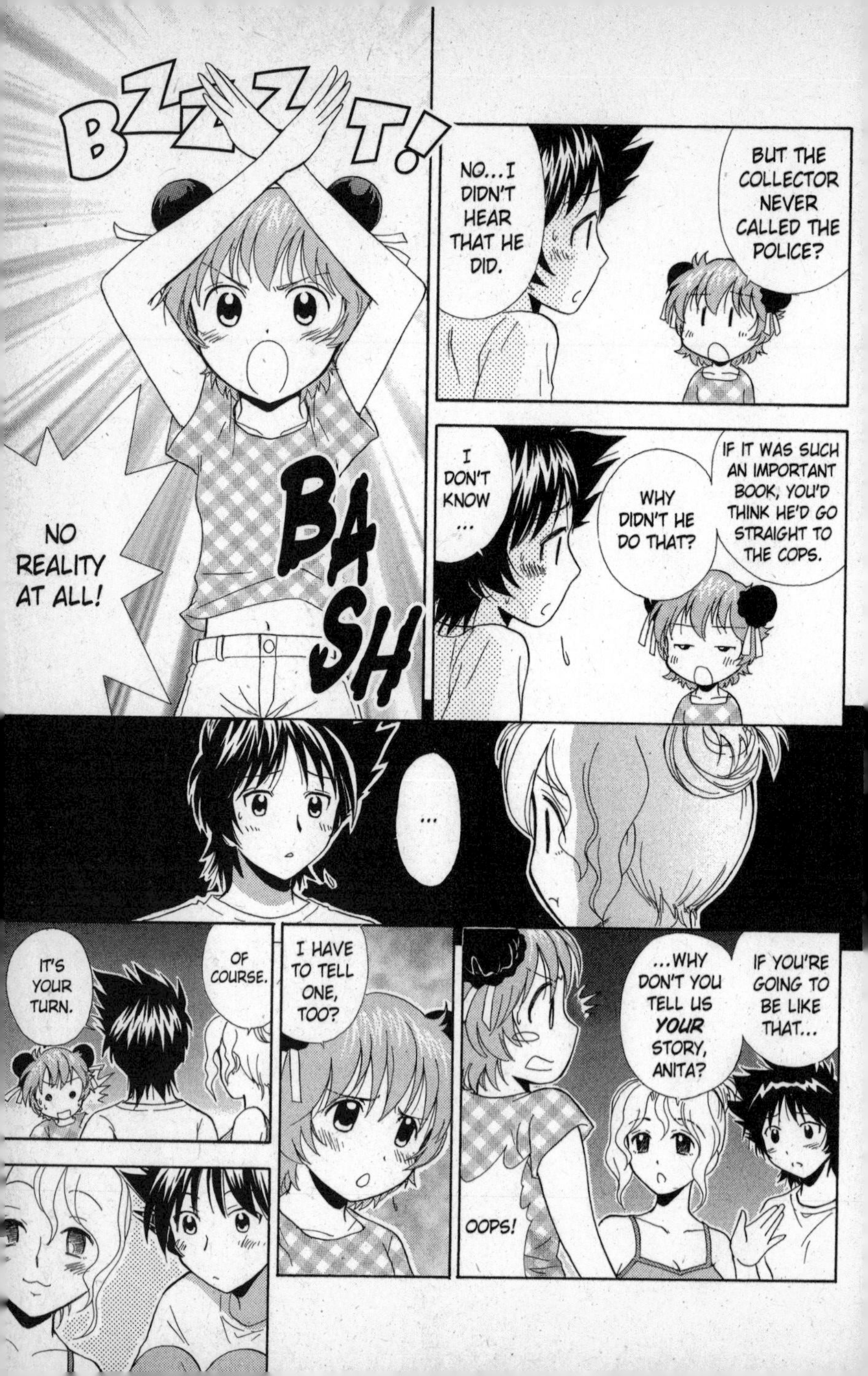
BUT THE COLLECTOR NEVER CALLED THE POLICE?
NO...I DIDN'T HEAR THAT HE DID.
IF IT WAS SUCH AN IMPORTANT BOOK, YOU'D THINK HE'D GO STRAIGHT TO THE COPS.
WHY DIDN'T HE DO THAT?
I DON'T KNOW ...
BZZZZT!
BASH
NO REALITY AT ALL!
...
IF YOU'RE GOING TO BE LIKE THAT...
...WHY DON'T YOU TELL US *YOUR* STORY, ANITA?
OOPS!
I HAVE TO TELL ONE, TOO?
OF COURSE.
IT'S YOUR TURN.

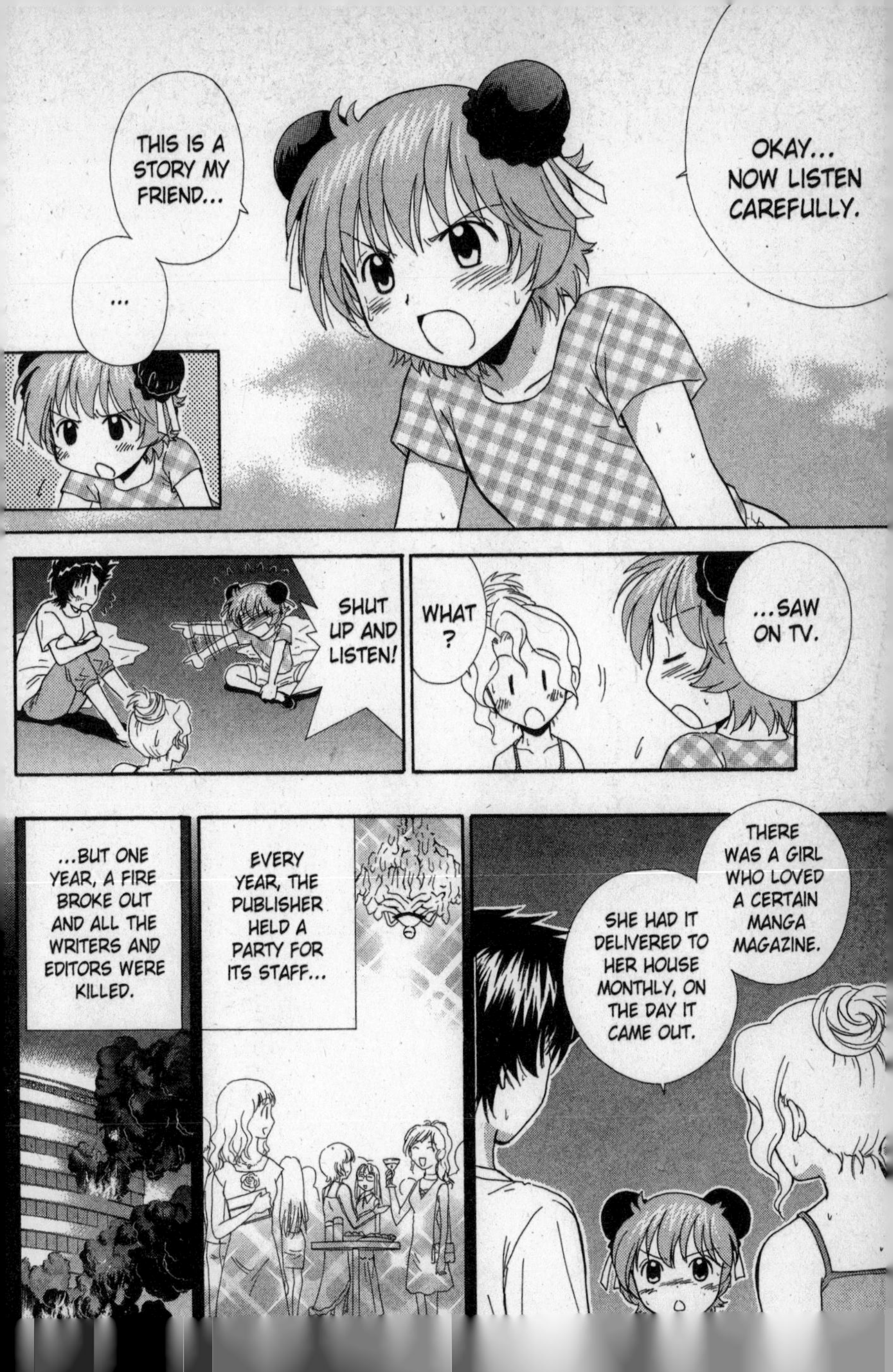
OKAY... NOW LISTEN CAREFULLY.
THIS IS A STORY MY FRIEND...
...
...SAW ON TV.
WHAT?
SHUT UP AND LISTEN!
THERE WAS A GIRL WHO LOVED A CERTAIN MANGA MAGAZINE.
SHE HAD IT DELIVERED TO HER HOUSE MONTHLY, ON THE DAY IT CAME OUT.
EVERY YEAR, THE PUBLISHER HELD A PARTY FOR ITS STAFF...
...BUT ONE YEAR, A FIRE BROKE OUT AND ALL THE WRITERS AND EDITORS WERE KILLED.

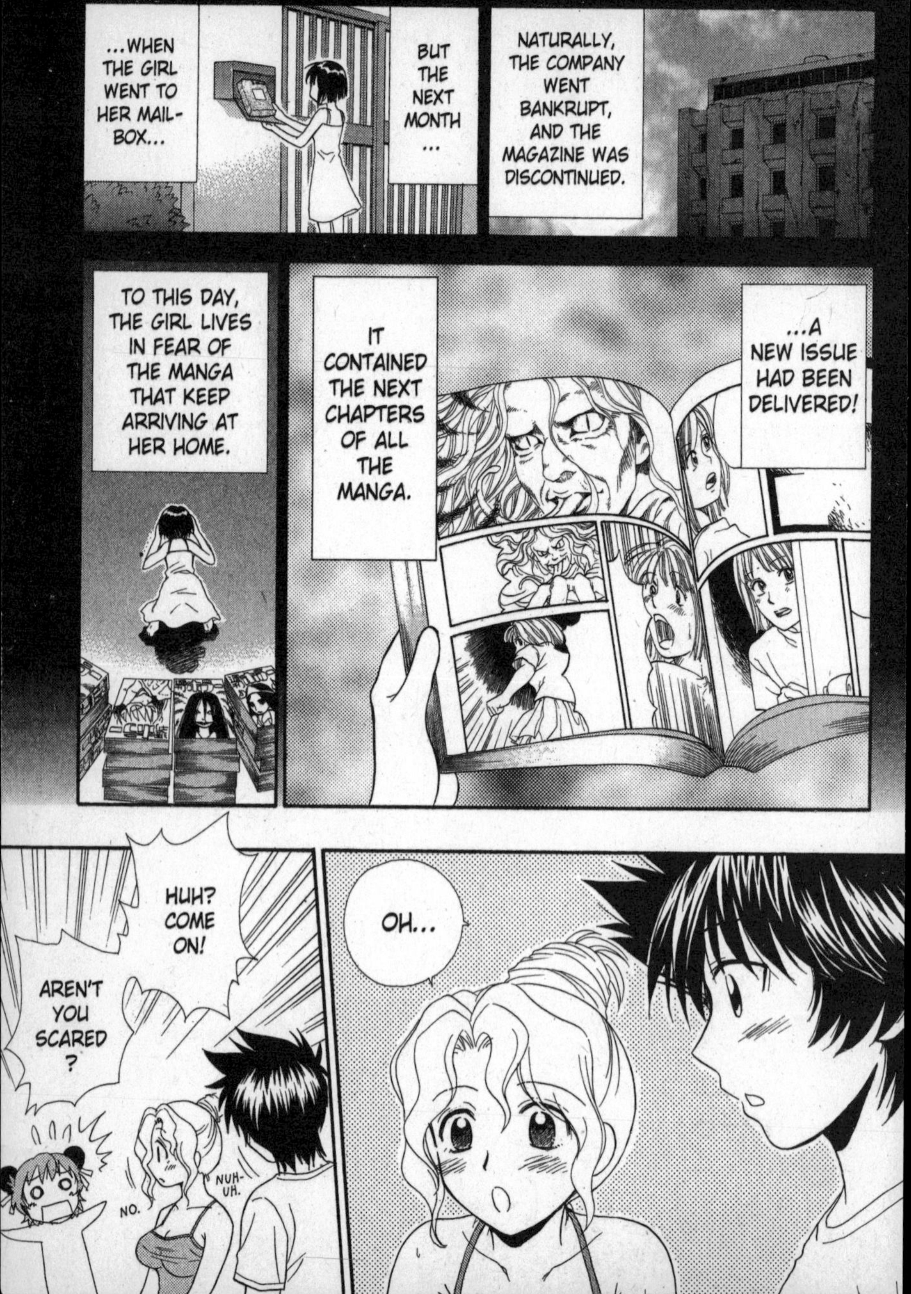
NATURALLY, THE COMPANY WENT BANKRUPT, AND THE MAGAZINE WAS DISCONTINUED.
BUT THE NEXT MONTH ...
...WHEN THE GIRL WENT TO HER MAIL-BOX...
...A NEW ISSUE HAD BEEN DELIVERED!
IT CONTAINED THE NEXT CHAPTERS OF ALL THE MANGA.
TO THIS DAY, THE GIRL LIVES IN FEAR OF THE MANGA THAT KEEP ARRIVING AT HER HOME.
OH...
HUH? COME ON!
AREN'T YOU SCARED?
NUH-UH.
NO.

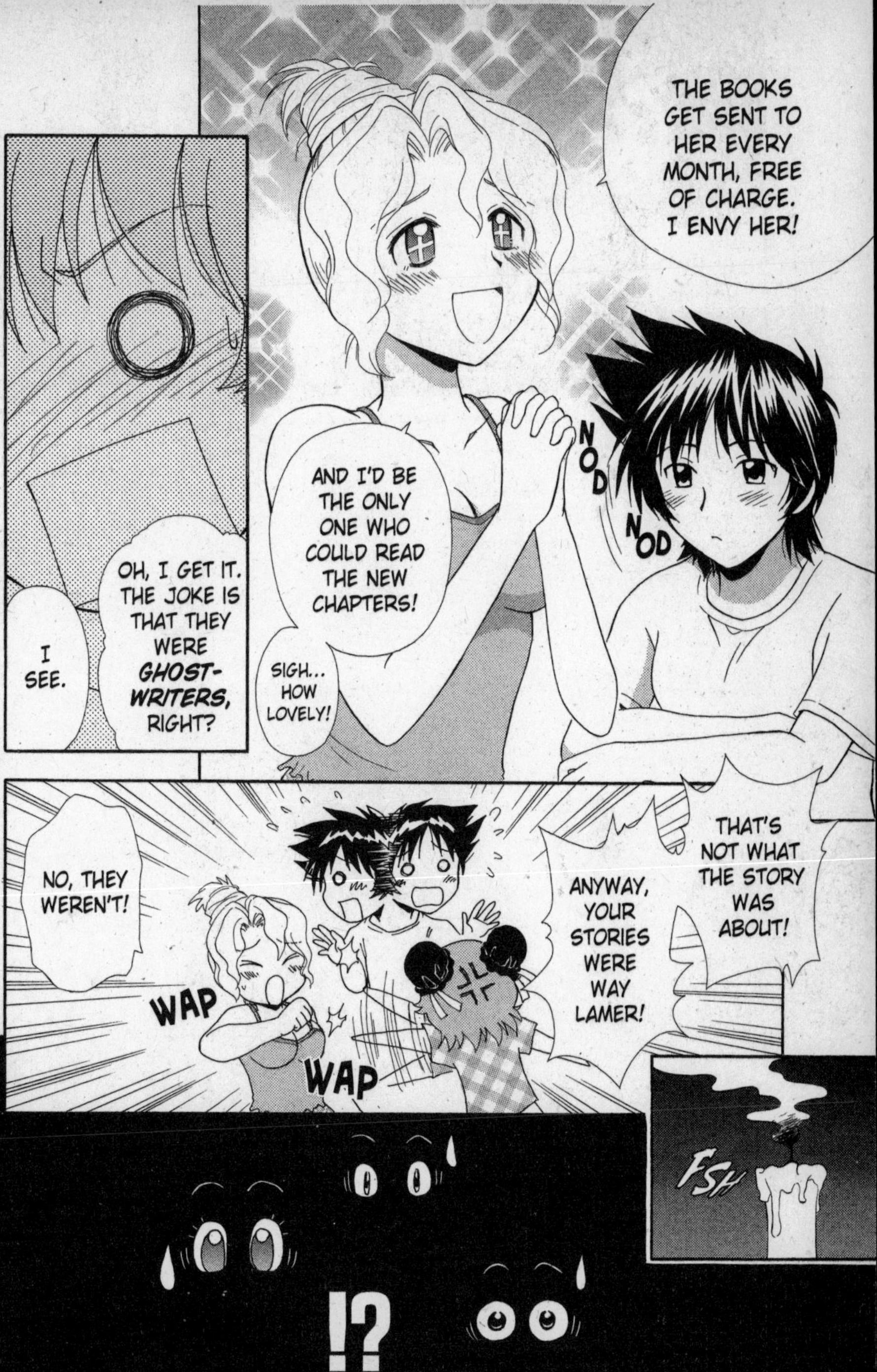
THE BOOKS GET SENT TO HER EVERY MONTH, FREE OF CHARGE. I ENVY HER!
AND I'D BE THE ONLY ONE WHO COULD READ THE NEW CHAPTERS!
NOD
NOD
SIGH... HOW LOVELY!
OH, I GET IT. THE JOKE IS THAT THEY WERE *GHOST-WRITERS*, RIGHT?
I SEE.
THAT'S NOT WHAT THE STORY WAS ABOUT!
ANYWAY, YOUR STORIES WERE WAY LAMER!
NO, THEY WEREN'T!
WAP
WAP
FSH
!?

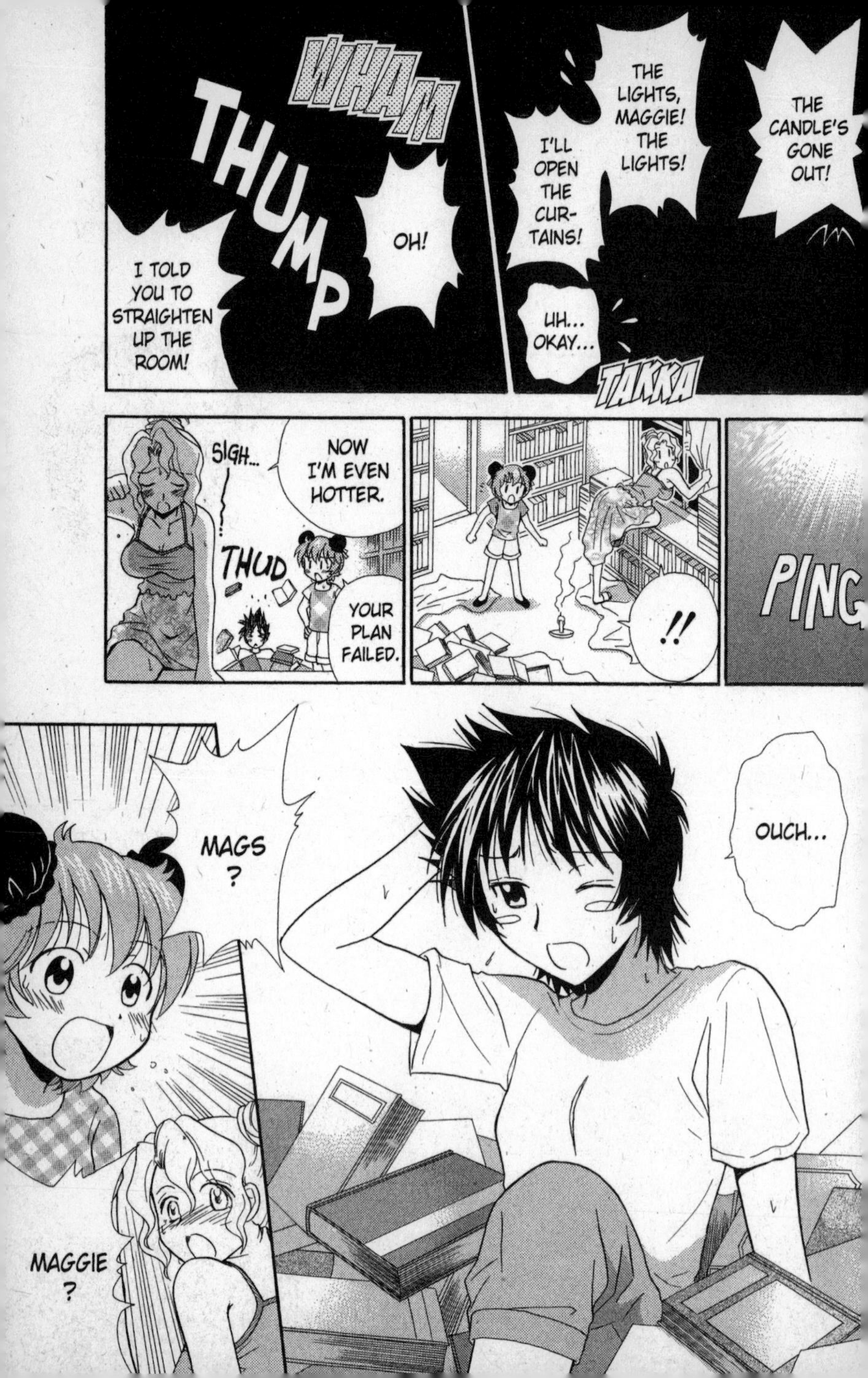
THE CANDLE'S GONE OUT!
THE LIGHTS, MAGGIE! THE LIGHTS!
I'LL OPEN THE CUR- TAINS!
UH... OKAY...
TAKKA
WHAM
OH!
THUMP
I TOLD YOU TO STRAIGHTEN UP THE ROOM!
PING
!!
NOW I'M EVEN HOTTER.
SIGH...
THUD
YOUR PLAN FAILED.
OUCH...
MAGS ?
MAGGIE ?

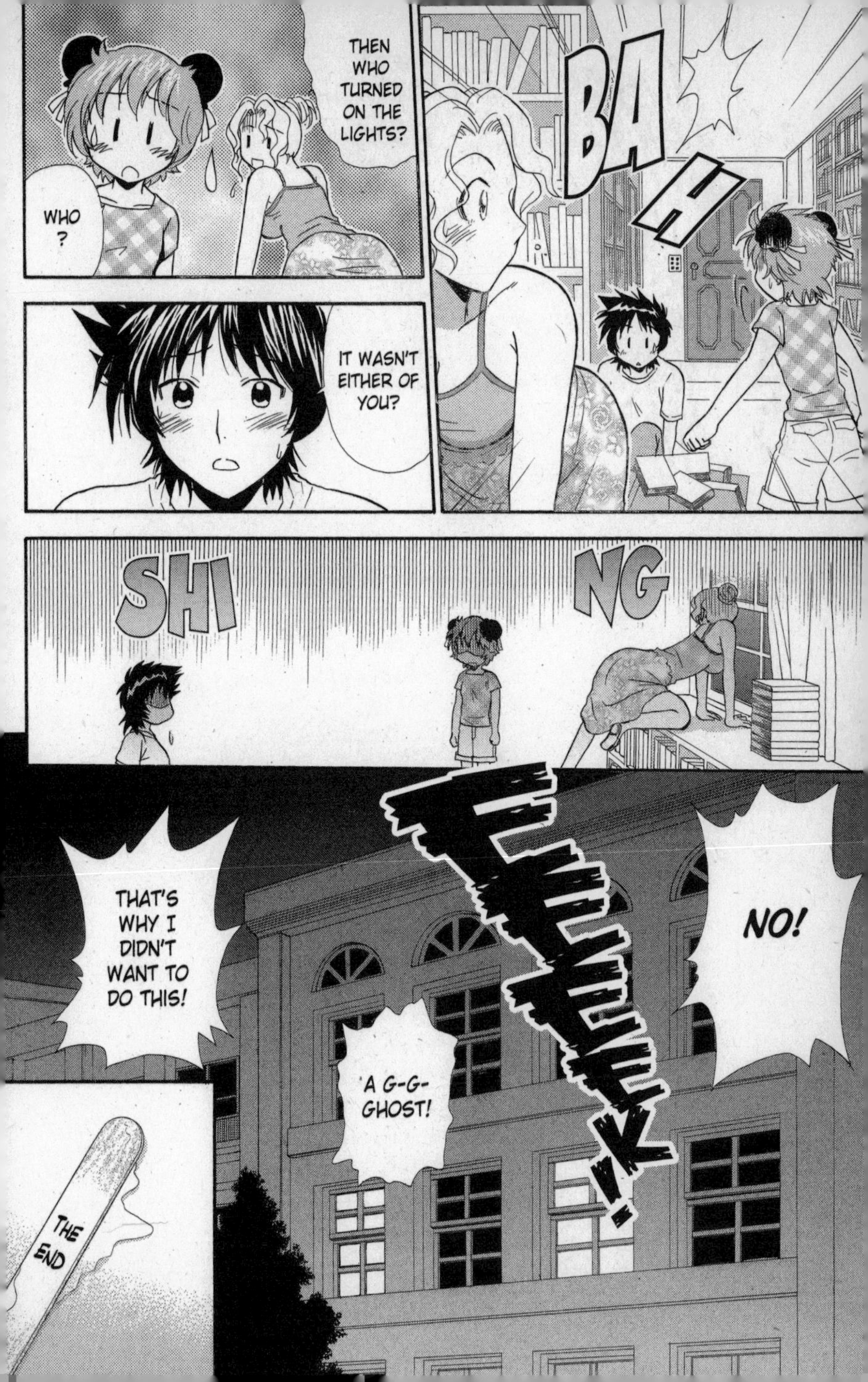
BAH
THEN WHO TURNED ON THE LIGHTS?
WHO?
IT WASN'T EITHER OF YOU?
SHING
NO!
'A G-G-GHOST!
THAT'S WHY I DIDN'T WANT TO DO THIS!
THE END

CHAPTER 12

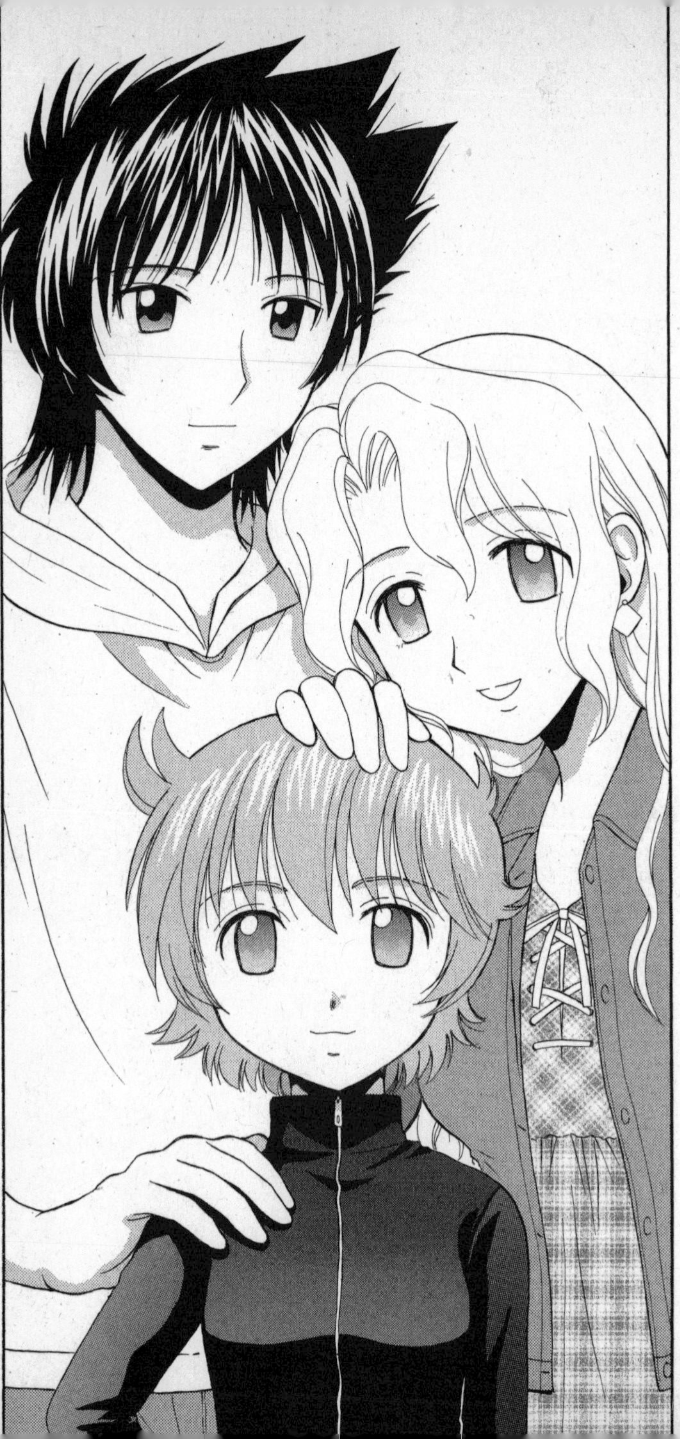

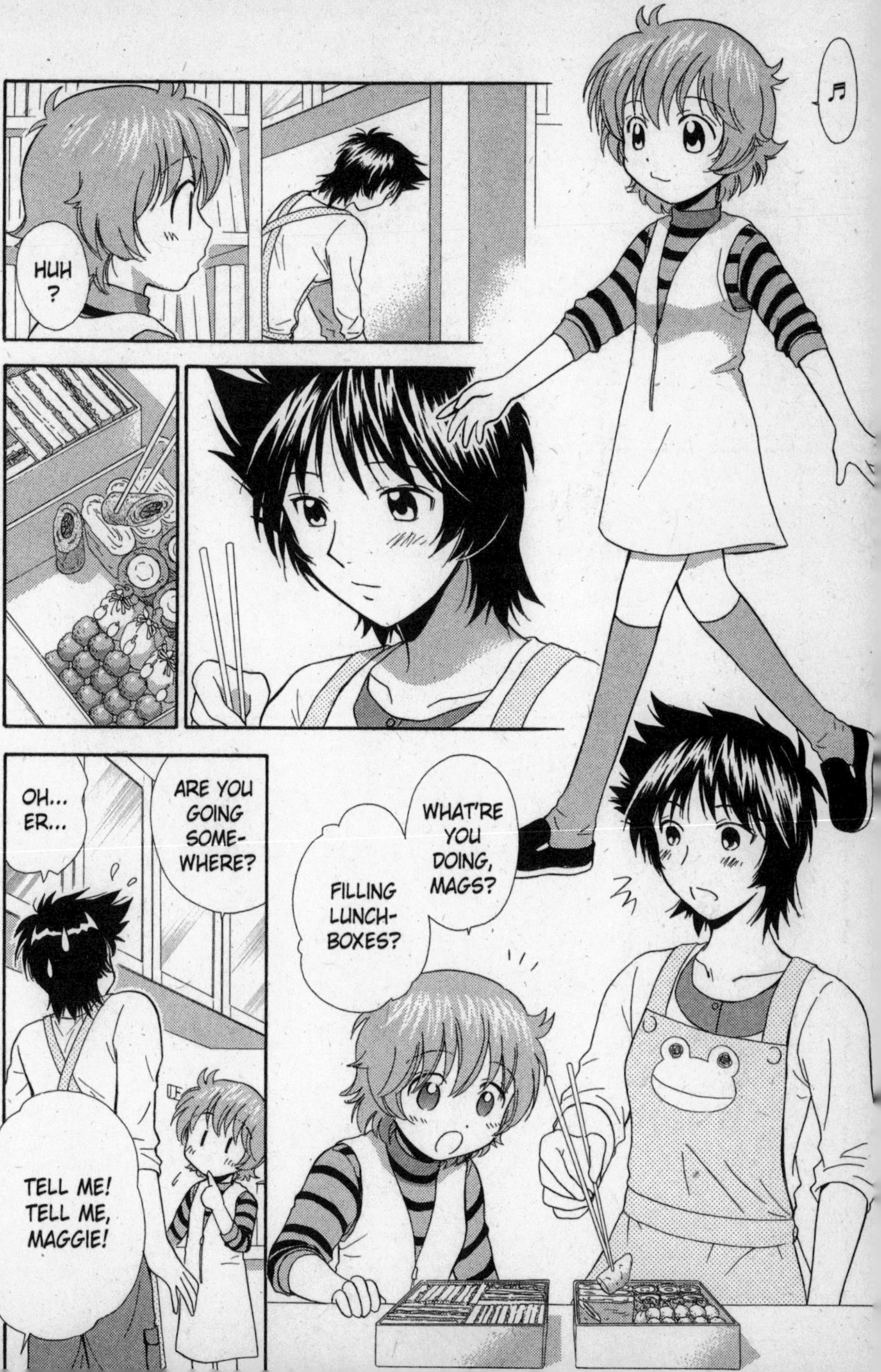
♬
HUH?
WHAT'RE YOU DOING, MAGS?
FILLING LUNCH-BOXES?
ARE YOU GOING SOME-WHERE?
OH... ER...
TELL ME! TELL ME, MAGGIE!

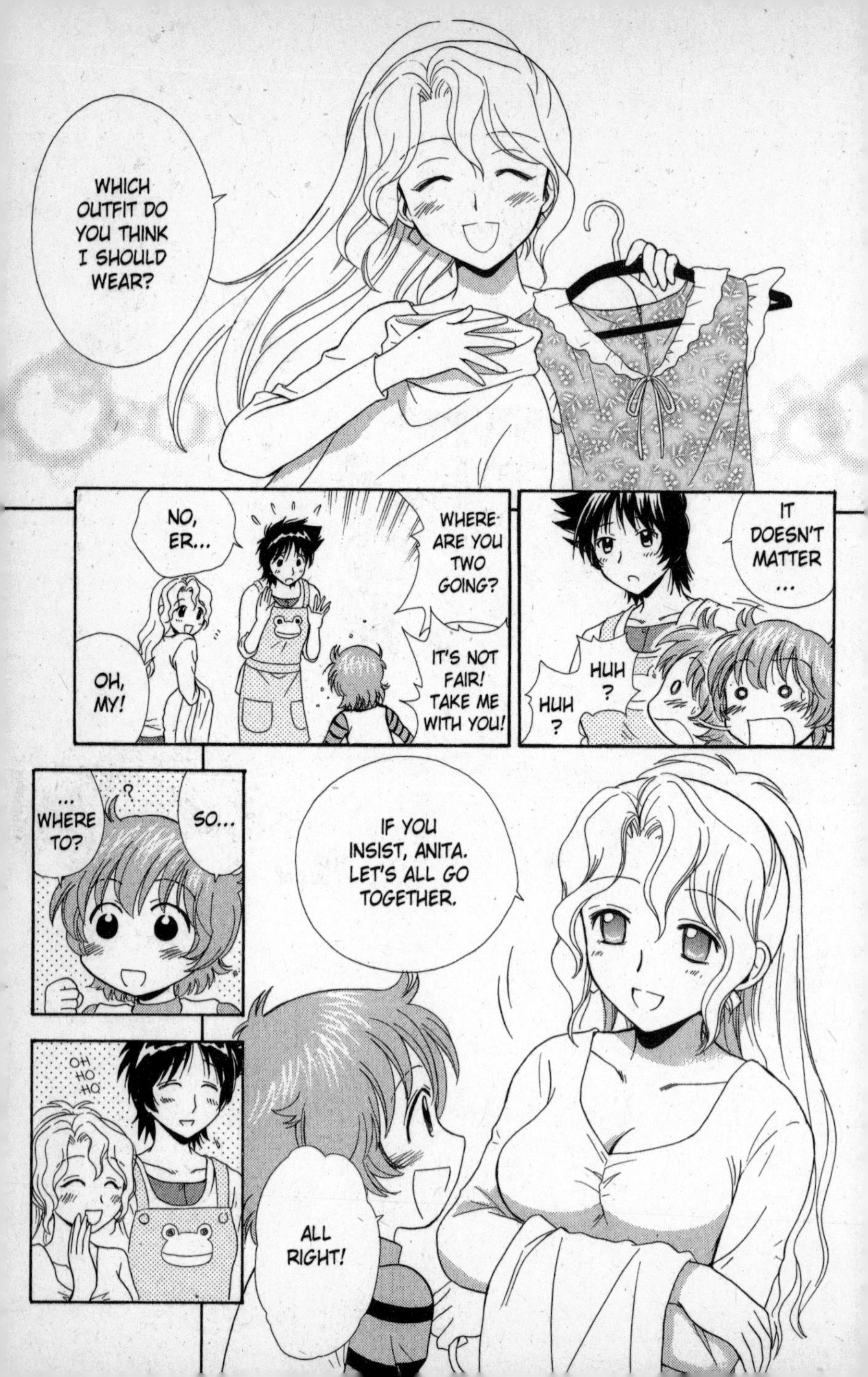
WHICH OUTFIT DO YOU THINK I SHOULD WEAR?
IT DOESN'T MATTER ...
HUH ?
HUH ?
WHERE ARE YOU TWO GOING?
IT'S NOT FAIR! TAKE ME WITH YOU!
NO, ER...
OH, MY!
IF YOU INSIST, ANITA. LET'S ALL GO TOGETHER.
ALL RIGHT!
SO...
... WHERE TO?
OH HO HO

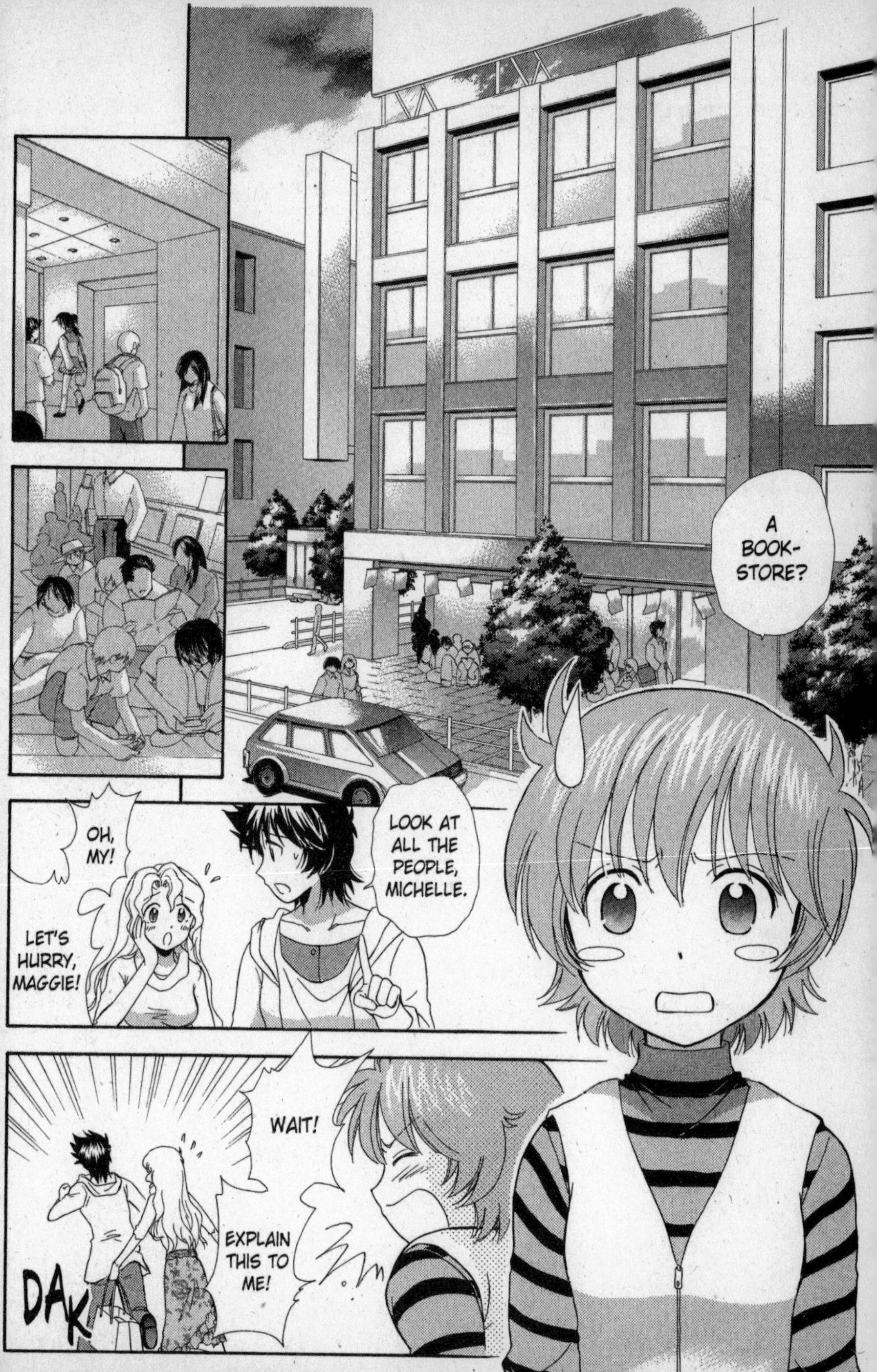
A BOOK-STORE?
LOOK AT ALL THE PEOPLE, MICHELLE.
OH, MY!
LET'S HURRY, MAGGIE!
WAIT!
EXPLAIN THIS TO ME!
DAK

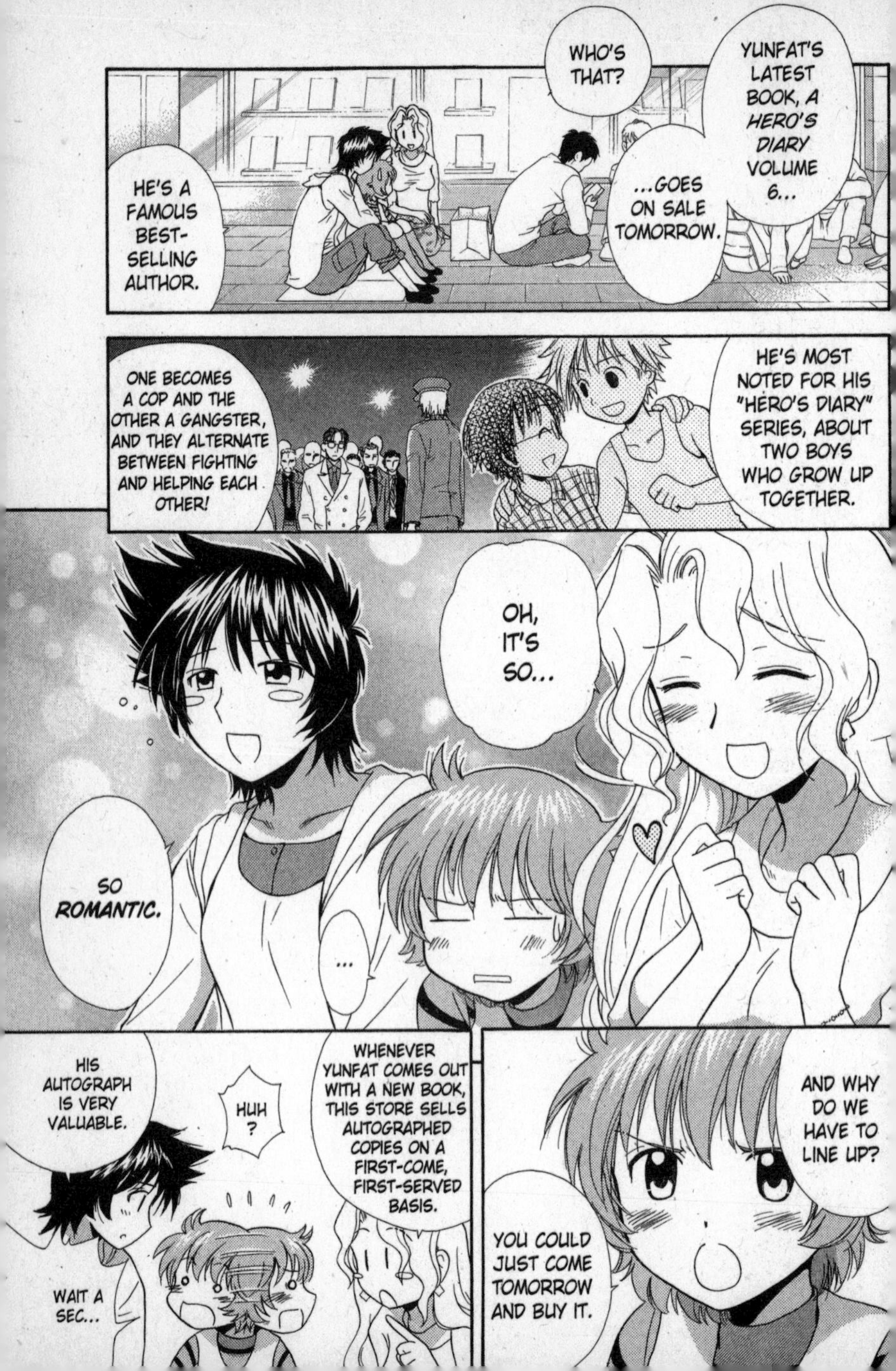
YUNFAT'S LATEST BOOK, A *HERO'S DIARY* VOLUME 6...
...GOES ON SALE TOMORROW.
WHO'S THAT?
HE'S A FAMOUS BEST-SELLING AUTHOR.
HE'S MOST NOTED FOR HIS "HERO'S DIARY" SERIES, ABOUT TWO BOYS WHO GROW UP TOGETHER.
ONE BECOMES A COP AND THE OTHER A GANGSTER, AND THEY ALTERNATE BETWEEN FIGHTING AND HELPING EACH OTHER!
OH, IT'S SO...
SO ***ROMANTIC.***
...
AND WHY DO WE HAVE TO LINE UP?
YOU COULD JUST COME TOMORROW AND BUY IT.
WHENEVER YUNFAT COMES OUT WITH A NEW BOOK, THIS STORE SELLS AUTOGRAPHED COPIES ON A FIRST-COME, FIRST-SERVED BASIS.
HUH?
HIS AUTOGRAPH IS VERY VALUABLE.
WAIT A SEC...

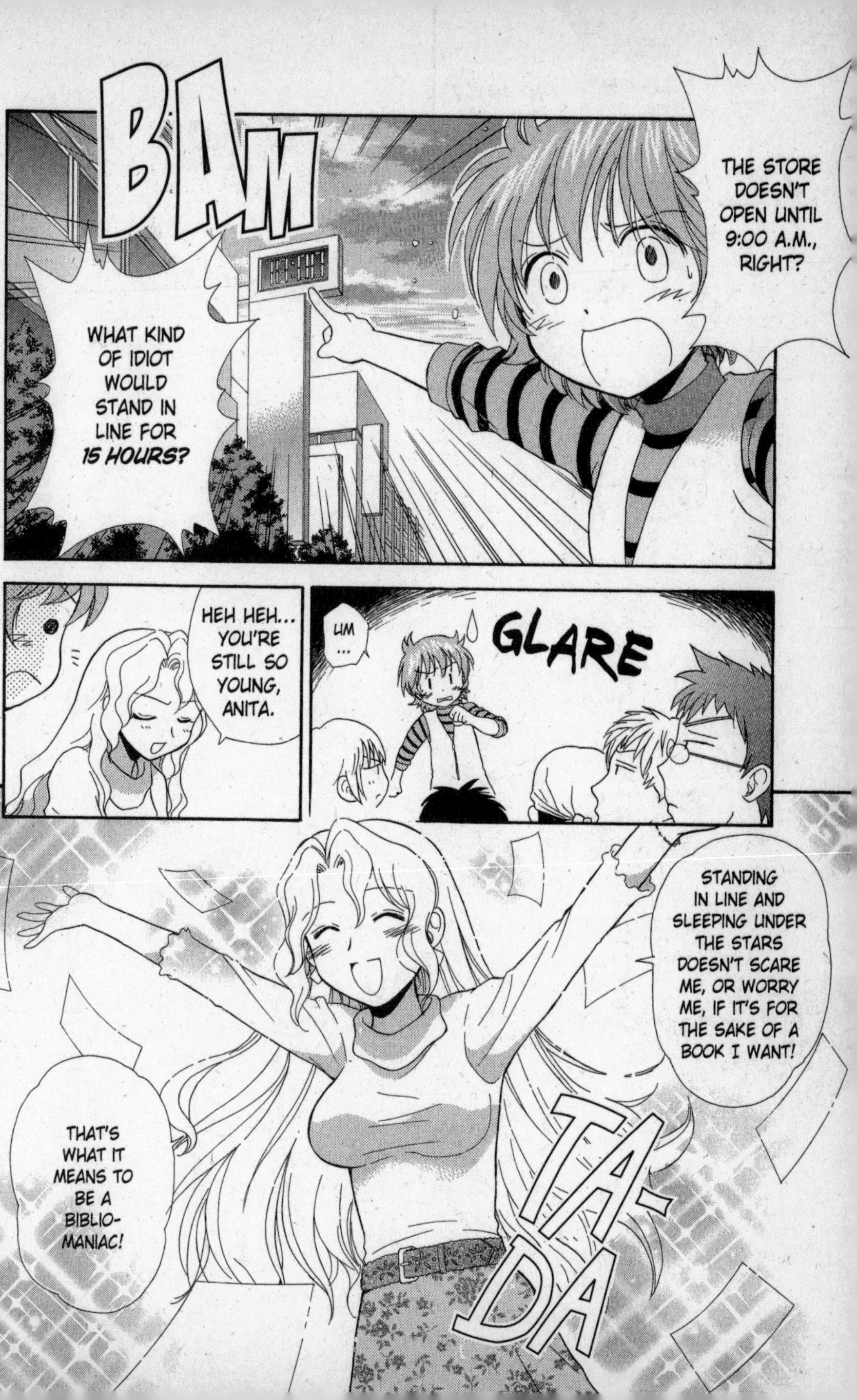
THE STORE DOESN'T OPEN UNTIL 9:00 A.M., RIGHT?
BAM
WHAT KIND OF IDIOT WOULD STAND IN LINE FOR *15 HOURS?*
UM ...
GLARE
HEH HEH... YOU'RE STILL SO YOUNG, ANITA.
STANDING IN LINE AND SLEEPING UNDER THE STARS DOESN'T SCARE ME, OR WORRY ME, IF IT'S FOR THE SAKE OF A BOOK I WANT!
TA-DA
THAT'S WHAT IT MEANS TO BE A BIBLIO-MANIAC!

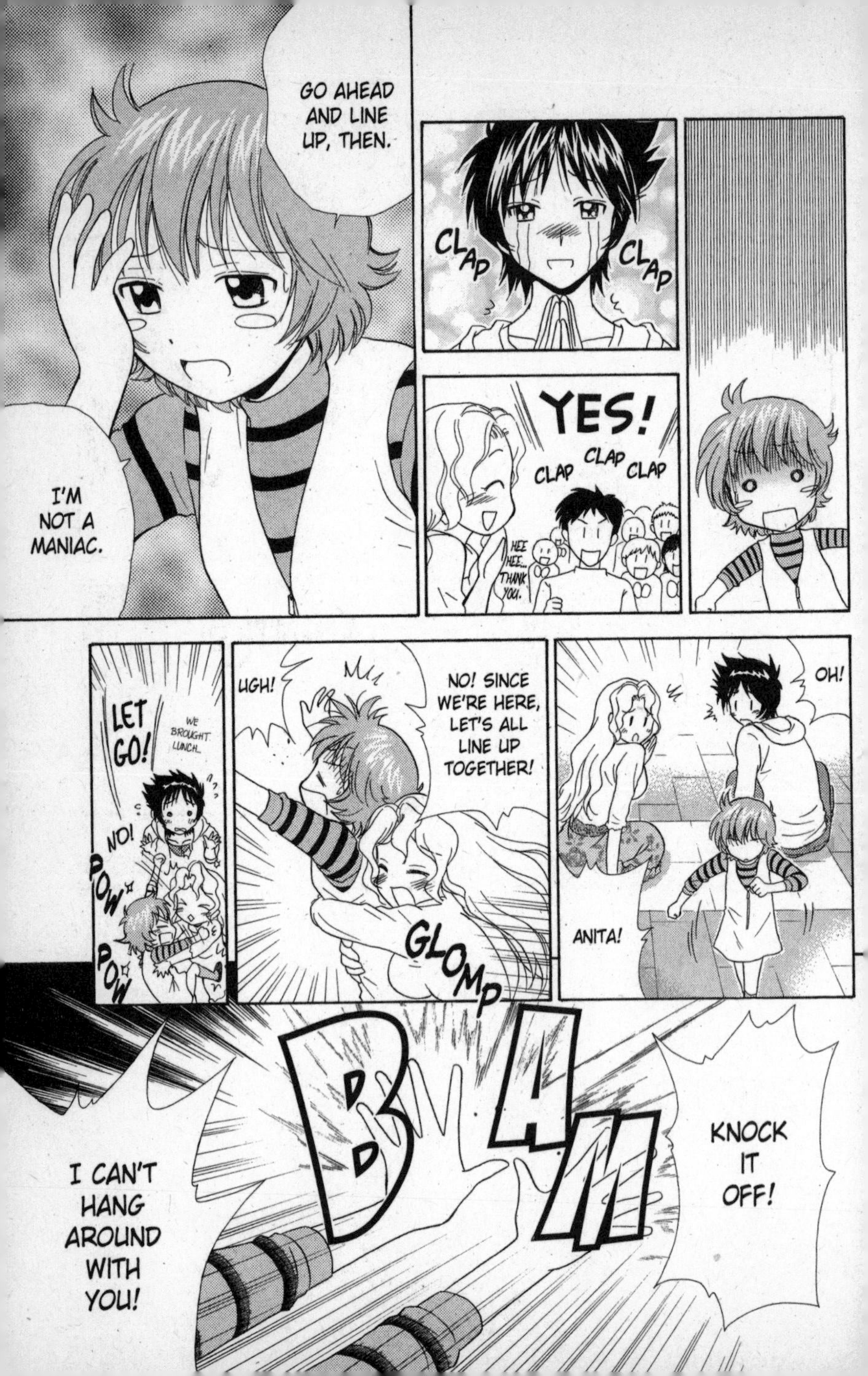
I'M NOT A MANIAC.
GO AHEAD AND LINE UP, THEN.
CLAP CLAP
YES!
CLAP CLAP CLAP
HEE HEE... THANK YOU.
OH!
ANITA!
NO! SINCE WE'RE HERE, LET'S ALL LINE UP TOGETHER!
UGH!
GLOMP
LET GO!
WE BROUGHT LUNCH.
NO!
POW POW
KNOCK IT OFF!
BAM
I CAN'T HANG AROUND WITH YOU!

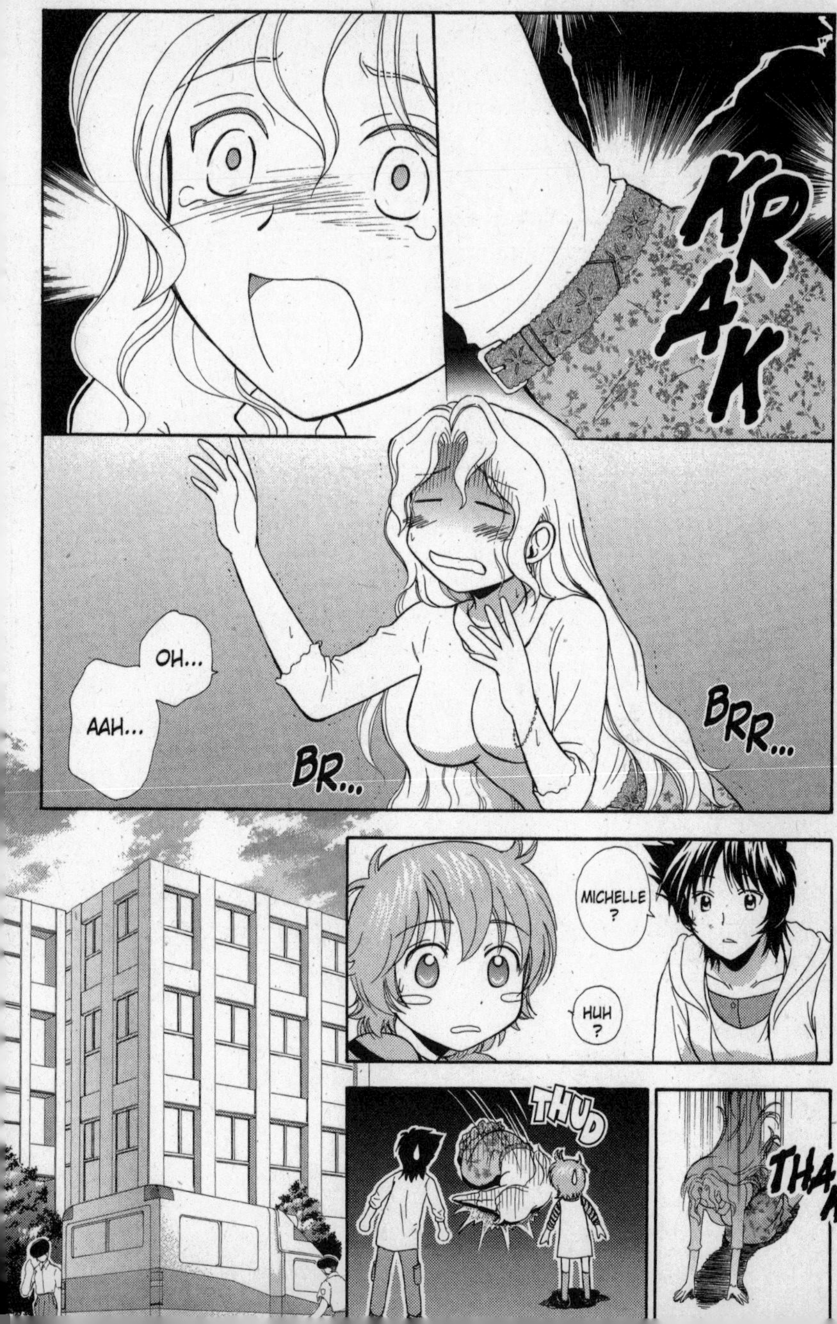
KRAK
BRRR...
OH...
AAH...
BR...
MICHELLE?
HUH?
THAK
THUD

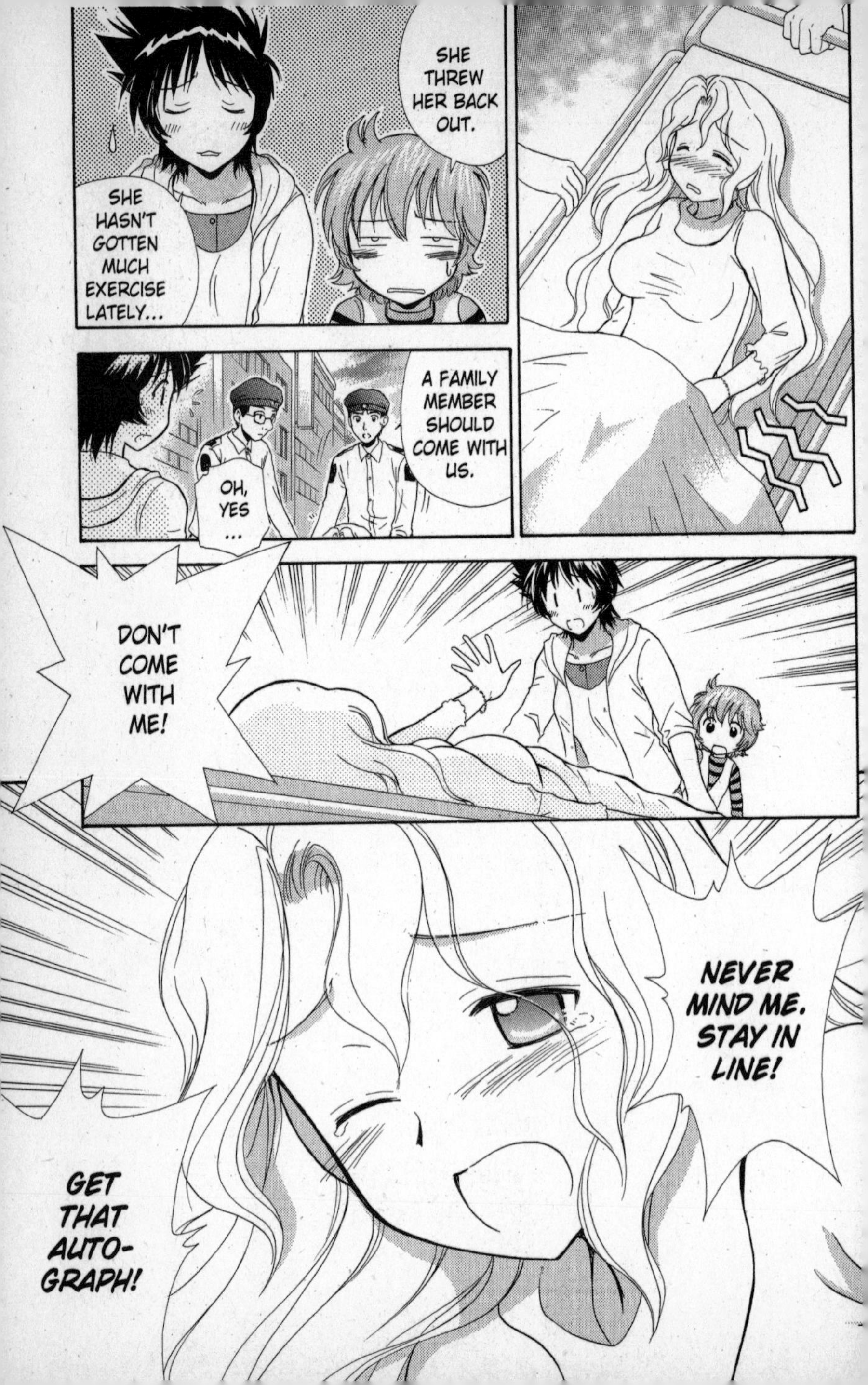
SHE THREW HER BACK OUT.
SHE HASN'T GOTTEN MUCH EXERCISE LATELY...
A FAMILY MEMBER SHOULD COME WITH US.
OH, YES ...
DON'T COME WITH ME!
NEVER MIND ME. STAY IN LINE!
GET THAT AUTO-GRAPH!

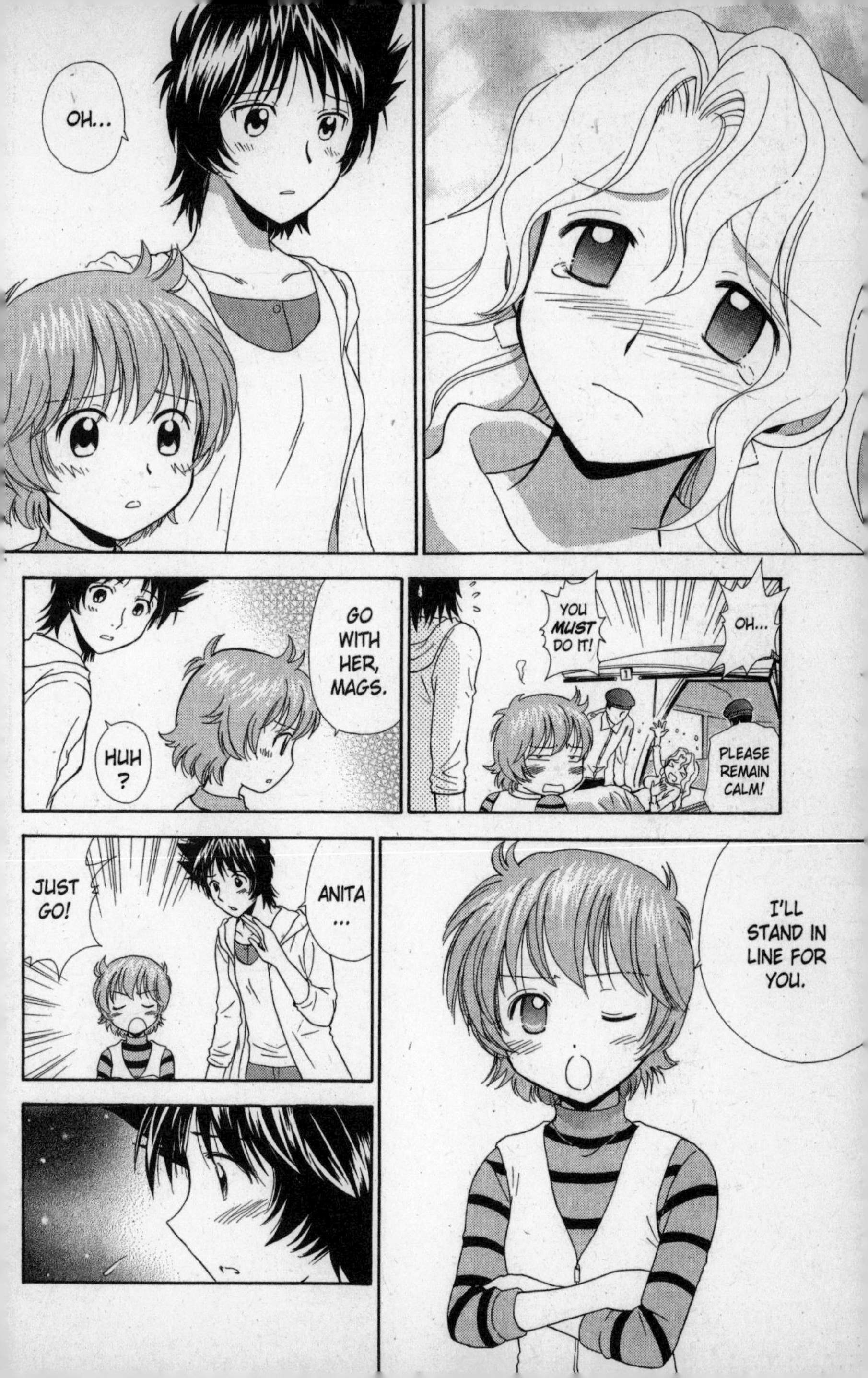
OH...
OH...
YOU MUST DO IT!
PLEASE REMAIN CALM!
GO WITH HER, MAGS.
HUH?
I'LL STAND IN LINE FOR YOU.
ANITA...
JUST GO!

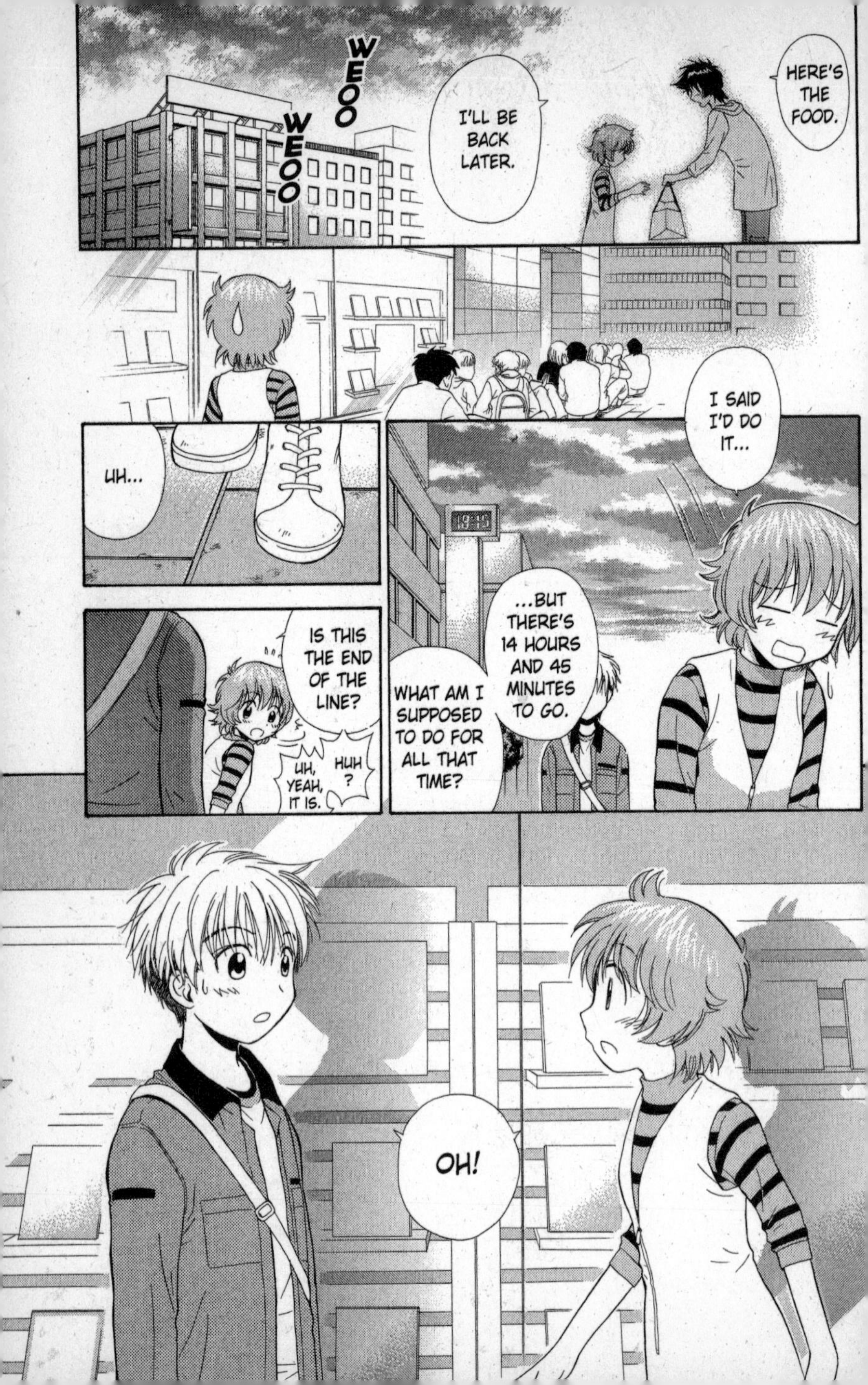
HERE'S THE FOOD.
I'LL BE BACK LATER.
WEOO
WEOO
I SAID I'D DO IT...
...BUT THERE'S 14 HOURS AND 45 MINUTES TO GO.
WHAT AM I SUPPOSED TO DO FOR ALL THAT TIME?
UH...
IS THIS THE END OF THE LINE?
HUH?
UH, YEAH, IT IS.
OH!

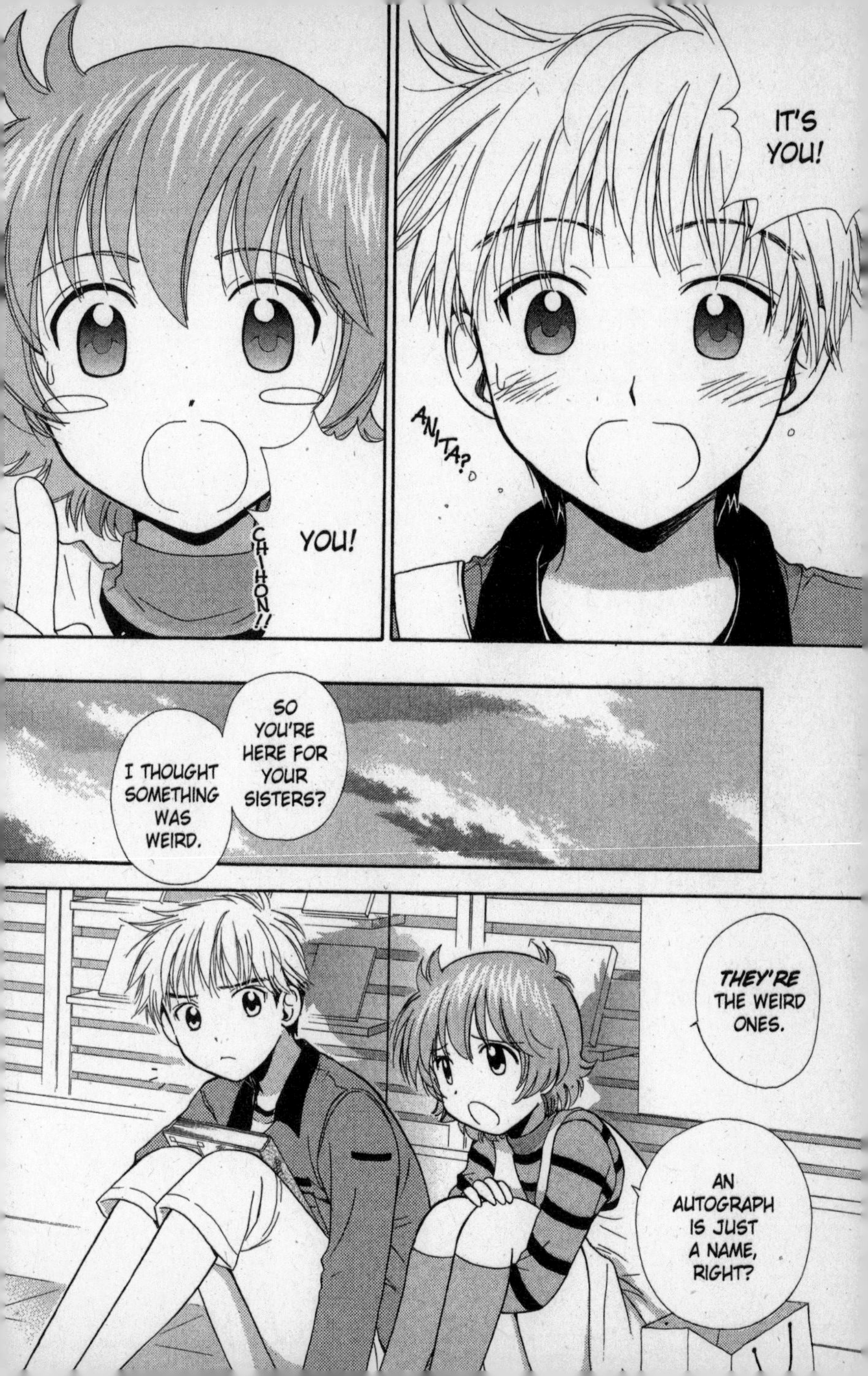
IT'S YOU!
ANITA?
YOU!
CHIHON!!
SO YOU'RE HERE FOR YOUR SISTERS?
I THOUGHT SOMETHING WAS WEIRD.
THEY'RE THE WEIRD ONES.
AN AUTOGRAPH IS JUST A NAME, RIGHT?

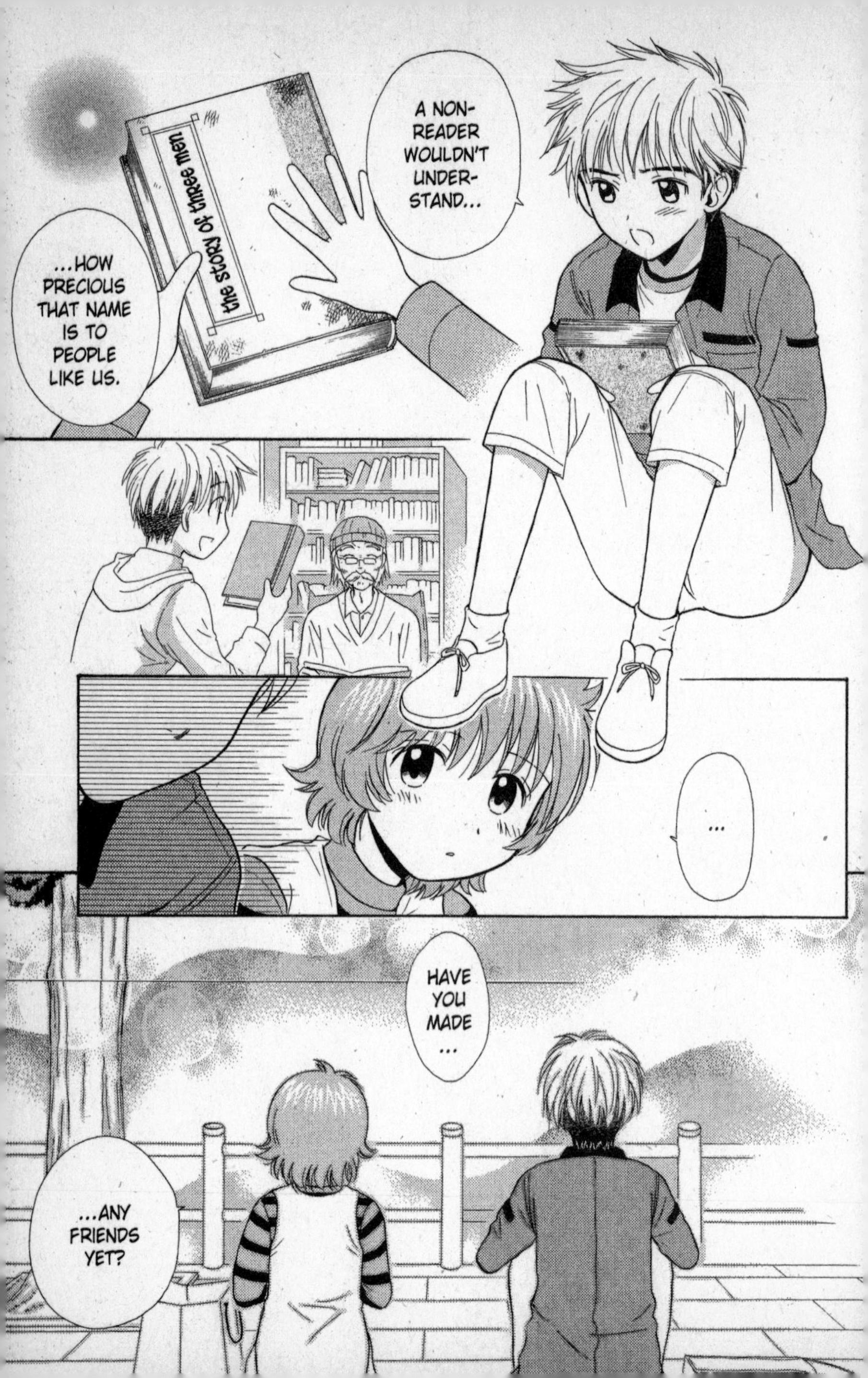
A NON-READER WOULDN'T UNDERSTAND...
the story of three men
...HOW PRECIOUS THAT NAME IS TO PEOPLE LIKE US.
...
HAVE YOU MADE ...
...ANY FRIENDS YET?

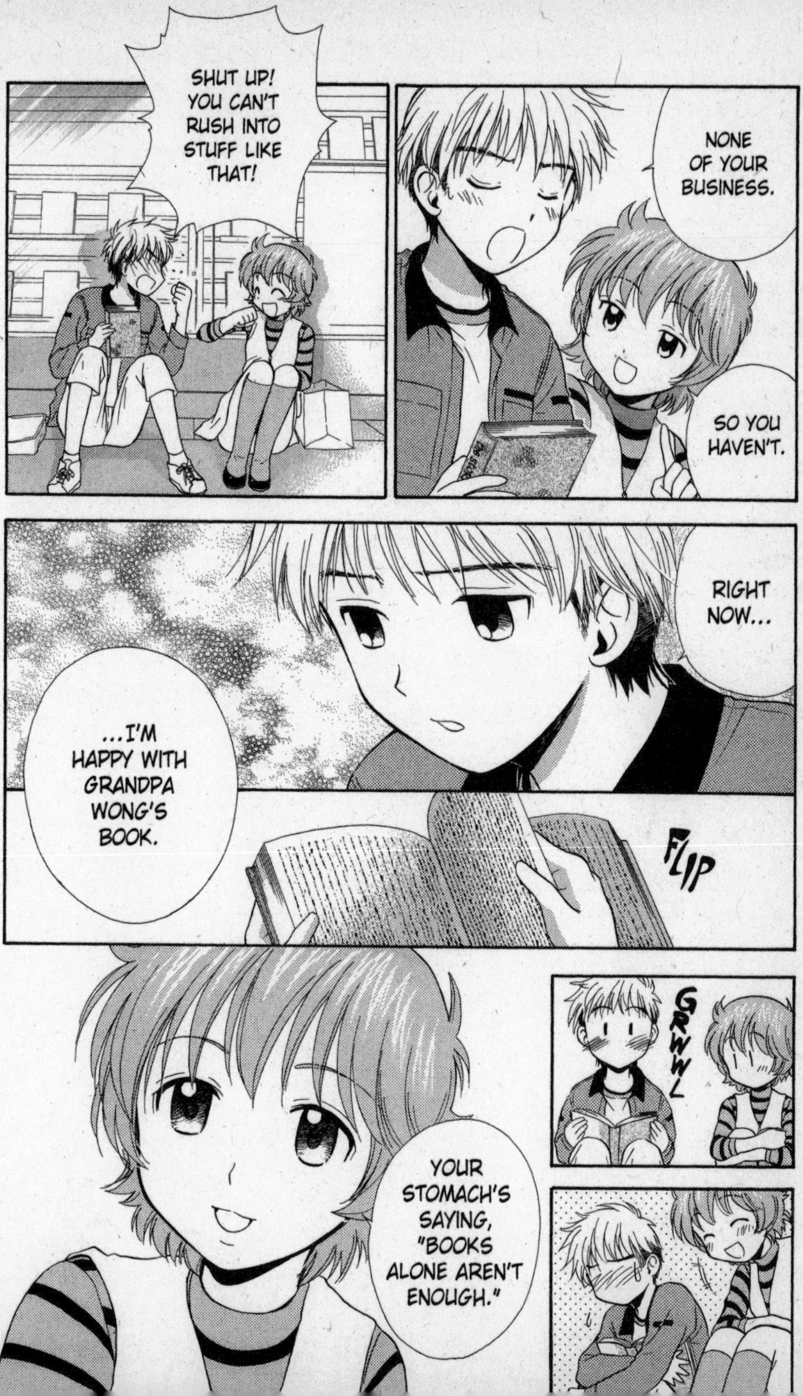
NONE OF YOUR BUSINESS.
SO YOU HAVEN'T.
SHUT UP! YOU CAN'T RUSH INTO STUFF LIKE THAT!
RIGHT NOW...
...I'M HAPPY WITH GRANDPA WONG'S BOOK.
FLIP
GRWWL
YOUR STOMACH'S SAYING, "BOOKS ALONE AREN'T ENOUGH."

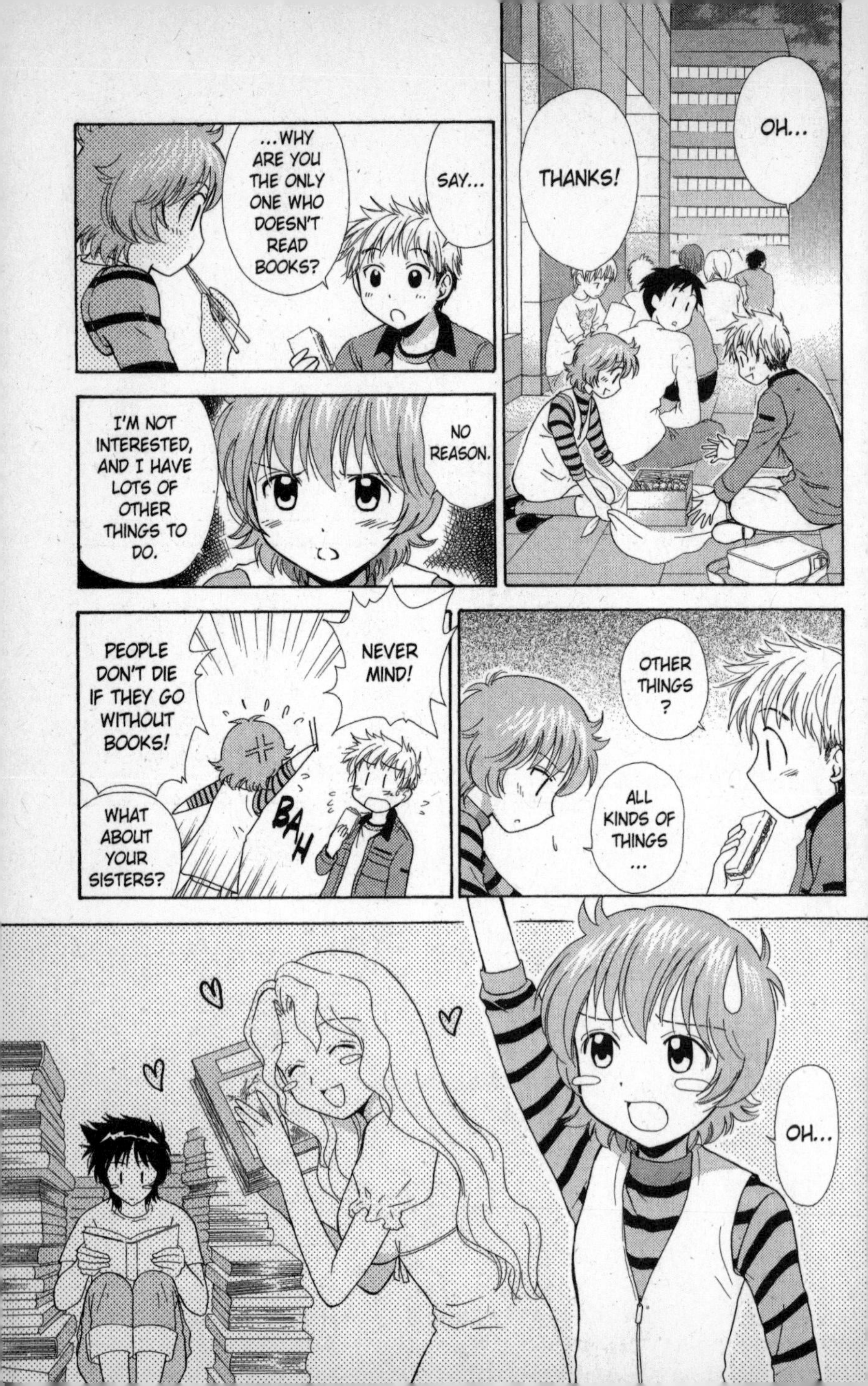
OH...
THANKS!
SAY...
...WHY ARE YOU THE ONLY ONE WHO DOESN'T READ BOOKS?
NO REASON.
I'M NOT INTERESTED, AND I HAVE LOTS OF OTHER THINGS TO DO.
OTHER THINGS ?
ALL KINDS OF THINGS ...
NEVER MIND!
PEOPLE DON'T DIE IF THEY GO WITHOUT BOOKS!
BAH
WHAT ABOUT YOUR SISTERS?
OH...

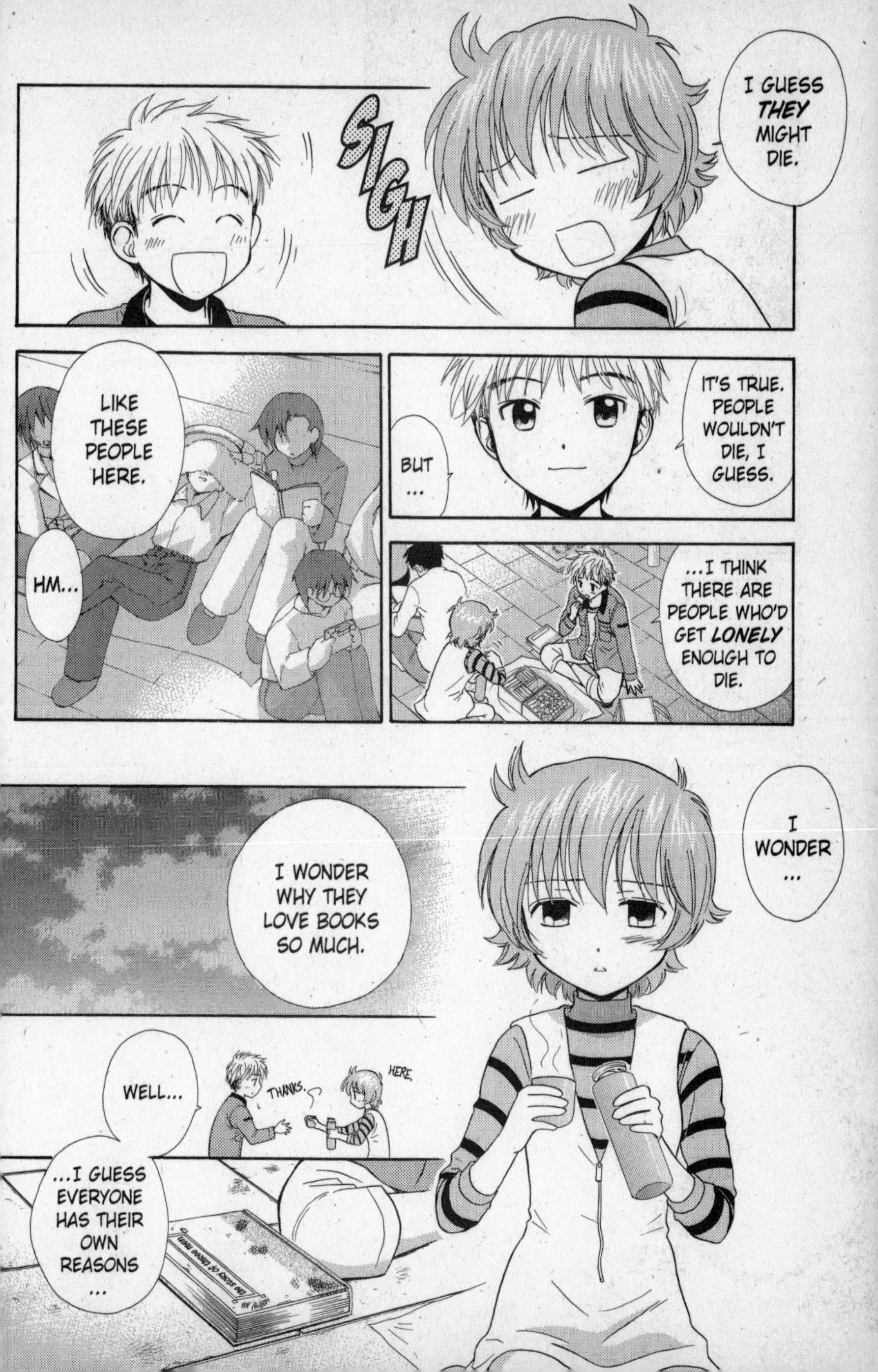
I GUESS THEY MIGHT DIE.
SIGH
IT'S TRUE. PEOPLE WOULDN'T DIE, I GUESS.
BUT ...
...I THINK THERE ARE PEOPLE WHO'D GET LONELY ENOUGH TO DIE.
LIKE THESE PEOPLE HERE.
HM...
I WONDER ...
I WONDER WHY THEY LOVE BOOKS SO MUCH.
HERE.
THANKS.
WELL...
...I GUESS EVERYONE HAS THEIR OWN REASONS ...

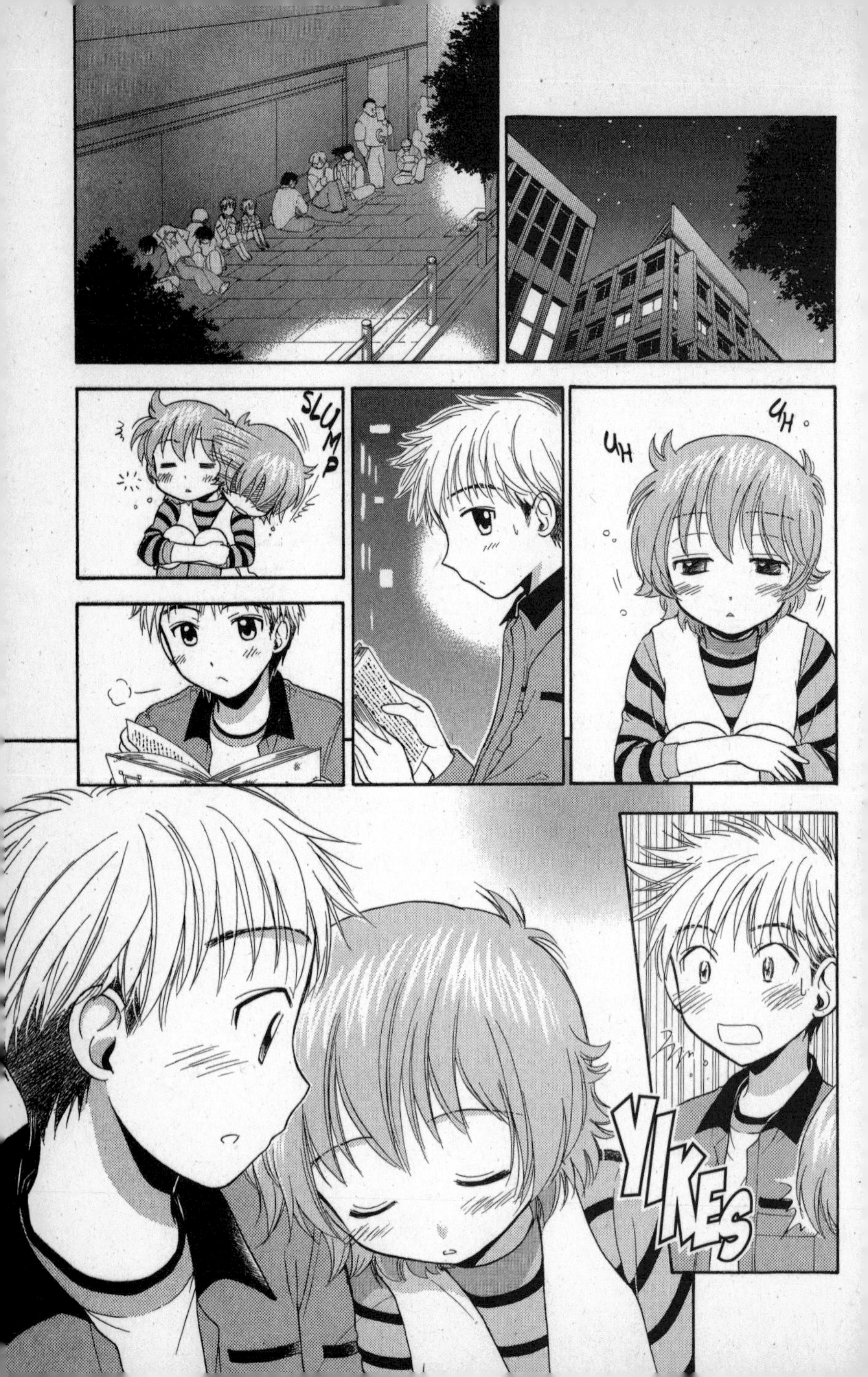

UH UH
SLUMP
YIKES

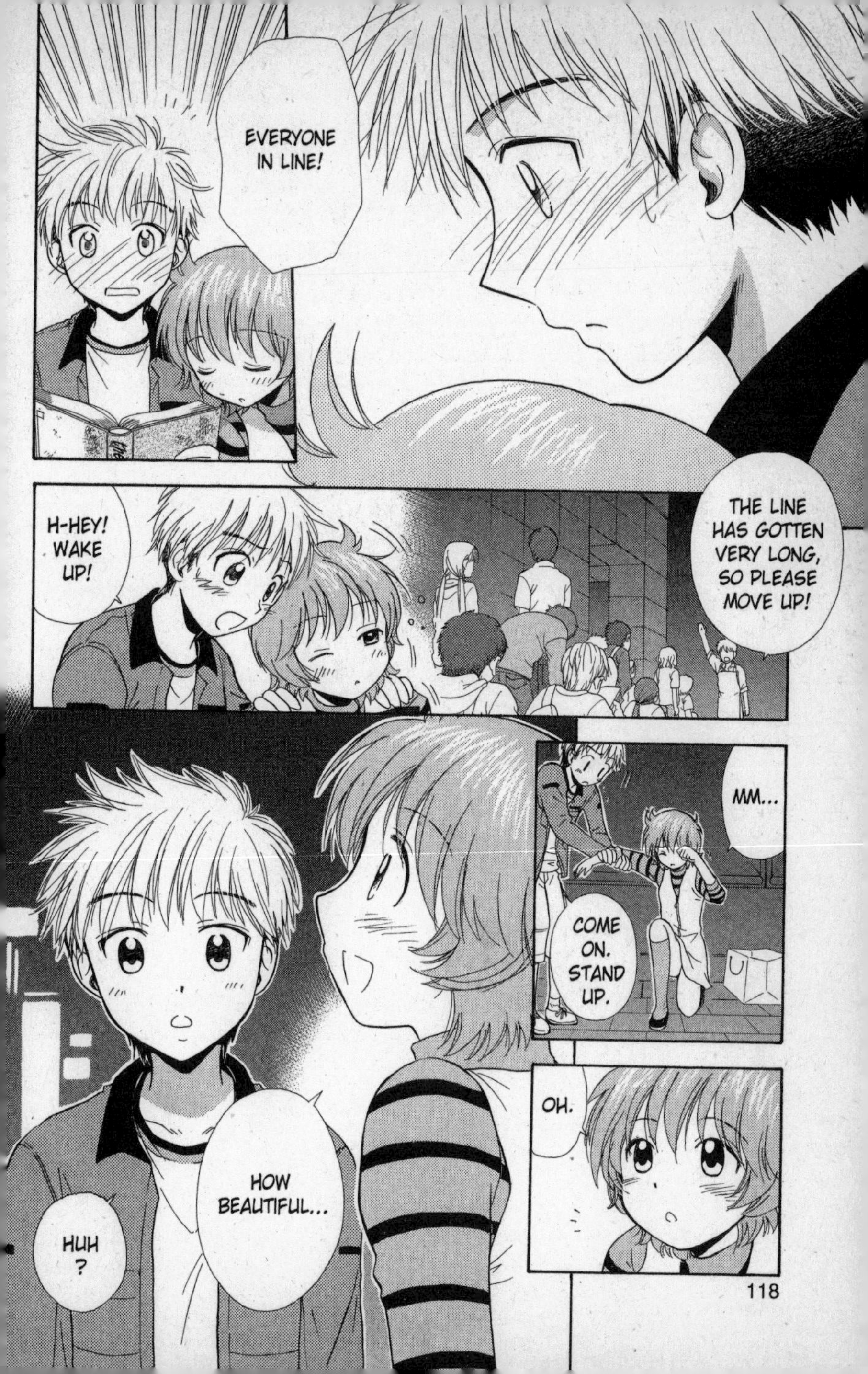
EVERYONE IN LINE!
THE LINE HAS GOTTEN VERY LONG, SO PLEASE MOVE UP!
H-HEY! WAKE UP!
MM...
COME ON. STAND UP.
OH.
HOW BEAUTIFUL...
HUH?

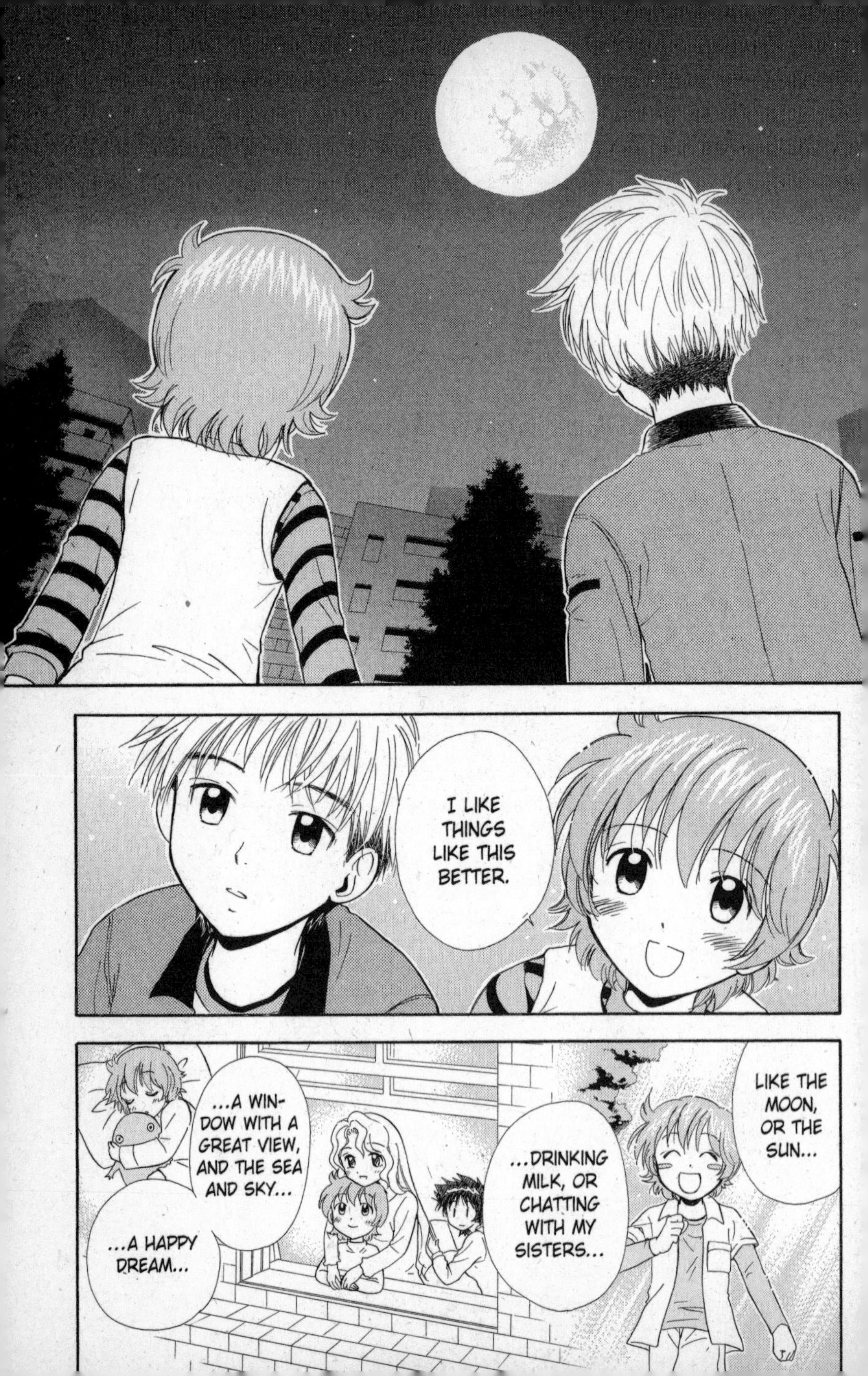
I LIKE THINGS LIKE THIS BETTER.
LIKE THE MOON, OR THE SUN...
...DRINKING MILK, OR CHATTING WITH MY SISTERS...
...A WIN-DOW WITH A GREAT VIEW, AND THE SEA AND SKY...
...A HAPPY DREAM...

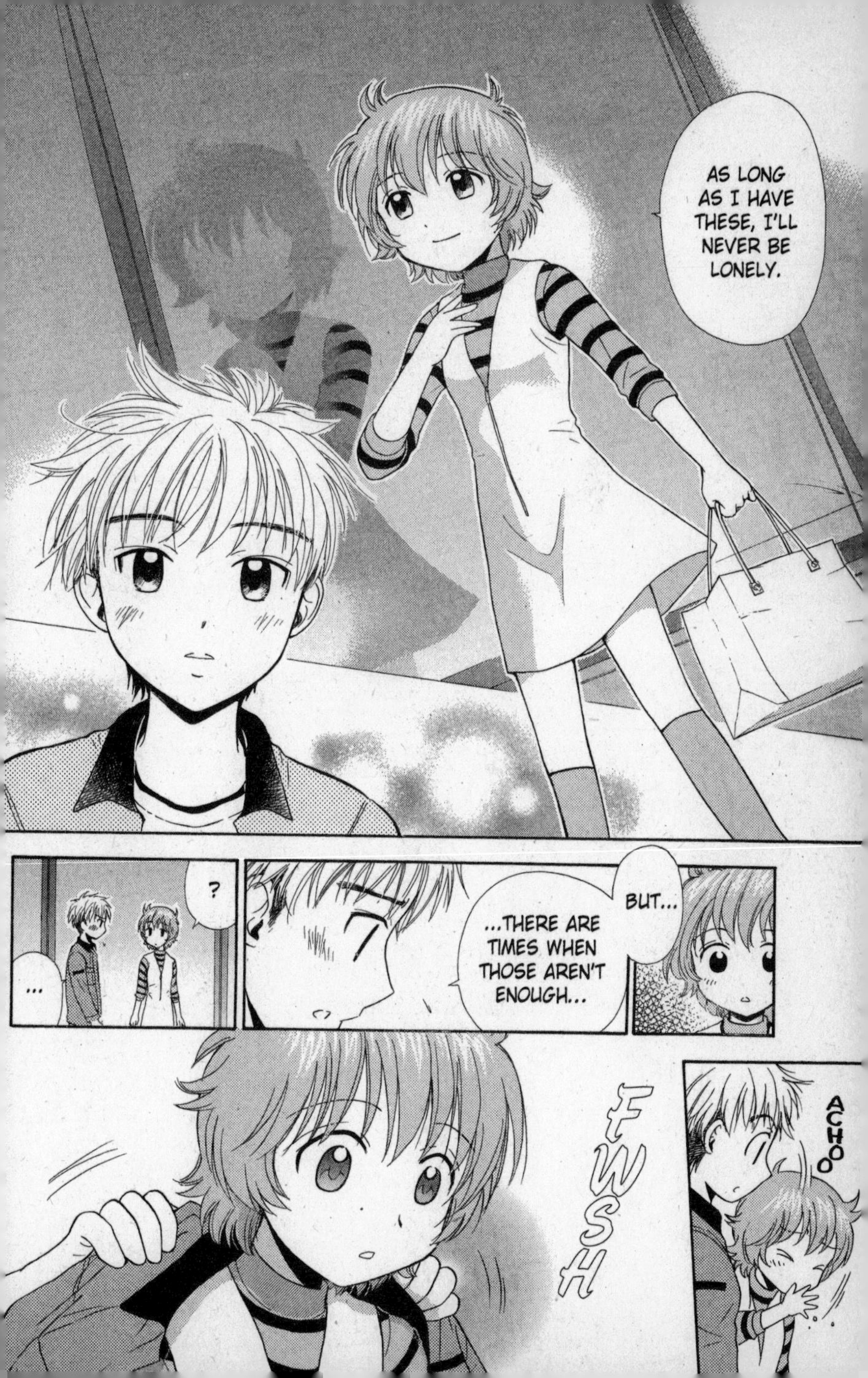

AS LONG AS I HAVE THESE, I'LL NEVER BE LONELY.
BUT...
...THERE ARE TIMES WHEN THOSE AREN'T ENOUGH...
?
...
ACHOO
FWSH

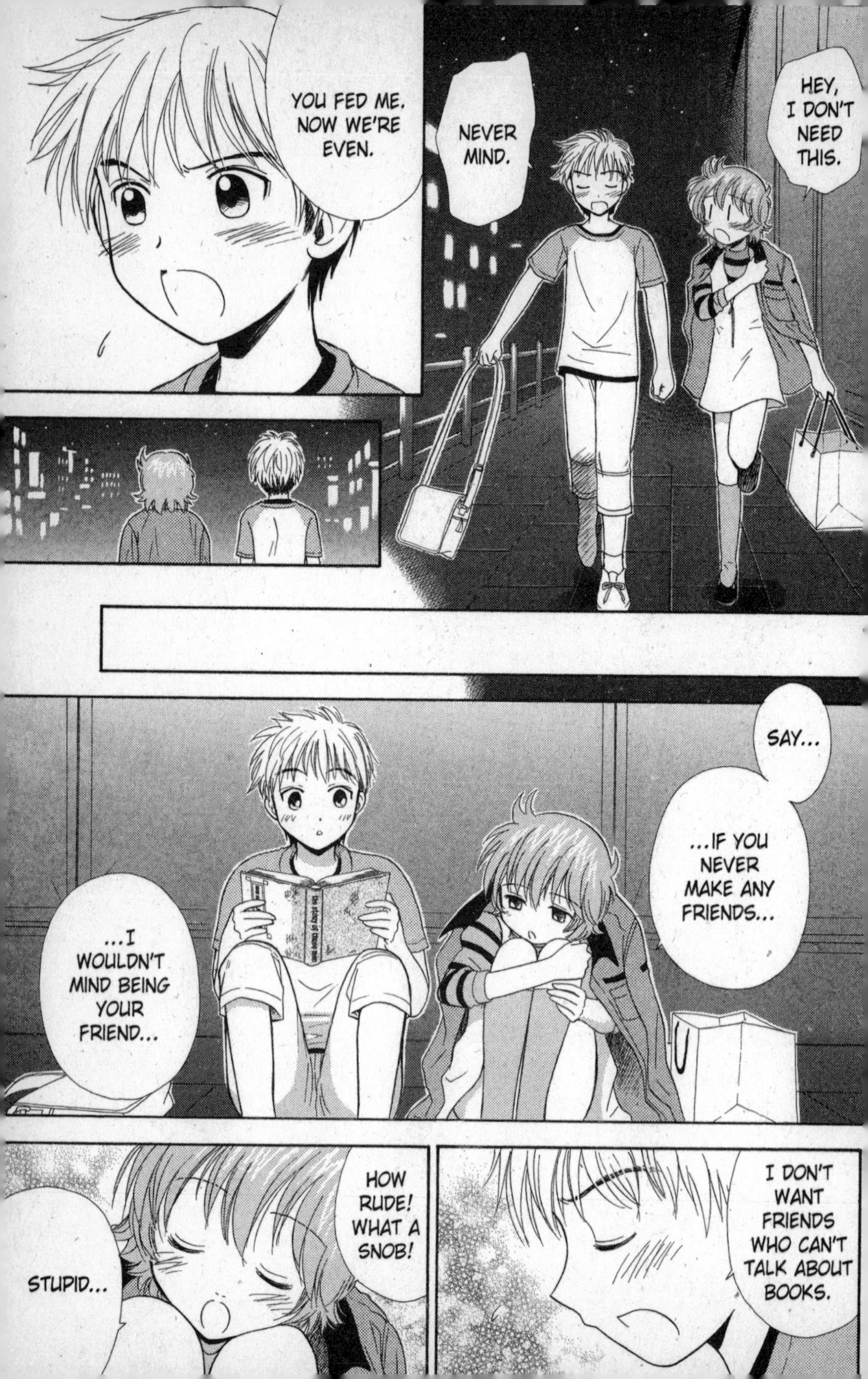
HEY, I DON'T NEED THIS.
NEVER MIND.
YOU FED ME. NOW WE'RE EVEN.
SAY...
...IF YOU NEVER MAKE ANY FRIENDS...
...I WOULDN'T MIND BEING YOUR FRIEND...
I DON'T WANT FRIENDS WHO CAN'T TALK ABOUT BOOKS.
HOW RUDE! WHAT A SNOB!
STUPID...

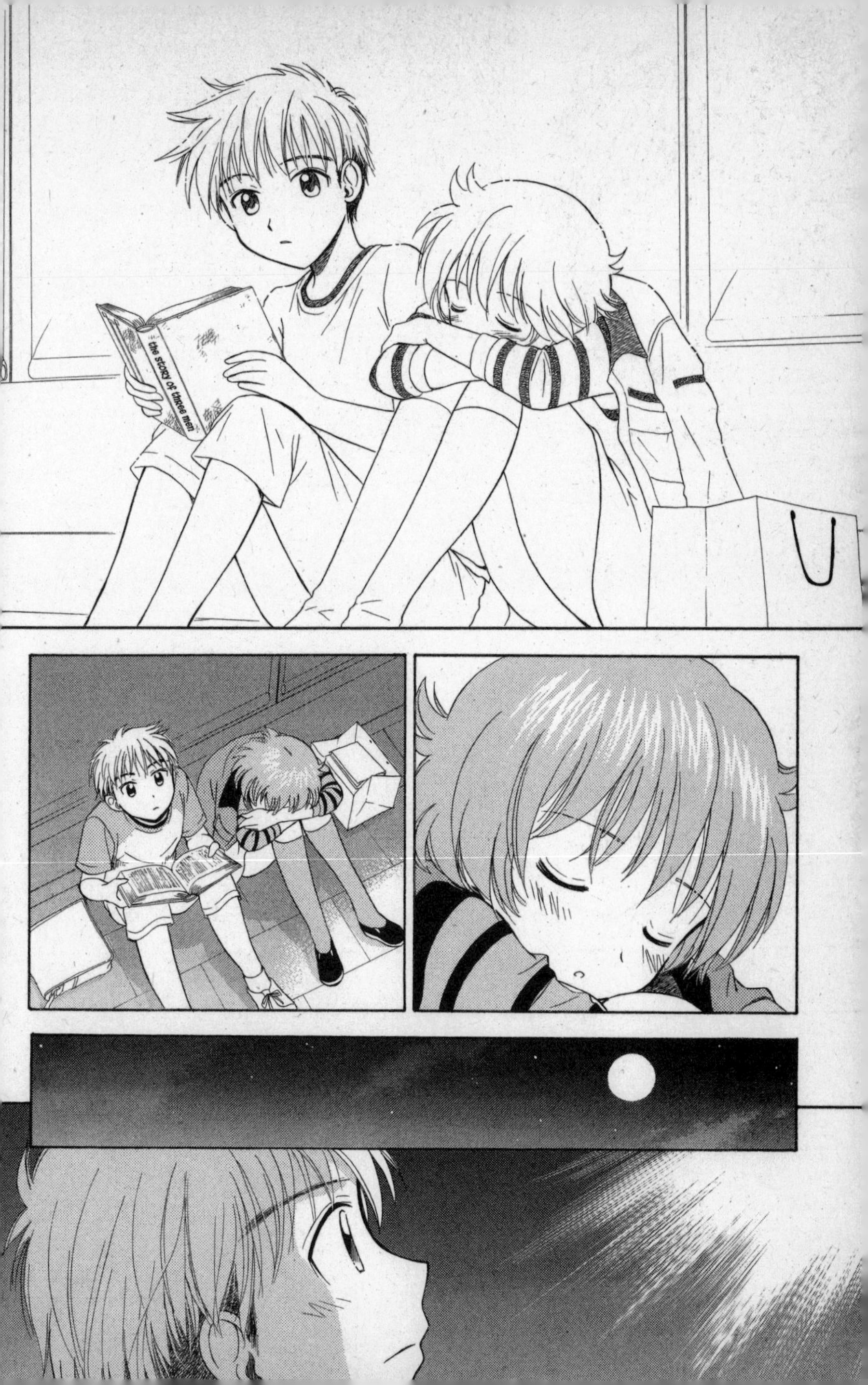
the story of three men

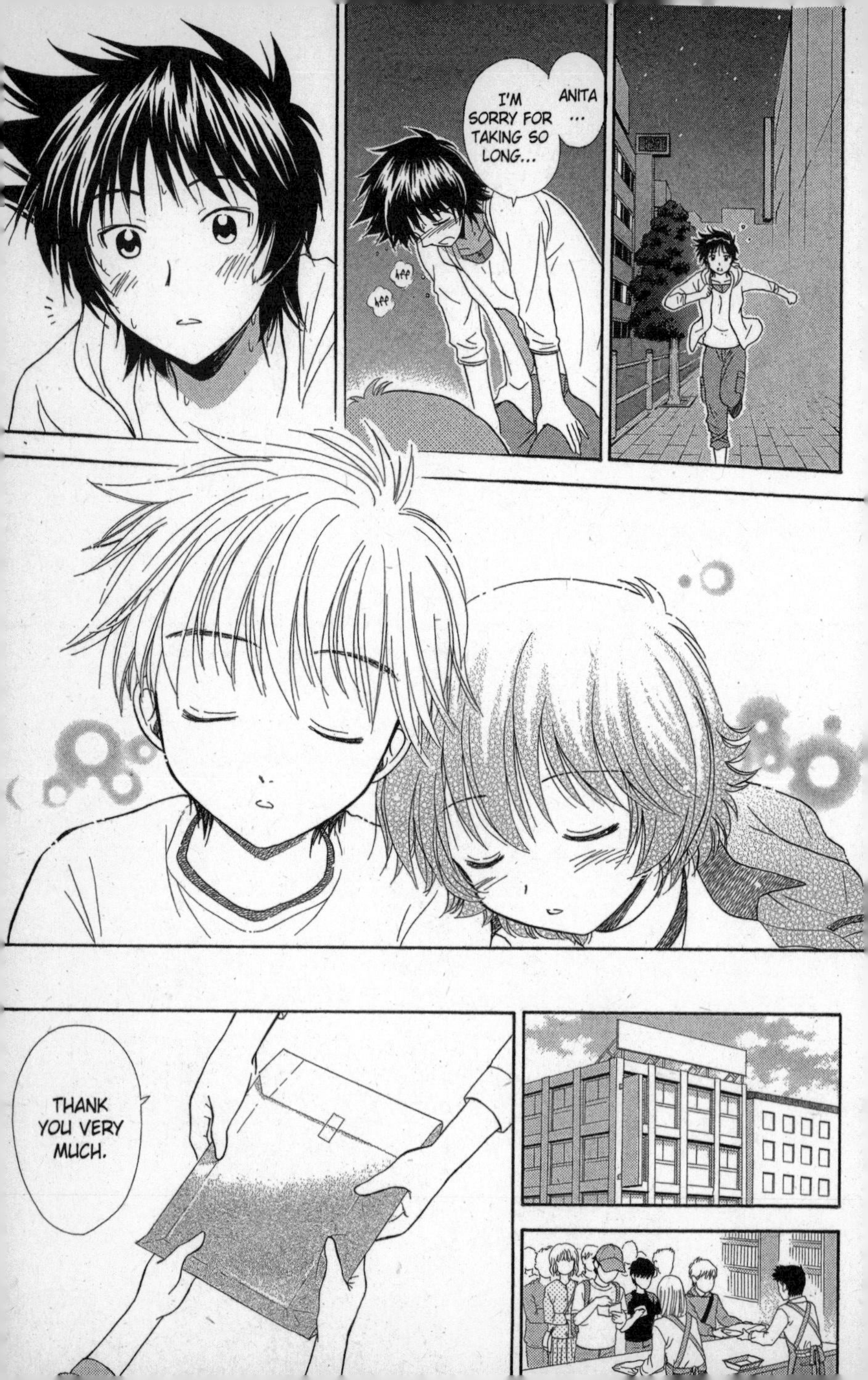
ANITA ...
I'M SORRY FOR TAKING SO LONG...
hff
hff
THANK YOU VERY MUCH.

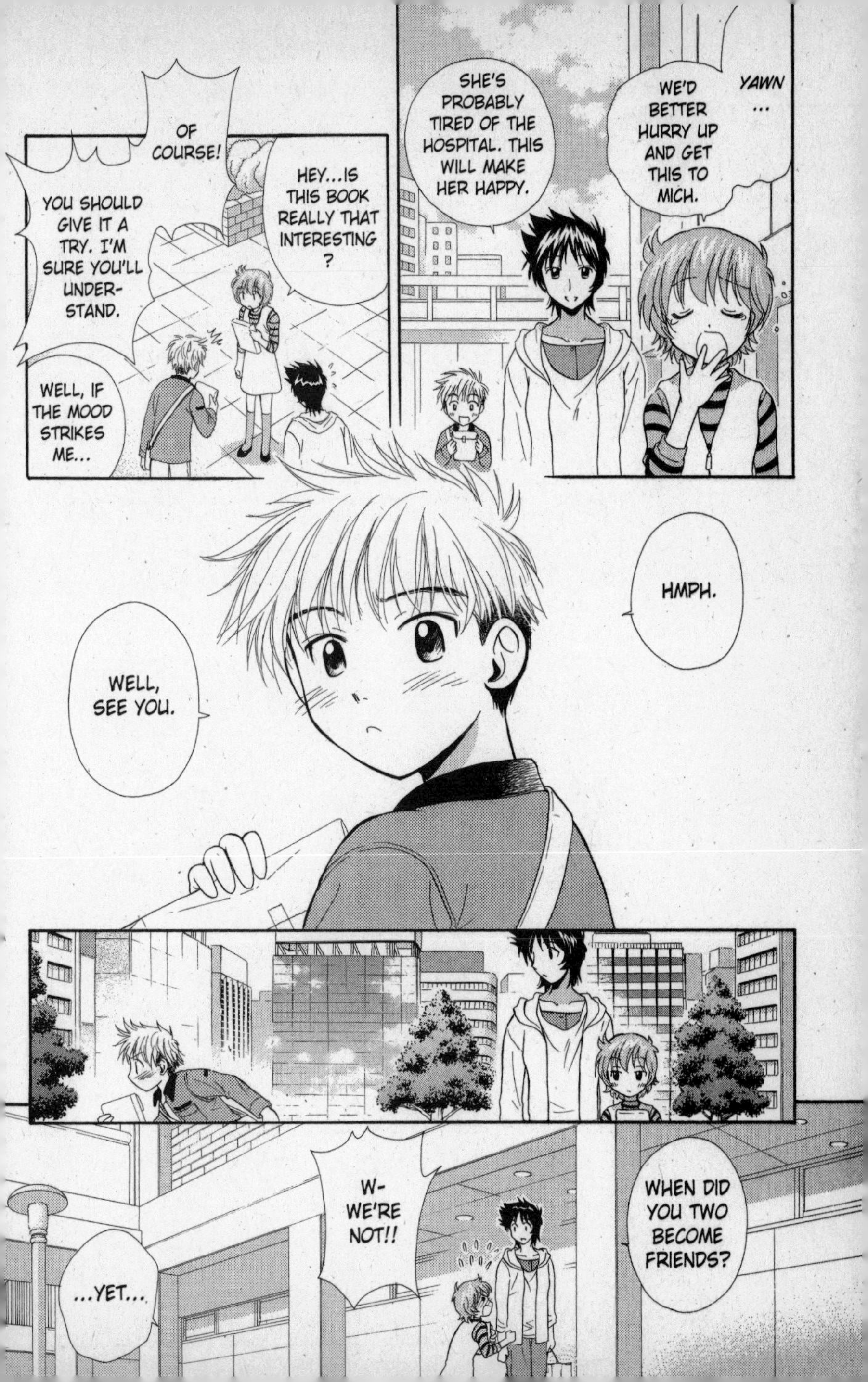
YAWN ...
WE'D BETTER HURRY UP AND GET THIS TO MICH.
SHE'S PROBABLY TIRED OF THE HOSPITAL. THIS WILL MAKE HER HAPPY.
HEY...IS THIS BOOK REALLY THAT INTERESTING?
OF COURSE!
YOU SHOULD GIVE IT A TRY. I'M SURE YOU'LL UNDER-STAND.
WELL, IF THE MOOD STRIKES ME...
HMPH.
WELL, SEE YOU.
WHEN DID YOU TWO BECOME FRIENDS?
W- WE'RE NOT!!
...YET...

CHAPTER 13

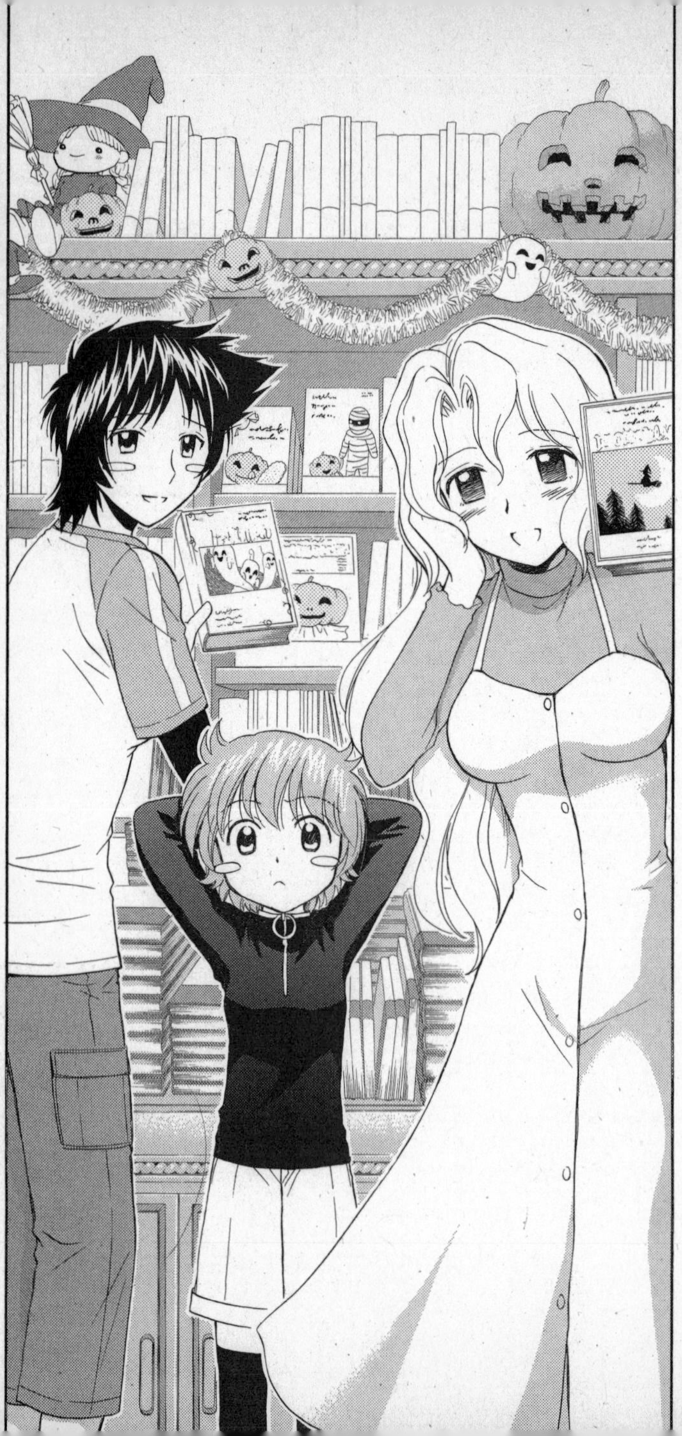

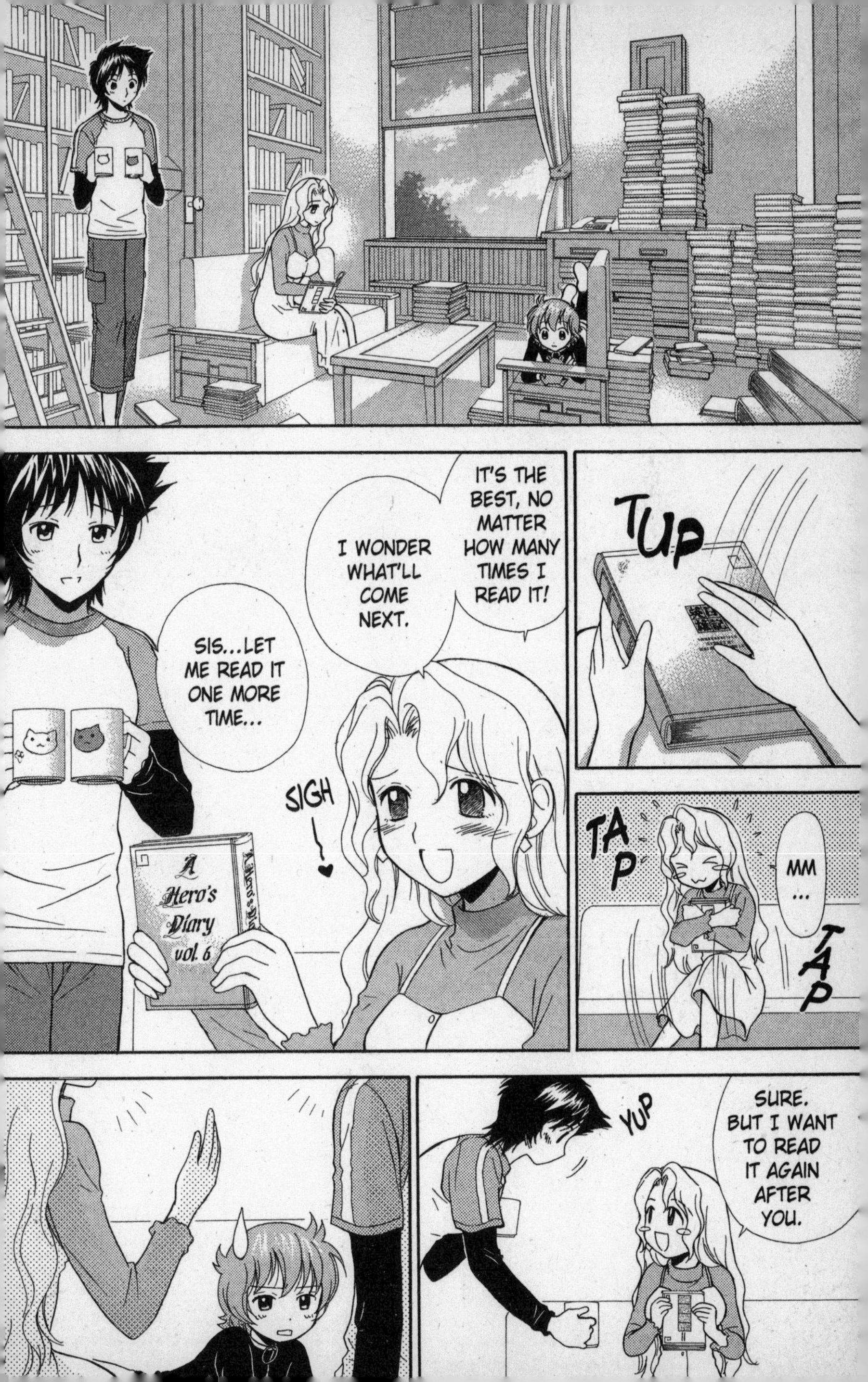
TUP
MM ...
TAP
TAP
IT'S THE BEST, NO MATTER HOW MANY TIMES I READ IT!
I WONDER WHAT'LL COME NEXT.
SIS...LET ME READ IT ONE MORE TIME...
SIGH
A Hero's Diary vol. 6
SURE. BUT I WANT TO READ IT AGAIN AFTER YOU.
YUP

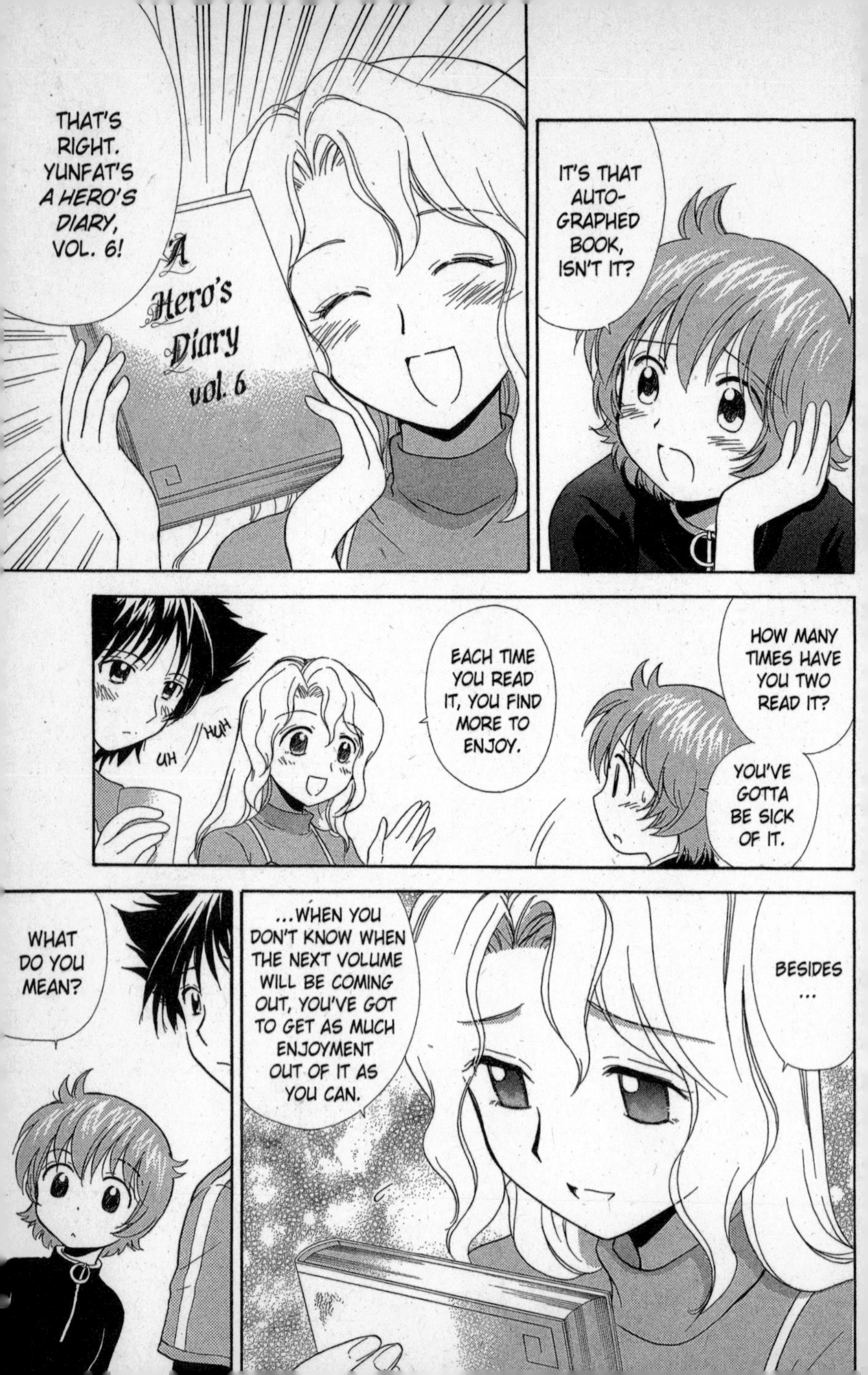
IT'S THAT AUTO-GRAPHED BOOK, ISN'T IT?
THAT'S RIGHT. YUNFAT'S A HERO'S DIARY, VOL. 6!
A Hero's Diary vol. 6
HOW MANY TIMES HAVE YOU TWO READ IT?
YOU'VE GOTTA BE SICK OF IT.
EACH TIME YOU READ IT, YOU FIND MORE TO ENJOY.
HUH
UH
BESIDES ...
...WHEN YOU DON'T KNOW WHEN THE NEXT VOLUME WILL BE COMING OUT, YOU'VE GOT TO GET AS MUCH ENJOYMENT OUT OF IT AS YOU CAN.
WHAT DO YOU MEAN?

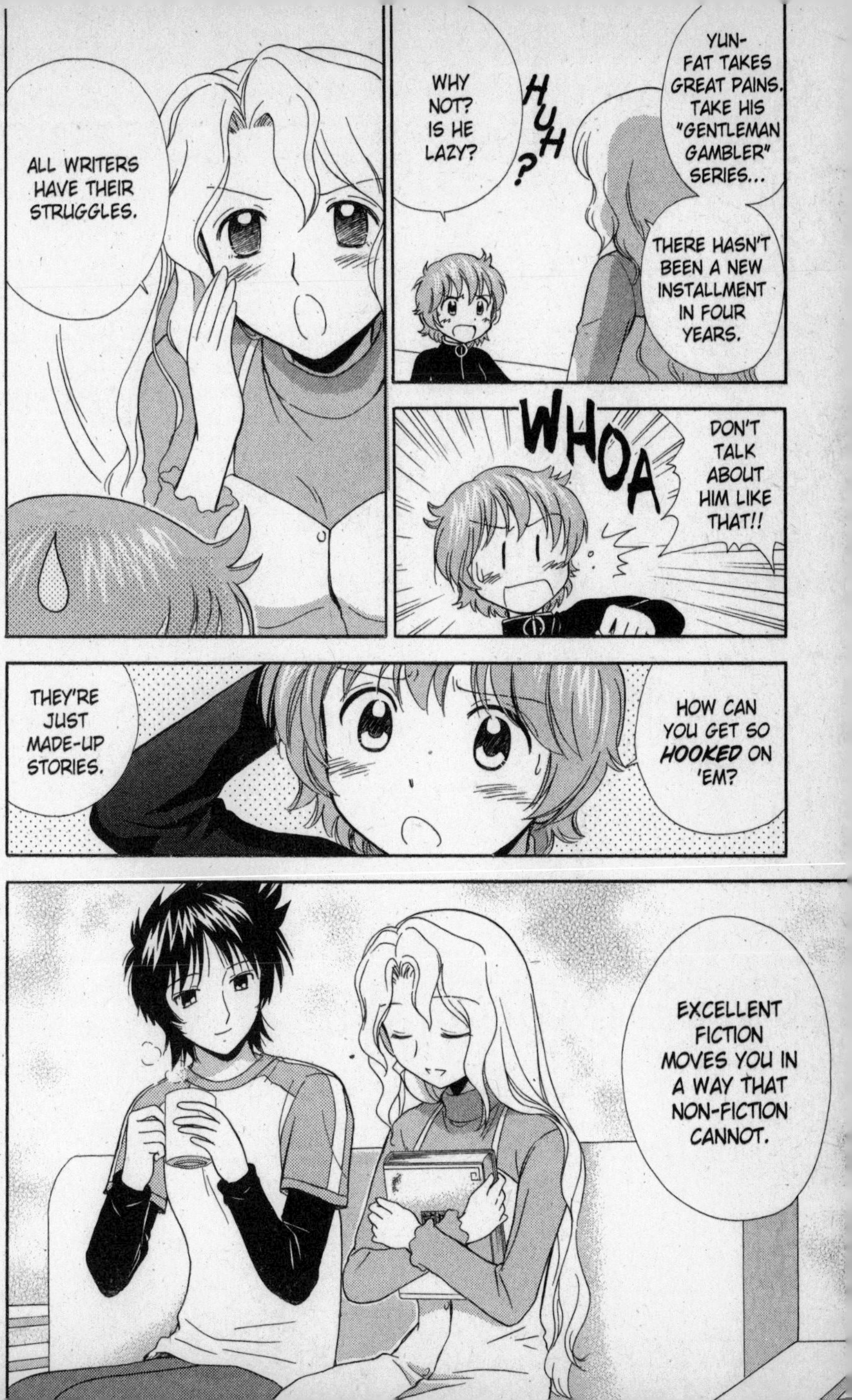
YUN-FAT TAKES GREAT PAINS. TAKE HIS "GENTLEMAN GAMBLER" SERIES...
THERE HASN'T BEEN A NEW INSTALLMENT IN FOUR YEARS.
HUH?
WHY NOT? IS HE LAZY?
WHOA
DON'T TALK ABOUT HIM LIKE THAT!!
ALL WRITERS HAVE THEIR STRUGGLES.
HOW CAN YOU GET SO ***HOOKED*** ON 'EM?
THEY'RE JUST MADE-UP STORIES.
EXCELLENT FICTION MOVES YOU IN A WAY THAT NON-FICTION CANNOT.

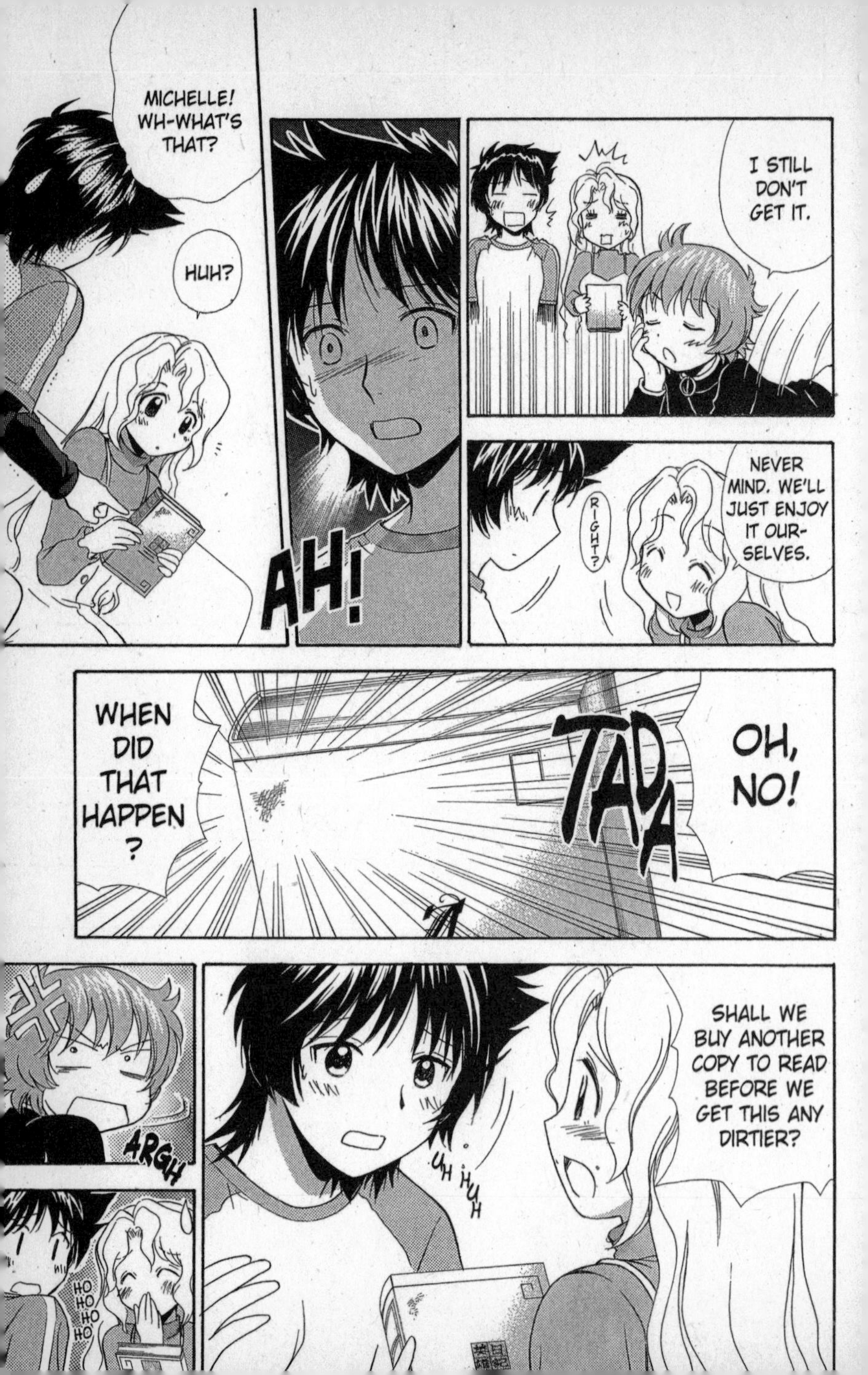
I STILL DON'T GET IT.
NEVER MIND. WE'LL JUST ENJOY IT OUR-SELVES.
RIGHT?
AH!
MICHELLE! WH-WHAT'S THAT?
HUH?
OH, NO!
TADA
WHEN DID THAT HAPPEN?
SHALL WE BUY ANOTHER COPY TO READ BEFORE WE GET THIS ANY DIRTIER?
UH HUH
ARGH
HO HO HO HO

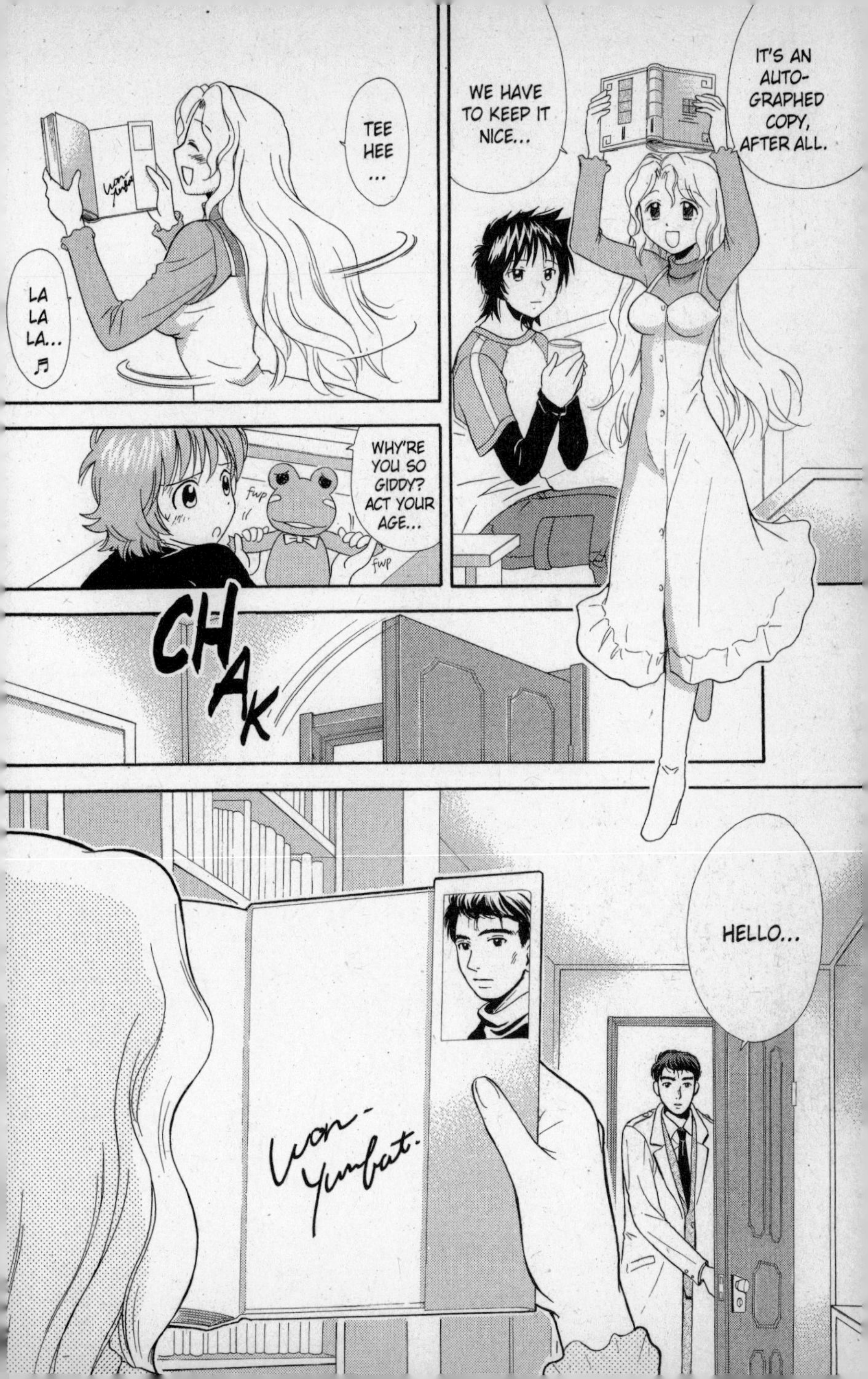
IT'S AN AUTO-GRAPHED COPY, AFTER ALL.
WE HAVE TO KEEP IT NICE...
TEE HEE ...
LA LA LA... ♬
WHY'RE YOU SO GIDDY? ACT YOUR AGE...
fwp
fwp
CHAK
HELLO...
won-Yumbat.

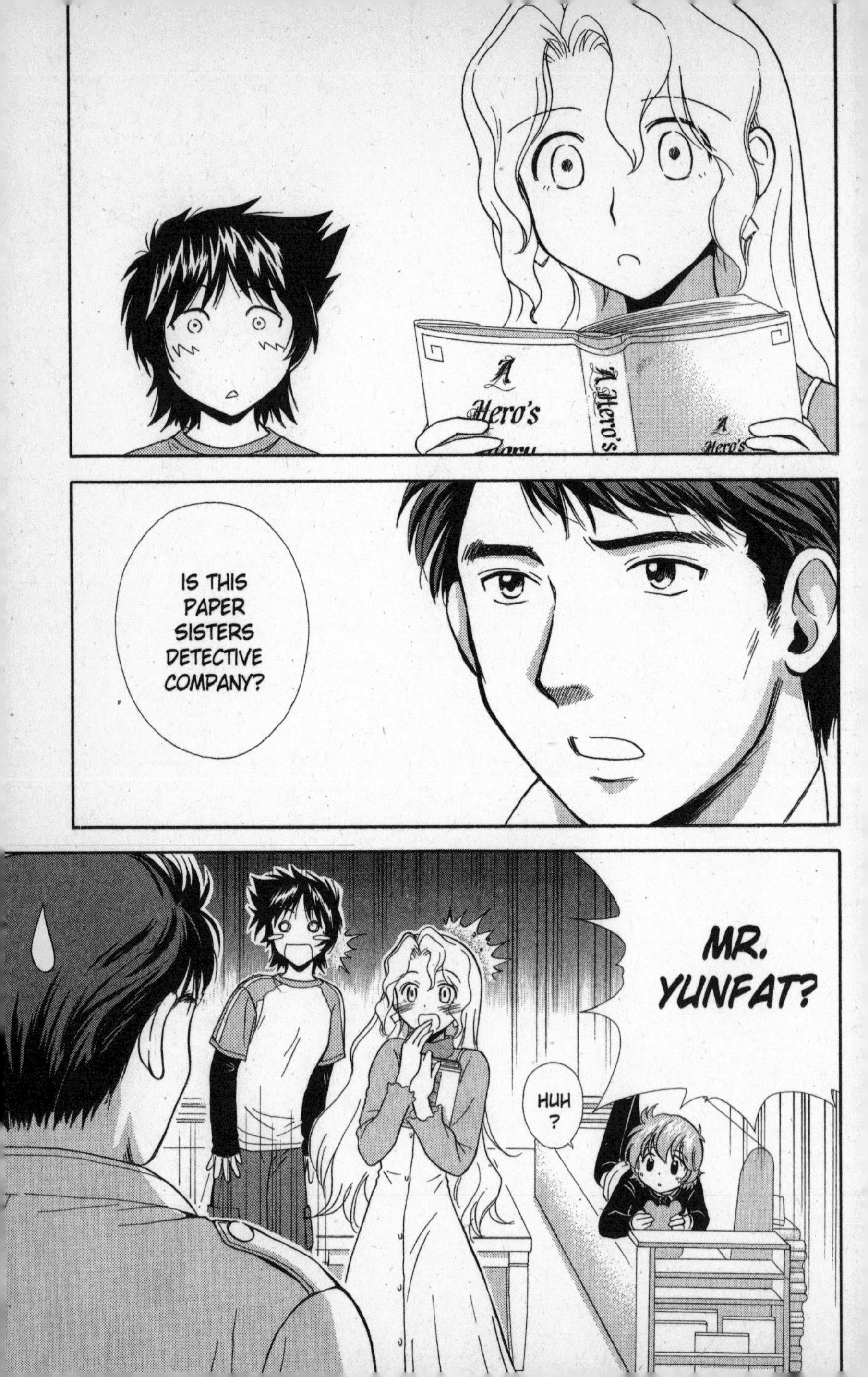
IS THIS PAPER SISTERS DETECTIVE COMPANY?
MR. YUNFAT?
HUH?

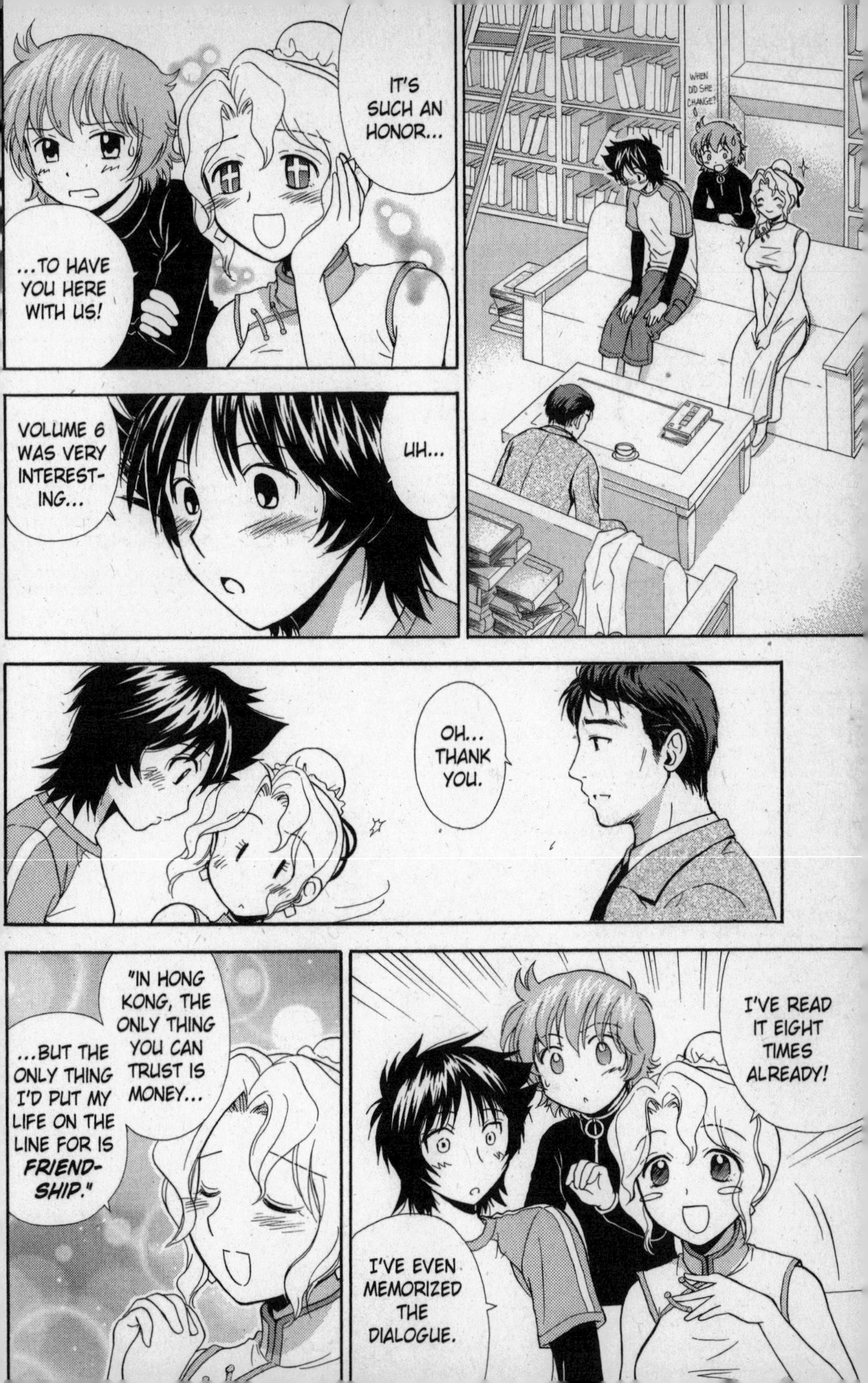
WHEN DID SHE CHANGE?
IT'S SUCH AN HONOR...
...TO HAVE YOU HERE WITH US!
VOLUME 6 WAS VERY INTERESTING...
UH...
OH... THANK YOU.
I'VE READ IT EIGHT TIMES ALREADY!
I'VE EVEN MEMORIZED THE DIALOGUE.
"IN HONG KONG, THE ONLY THING YOU CAN TRUST IS MONEY...
...BUT THE ONLY THING I'D PUT MY LIFE ON THE LINE FOR IS *FRIENDSHIP.*"

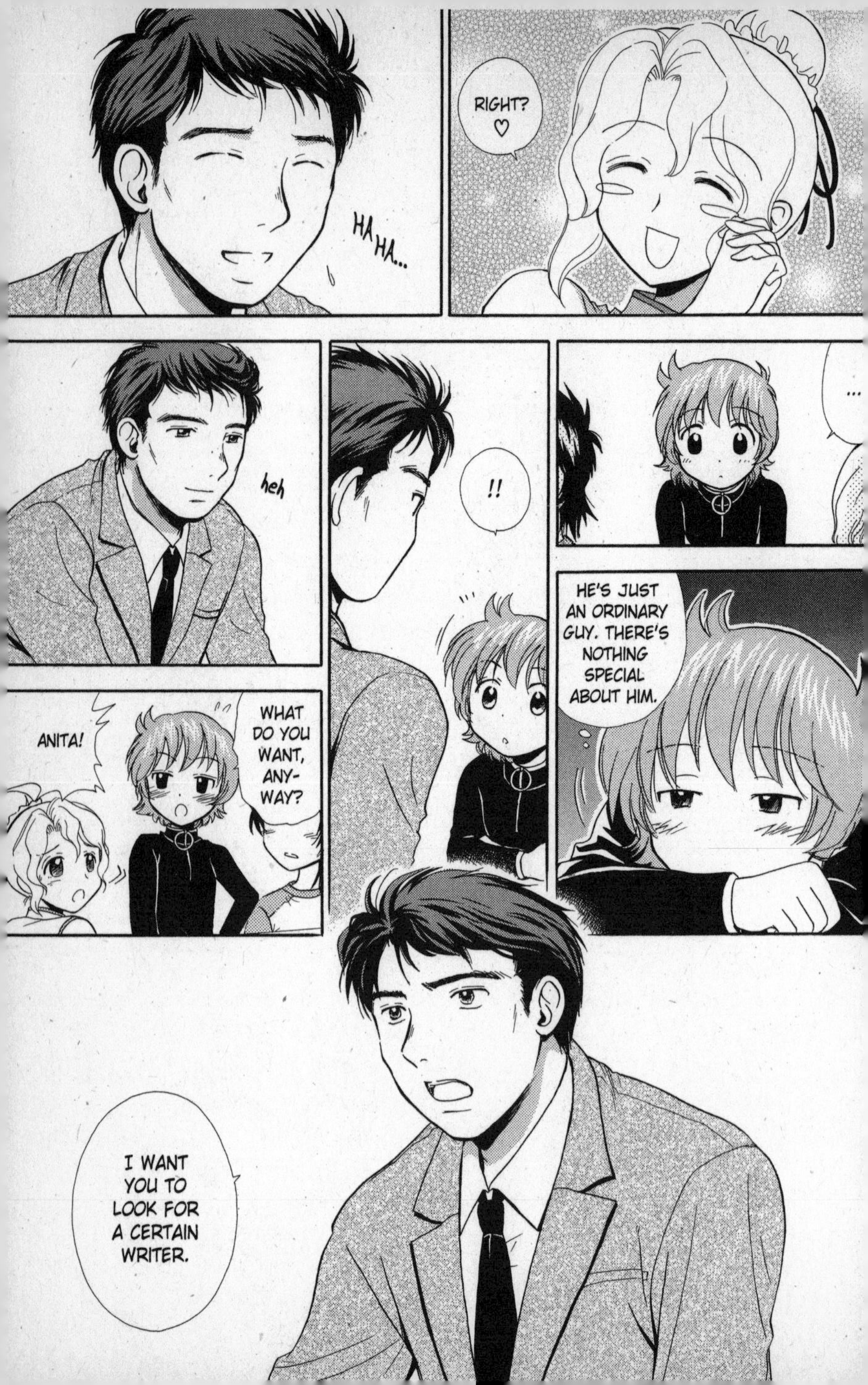
RIGHT? ♡
HA HA...
...
HE'S JUST AN ORDINARY GUY. THERE'S NOTHING SPECIAL ABOUT HIM.
!!
heh
WHAT DO YOU WANT, ANY-WAY?
ANITA!
I WANT YOU TO LOOK FOR A CERTAIN WRITER.

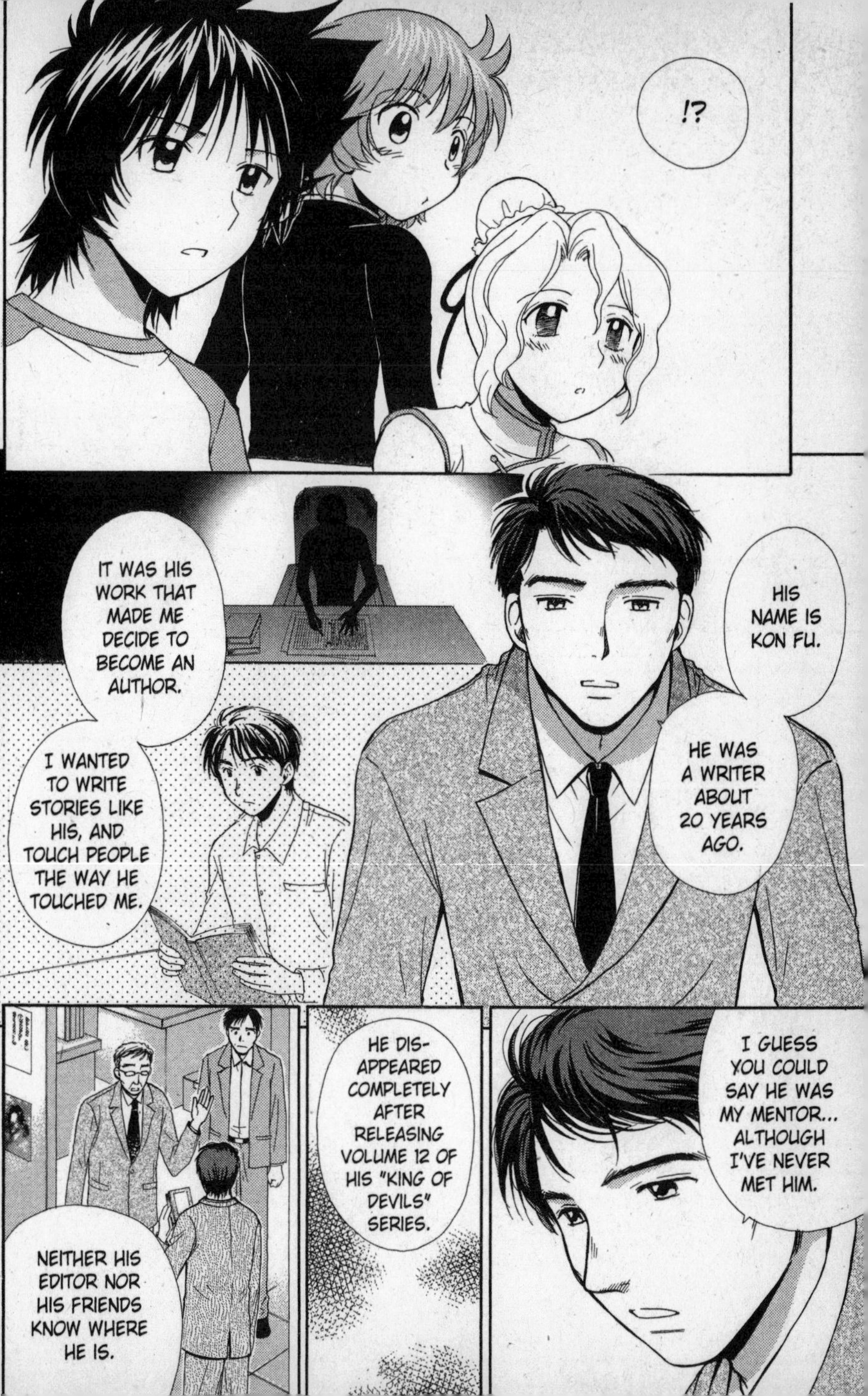
!?
HIS NAME IS KON FU.
HE WAS A WRITER ABOUT 20 YEARS AGO.
IT WAS HIS WORK THAT MADE ME DECIDE TO BECOME AN AUTHOR.
I WANTED TO WRITE STORIES LIKE HIS, AND TOUCH PEOPLE THE WAY HE TOUCHED ME.
I GUESS YOU COULD SAY HE WAS MY MENTOR... ALTHOUGH I'VE NEVER MET HIM.
HE DIS-APPEARED COMPLETELY AFTER RELEASING VOLUME 12 OF HIS "KING OF DEVILS" SERIES.
NEITHER HIS EDITOR NOR HIS FRIENDS KNOW WHERE HE IS.

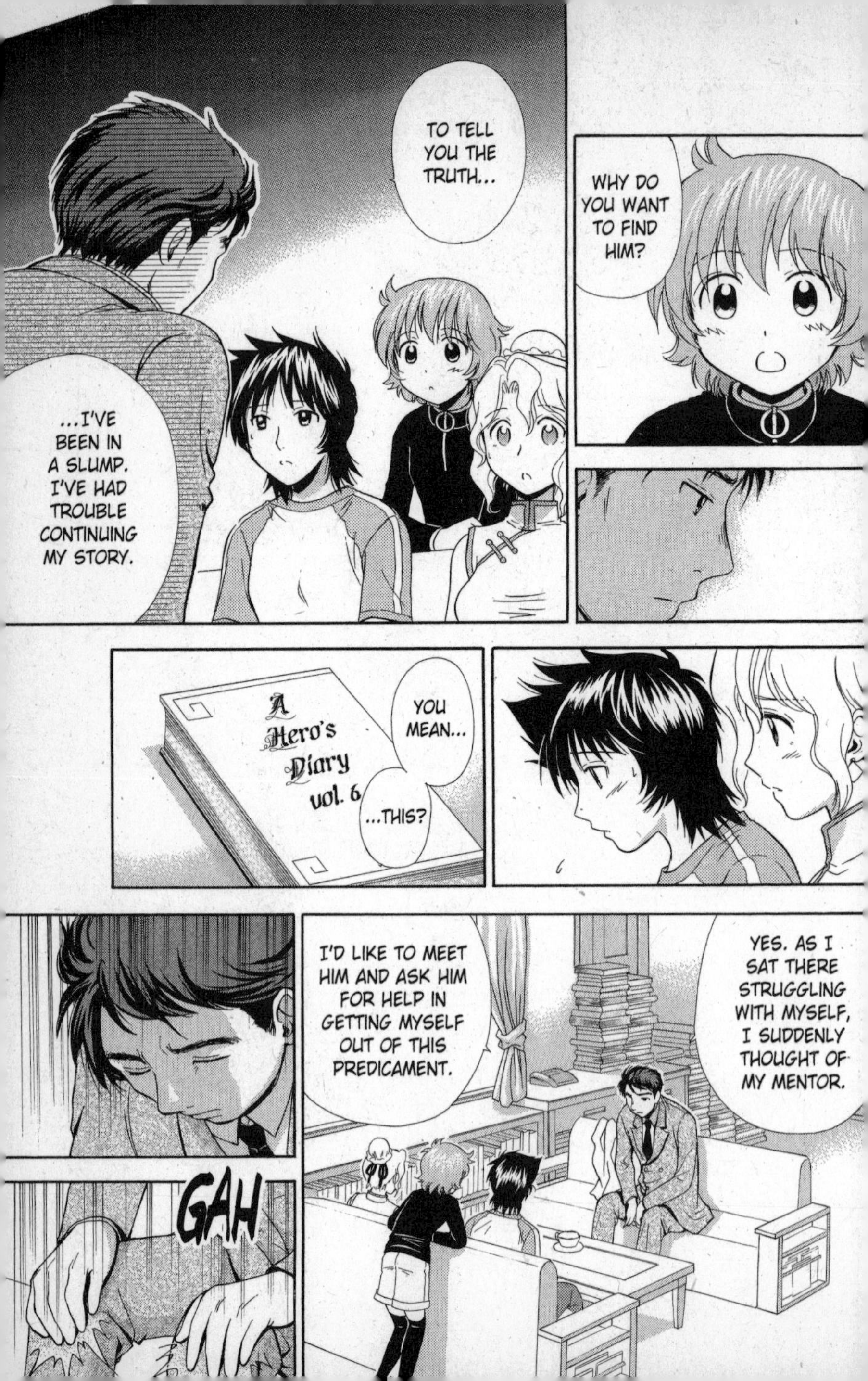
WHY DO YOU WANT TO FIND HIM?
TO TELL YOU THE TRUTH...
...I'VE BEEN IN A SLUMP. I'VE HAD TROUBLE CONTINUING MY STORY.
A Hero's Diary vol. 6
YOU MEAN...
...THIS?
YES. AS I SAT THERE STRUGGLING WITH MYSELF, I SUDDENLY THOUGHT OF MY MENTOR.
I'D LIKE TO MEET HIM AND ASK HIM FOR HELP IN GETTING MYSELF OUT OF THIS PREDICAMENT.
GAH

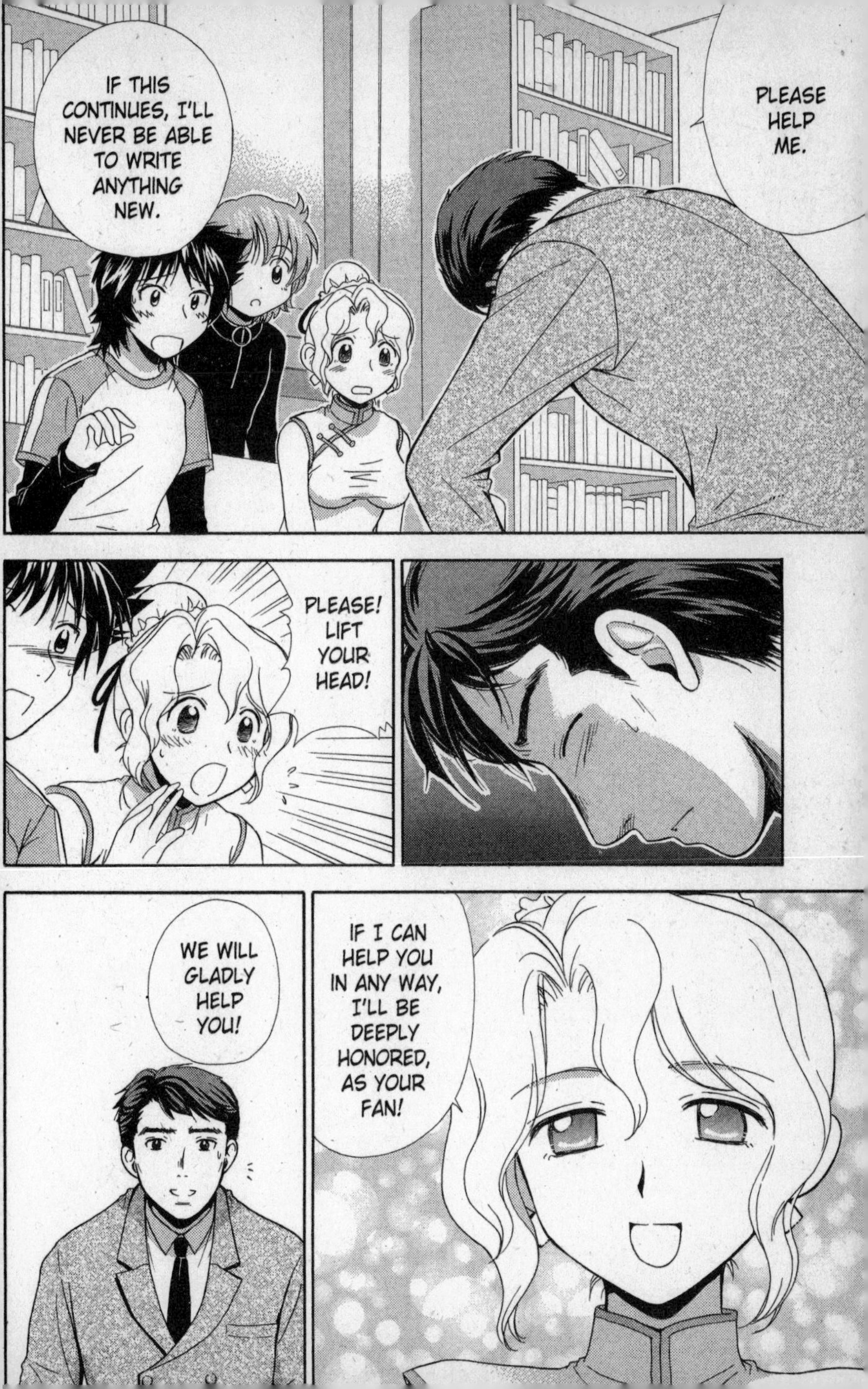
PLEASE HELP ME.
IF THIS CONTINUES, I'LL NEVER BE ABLE TO WRITE ANYTHING NEW.
PLEASE! LIFT YOUR HEAD!
IF I CAN HELP YOU IN ANY WAY, I'LL BE DEEPLY HONORED, AS YOUR FAN!
WE WILL GLADLY HELP YOU!

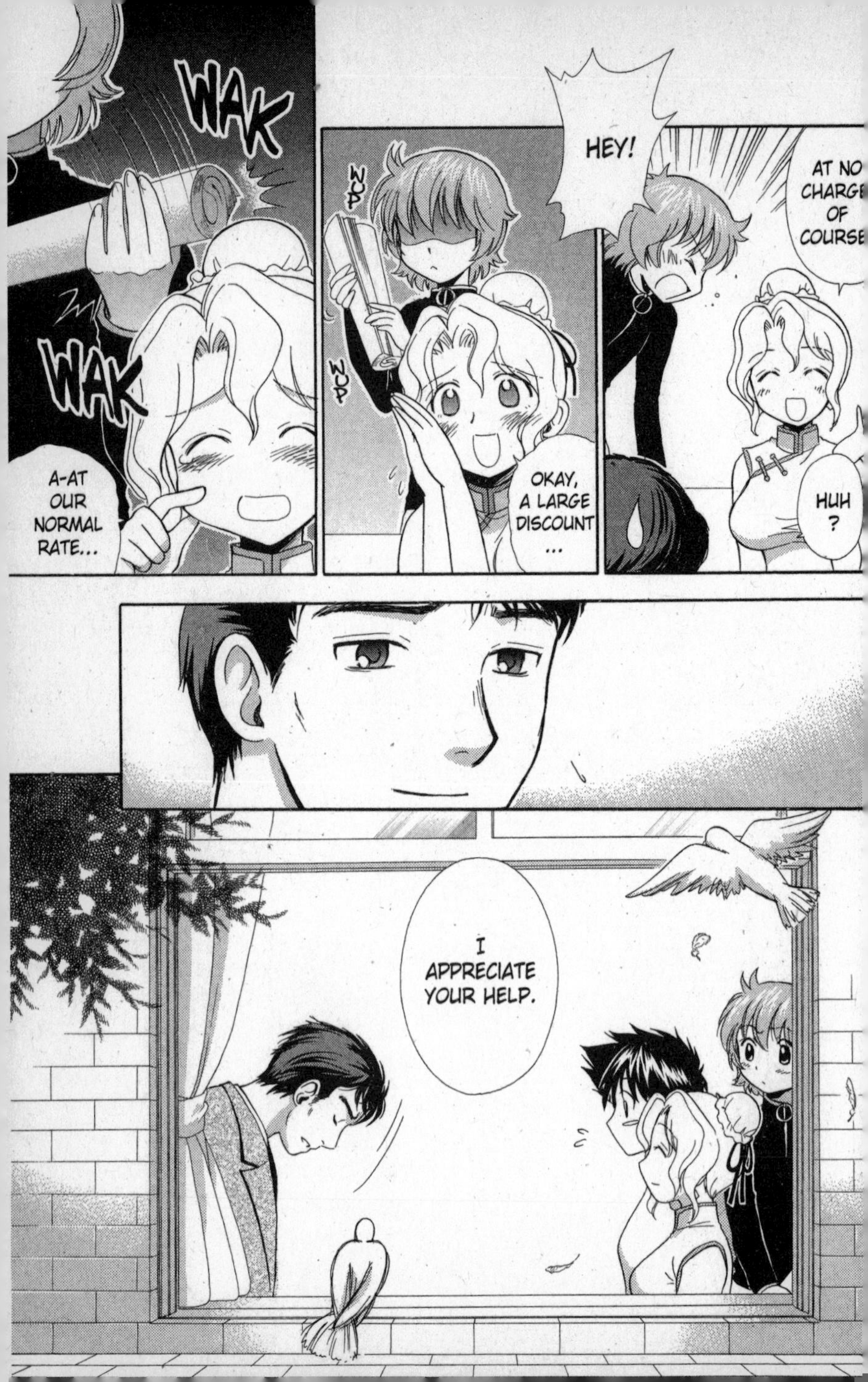
AT NO CHARG OF COURSE
HEY!
HUH?
WUP
WUP
OKAY, A LARGE DISCOUNT...
WAK
WAK
A-AT OUR NORMAL RATE...
I APPRECIATE YOUR HELP.

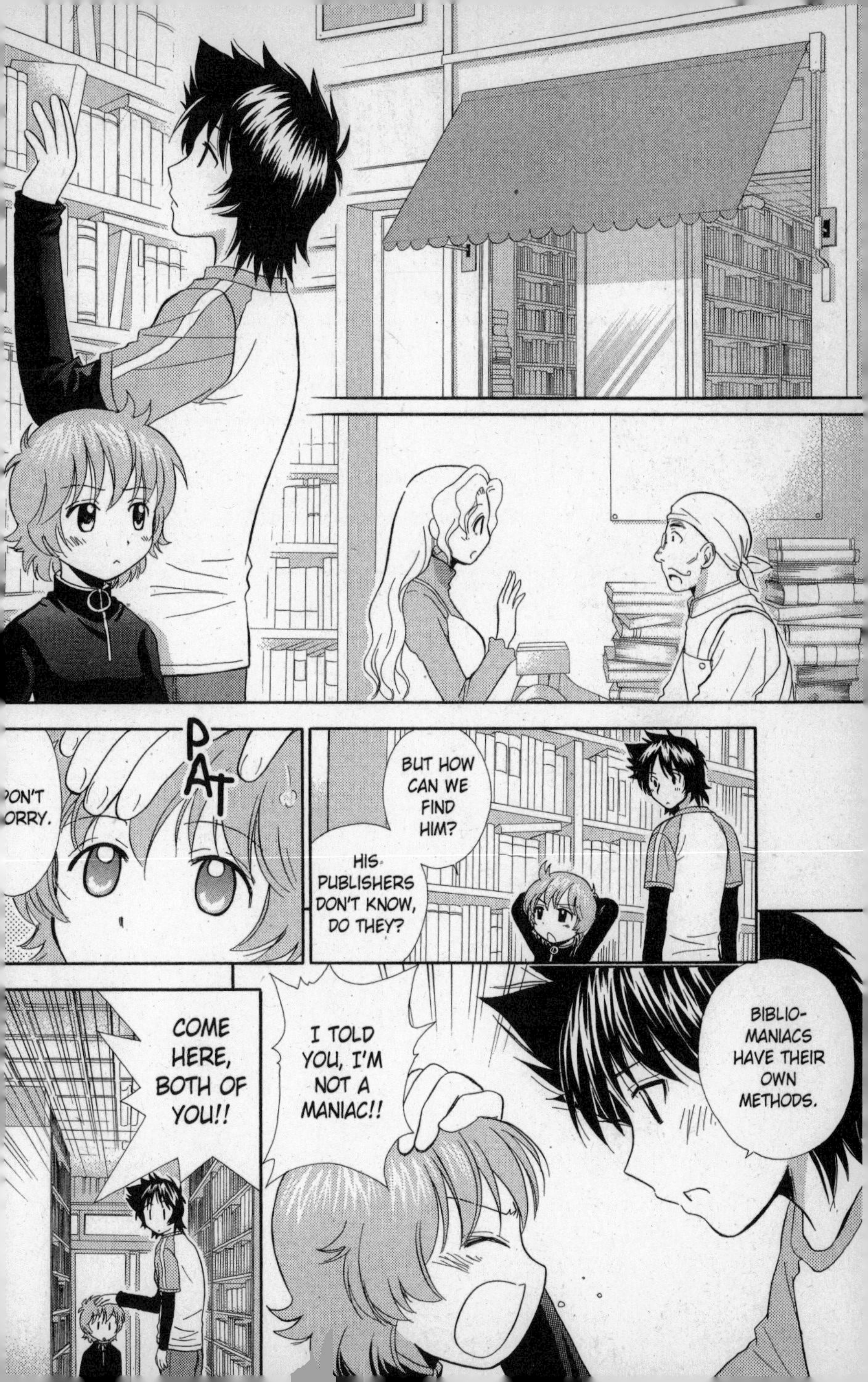
BUT HOW CAN WE FIND HIM?
HIS PUBLISHERS DON'T KNOW, DO THEY?
PAT
ON'T ORRY.
BIBLIO-MANIACS HAVE THEIR OWN METHODS.
I TOLD YOU, I'M NOT A MANIAC!!
COME HERE, BOTH OF YOU!!

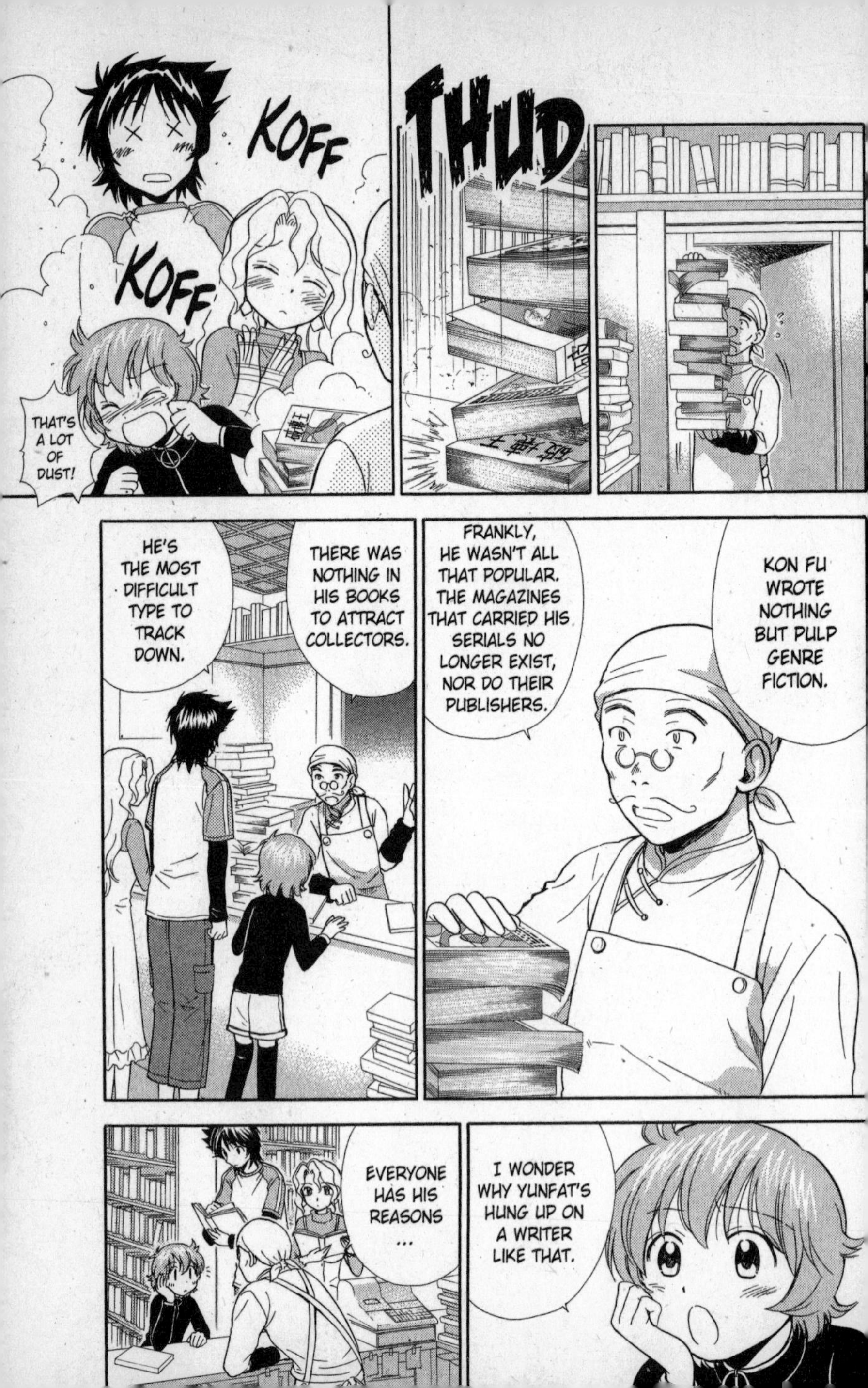
THUD
KOFF
KOFF
THAT'S A LOT OF DUST!
KON FU WROTE NOTHING BUT PULP GENRE FICTION.
FRANKLY, HE WASN'T ALL THAT POPULAR. THE MAGAZINES THAT CARRIED HIS SERIALS NO LONGER EXIST, NOR DO THEIR PUBLISHERS.
THERE WAS NOTHING IN HIS BOOKS TO ATTRACT COLLECTORS.
HE'S THE MOST DIFFICULT TYPE TO TRACK DOWN.
I WONDER WHY YUNFAT'S HUNG UP ON A WRITER LIKE THAT.
EVERYONE HAS HIS REASONS ...

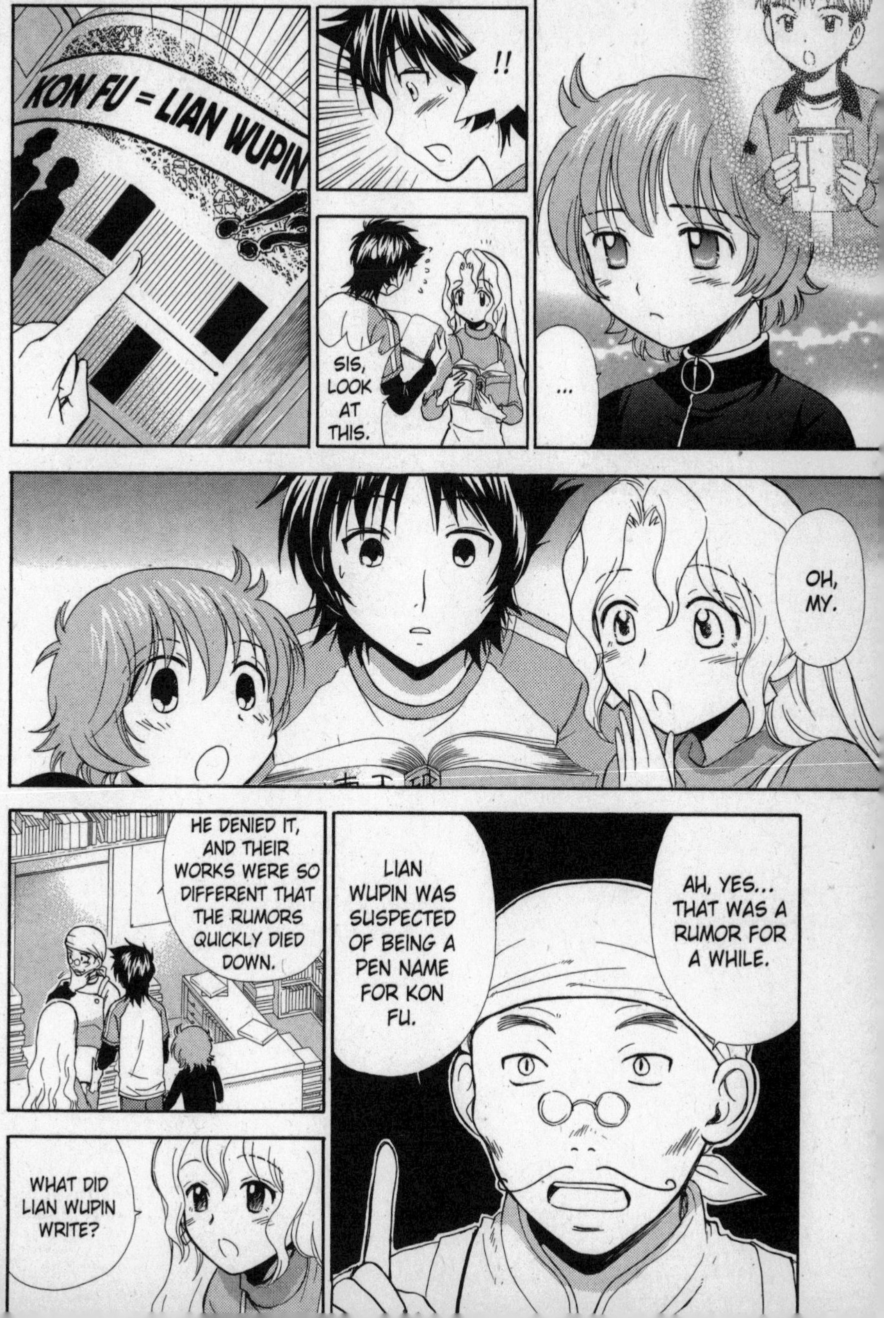
...
!!
SIS, LOOK AT THIS.
KON FU = LIAN WUPIN
OH, MY.
AH, YES... THAT WAS A RUMOR FOR A WHILE.
LIAN WUPIN WAS SUSPECTED OF BEING A PEN NAME FOR KON FU.
HE DENIED IT, AND THEIR WORKS WERE SO DIFFERENT THAT THE RUMORS QUICKLY DIED DOWN.
WHAT DID LIAN WUPIN WRITE?

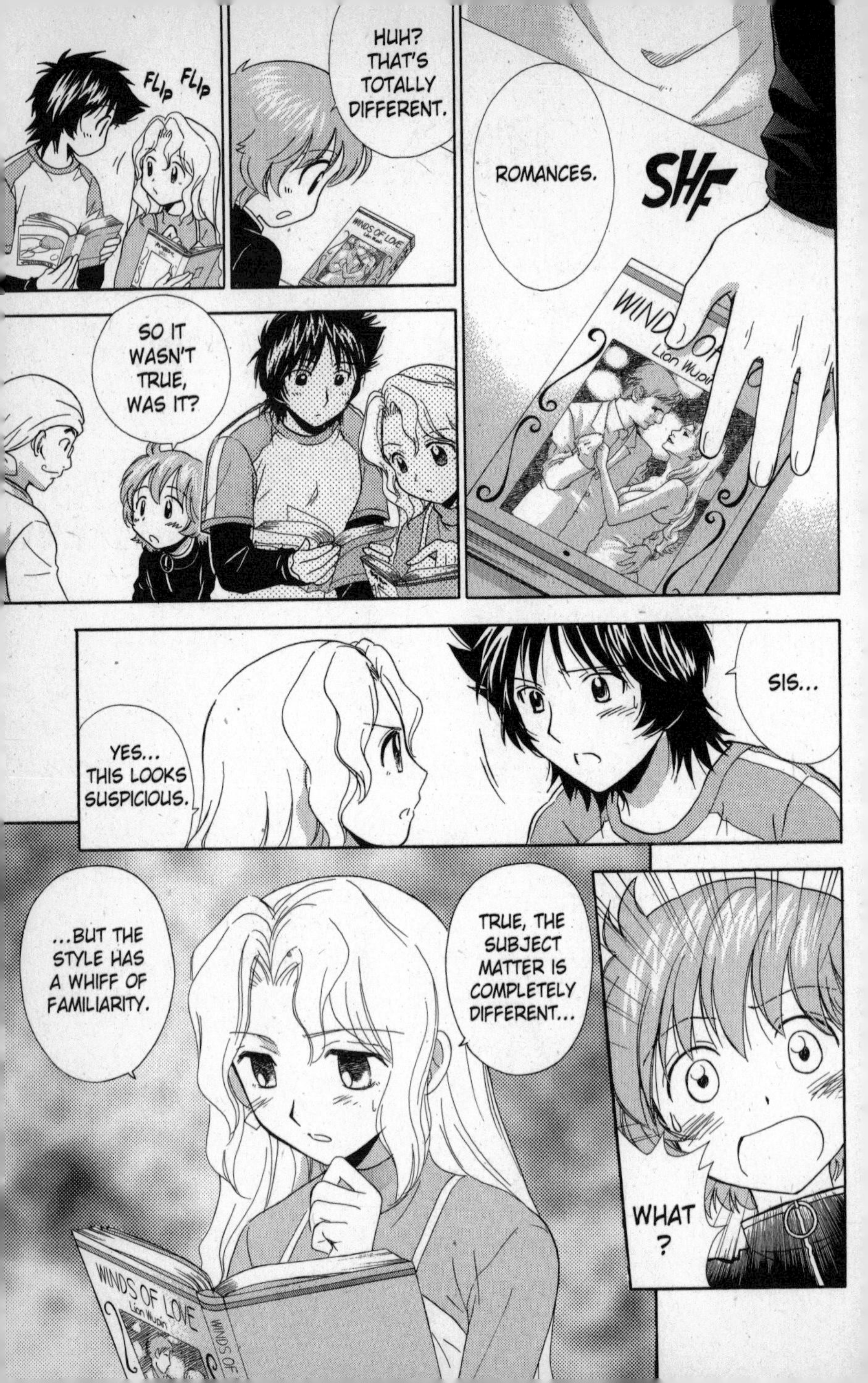
ROMANCES.
SHF
WINDS OF
Lion Wupin
HUH? THAT'S TOTALLY DIFFERENT.
WINDS OF LOVE
FLIP FLIP
SO IT WASN'T TRUE, WAS IT?
SIS...
YES... THIS LOOKS SUSPICIOUS.
WHAT?
TRUE, THE SUBJECT MATTER IS COMPLETELY DIFFERENT...
...BUT THE STYLE HAS A WHIFF OF FAMILIARITY.
WINDS OF LOVE
Lion Wupin
WINDS OF

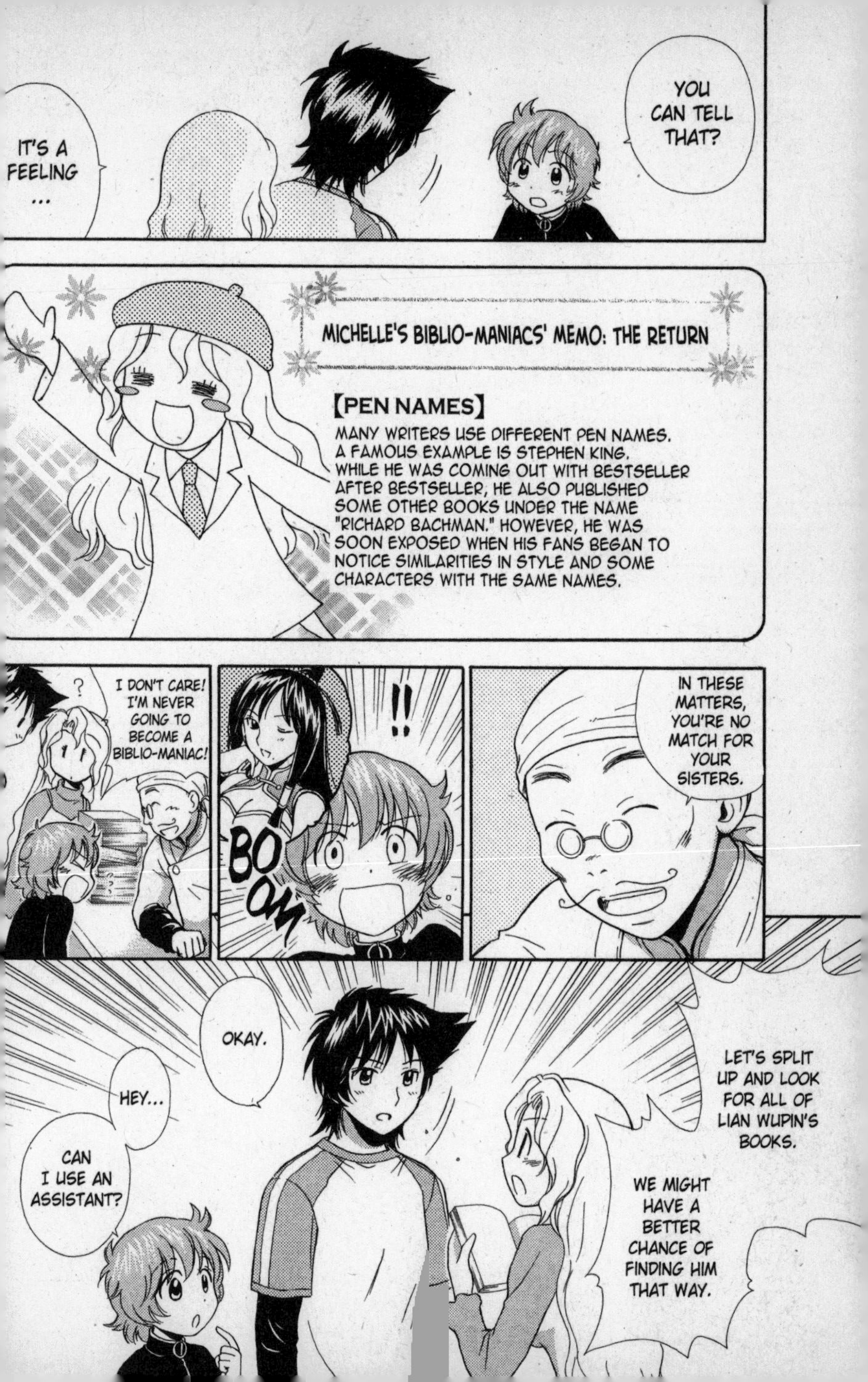
YOU CAN TELL THAT?
IT'S A FEELING ...
MICHELLE'S BIBLIO-MANIACS' MEMO: THE RETURN
【PEN NAMES】
MANY WRITERS USE DIFFERENT PEN NAMES. A FAMOUS EXAMPLE IS STEPHEN KING. WHILE HE WAS COMING OUT WITH BESTSELLER AFTER BESTSELLER, HE ALSO PUBLISHED SOME OTHER BOOKS UNDER THE NAME "RICHARD BACHMAN." HOWEVER, HE WAS SOON EXPOSED WHEN HIS FANS BEGAN TO NOTICE SIMILARITIES IN STYLE AND SOME CHARACTERS WITH THE SAME NAMES.
IN THESE MATTERS, YOU'RE NO MATCH FOR YOUR SISTERS.
!!
BOOM
?
I DON'T CARE! I'M NEVER GOING TO BECOME A BIBLIO-MANIAC!
LET'S SPLIT UP AND LOOK FOR ALL OF LIAN WUPIN'S BOOKS.
WE MIGHT HAVE A BETTER CHANCE OF FINDING HIM THAT WAY.
OKAY.
HEY...
CAN I USE AN ASSISTANT?

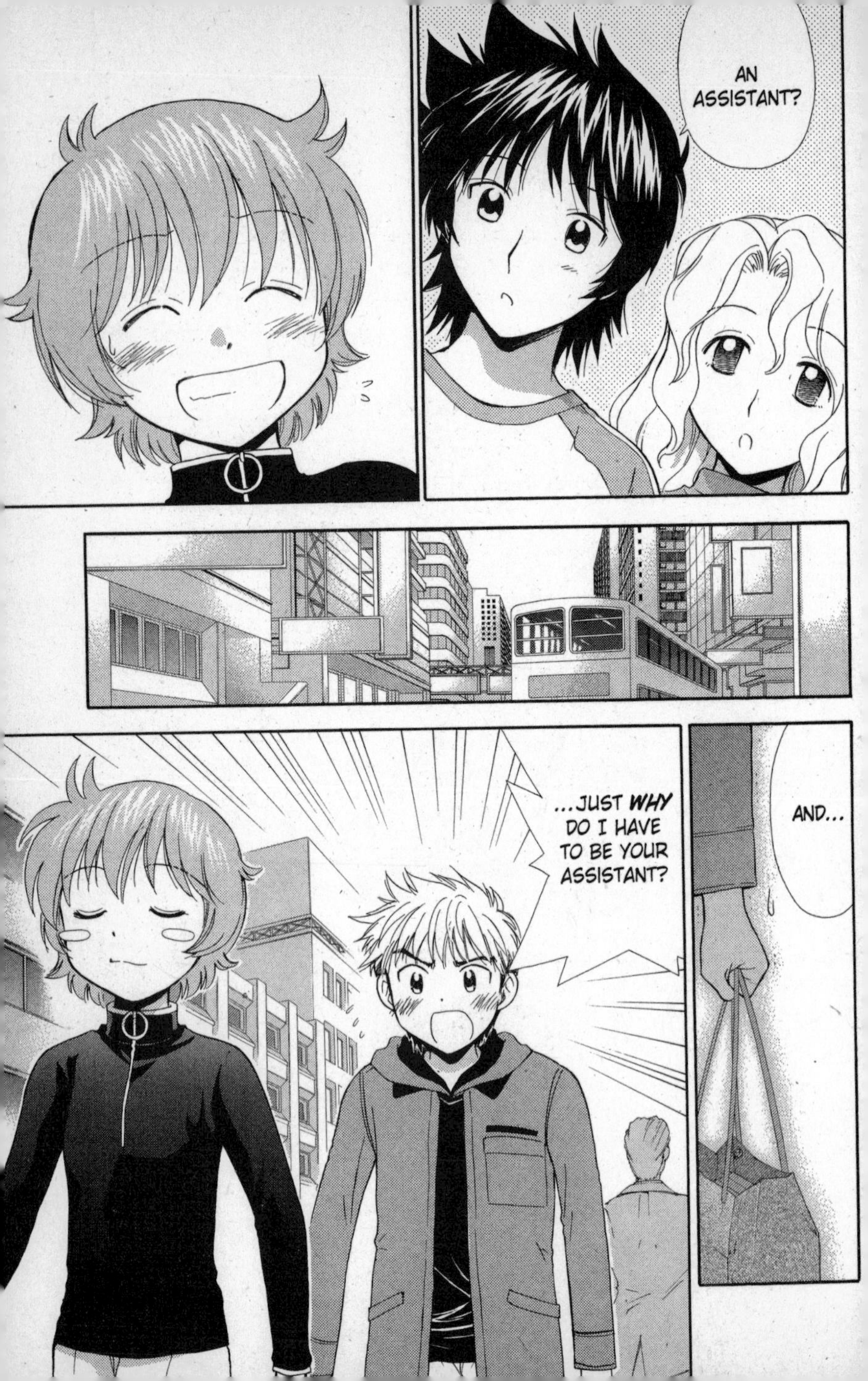
AN ASSISTANT?
AND...
...JUST WHY DO I HAVE TO BE YOUR ASSISTANT?

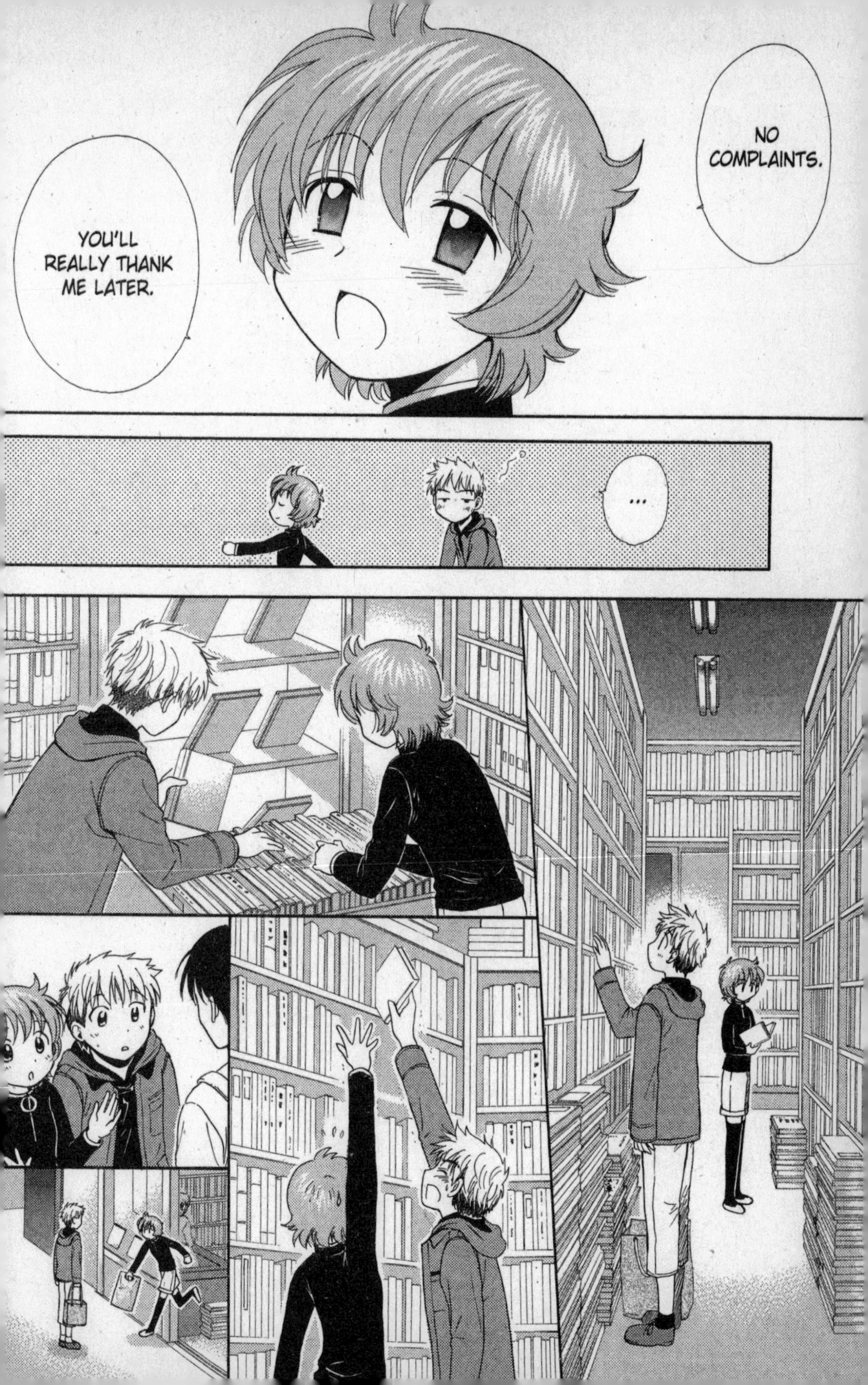
NO COMPLAINTS.
YOU'LL REALLY THANK ME LATER.
...

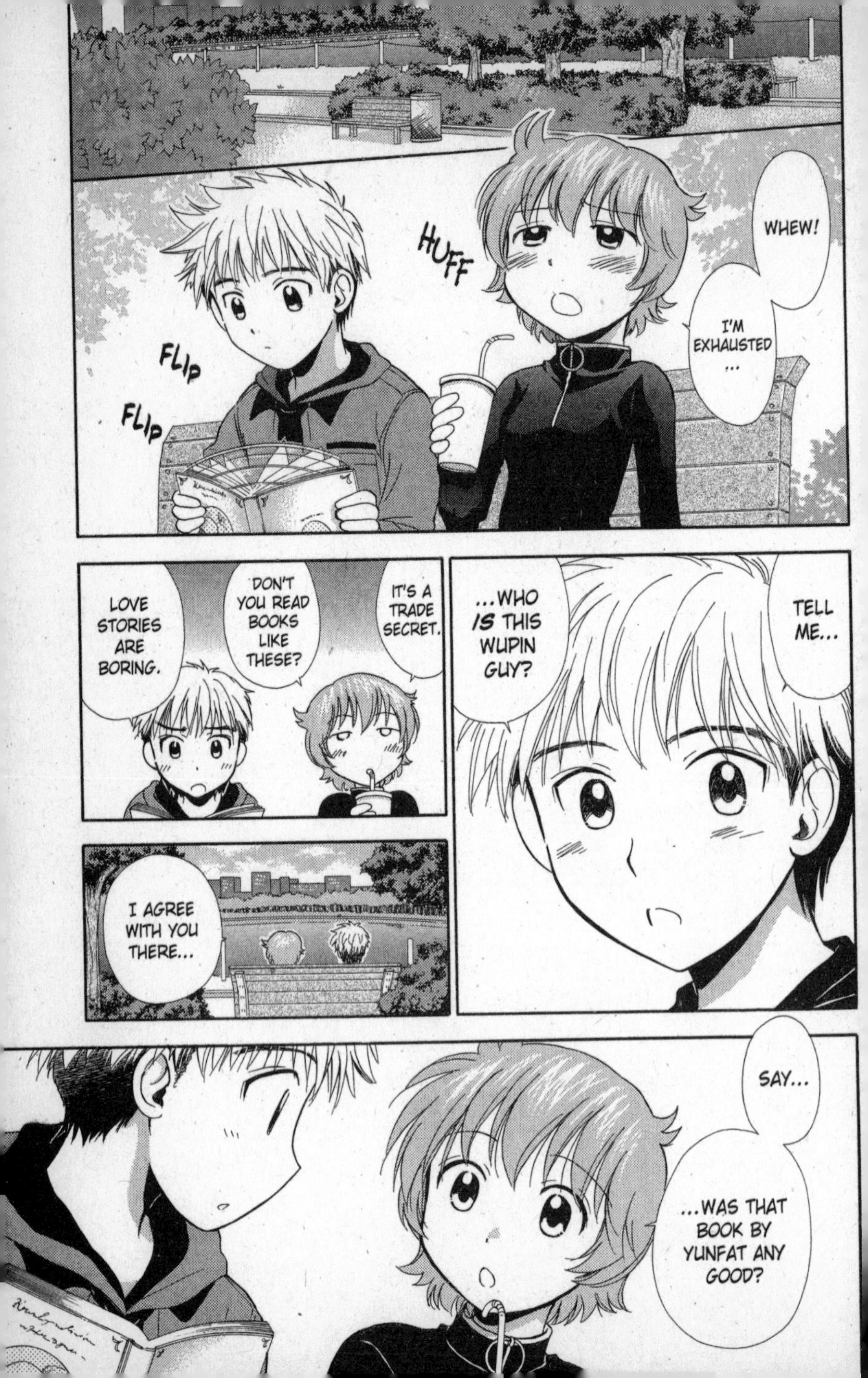
WHEW!
I'M EXHAUSTED ...
HUFF
FLIP
FLIP
TELL ME...
...WHO IS THIS WUPIN GUY?
IT'S A TRADE SECRET.
DON'T YOU READ BOOKS LIKE THESE?
LOVE STORIES ARE BORING.
I AGREE WITH YOU THERE...
SAY...
...WAS THAT BOOK BY YUNFAT ANY GOOD?

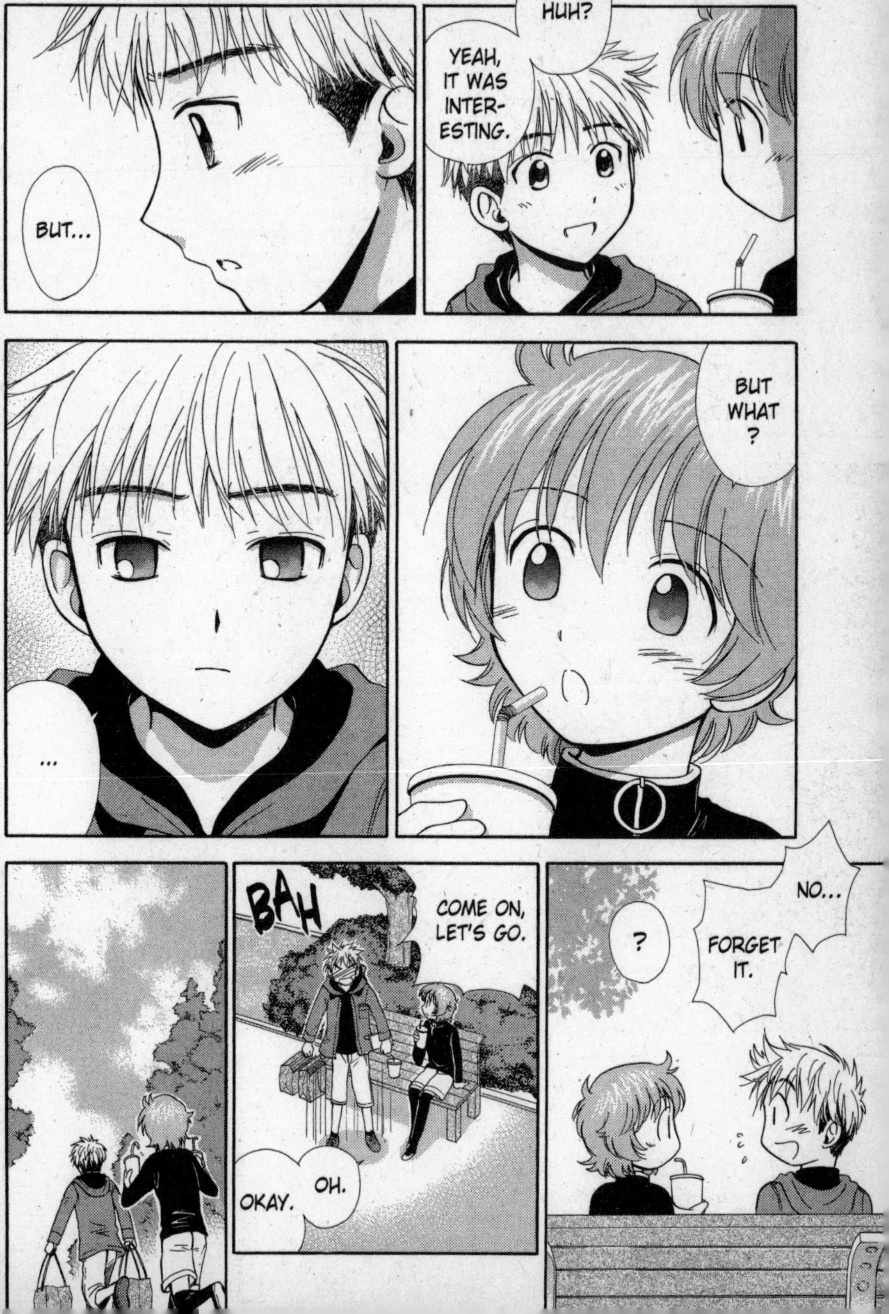
HUH?
YEAH, IT WAS INTER-ESTING.
BUT...
BUT WHAT?
...
NO... FORGET IT.
?
COME ON, LET'S GO.
BAH
OH.
OKAY.

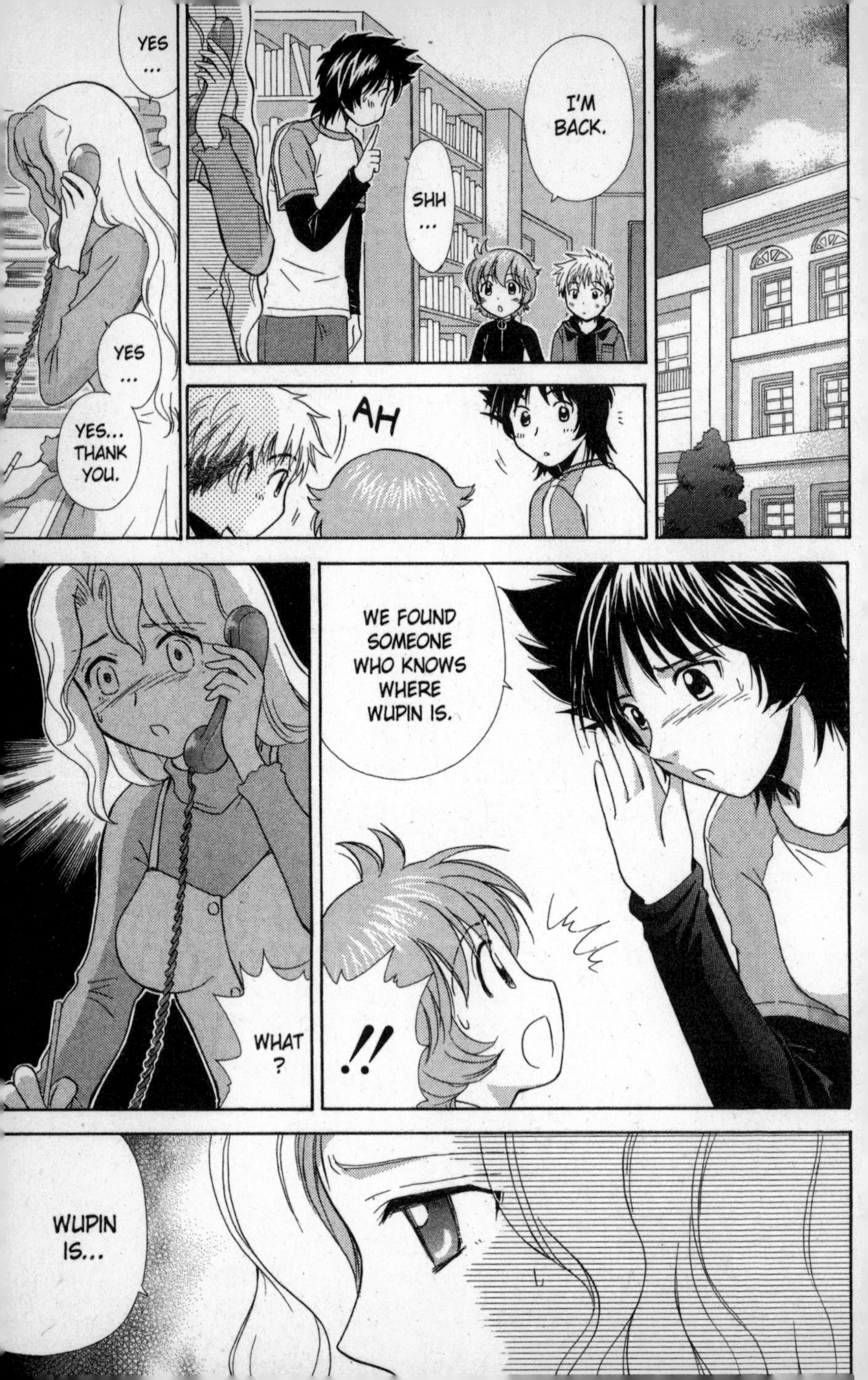
I'M BACK.
SHH ...
AH
YES ...
YES ...
YES... THANK YOU.
WE FOUND SOMEONE WHO KNOWS WHERE WUPIN IS.
!!
WHAT ?
WUPIN IS...

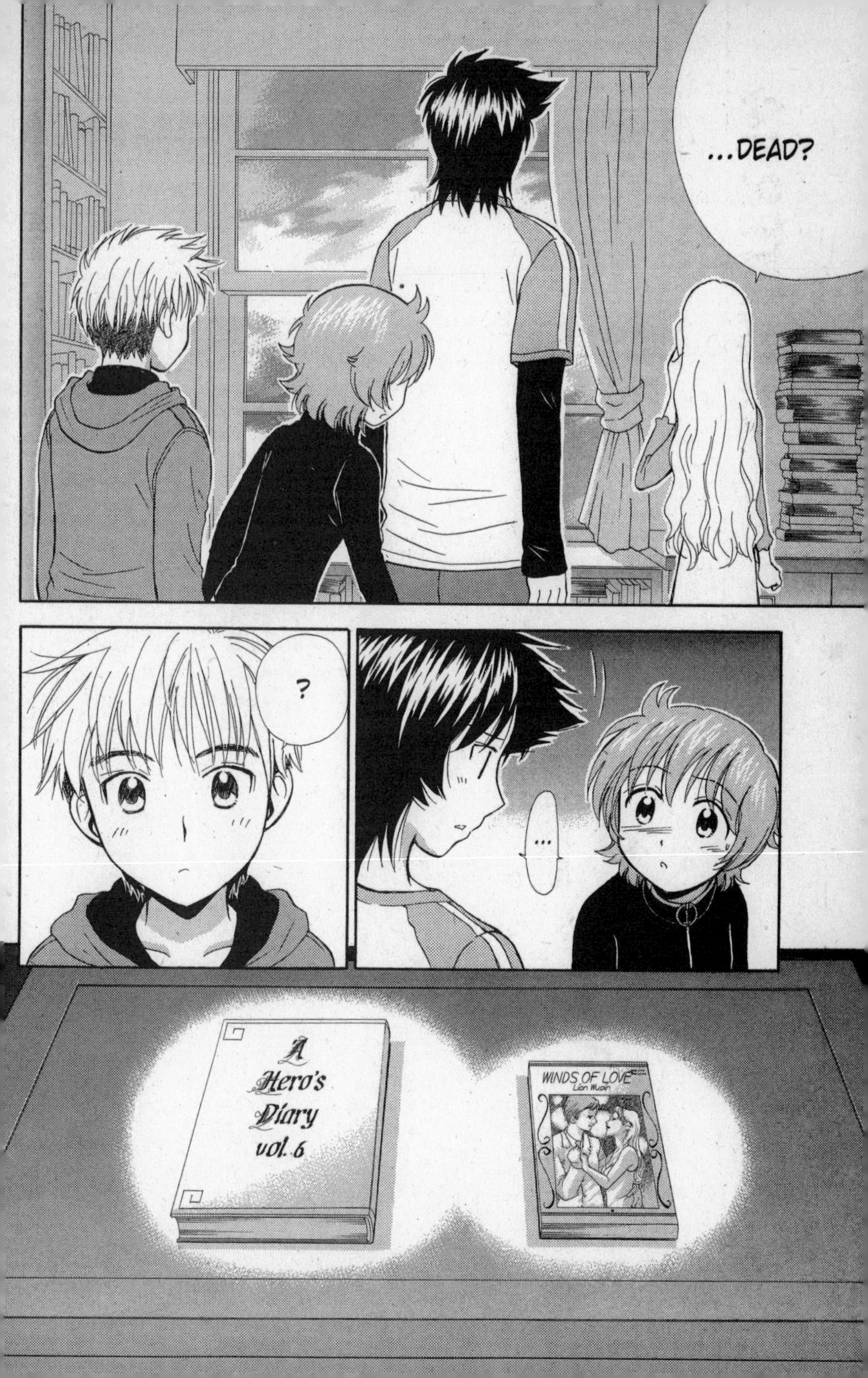
...DEAD?
...
?
WINDS OF LOVE
A Hero's Diary vol. 6

CHAPTER 14

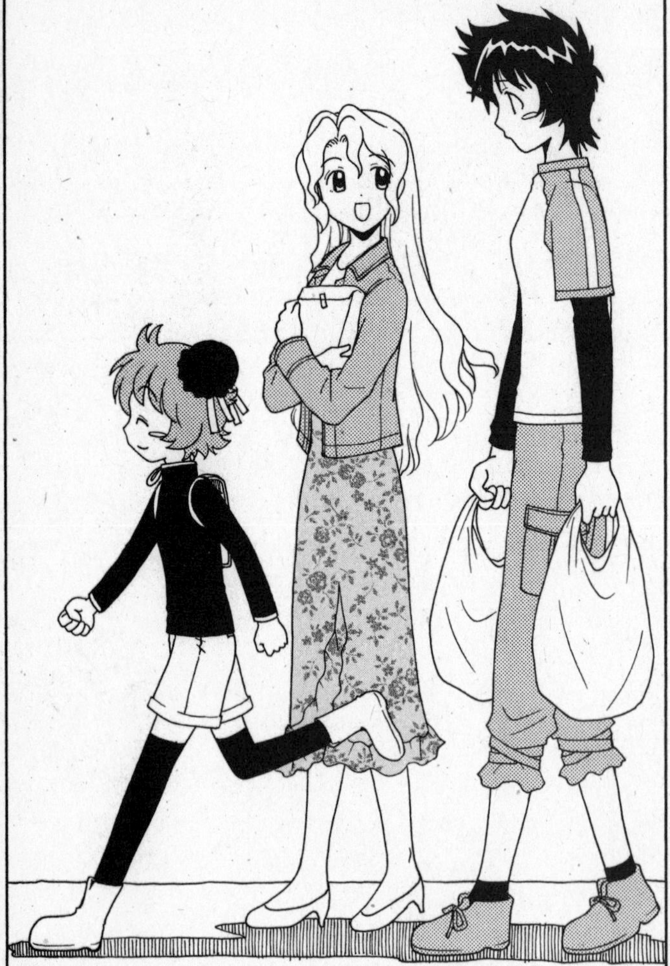

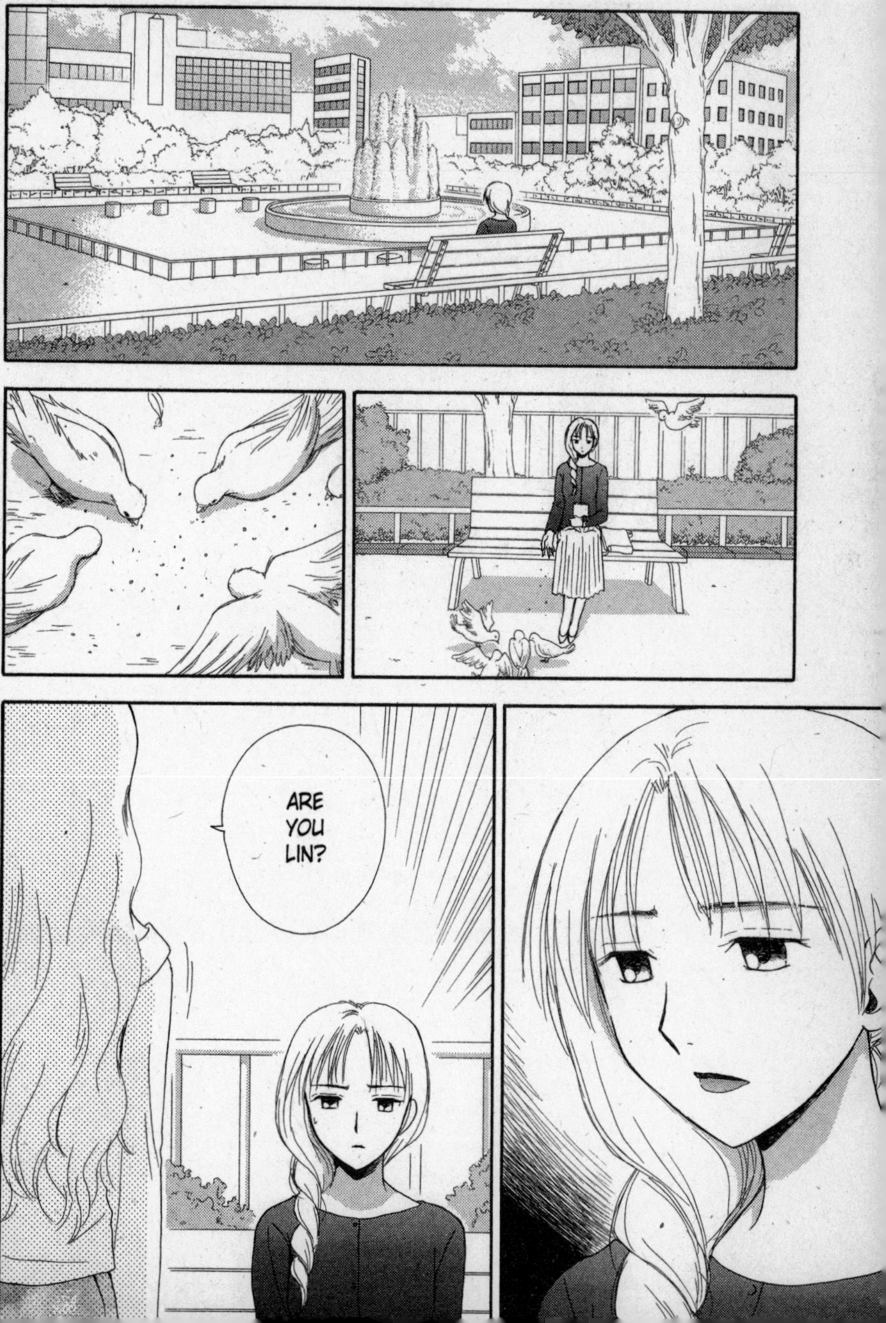
ARE YOU LIN?

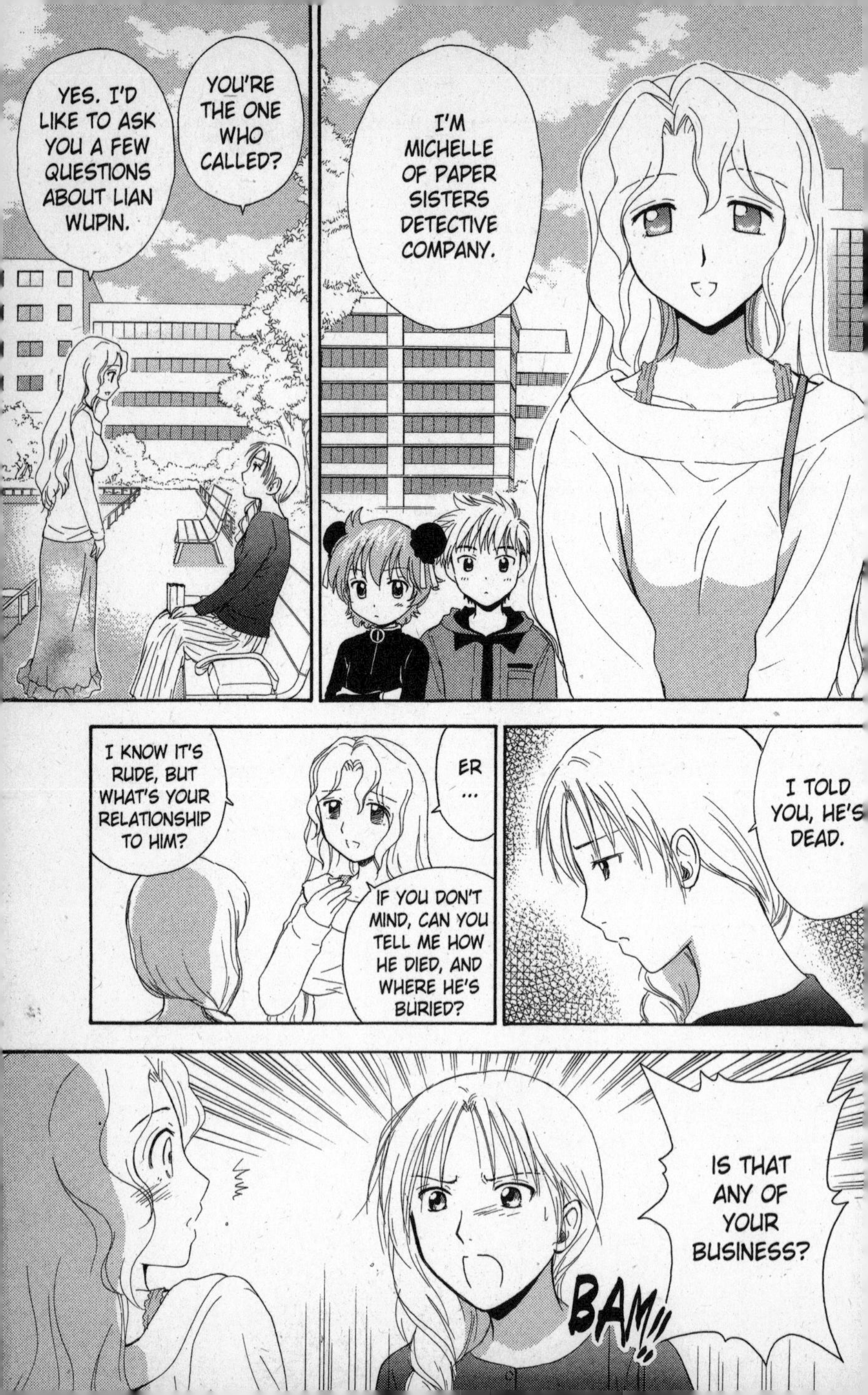
I'M MICHELLE OF PAPER SISTERS DETECTIVE COMPANY.
YOU'RE THE ONE WHO CALLED?
YES. I'D LIKE TO ASK YOU A FEW QUESTIONS ABOUT LIAN WUPIN.
I TOLD YOU, HE'S DEAD.
ER ...
I KNOW IT'S RUDE, BUT WHAT'S YOUR RELATIONSHIP TO HIM?
IF YOU DON'T MIND, CAN YOU TELL ME HOW HE DIED, AND WHERE HE'S BURIED?
IS THAT ANY OF YOUR BUSINESS?
BAM!!

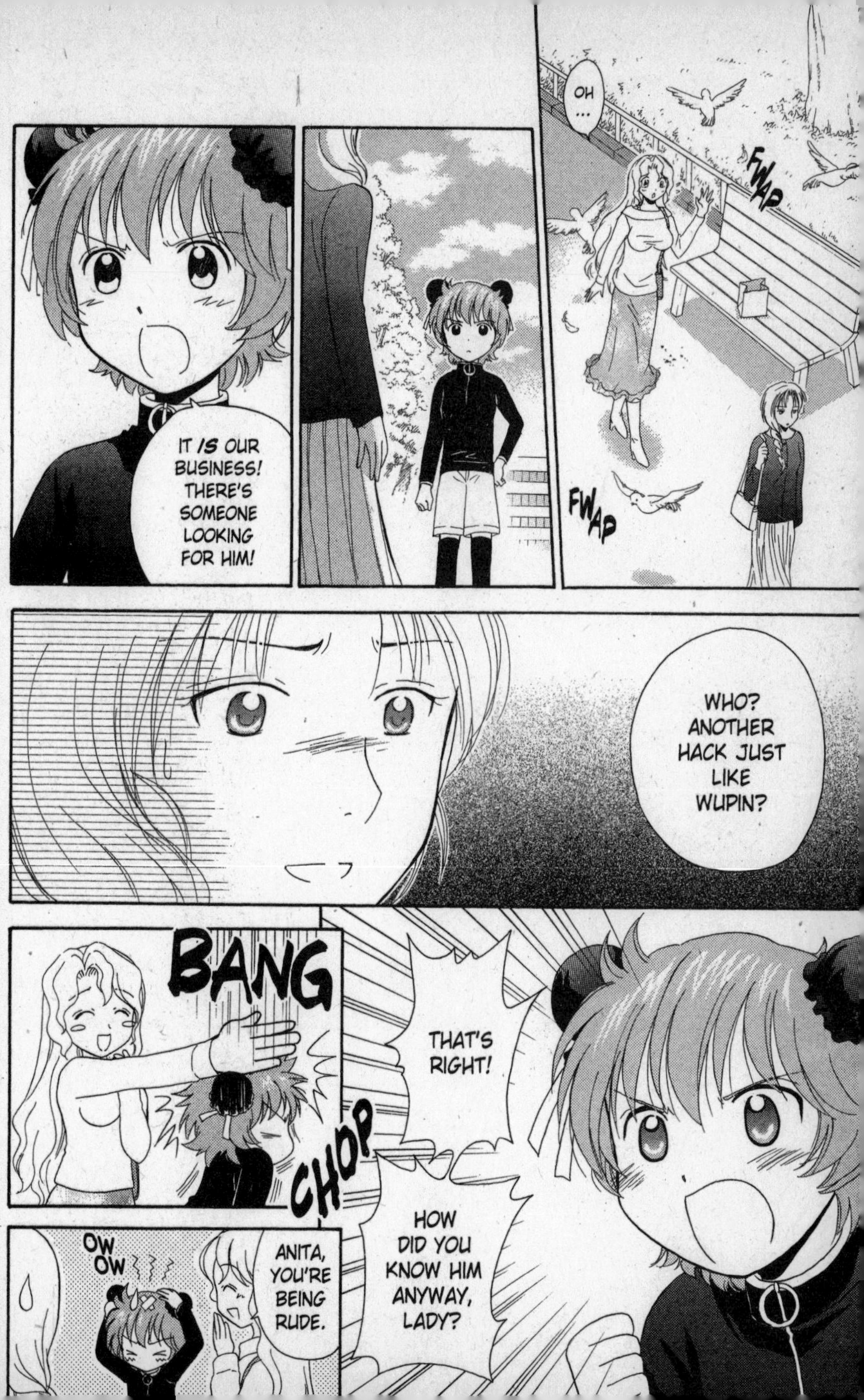
OH ...
FWAP
FWAP
IT *IS* OUR BUSINESS! THERE'S SOMEONE LOOKING FOR HIM!
WHO? ANOTHER HACK JUST LIKE WUPIN?
THAT'S RIGHT!
HOW DID YOU KNOW HIM ANYWAY, LADY?
BANG
CHOP
ANITA, YOU'RE BEING RUDE.
OW OW

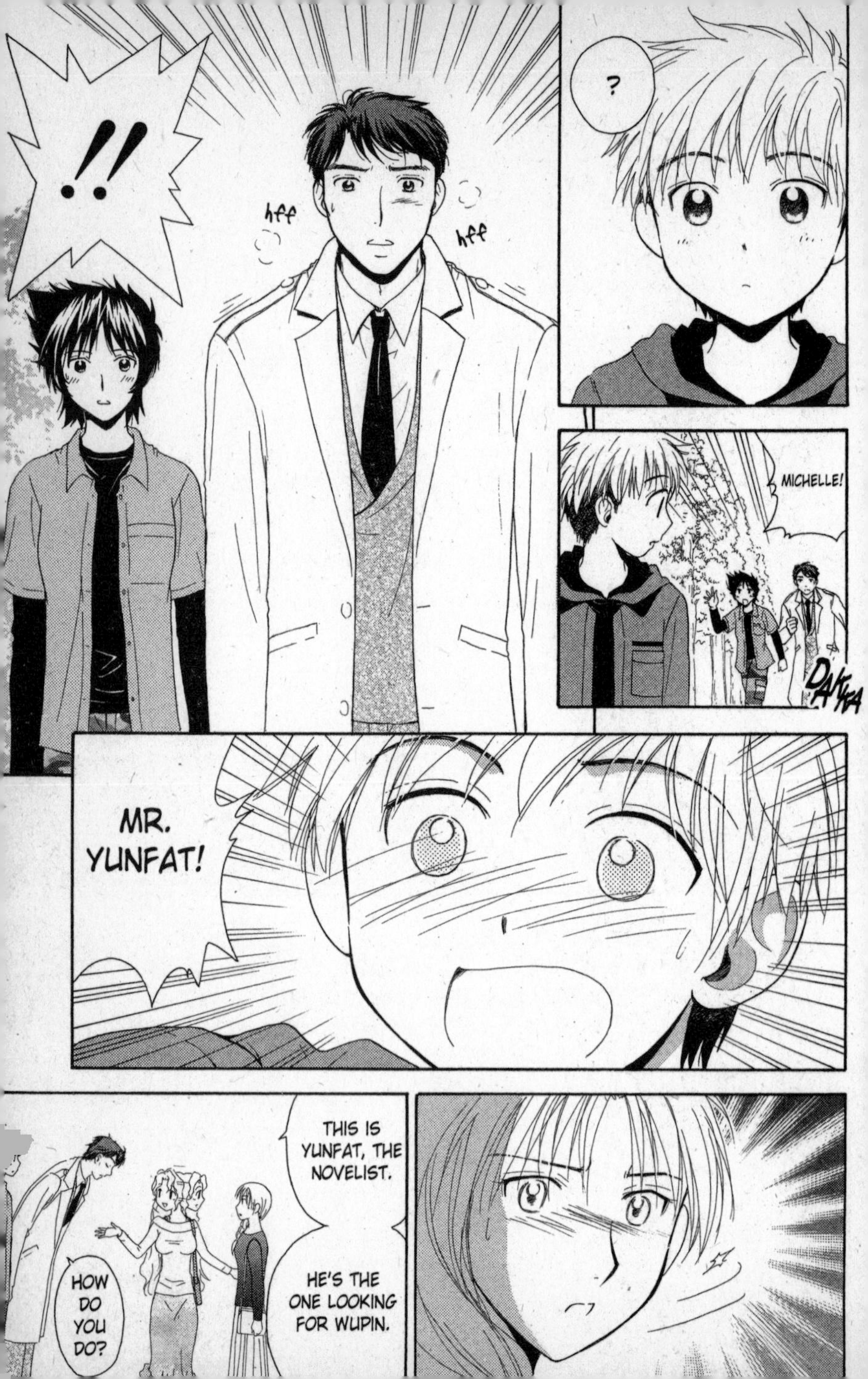
?
MICHELLE!
DAKKA
!!
hff
hff
MR. YUNFAT!
THIS IS YUNFAT, THE NOVELIST.
HE'S THE ONE LOOKING FOR WUPIN.
HOW DO YOU DO?

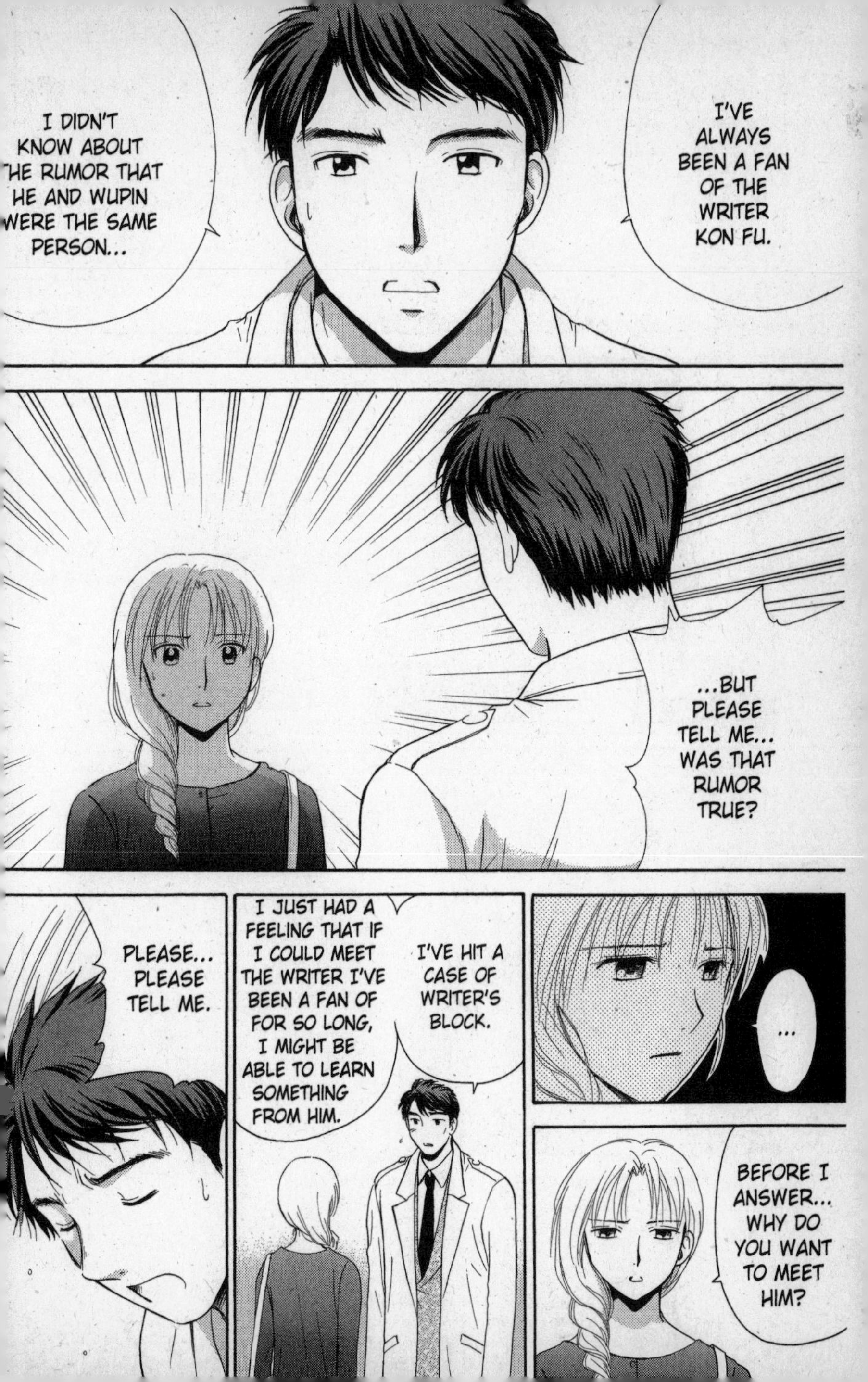
I'VE ALWAYS BEEN A FAN OF THE WRITER KON FU.
I DIDN'T KNOW ABOUT THE RUMOR THAT HE AND WUPIN WERE THE SAME PERSON...
...BUT PLEASE TELL ME... WAS THAT RUMOR TRUE?
...
BEFORE I ANSWER... WHY DO YOU WANT TO MEET HIM?
I'VE HIT A CASE OF WRITER'S BLOCK.
I JUST HAD A FEELING THAT IF I COULD MEET THE WRITER I'VE BEEN A FAN OF FOR SO LONG, I MIGHT BE ABLE TO LEARN SOMETHING FROM HIM.
PLEASE... PLEASE TELL ME.

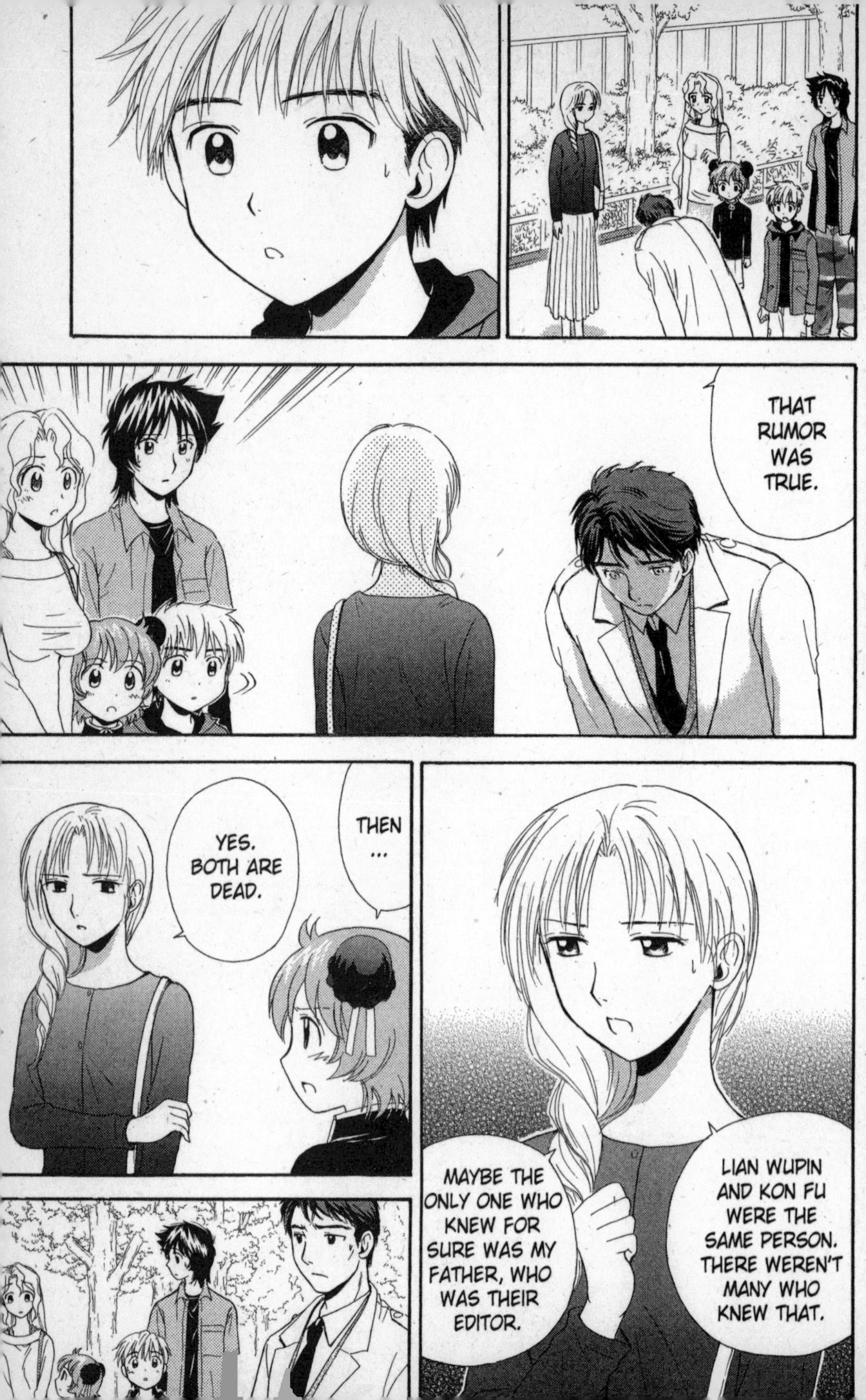
THAT RUMOR WAS TRUE.
LIAN WUPIN AND KON FU WERE THE SAME PERSON. THERE WEREN'T MANY WHO KNEW THAT.
MAYBE THE ONLY ONE WHO KNEW FOR SURE WAS MY FATHER, WHO WAS THEIR EDITOR.
THEN ...
YES. BOTH ARE DEAD.

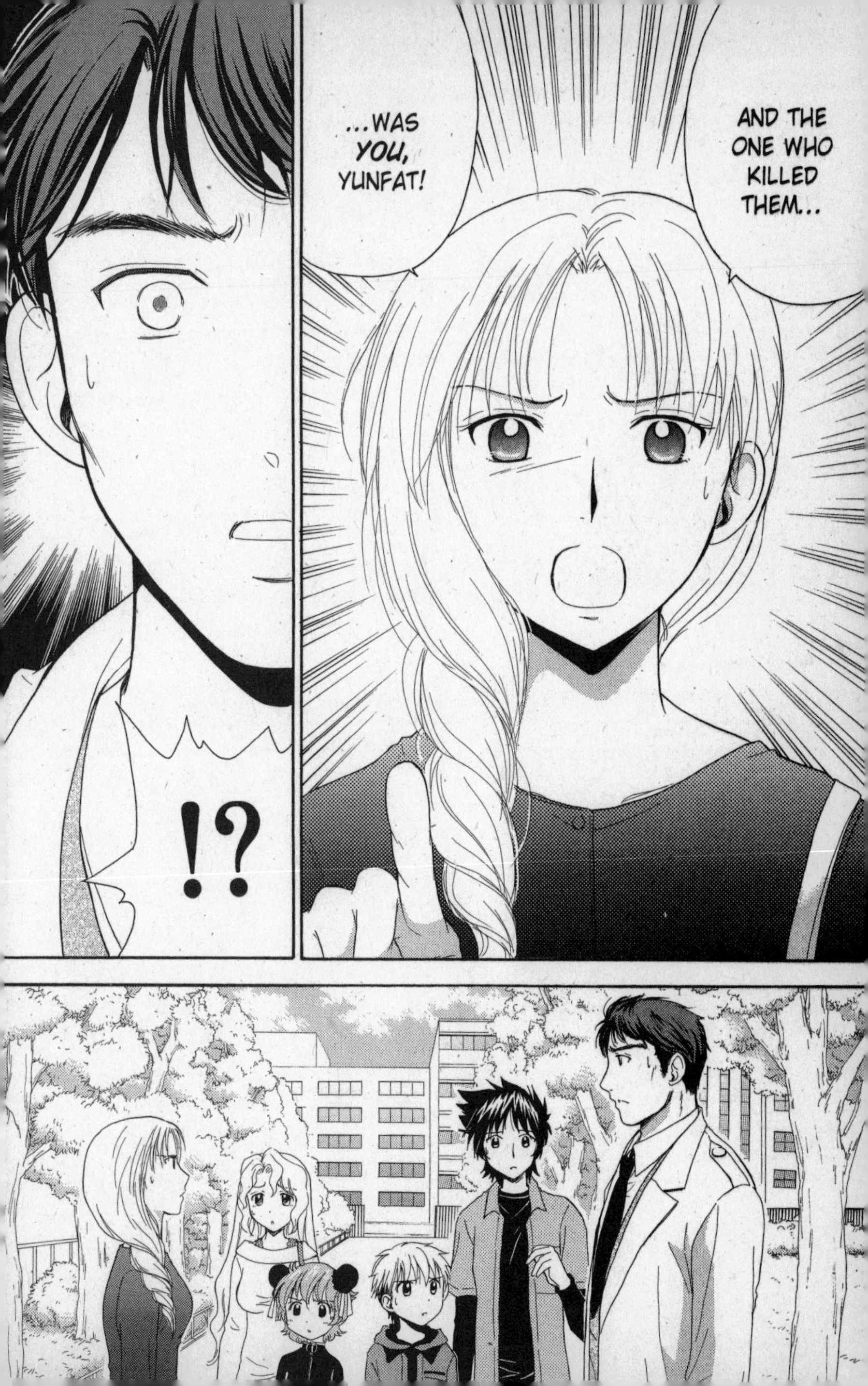
AND THE ONE WHO KILLED THEM...
...WAS *YOU*, YUNFAT!
!?

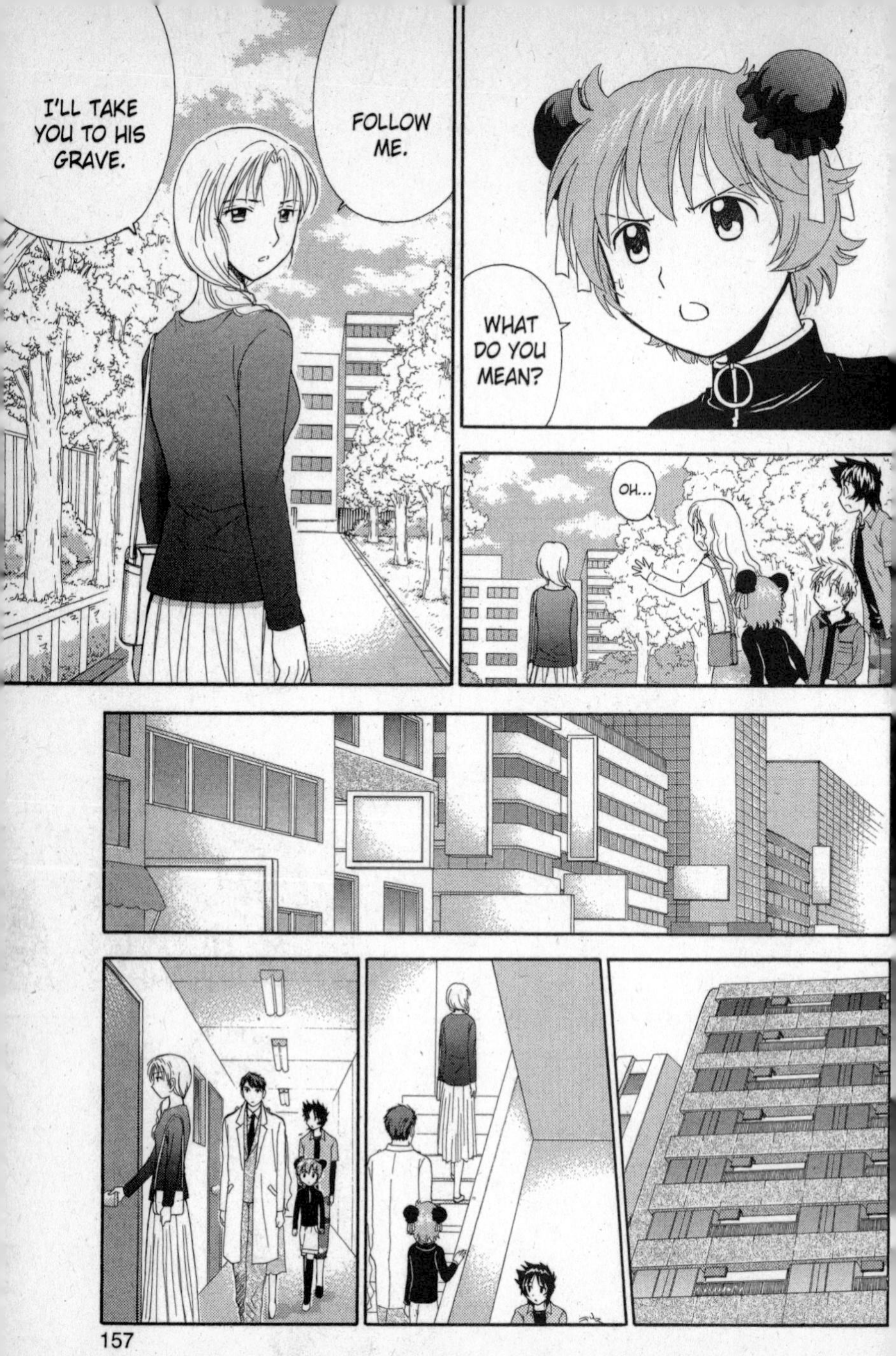
WHAT DO YOU MEAN?
OH...
FOLLOW ME.
I'LL TAKE YOU TO HIS GRAVE.

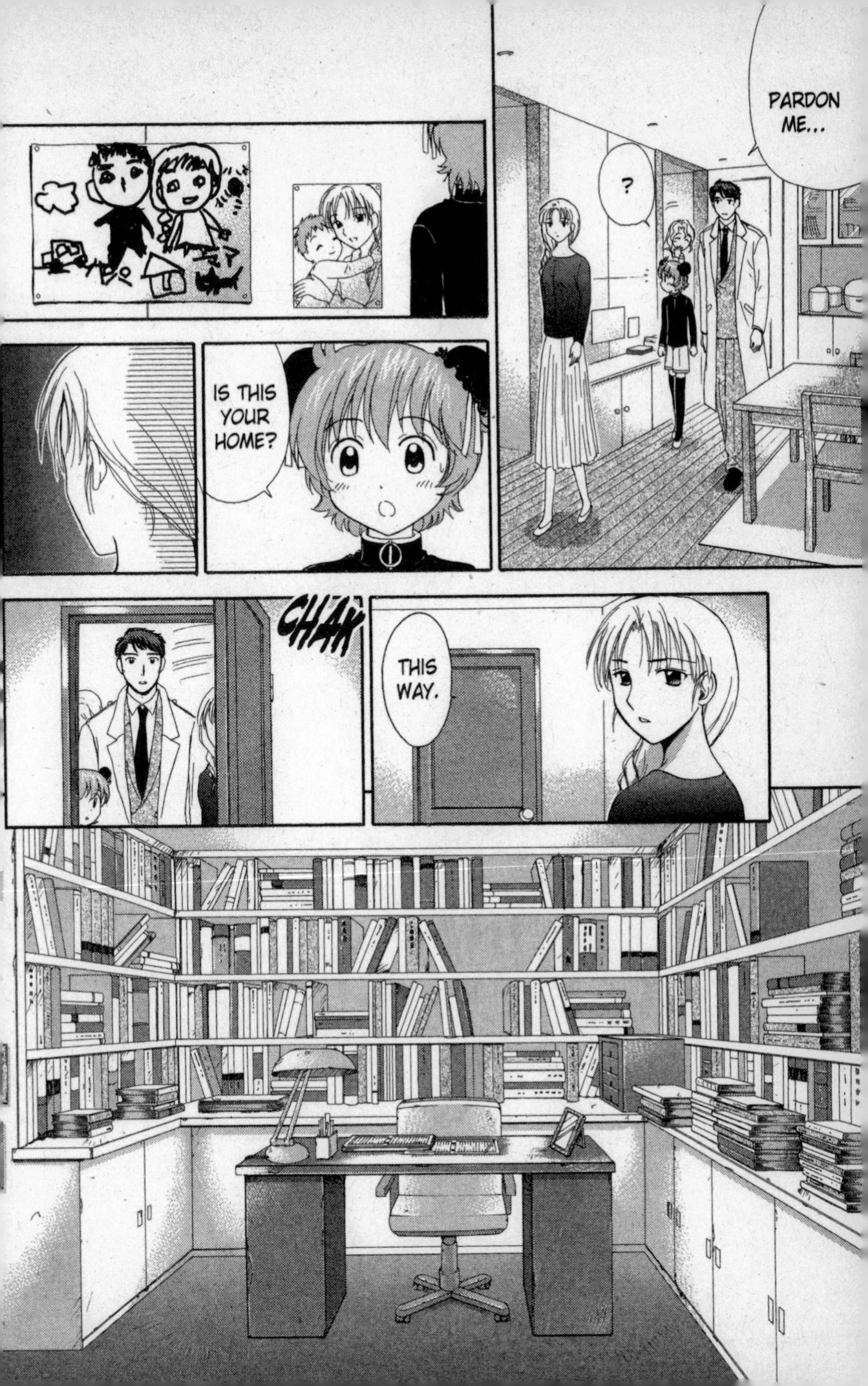
PARDON ME...
?
IS THIS YOUR HOME?
THIS WAY.
CHAK

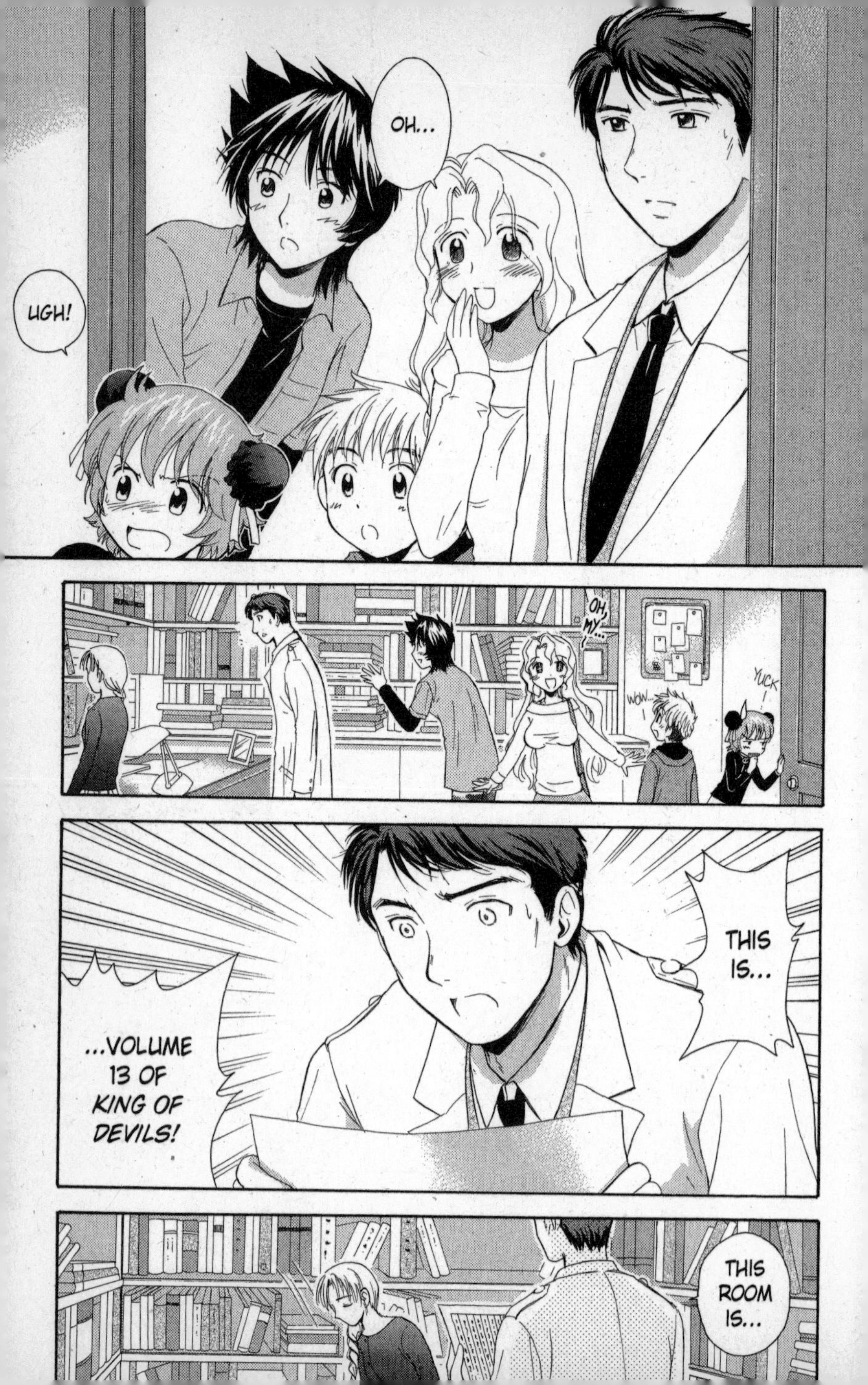
OH...
UGH!
YUCK!
WOW...!
OH, MY...!
THIS IS...
...VOLUME 13 OF KING OF DEVILS!
THIS ROOM IS...

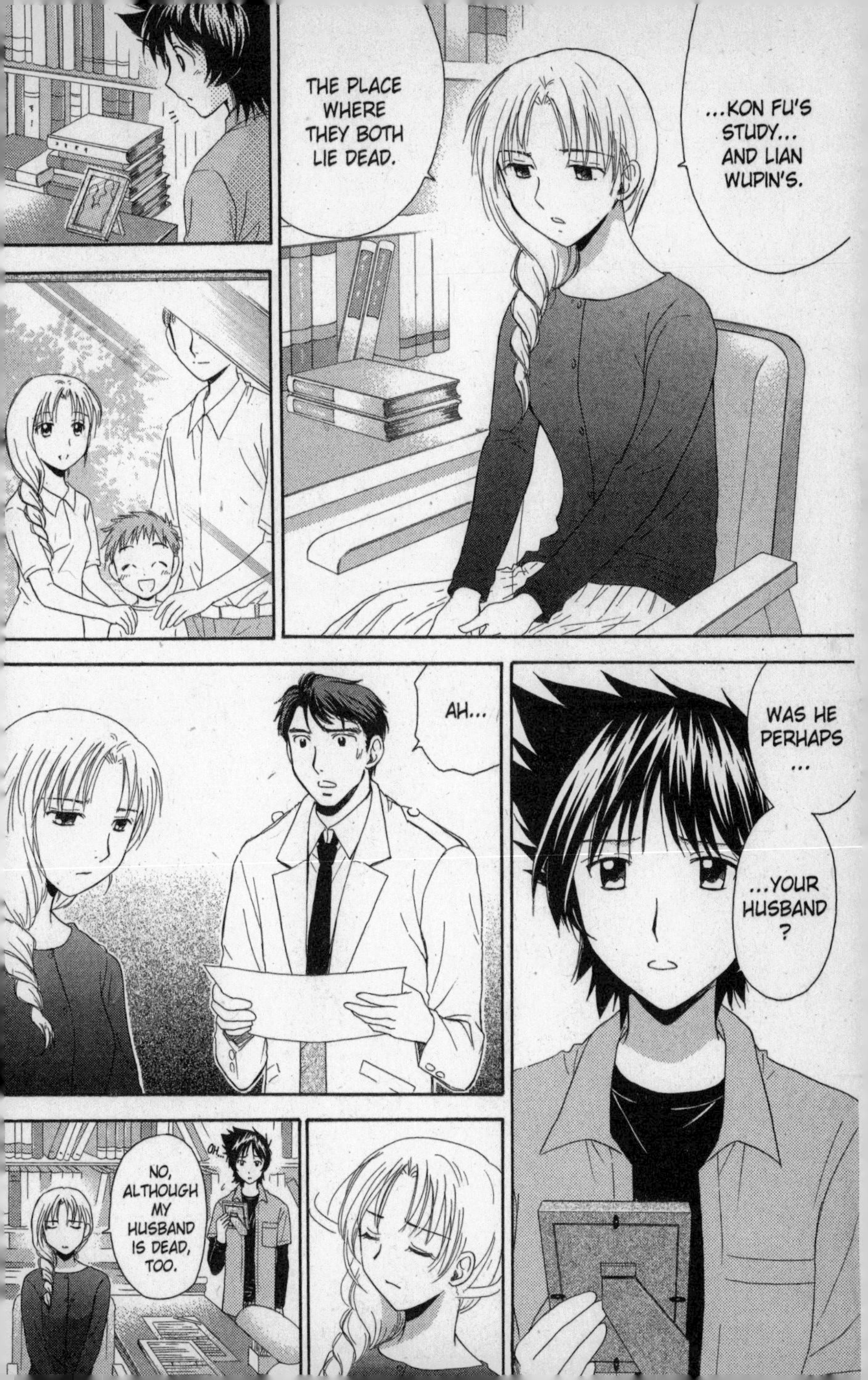
...KON FU'S STUDY... AND LIAN WUPIN'S.
THE PLACE WHERE THEY BOTH LIE DEAD.
WAS HE PERHAPS ...
...YOUR HUSBAND ?
AH...
OH...
NO, ALTHOUGH MY HUSBAND IS DEAD, TOO.

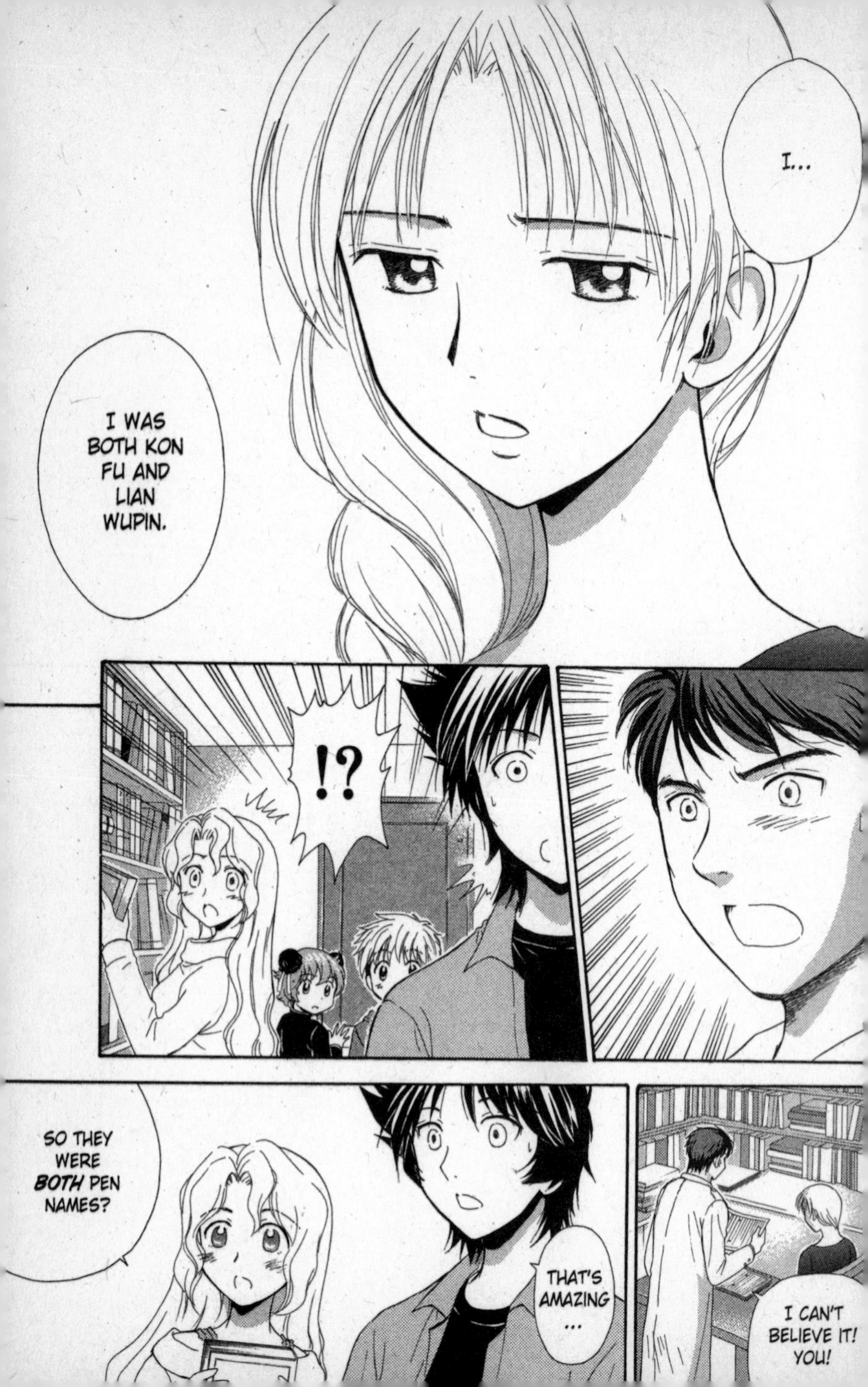
I...
I WAS BOTH KON FU AND LIAN WUPIN.
!?
I CAN'T BELIEVE IT! YOU!
SO THEY WERE BOTH PEN NAMES?
THAT'S AMAZING ...

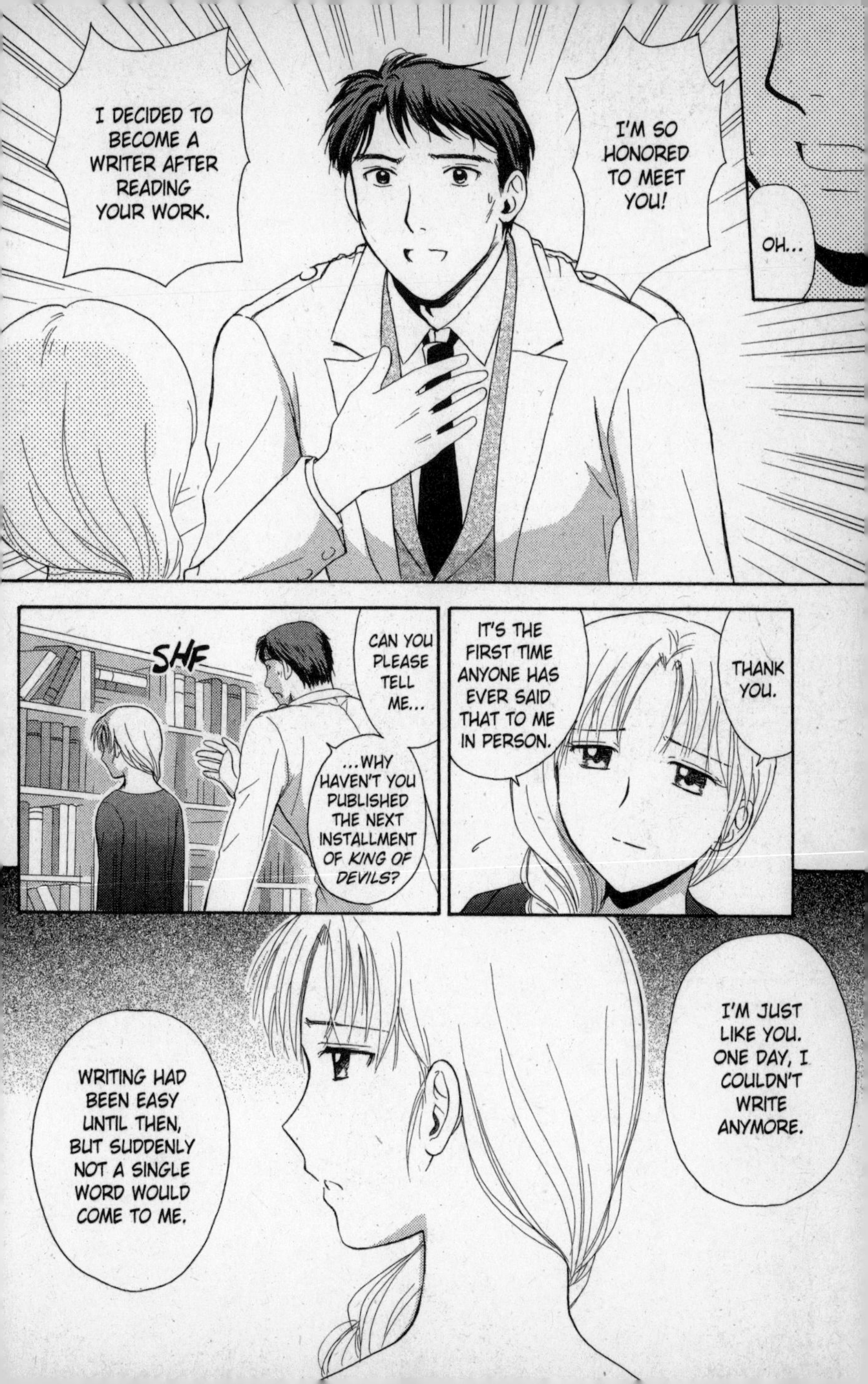
OH...
I'M SO HONORED TO MEET YOU!
I DECIDED TO BECOME A WRITER AFTER READING YOUR WORK.
THANK YOU.
IT'S THE FIRST TIME ANYONE HAS EVER SAID THAT TO ME IN PERSON.
CAN YOU PLEASE TELL ME...
...WHY HAVEN'T YOU PUBLISHED THE NEXT INSTALLMENT OF *KING OF DEVILS*?
SHF
I'M JUST LIKE YOU. ONE DAY, I COULDN'T WRITE ANYMORE.
WRITING HAD BEEN EASY UNTIL THEN, BUT SUDDENLY NOT A SINGLE WORD WOULD COME TO ME.

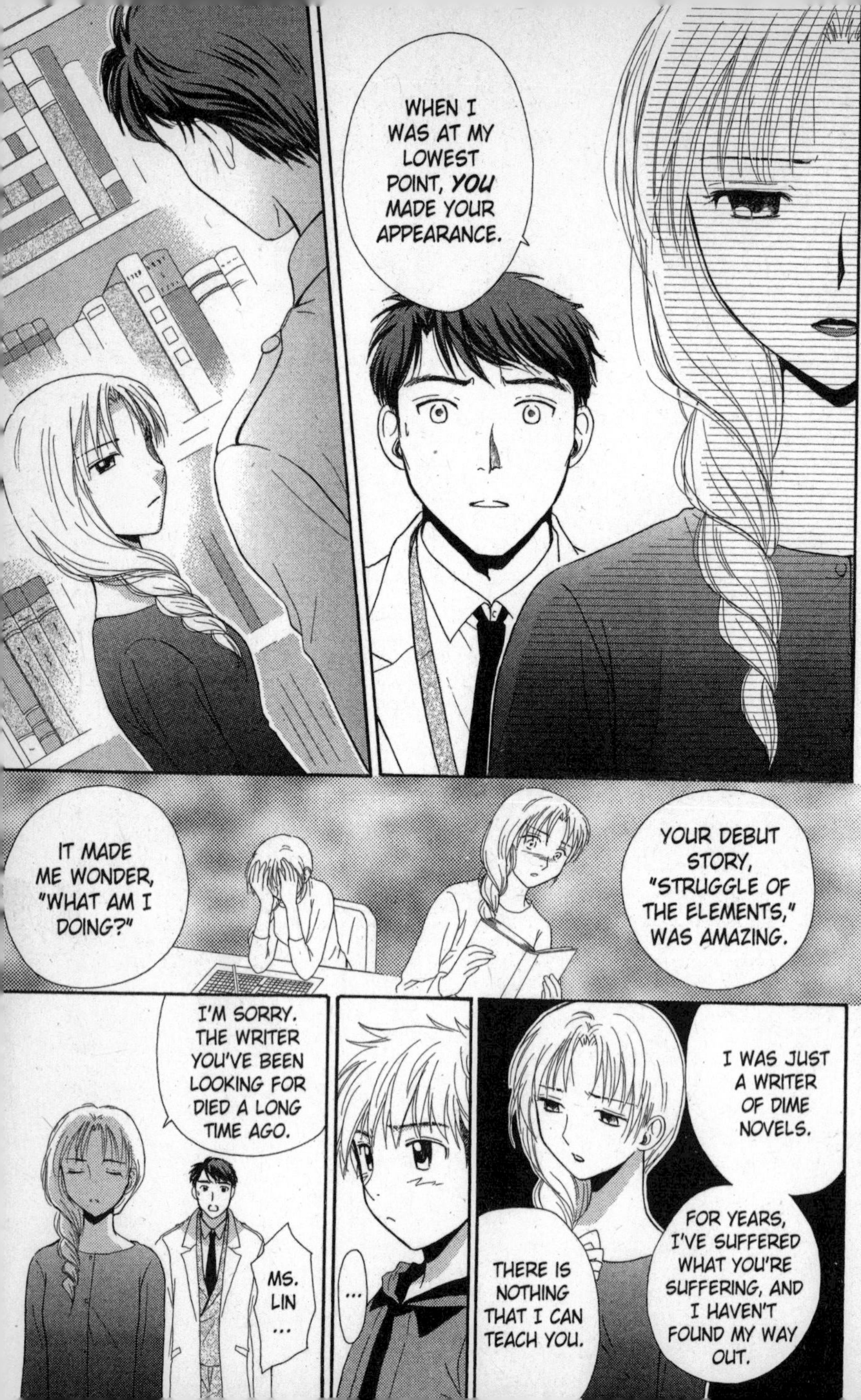
WHEN I WAS AT MY LOWEST POINT, *YOU* MADE YOUR APPEARANCE.
YOUR DEBUT STORY, "STRUGGLE OF THE ELEMENTS," WAS AMAZING.
IT MADE ME WONDER, "WHAT AM I DOING?"
I WAS JUST A WRITER OF DIME NOVELS.
FOR YEARS, I'VE SUFFERED WHAT YOU'RE SUFFERING, AND I HAVEN'T FOUND MY WAY OUT.
THERE IS NOTHING THAT I CAN TEACH YOU.
...
I'M SORRY. THE WRITER YOU'VE BEEN LOOKING FOR DIED A LONG TIME AGO.
MS. LIN ...

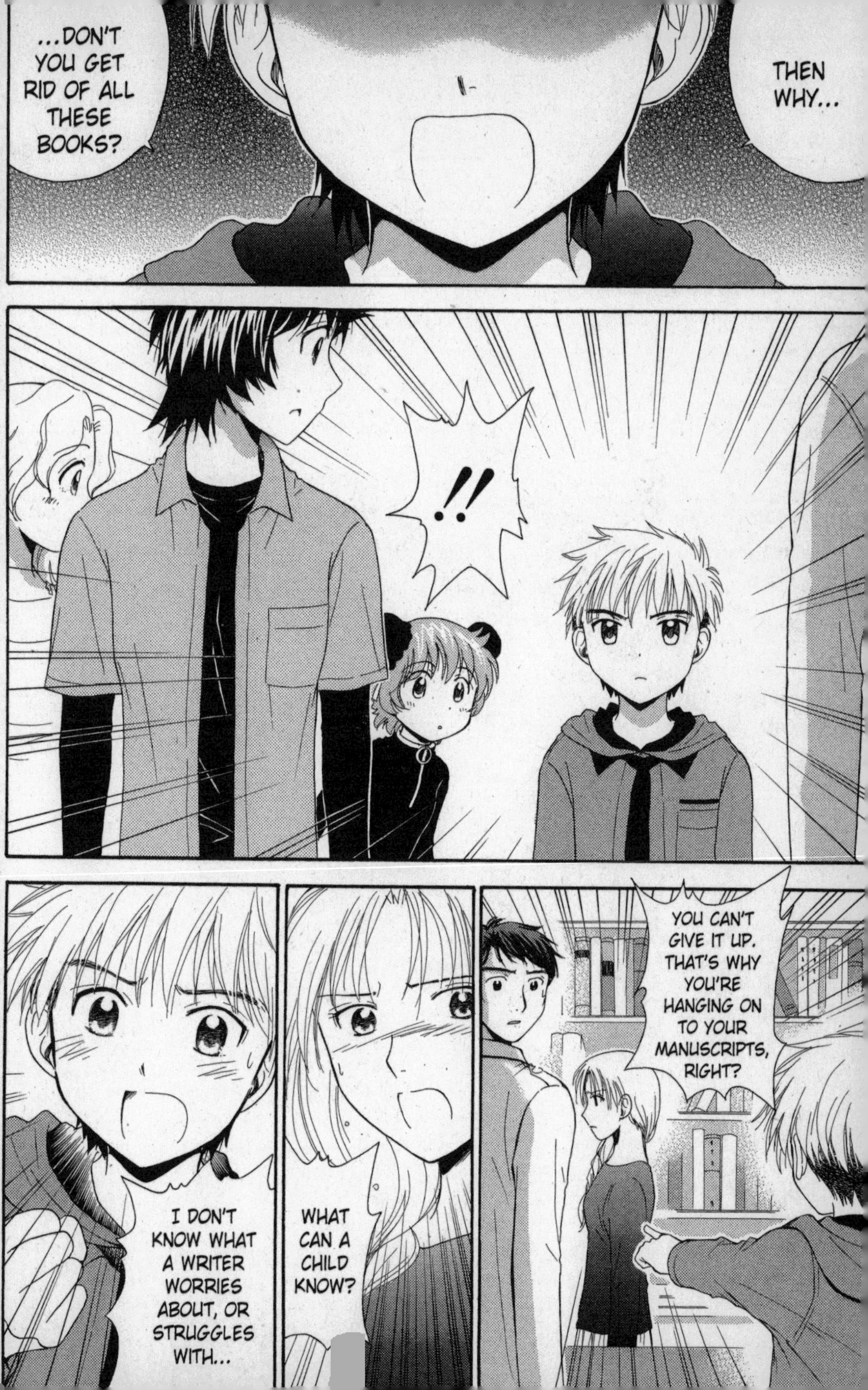
THEN WHY...
...DON'T YOU GET RID OF ALL THESE BOOKS?
!!
YOU CAN'T GIVE IT UP. THAT'S WHY YOU'RE HANGING ON TO YOUR MANUSCRIPTS, RIGHT?
WHAT CAN A CHILD KNOW?
I DON'T KNOW WHAT A WRITER WORRIES ABOUT, OR STRUGGLES WITH...

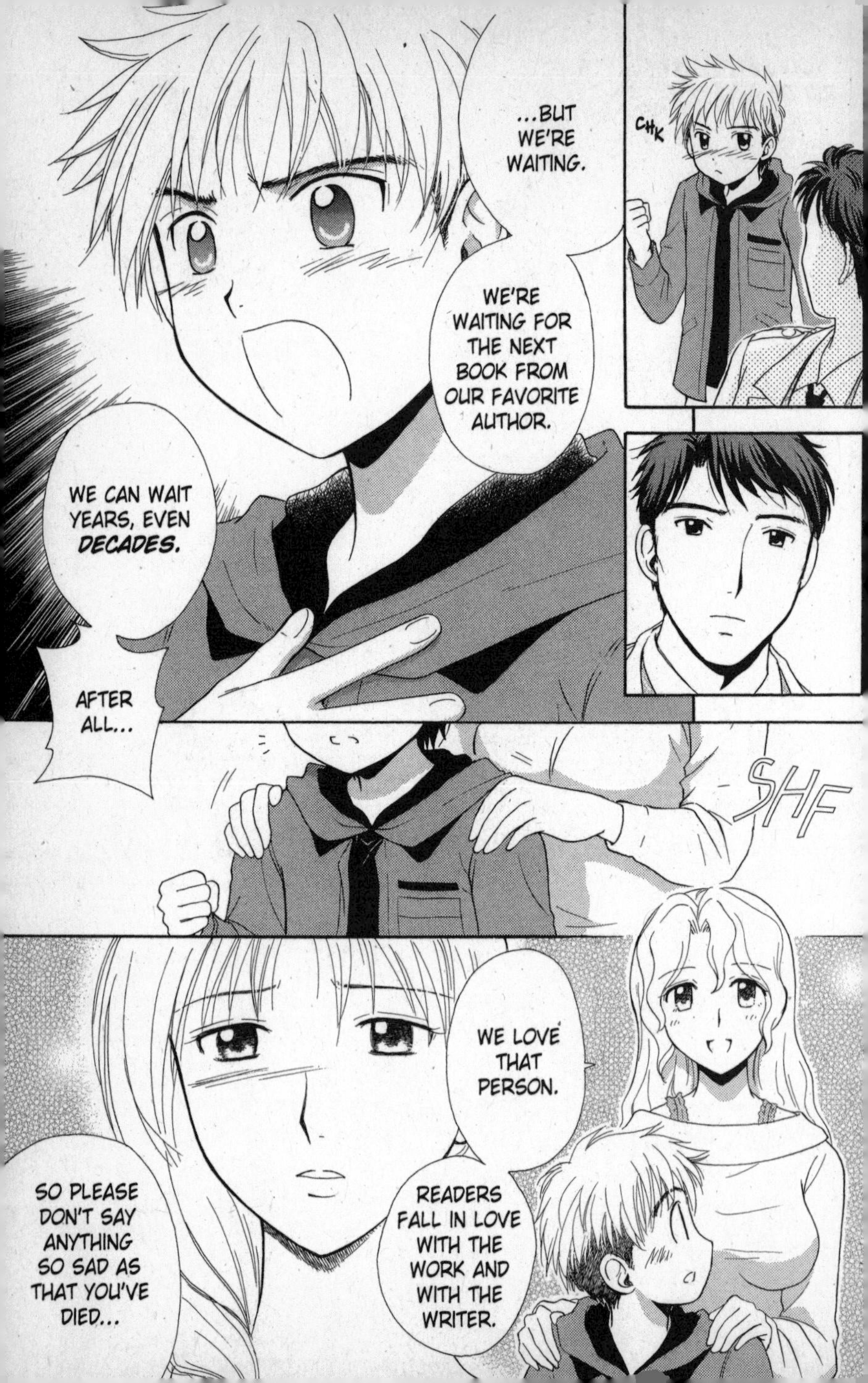
CHK
...BUT WE'RE WAITING.
WE'RE WAITING FOR THE NEXT BOOK FROM OUR FAVORITE AUTHOR.
WE CAN WAIT YEARS, EVEN *DECADES.*
AFTER ALL...
SHF
WE LOVE THAT PERSON.
READERS FALL IN LOVE WITH THE WORK AND WITH THE WRITER.
SO PLEASE DON'T SAY ANYTHING SO SAD AS THAT YOU'VE DIED...

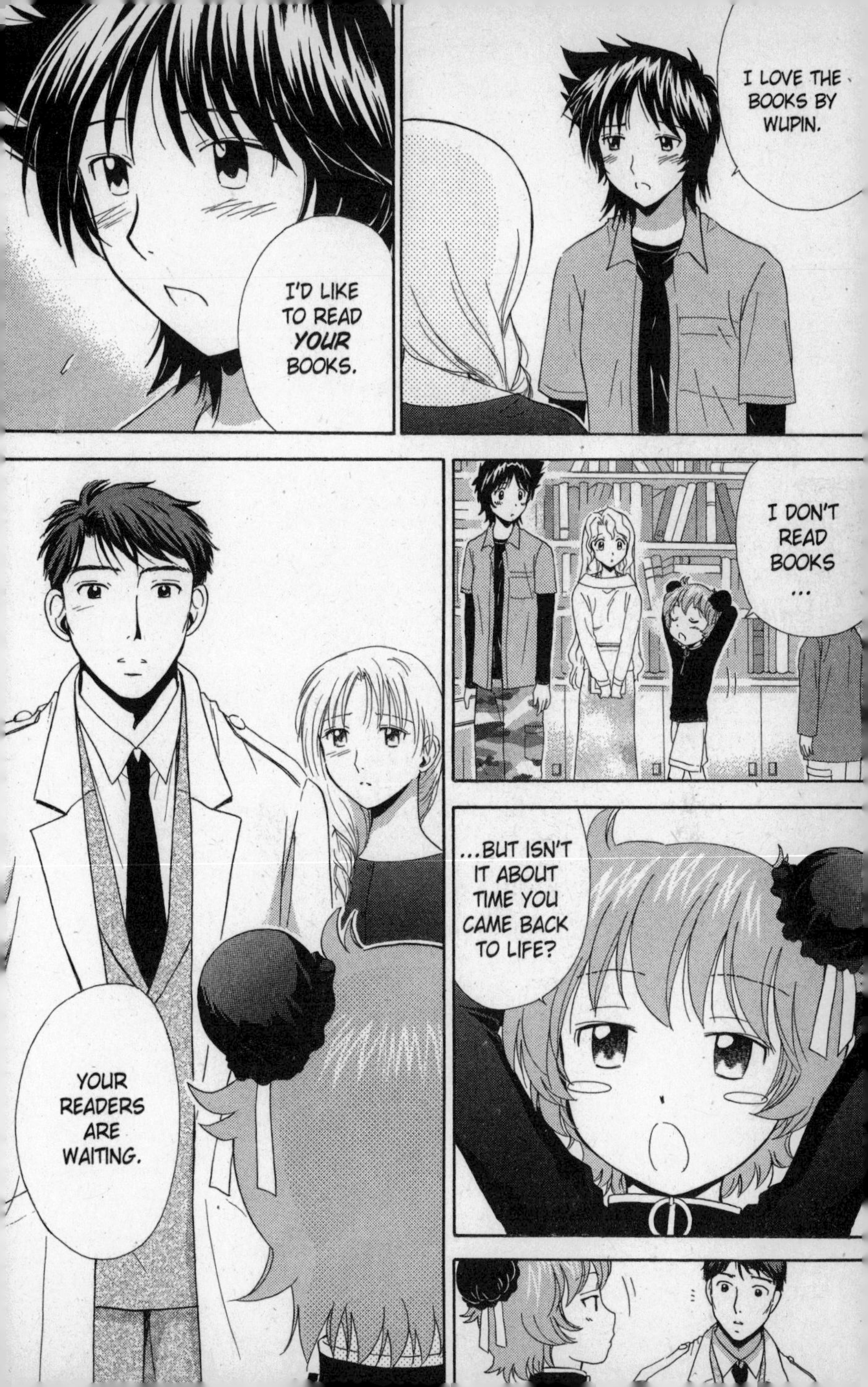
I LOVE THE BOOKS BY WUPIN.
I'D LIKE TO READ *YOUR* BOOKS.
I DON'T READ BOOKS ...
...BUT ISN'T IT ABOUT TIME YOU CAME BACK TO LIFE?
YOUR READERS ARE WAITING.

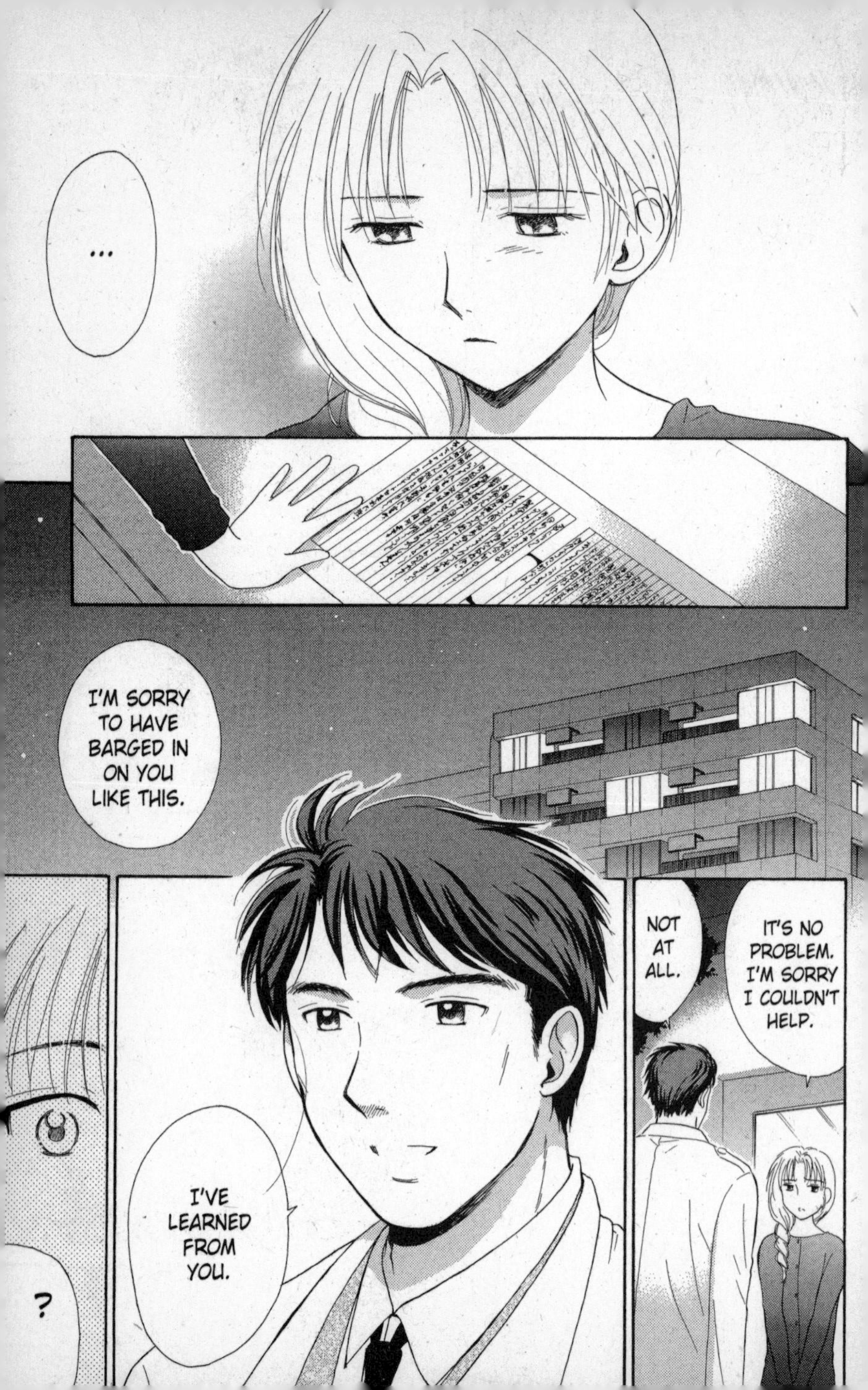
...
I'M SORRY TO HAVE BARGED IN ON YOU LIKE THIS.
IT'S NO PROBLEM. I'M SORRY I COULDN'T HELP.
NOT AT ALL.
I'VE LEARNED FROM YOU.
?

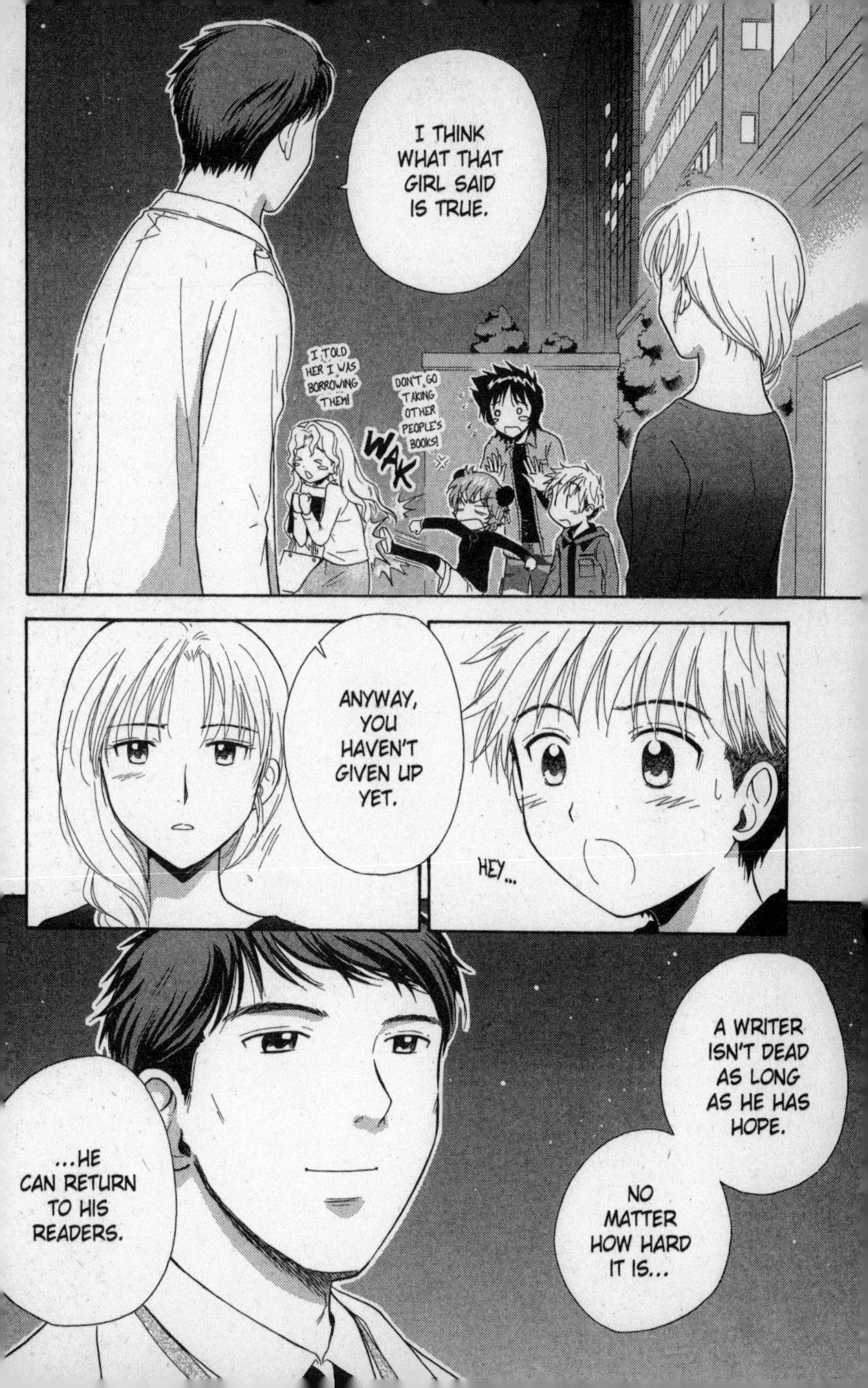
I THINK WHAT THAT GIRL SAID IS TRUE.
DON'T GO TAKING OTHER PEOPLE'S BOOKS!
WAK
I TOLD HER I WAS BORROWING THEM!
HEY...
ANYWAY, YOU HAVEN'T GIVEN UP YET.
A WRITER ISN'T DEAD AS LONG AS HE HAS HOPE.
NO MATTER HOW HARD IT IS...
...HE CAN RETURN TO HIS READERS.

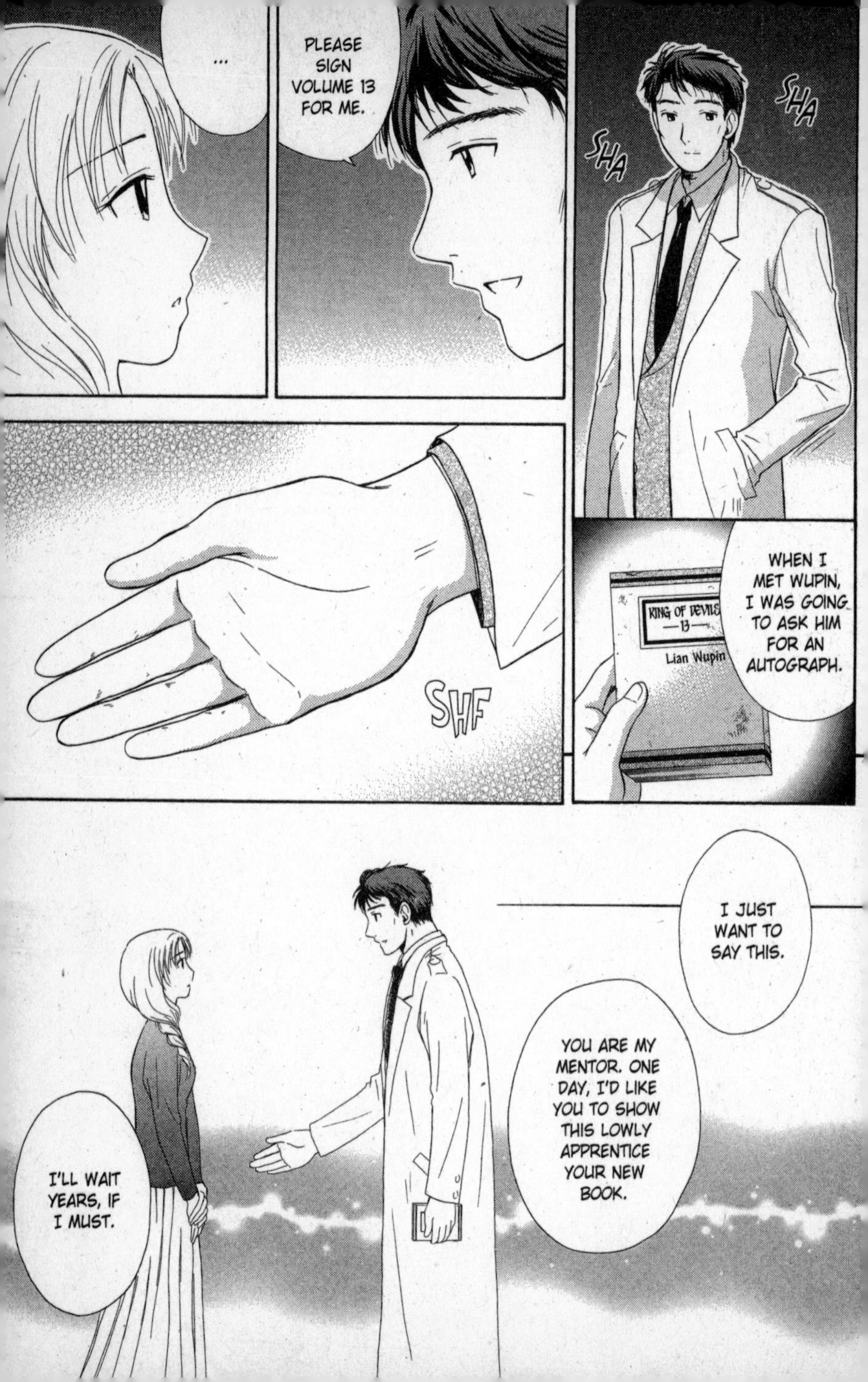
SHA
SHA
PLEASE SIGN VOLUME 13 FOR ME.
...
KING OF DEVILS —13— Lian Wupin
WHEN I MET WUPIN, I WAS GOING TO ASK HIM FOR AN AUTOGRAPH.
SHF
I JUST WANT TO SAY THIS.
YOU ARE MY MENTOR. ONE DAY, I'D LIKE YOU TO SHOW THIS LOWLY APPRENTICE YOUR NEW BOOK.
I'LL WAIT YEARS, IF I MUST.

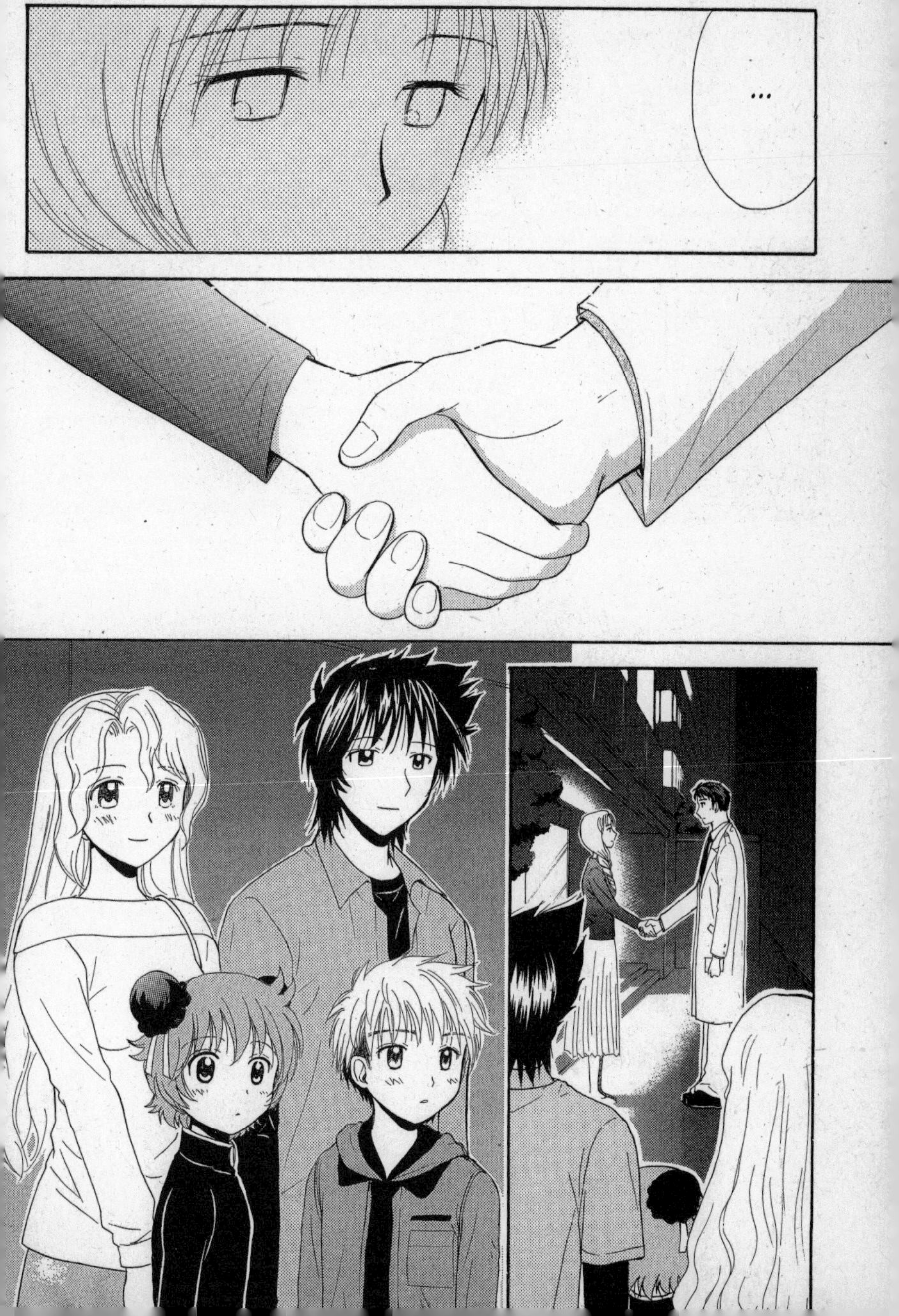
...

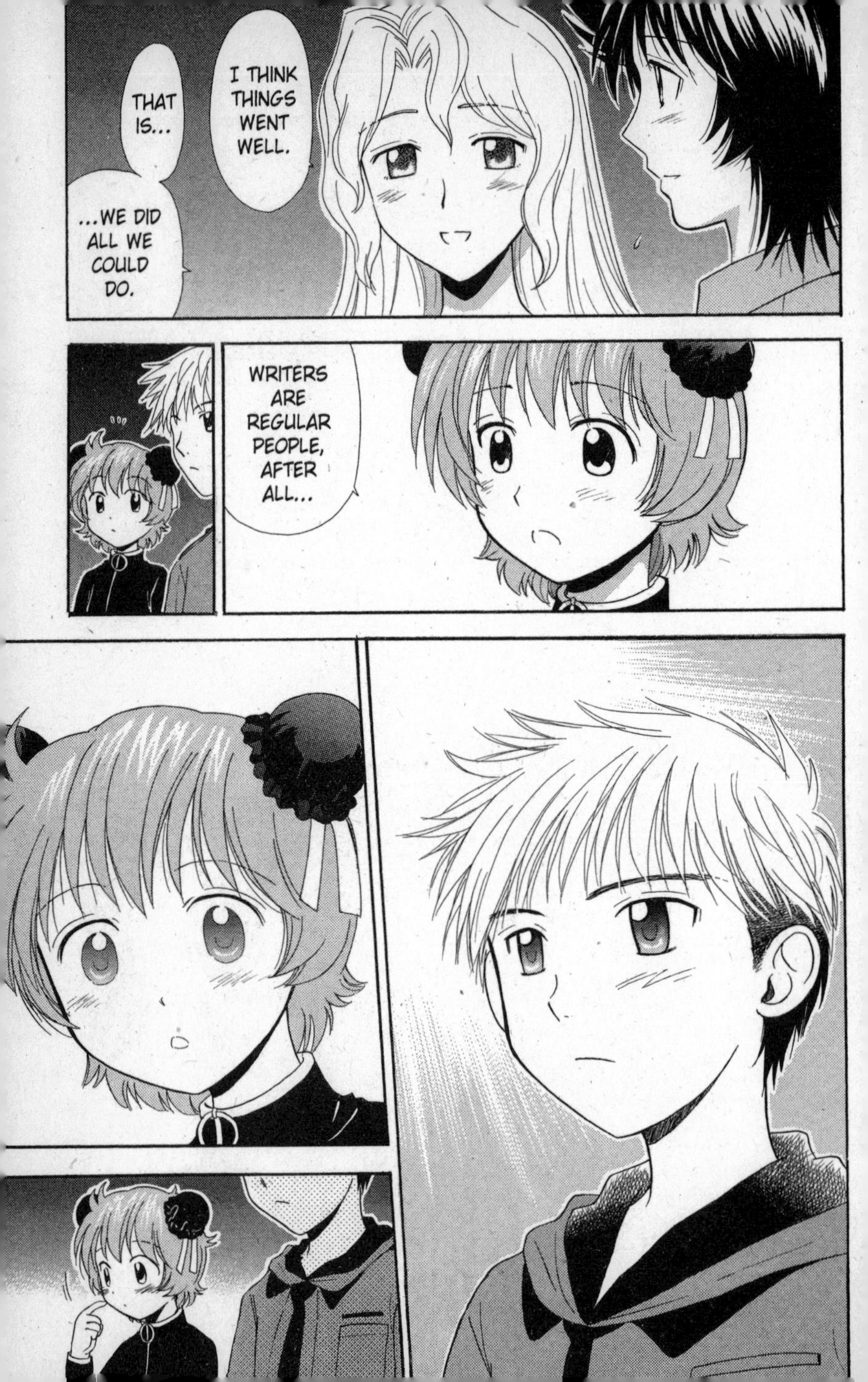
I THINK THINGS WENT WELL.
THAT IS...
...WE DID ALL WE COULD DO.
WRITERS ARE REGULAR PEOPLE, AFTER ALL...

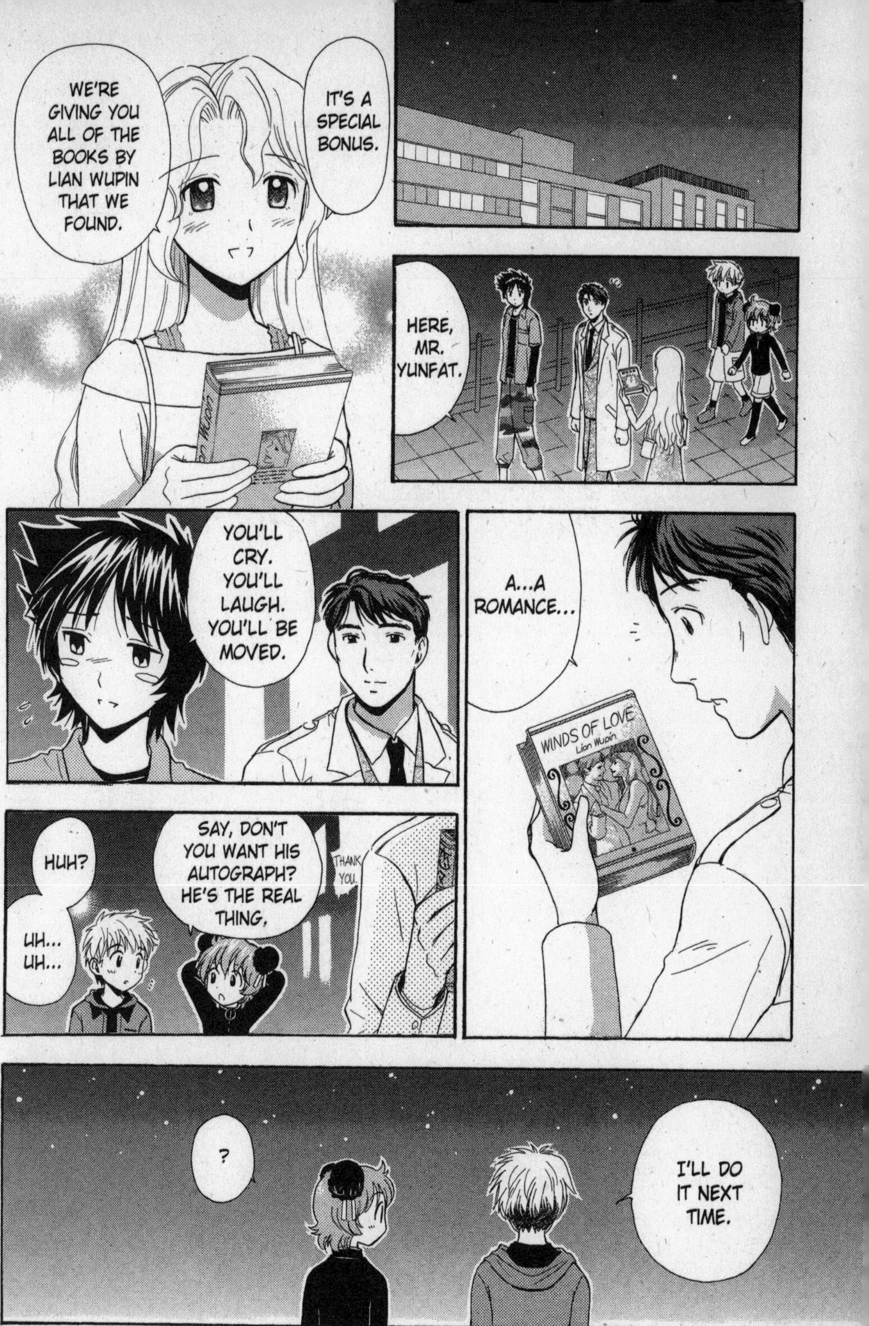
HERE, MR. YUNFAT.
IT'S A SPECIAL BONUS.
WE'RE GIVING YOU ALL OF THE BOOKS BY LIAN WUPIN THAT WE FOUND.
A...A ROMANCE...
WINDS OF LOVE
Lion Wupin
YOU'LL CRY. YOU'LL LAUGH. YOU'LL BE MOVED.
THANK YOU.
SAY, DON'T YOU WANT HIS AUTOGRAPH? HE'S THE REAL THING.
HUH?
UH... UH...
I'LL DO IT NEXT TIME.
?

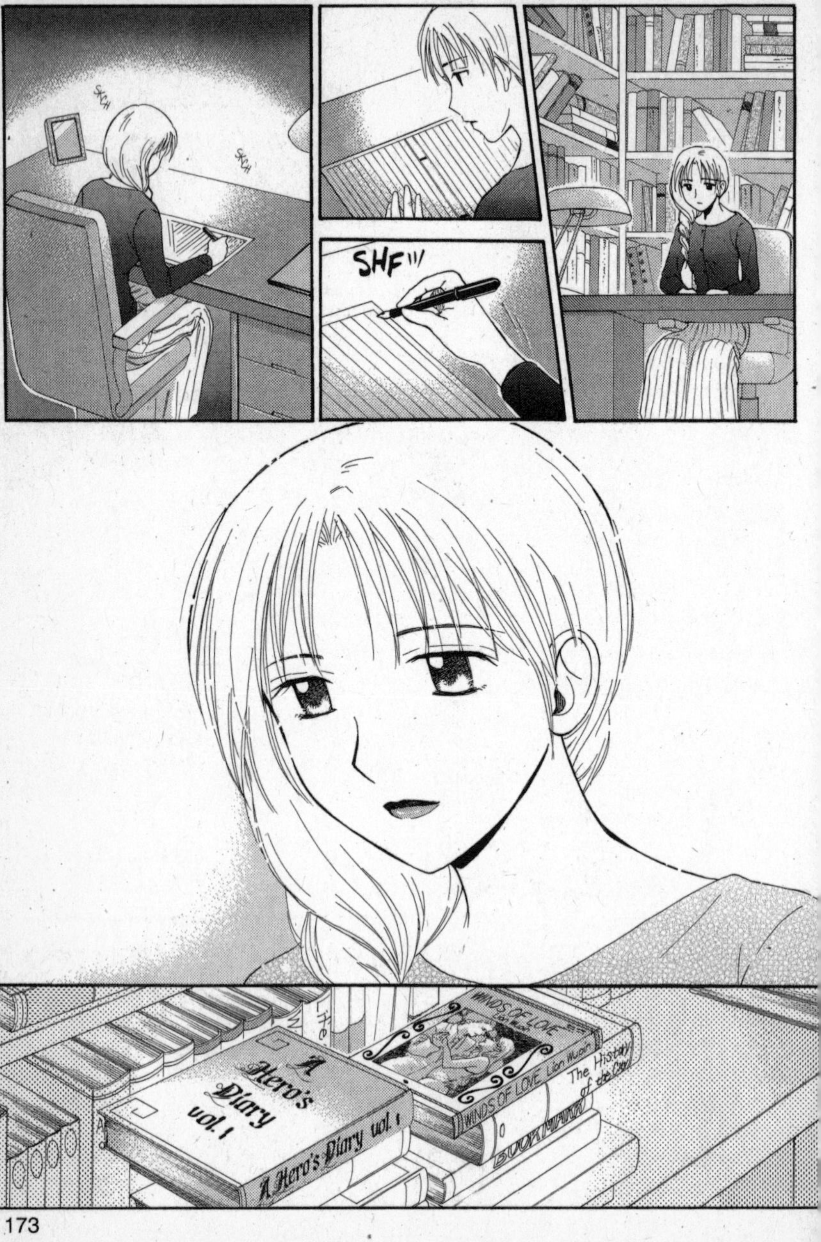
SHF
SKSH
SKSH
Life
A Hero's Diary vol. 1
A Hero's Diary vol. 1
WINDS OF LOVE
WINDS OF LOVE Lion Muan
The History of the City
BOOKMARK

DESERT ISLE ①

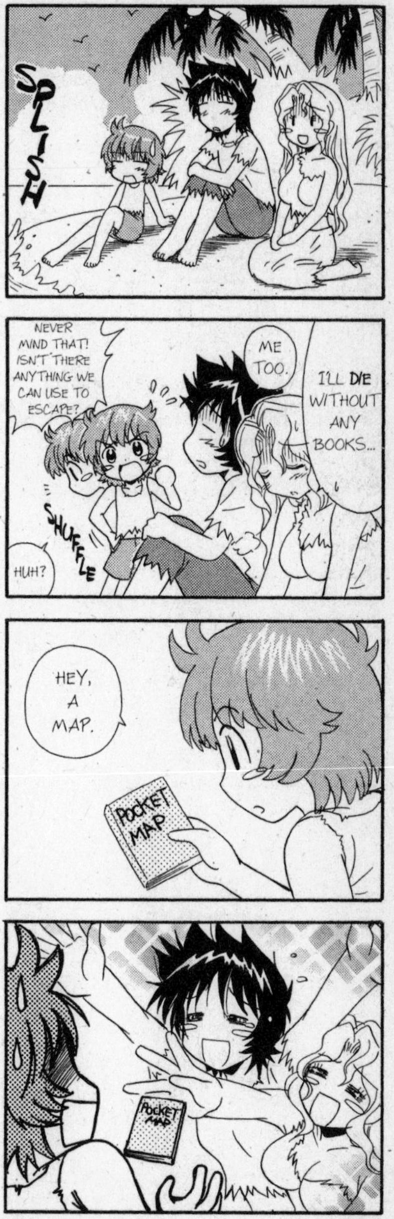
SPLISH
I'LL DIE WITHOUT ANY BOOKS...
ME TOO.
NEVER MIND THAT! ISN'T THERE ANYTHING WE CAN USE TO ESCAPE?
SHUFFLE
HUH?
HEY, A MAP.
POCKET MAP
POCKET MAP

DESERT ISLE ②

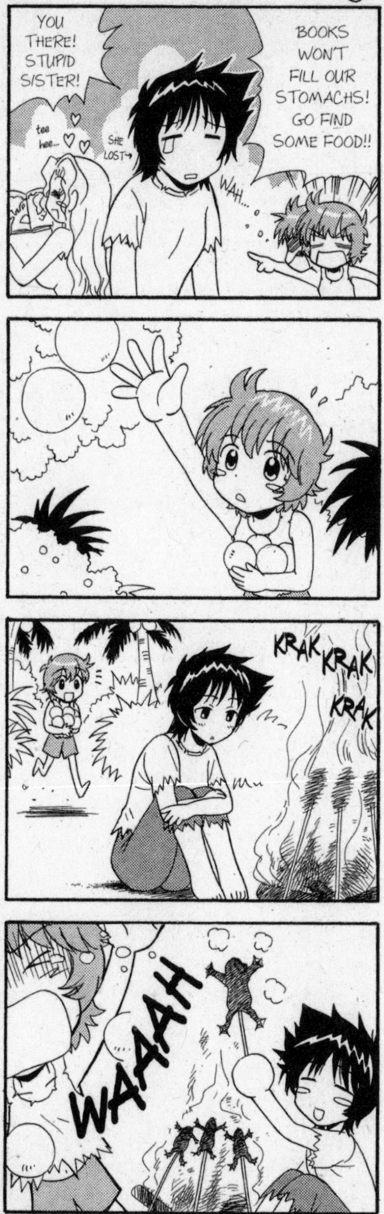
BOOKS WON'T FILL OUR STOMACHS! GO FIND SOME FOOD!!
YOU THERE! STUPID SISTER!
SHE LOST→
WAH...
tee hee...
KRAK KRAK KRAK
WAAAH

THE END

CHAPTER 15

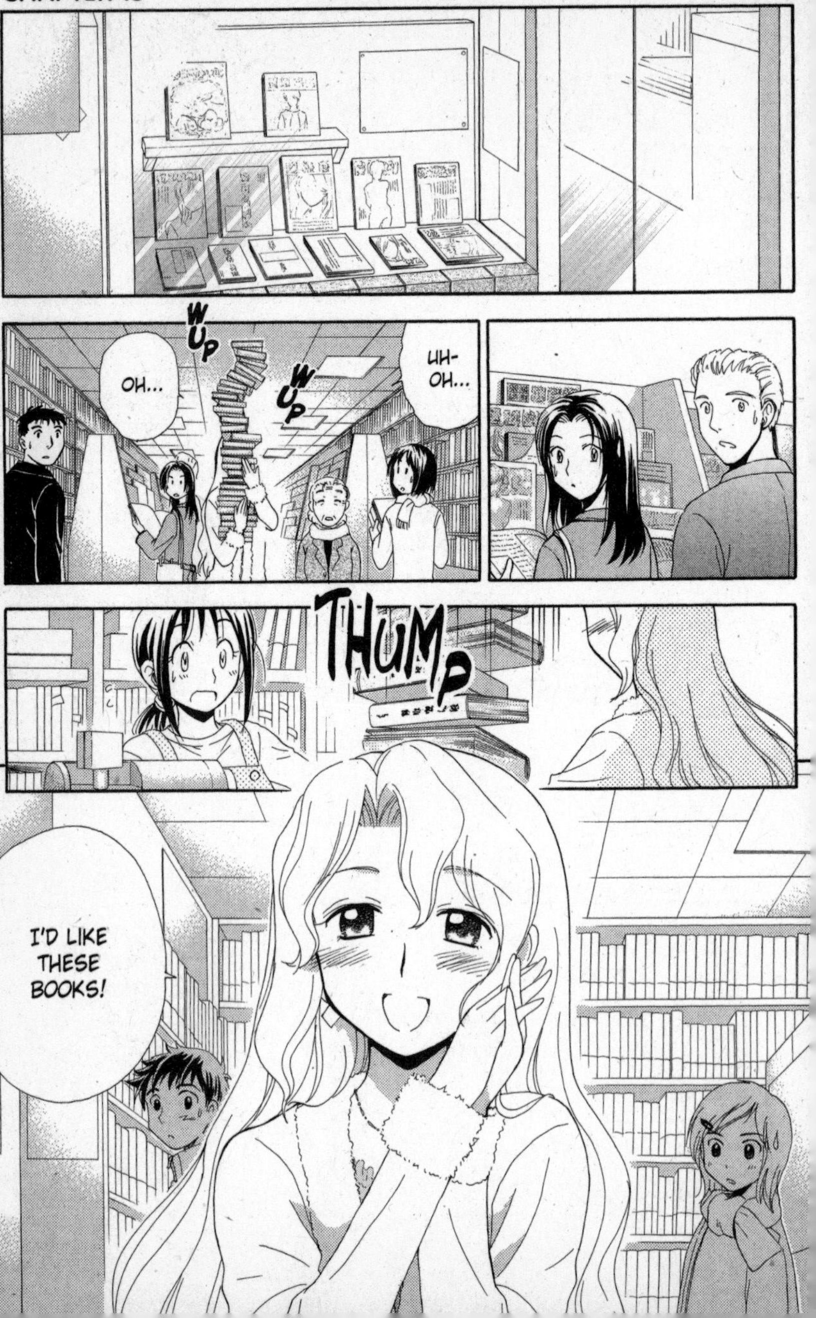
UH-OH...
WUP
WUP
OH...
THUMP
I'D LIKE THESE BOOKS!

CHAPTER 15

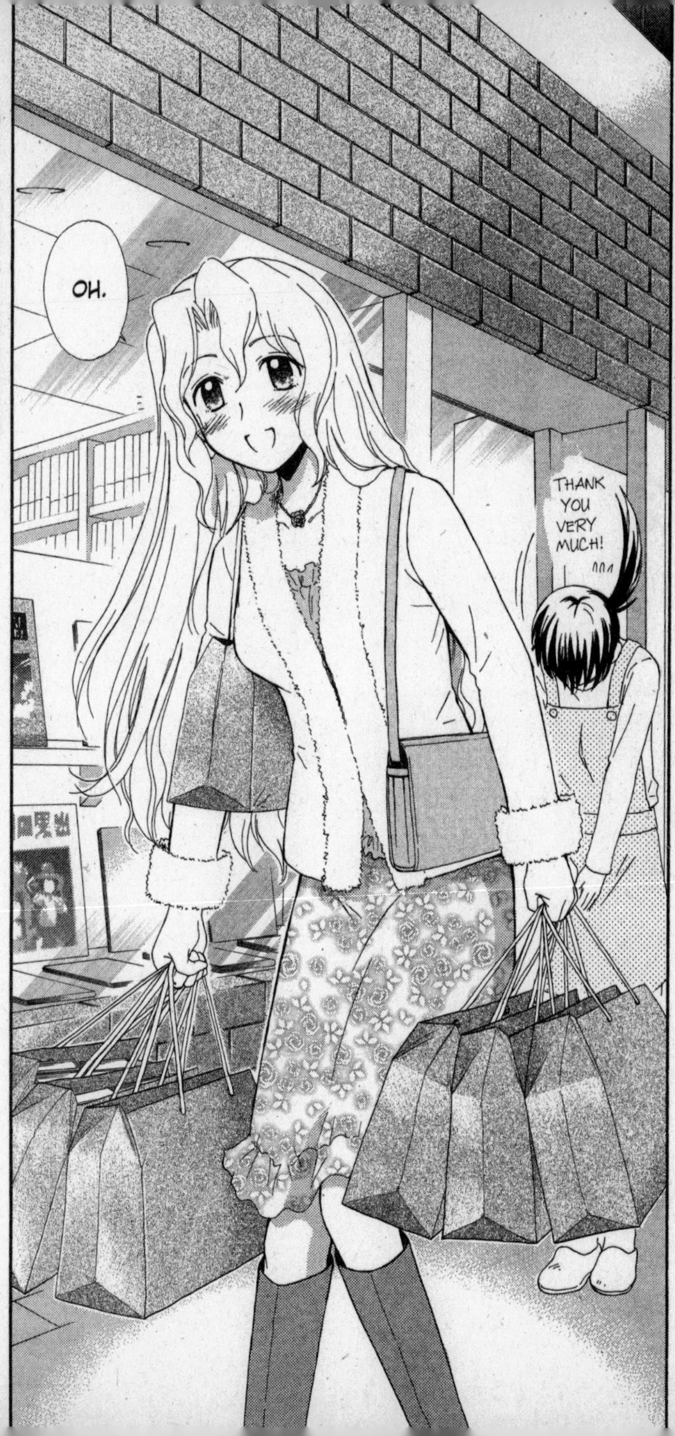
THANK YOU VERY MUCH!
OH.

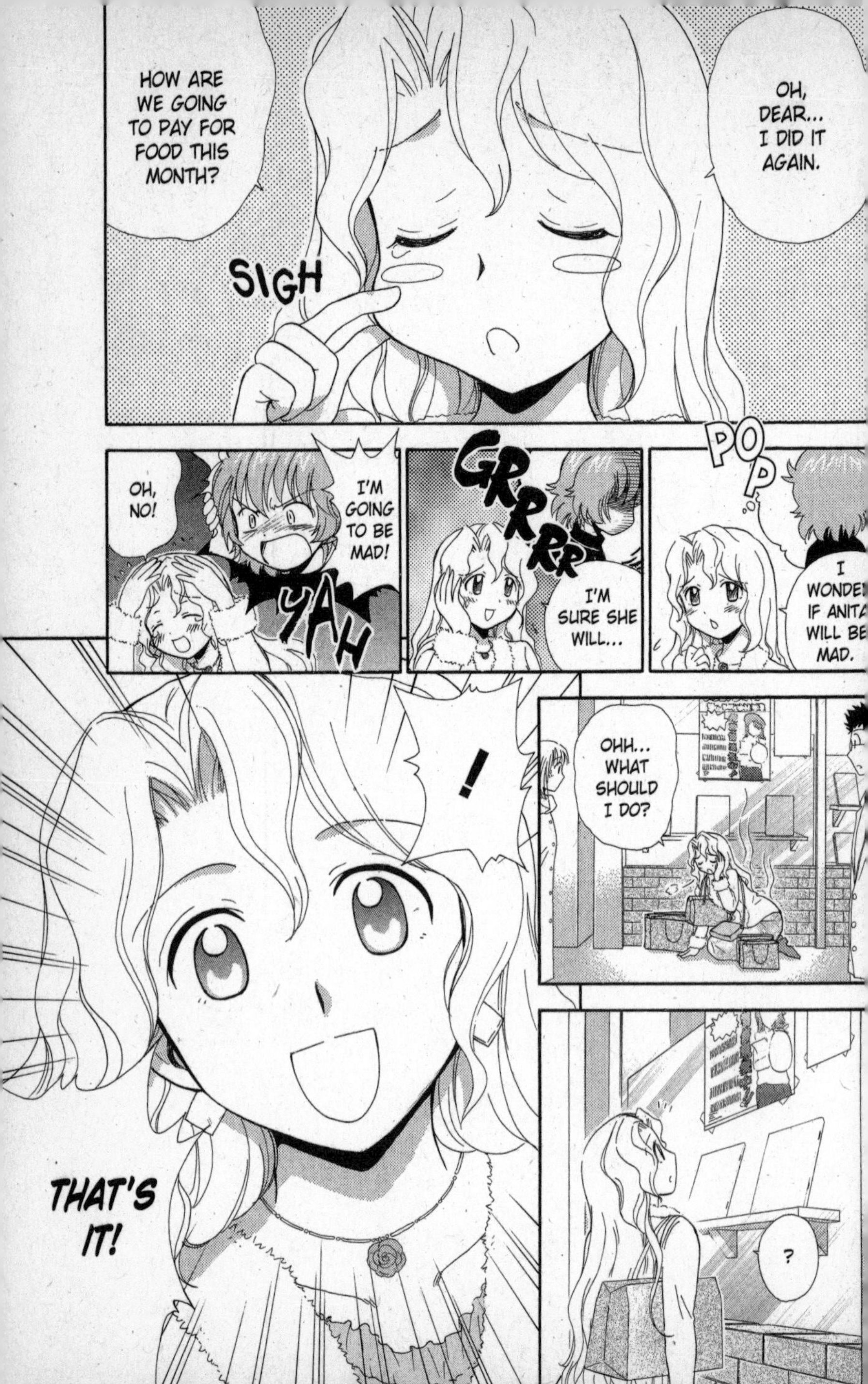
OH, DEAR... I DID IT AGAIN.
HOW ARE WE GOING TO PAY FOR FOOD THIS MONTH?
SIGH
POP
I WONDE IF ANITA WILL BE MAD.
GRRRR
I'M SURE SHE WILL...
I'M GOING TO BE MAD!
OH, NO!
YAH
OHH... WHAT SHOULD I DO?
?
!
THAT'S IT!

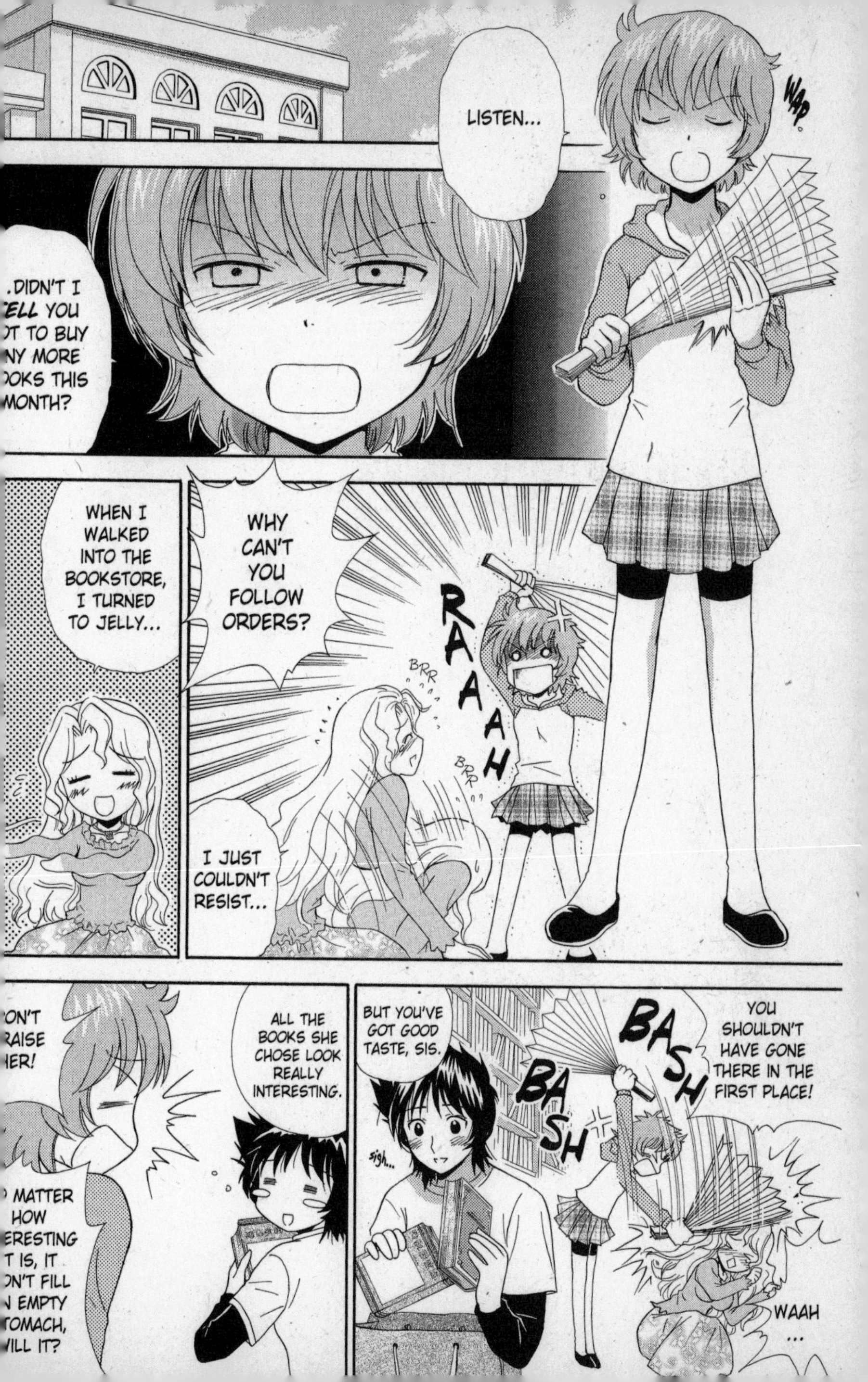
WAP
LISTEN...
.DIDN'T I ELL YOU OT TO BUY NY MORE OOKS THIS MONTH?
WHY CAN'T YOU FOLLOW ORDERS?
RAAAAH
BRR
BRR
I JUST COULDN'T RESIST...
WHEN I WALKED INTO THE BOOKSTORE, I TURNED TO JELLY...
BASH
BASH
YOU SHOULDN'T HAVE GONE THERE IN THE FIRST PLACE!
WAAH ...
BUT YOU'VE GOT GOOD TASTE, SIS.
sigh...
ALL THE BOOKS SHE CHOSE LOOK REALLY INTERESTING.
ON'T RAISE HER!
MATTER HOW ERESTING T IS, IT ON'T FILL N EMPTY TOMACH, ILL IT?

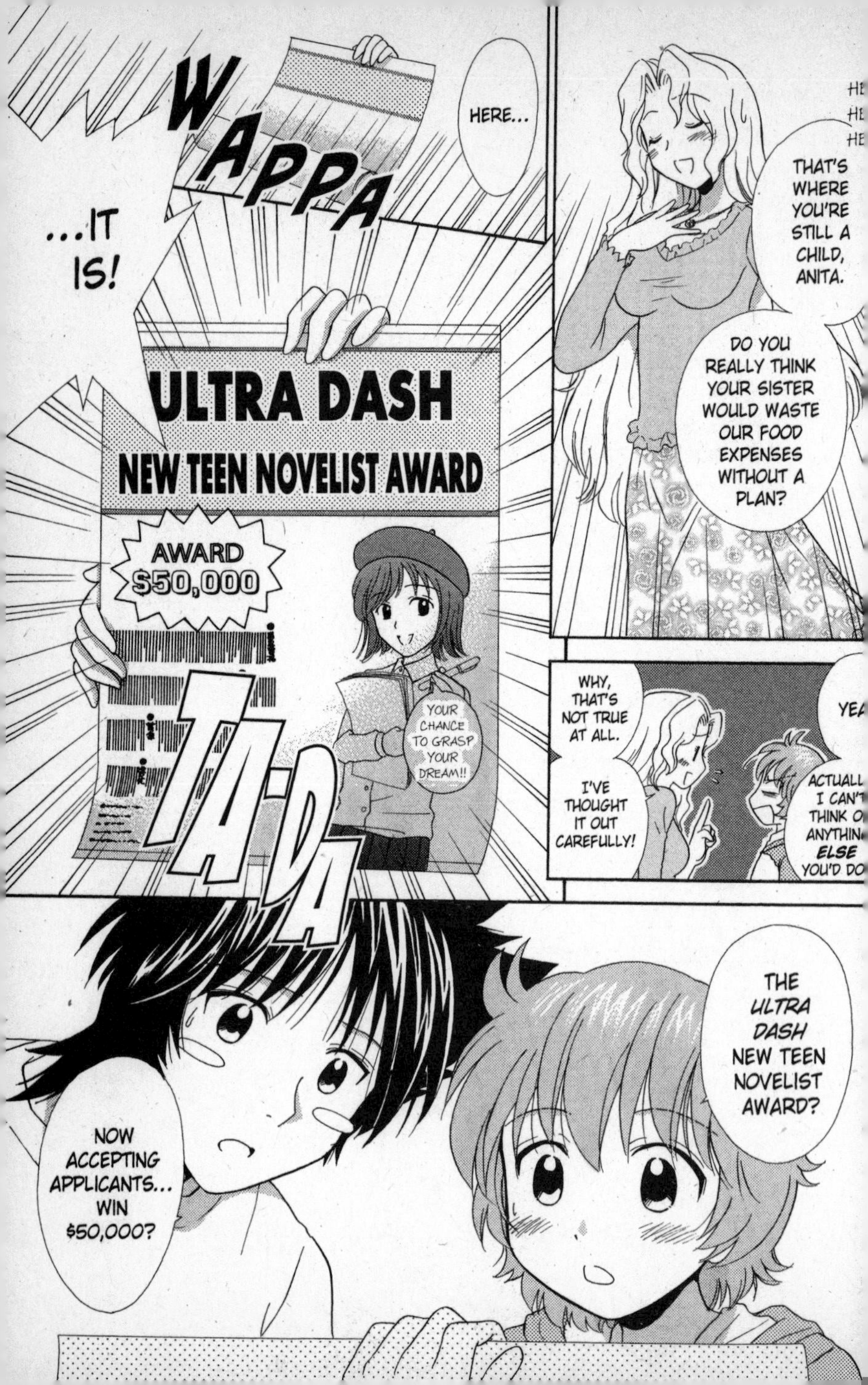
HE
HE
HE
THAT'S WHERE YOU'RE STILL A CHILD, ANITA.
DO YOU REALLY THINK YOUR SISTER WOULD WASTE OUR FOOD EXPENSES WITHOUT A PLAN?
YEA
ACTUALL I CAN'T THINK O ANYTHIN *ELSE* YOU'D DO
WHY, THAT'S NOT TRUE AT ALL.
I'VE THOUGHT IT OUT CAREFULLY!
HERE...
WAPPA
...IT IS!
ULTRA DASH
NEW TEEN NOVELIST AWARD
AWARD $50,000
YOUR CHANCE TO GRASP YOUR DREAM!!
TA-DA
THE *ULTRA DASH* NEW TEEN NOVELIST AWARD?
NOW ACCEPTING APPLICANTS... WIN $50,000?

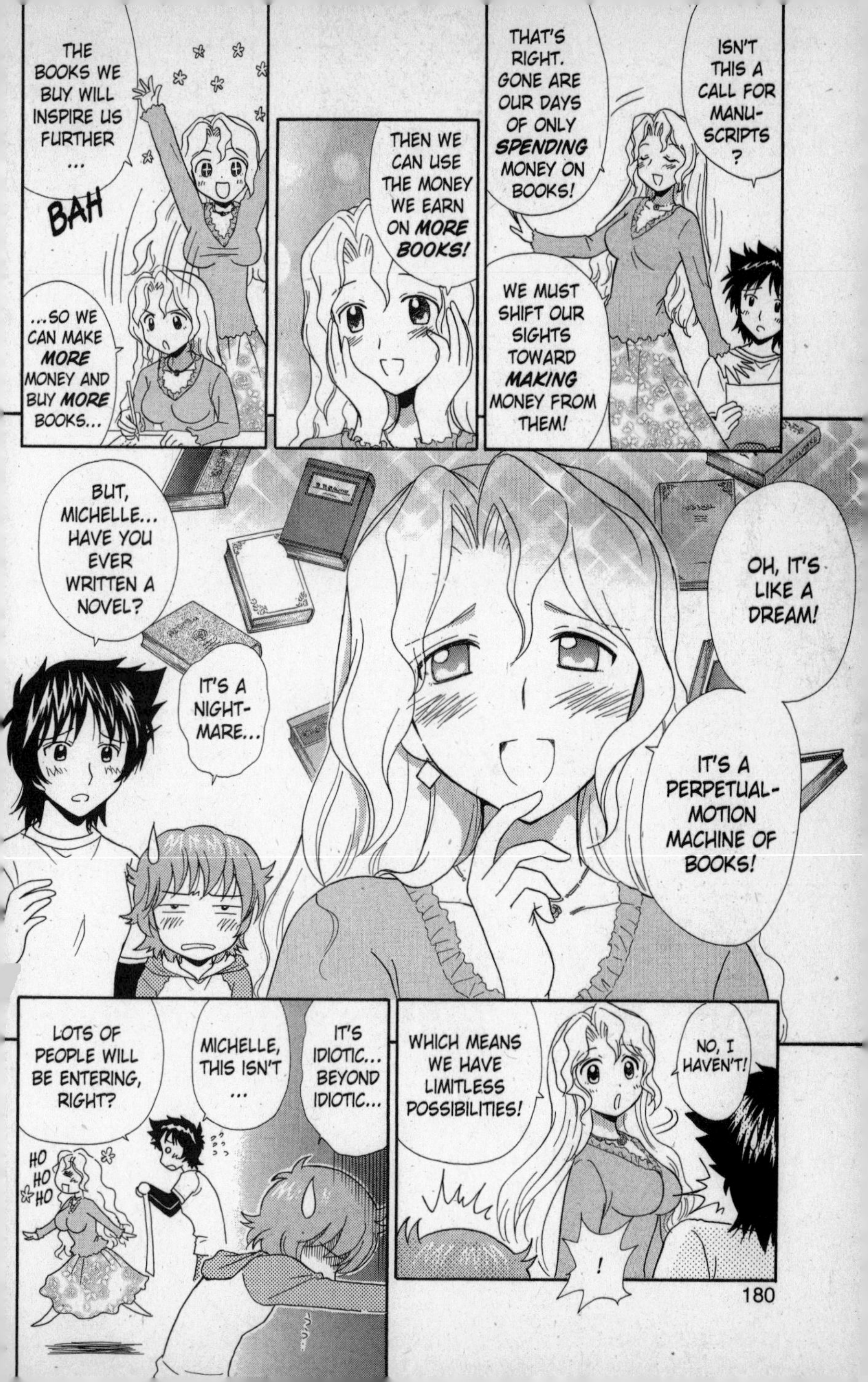
ISN'T THIS A CALL FOR MANU-SCRIPTS?
THAT'S RIGHT. GONE ARE OUR DAYS OF ONLY SPENDING MONEY ON BOOKS!
WE MUST SHIFT OUR SIGHTS TOWARD MAKING MONEY FROM THEM!
THEN WE CAN USE THE MONEY WE EARN ON MORE BOOKS!
THE BOOKS WE BUY WILL INSPIRE US FURTHER...
BAH
...SO WE CAN MAKE MORE MONEY AND BUY MORE BOOKS...
OH, IT'S LIKE A DREAM!
IT'S A PERPETUAL-MOTION MACHINE OF BOOKS!
IT'S A NIGHT-MARE...
BUT, MICHELLE... HAVE YOU EVER WRITTEN A NOVEL?
NO, I HAVEN'T!
WHICH MEANS WE HAVE LIMITLESS POSSIBILITIES!
!
IT'S IDIOTIC... BEYOND IDIOTIC...
MICHELLE, THIS ISN'T...
LOTS OF PEOPLE WILL BE ENTERING, RIGHT?
HO HO HO

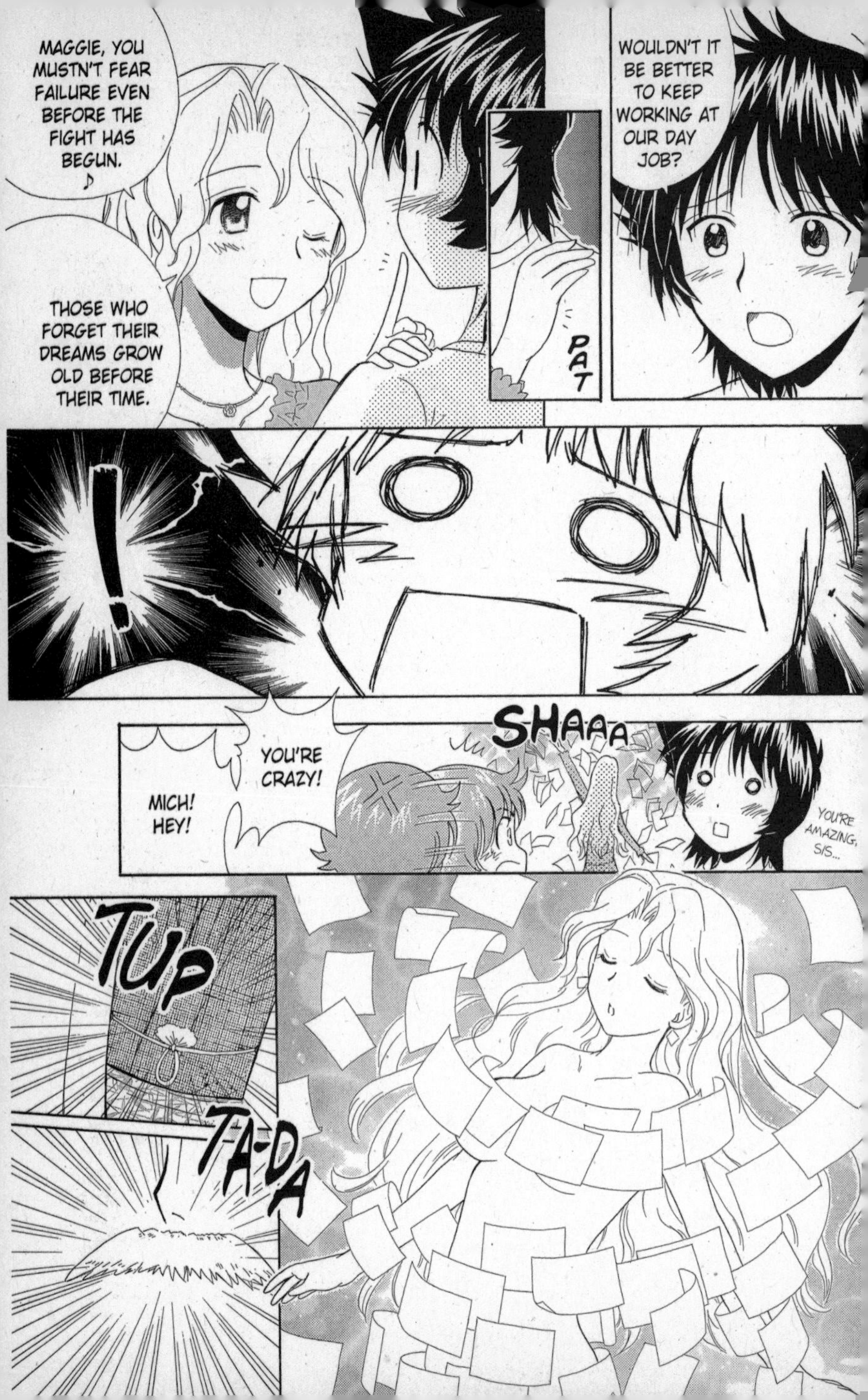
WOULDN'T IT BE BETTER TO KEEP WORKING AT OUR DAY JOB?
PAT
MAGGIE, YOU MUSTN'T FEAR FAILURE EVEN BEFORE THE FIGHT HAS BEGUN. ♪
THOSE WHO FORGET THEIR DREAMS GROW OLD BEFORE THEIR TIME.
!
YOU'RE AMAZING, SIS...
SHAAA
YOU'RE CRAZY!
MICH! HEY!
TUP
TA-DA

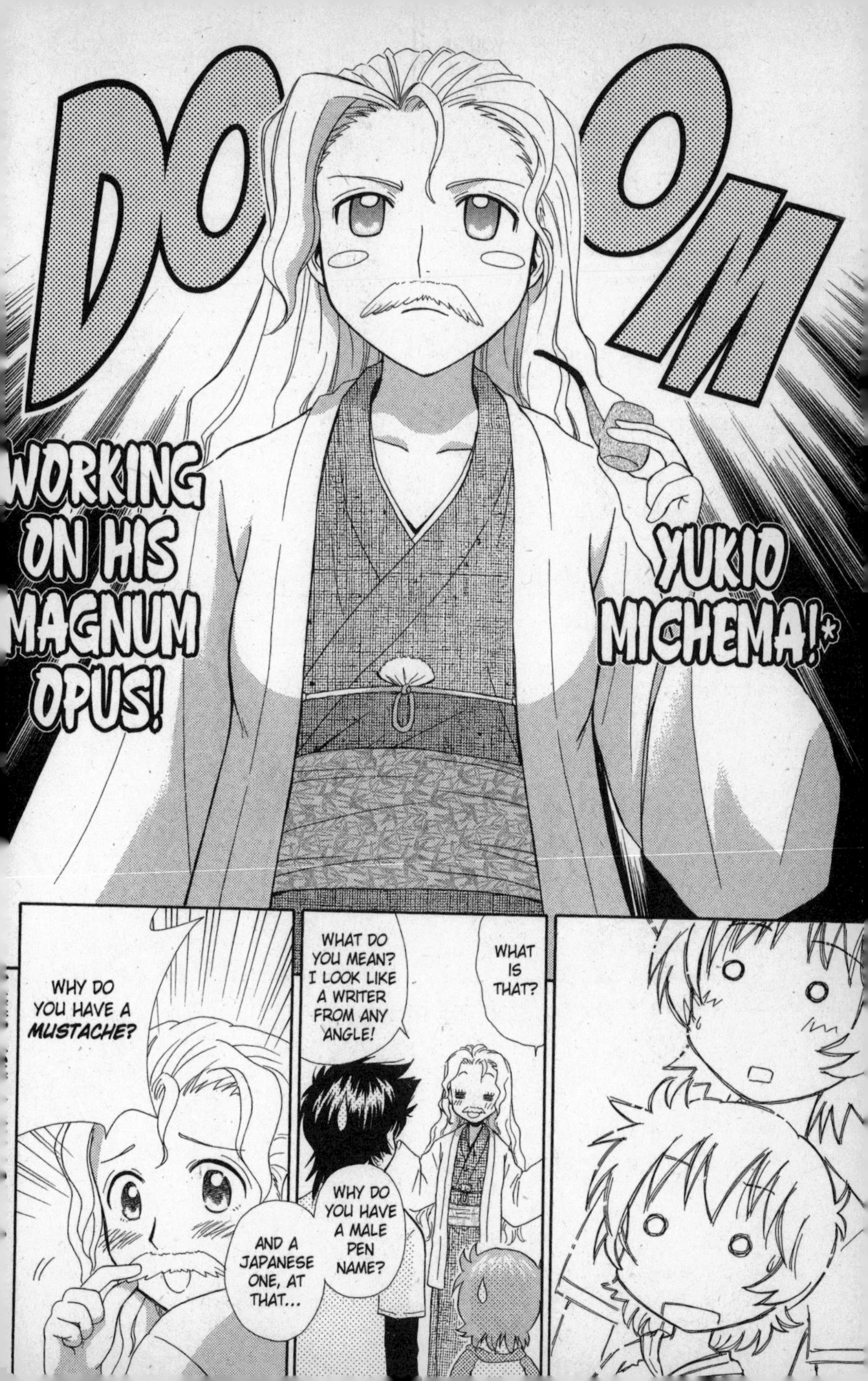
DOOM
YUKIO MICHEMA!*
WORKING ON HIS MAGNUM OPUS!
WHAT IS THAT?
WHAT DO YOU MEAN? I LOOK LIKE A WRITER FROM ANY ANGLE!
WHY DO YOU HAVE A MALE PEN NAME?
AND A JAPANESE ONE, AT THAT...
WHY DO YOU HAVE A *MUSTACHE?*

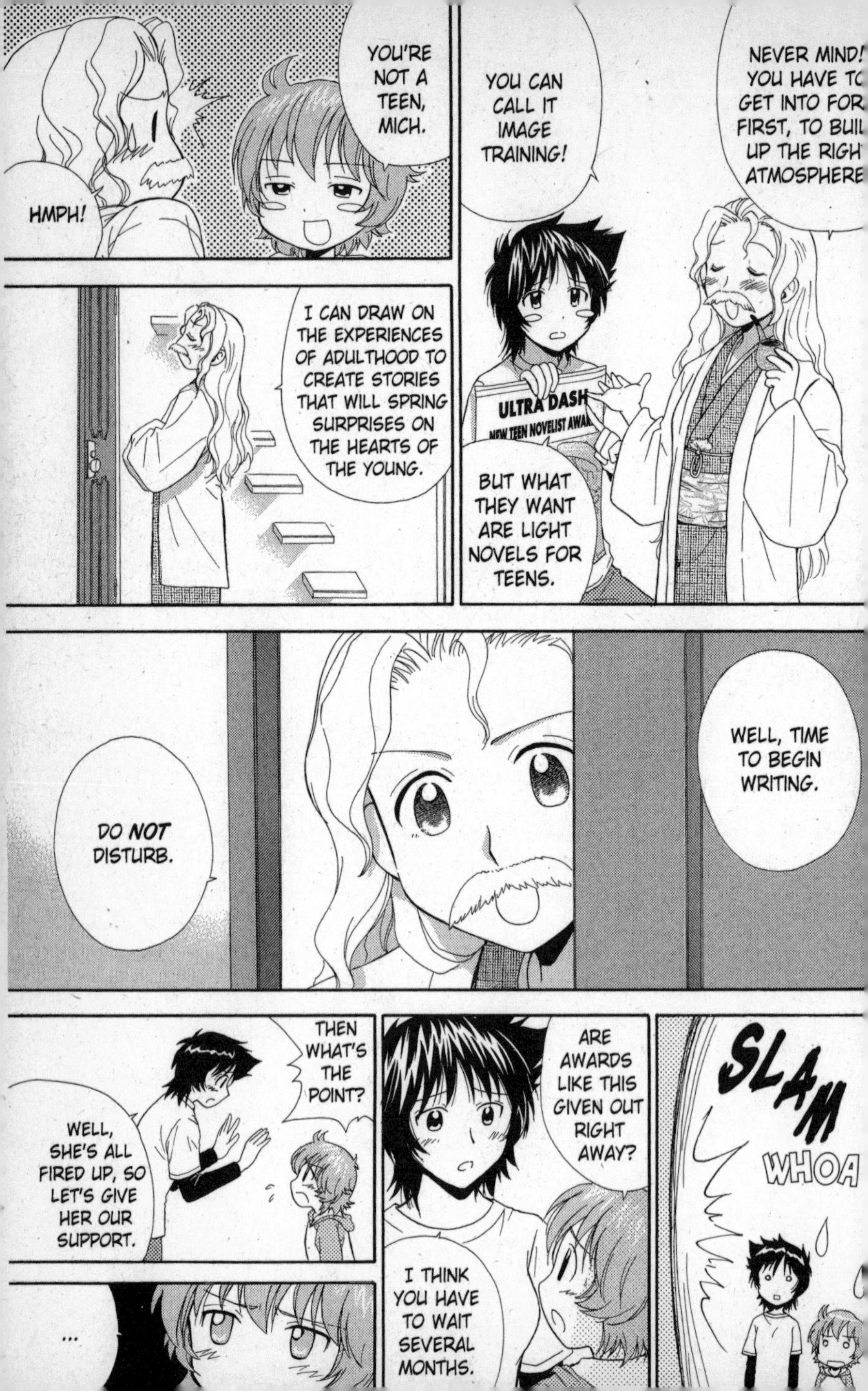
NEVER MIND! YOU HAVE T GET INTO FOR FIRST, TO BUIL UP THE RIGH ATMOSPHERE
YOU CAN CALL IT IMAGE TRAINING!
ULTRA DASH
NEW TEEN NOVELIST AWA
BUT WHAT THEY WANT ARE LIGHT NOVELS FOR TEENS.
YOU'RE NOT A TEEN, MICH.
HMPH!
I CAN DRAW ON THE EXPERIENCES OF ADULTHOOD TO CREATE STORIES THAT WILL SPRING SURPRISES ON THE HEARTS OF THE YOUNG.
WELL, TIME TO BEGIN WRITING.
DO *NOT* DISTURB.
SLAM
WHOA
ARE AWARDS LIKE THIS GIVEN OUT RIGHT AWAY?
I THINK YOU HAVE TO WAIT SEVERAL MONTHS.
THEN WHAT'S THE POINT?
WELL, SHE'S ALL FIRED UP, SO LET'S GIVE HER OUR SUPPORT.
...

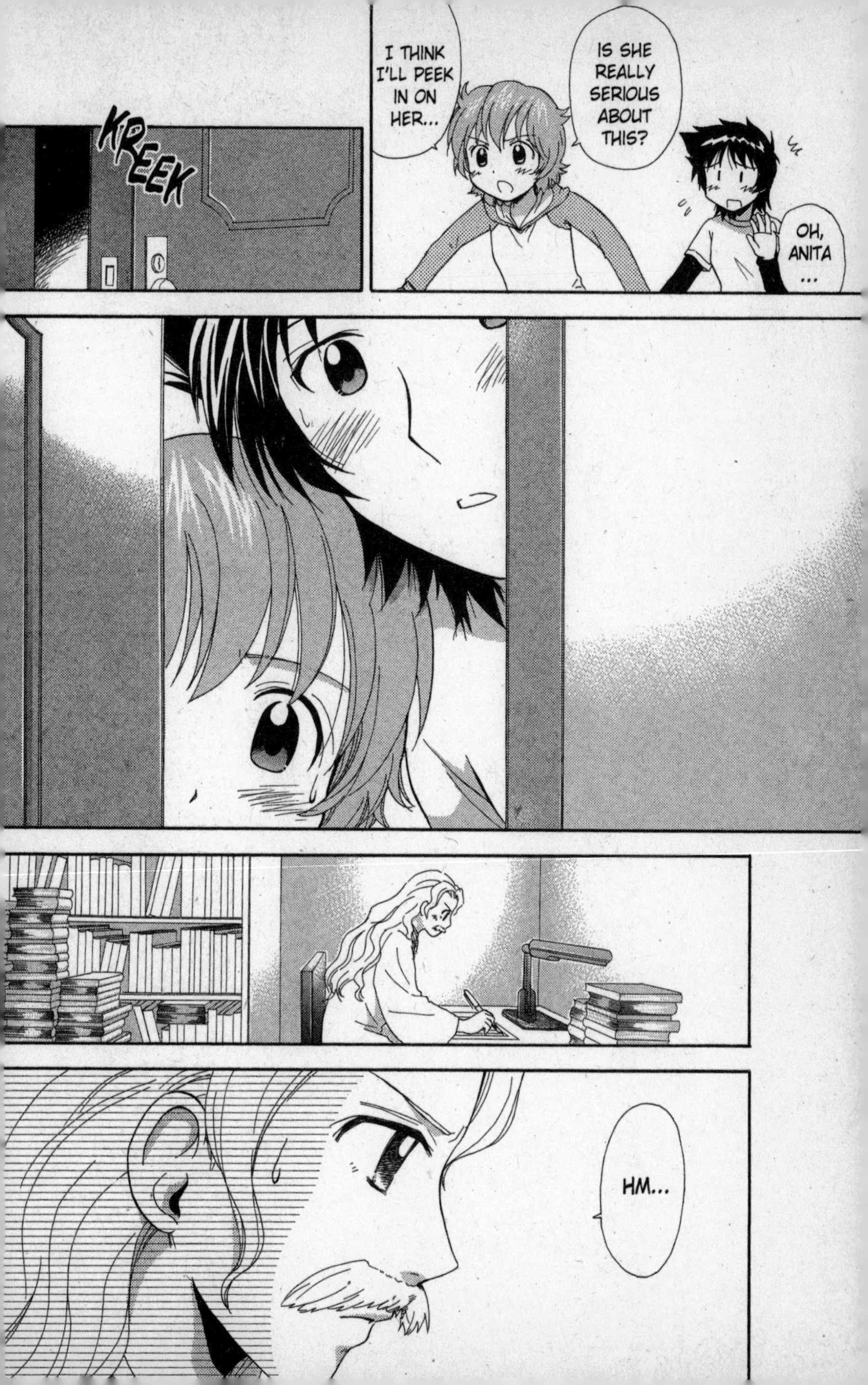
IS SHE REALLY SERIOUS ABOUT THIS?
OH, ANITA ...
I THINK I'LL PEEK IN ON HER...
KREEK
HM...

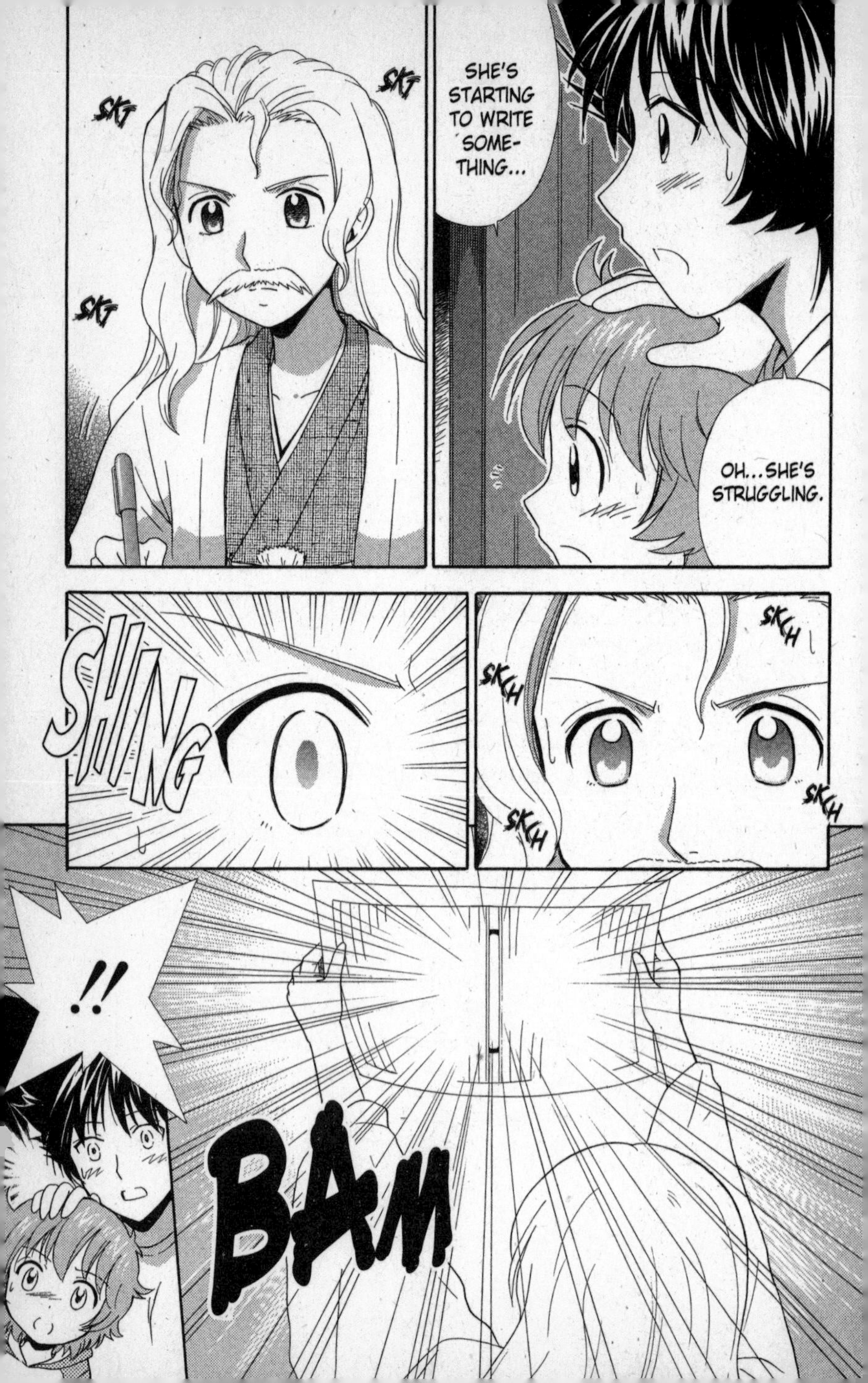
SHE'S STARTING TO WRITE SOME-THING...
OH...SHE'S STRUGGLING.
SKT
SKT
SKT
SKCH
SKCH
SKCH
SKCH
SHING
!!
BAM

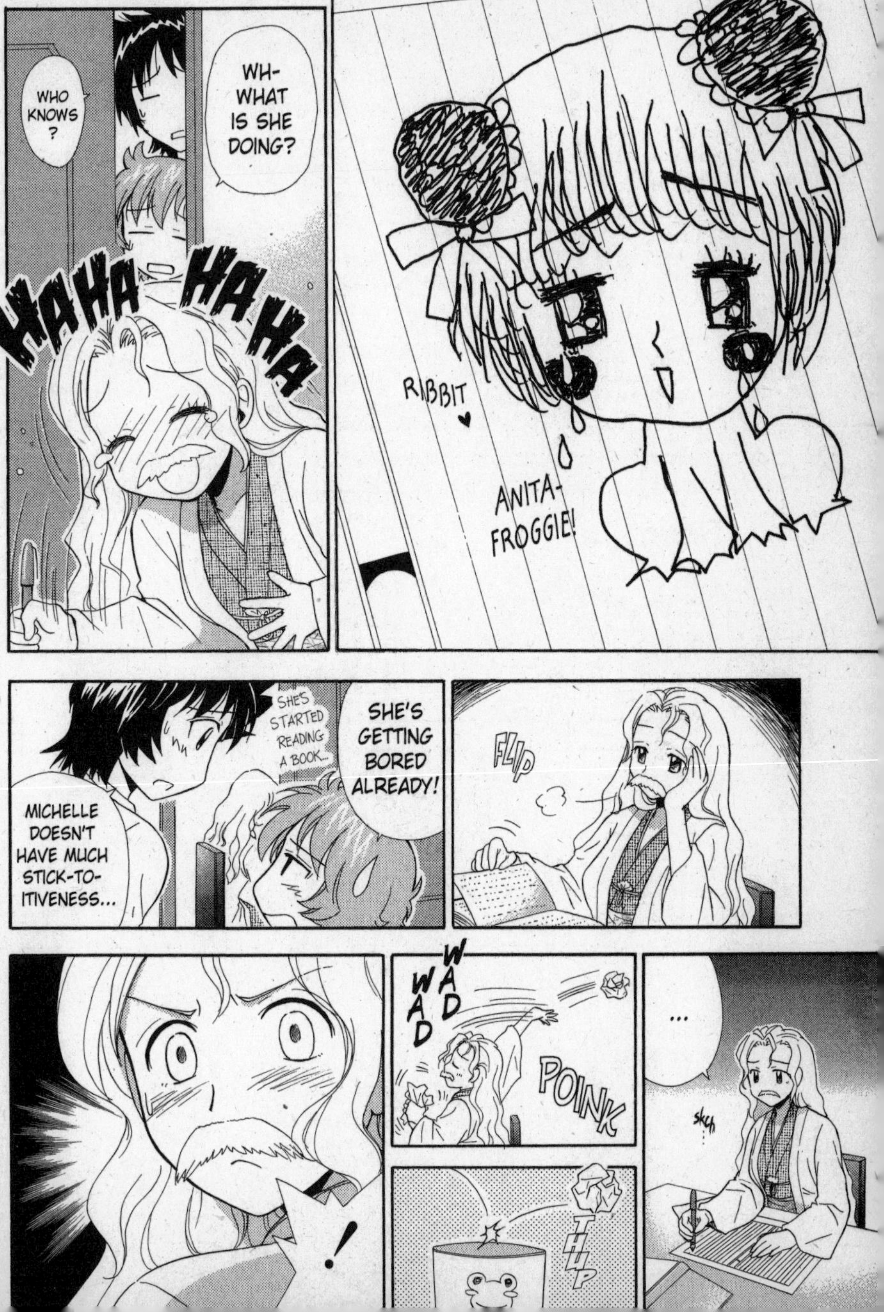
RIBBIT ♥
ANITA-FROGGIE!
WH-WHAT IS SHE DOING?
WHO KNOWS?
HAHA HAHAHA
FLIP
SHE'S GETTING BORED ALREADY!
SHE'S STARTED READING A BOOK...
MICHELLE DOESN'T HAVE MUCH STICK-TO-ITIVENESS...
...
skch
WAD WAD
POINK
THUP
!

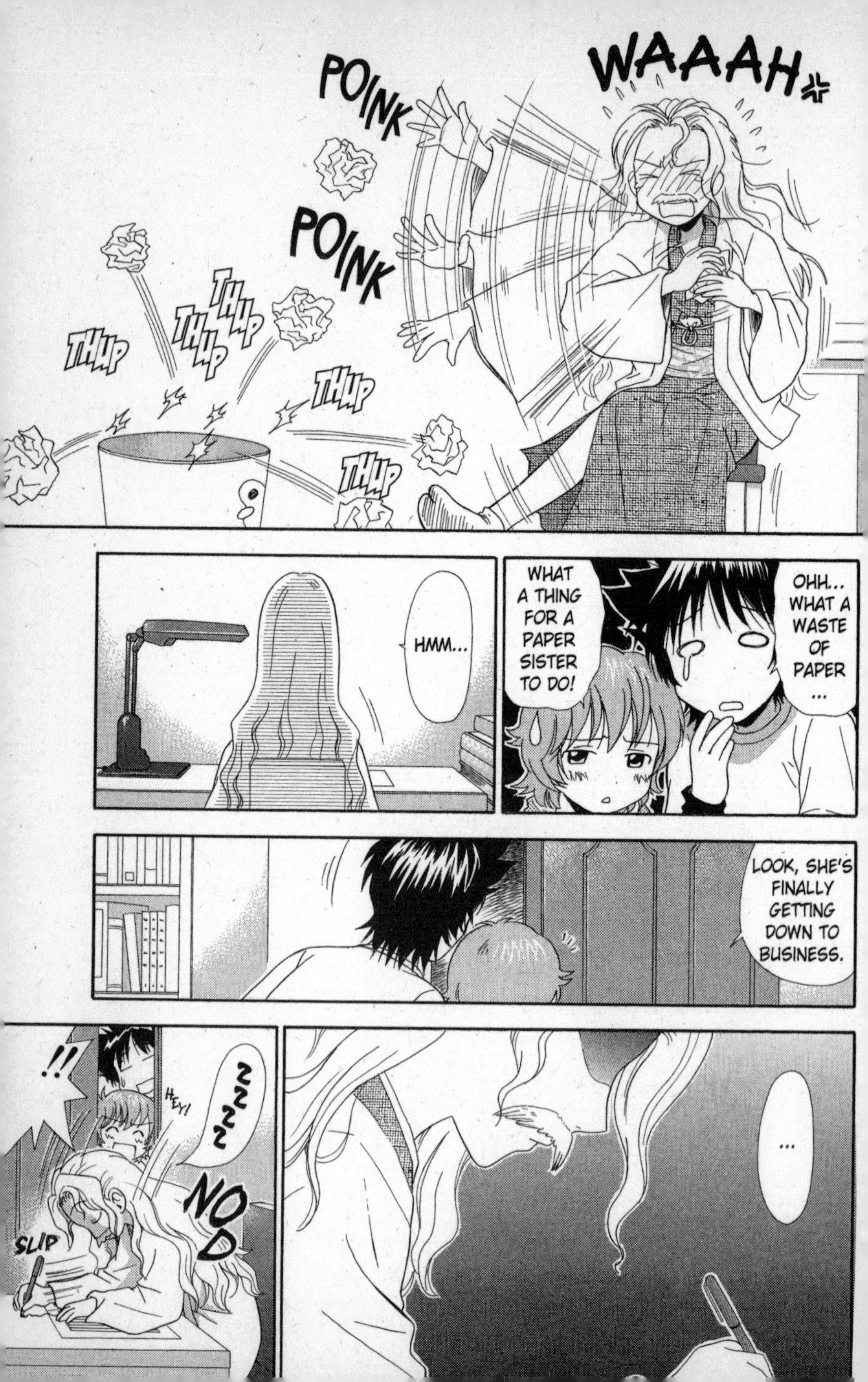
WAAAH
POINK
POINK
THUP
THUP
THUP
THUP
THUP
OHH... WHAT A WASTE OF PAPER ...
WHAT A THING FOR A PAPER SISTER TO DO!
HMM...
LOOK, SHE'S FINALLY GETTING DOWN TO BUSINESS.
...
!!
HEY!
ZZZZ
NOD
SLIP

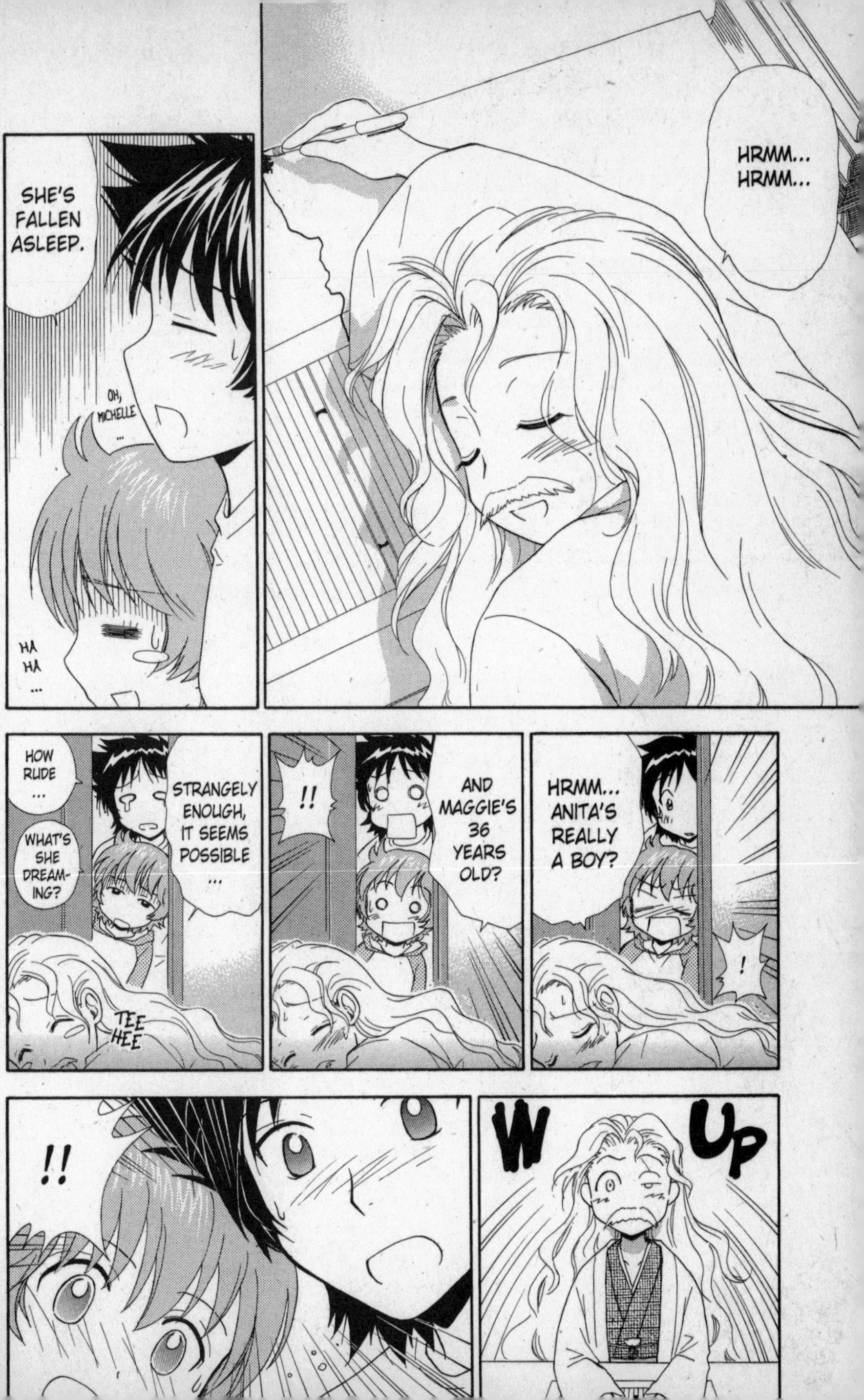
HRMM... HRMM...
SHE'S FALLEN ASLEEP.
OH, MICHELLE ...
HA HA ...
HRMM... ANITA'S REALLY A BOY?
!
AND MAGGIE'S 36 YEARS OLD?
!!
STRANGELY ENOUGH, IT SEEMS POSSIBLE ...
HOW RUDE ...
WHAT'S SHE DREAMING?
TEE HEE
W UP
!!

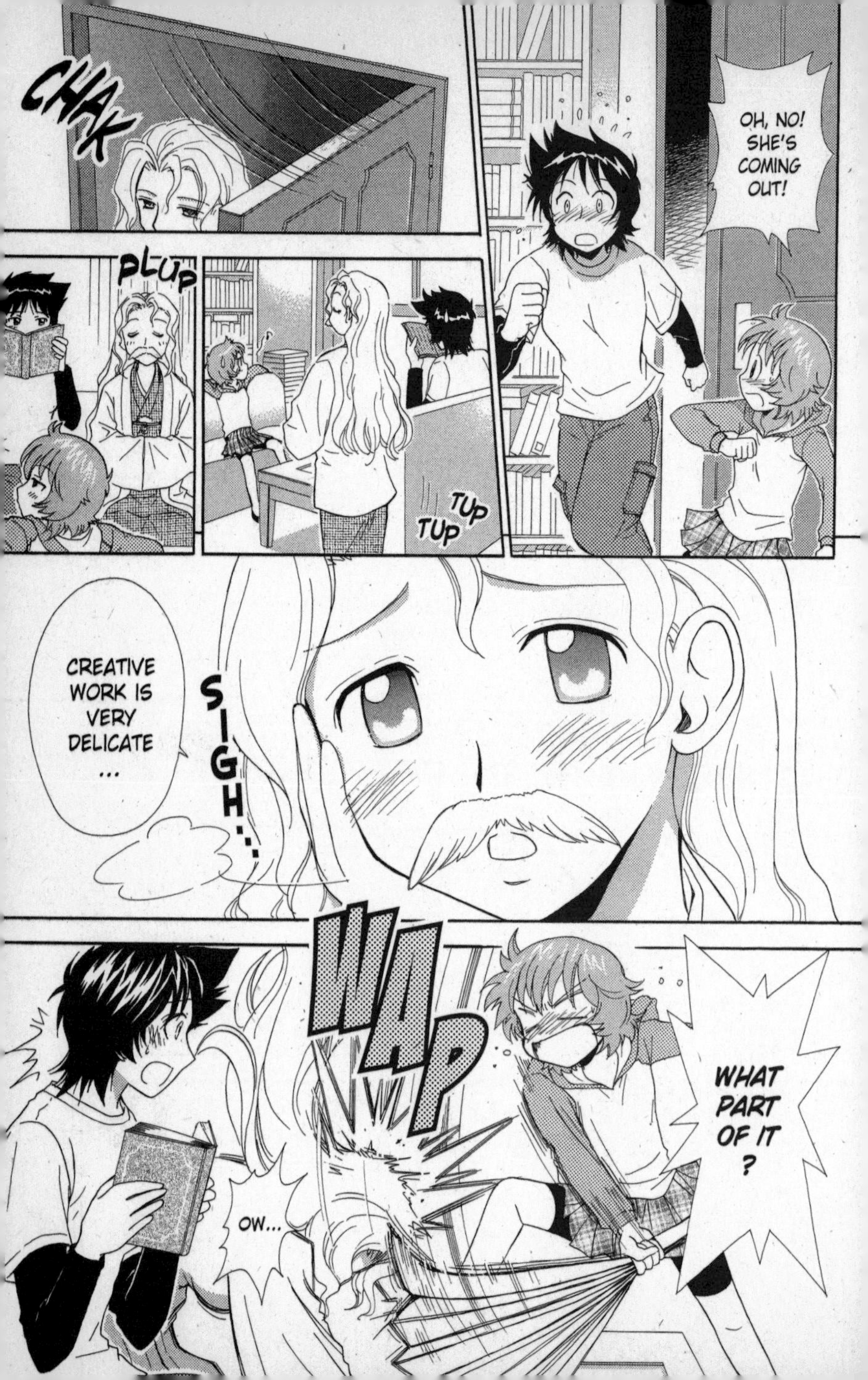
OH, NO! SHE'S COMING OUT!
CHAK
TUP TUP
PLUP
SIGH...
CREATIVE WORK IS VERY DELICATE ...
WHAT PART OF IT ?
WAP
OW...

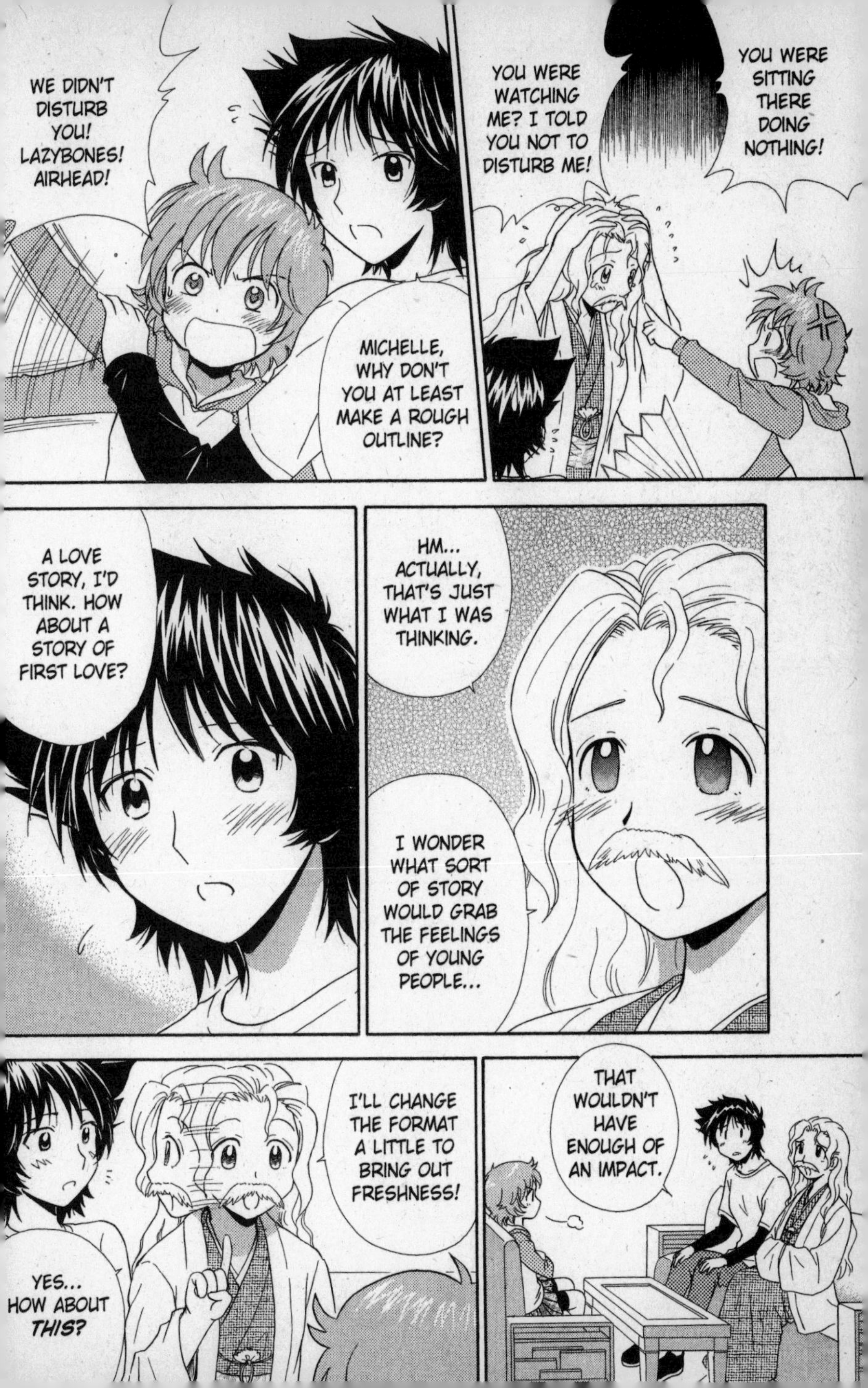
YOU WERE SITTING THERE DOING NOTHING!
YOU WERE WATCHING ME? I TOLD YOU NOT TO DISTURB ME!
WE DIDN'T DISTURB YOU! LAZYBONES! AIRHEAD!
MICHELLE, WHY DON'T YOU AT LEAST MAKE A ROUGH OUTLINE?
HM... ACTUALLY, THAT'S JUST WHAT I WAS THINKING.
I WONDER WHAT SORT OF STORY WOULD GRAB THE FEELINGS OF YOUNG PEOPLE...
A LOVE STORY, I'D THINK. HOW ABOUT A STORY OF FIRST LOVE?
THAT WOULDN'T HAVE ENOUGH OF AN IMPACT.
I'LL CHANGE THE FORMAT A LITTLE TO BRING OUT FRESHNESS!
YES... HOW ABOUT *THIS*?

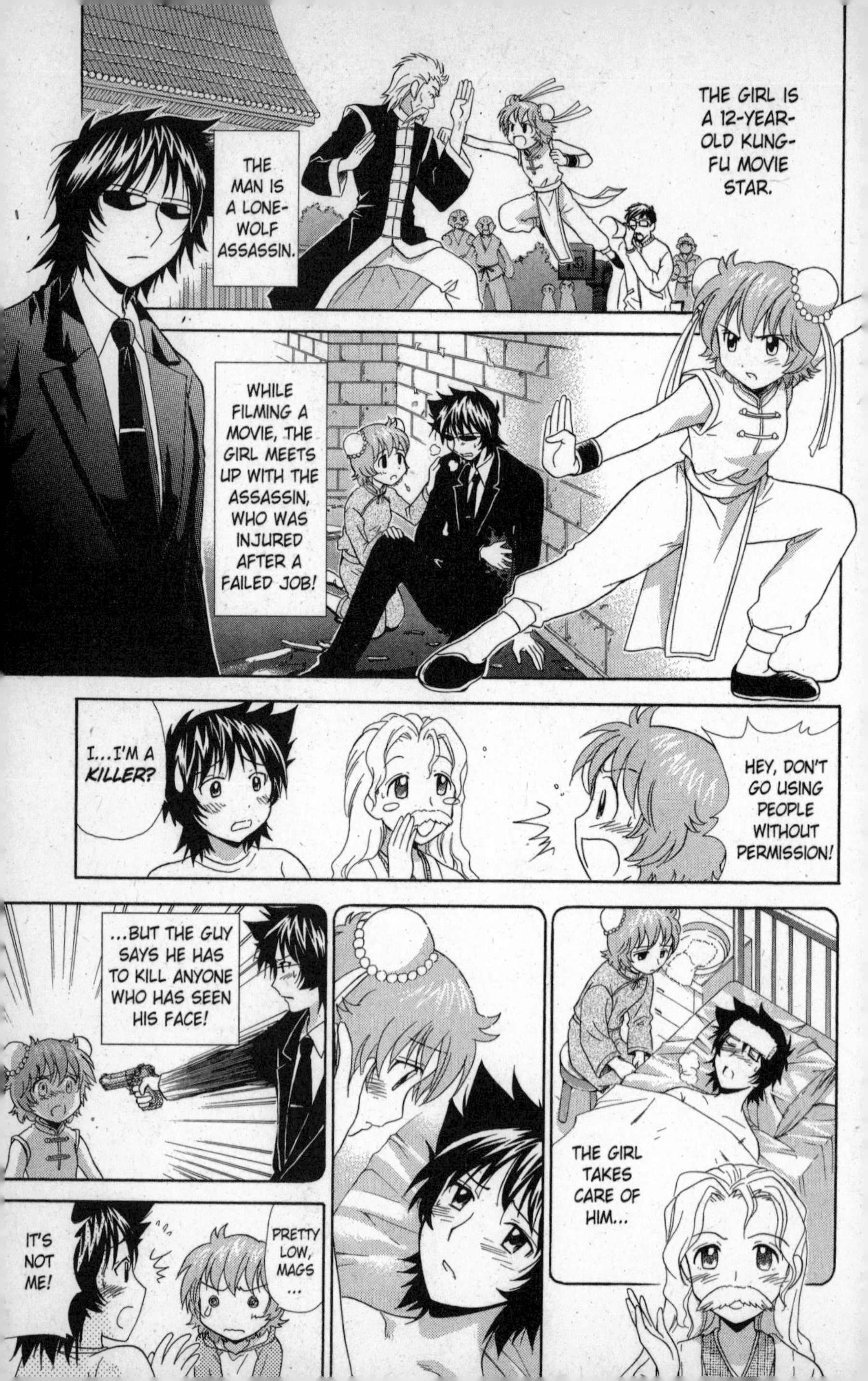
THE GIRL IS A 12-YEAR-OLD KUNG-FU MOVIE STAR.
THE MAN IS A LONE-WOLF ASSASSIN.
WHILE FILMING A MOVIE, THE GIRL MEETS UP WITH THE ASSASSIN, WHO WAS INJURED AFTER A FAILED JOB!
HEY, DON'T GO USING PEOPLE WITHOUT PERMISSION!
I...I'M A *KILLER?*
THE GIRL TAKES CARE OF HIM...
...BUT THE GUY SAYS HE HAS TO KILL ANYONE WHO HAS SEEN HIS FACE!
PRETTY LOW, MAGS...
IT'S NOT ME!

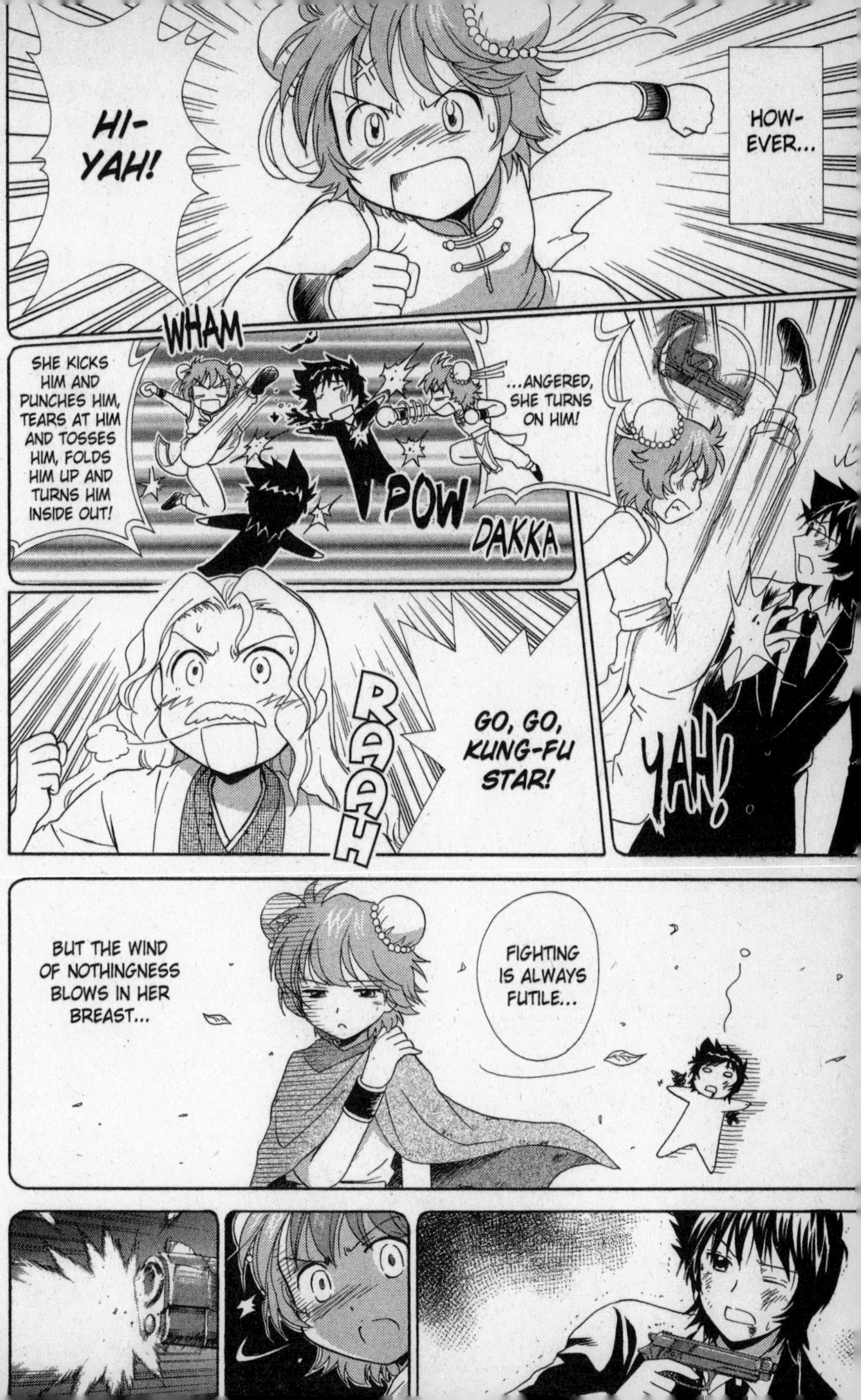
HOW-EVER...
HI-YAH!
YAH!
...ANGERED, SHE TURNS ON HIM!
WHAM
SHE KICKS HIM AND PUNCHES HIM, TEARS AT HIM AND TOSSES HIM, FOLDS HIM UP AND TURNS HIM INSIDE OUT!
POW
DAKKA
GO, GO, KUNG-FU STAR!
RAAAH
FIGHTING IS ALWAYS FUTILE...
BUT THE WIND OF NOTHINGNESS BLOWS IN HER BREAST...

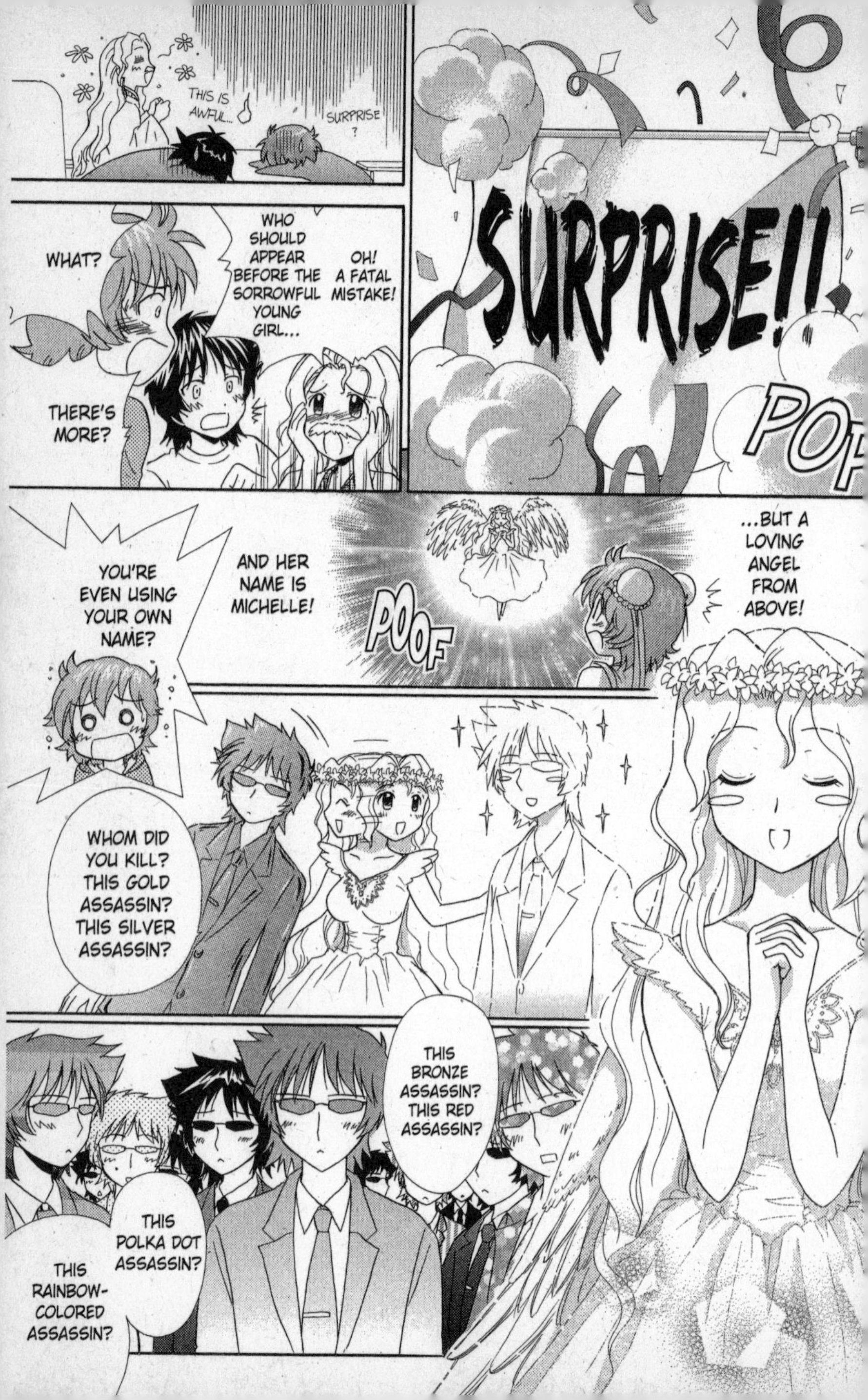
SURPRISE!!
POP
THIS IS AWFUL...
SURPRISE?
OH! A FATAL MISTAKE!
WHO SHOULD APPEAR BEFORE THE SORROWFUL YOUNG GIRL...
WHAT?
THERE'S MORE?
...BUT A LOVING ANGEL FROM ABOVE!
POOF
AND HER NAME IS MICHELLE!
YOU'RE EVEN USING YOUR OWN NAME?
WHOM DID YOU KILL? THIS GOLD ASSASSIN? THIS SILVER ASSASSIN?
THIS BRONZE ASSASSIN? THIS RED ASSASSIN?
THIS POLKA DOT ASSASSIN?
THIS RAINBOW-COLORED ASSASSIN?

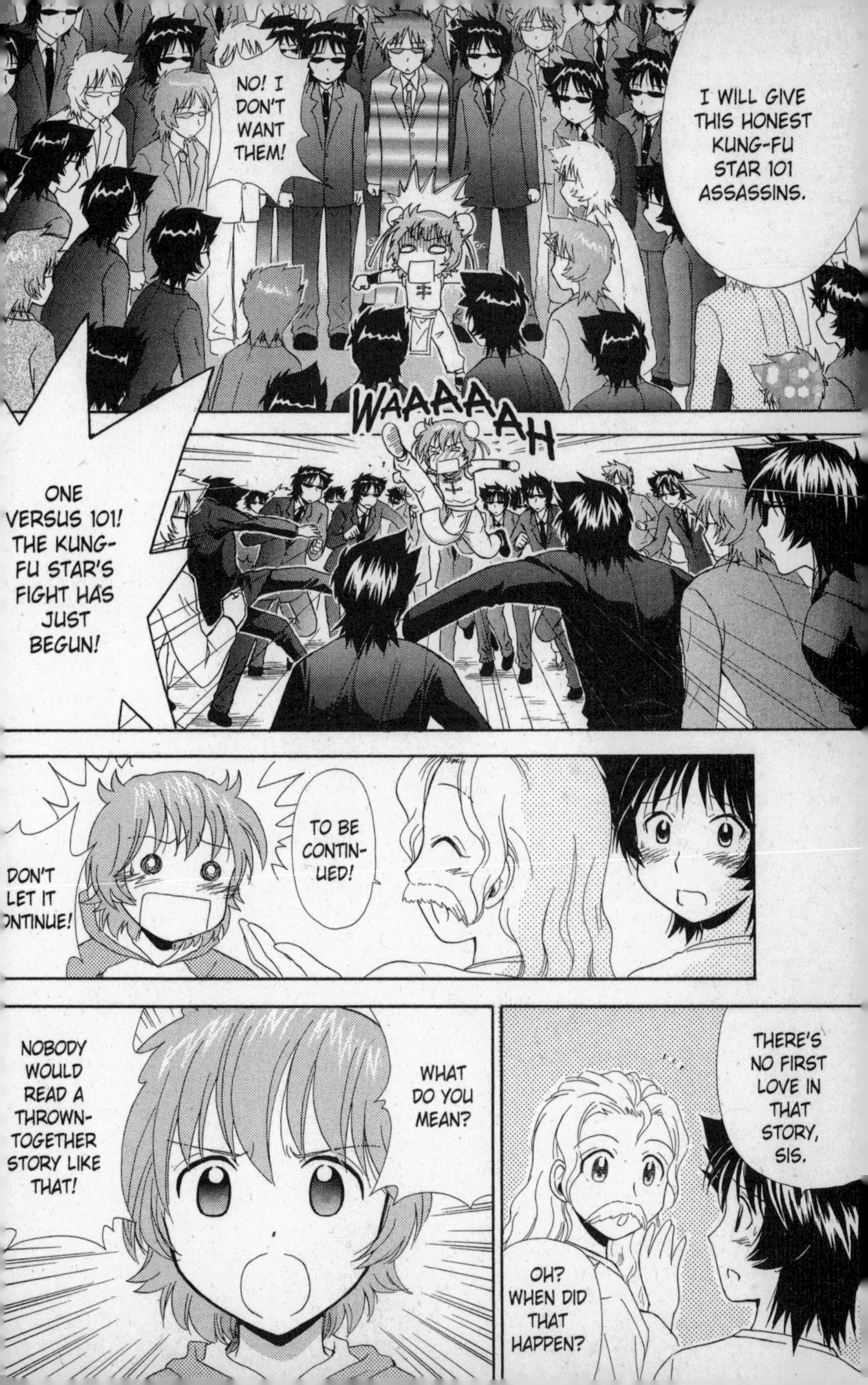
I WILL GIVE THIS HONEST KUNG-FU STAR 101 ASSASSINS.
NO! I DON'T WANT THEM!
WAAAAAH
ONE VERSUS 101! THE KUNG-FU STAR'S FIGHT HAS JUST BEGUN!
TO BE CONTIN-UED!
DON'T LET IT ONTINUE!
THERE'S NO FIRST LOVE IN THAT STORY, SIS.
OH? WHEN DID THAT HAPPEN?
WHAT DO YOU MEAN?
NOBODY WOULD READ A THROWN-TOGETHER STORY LIKE THAT!

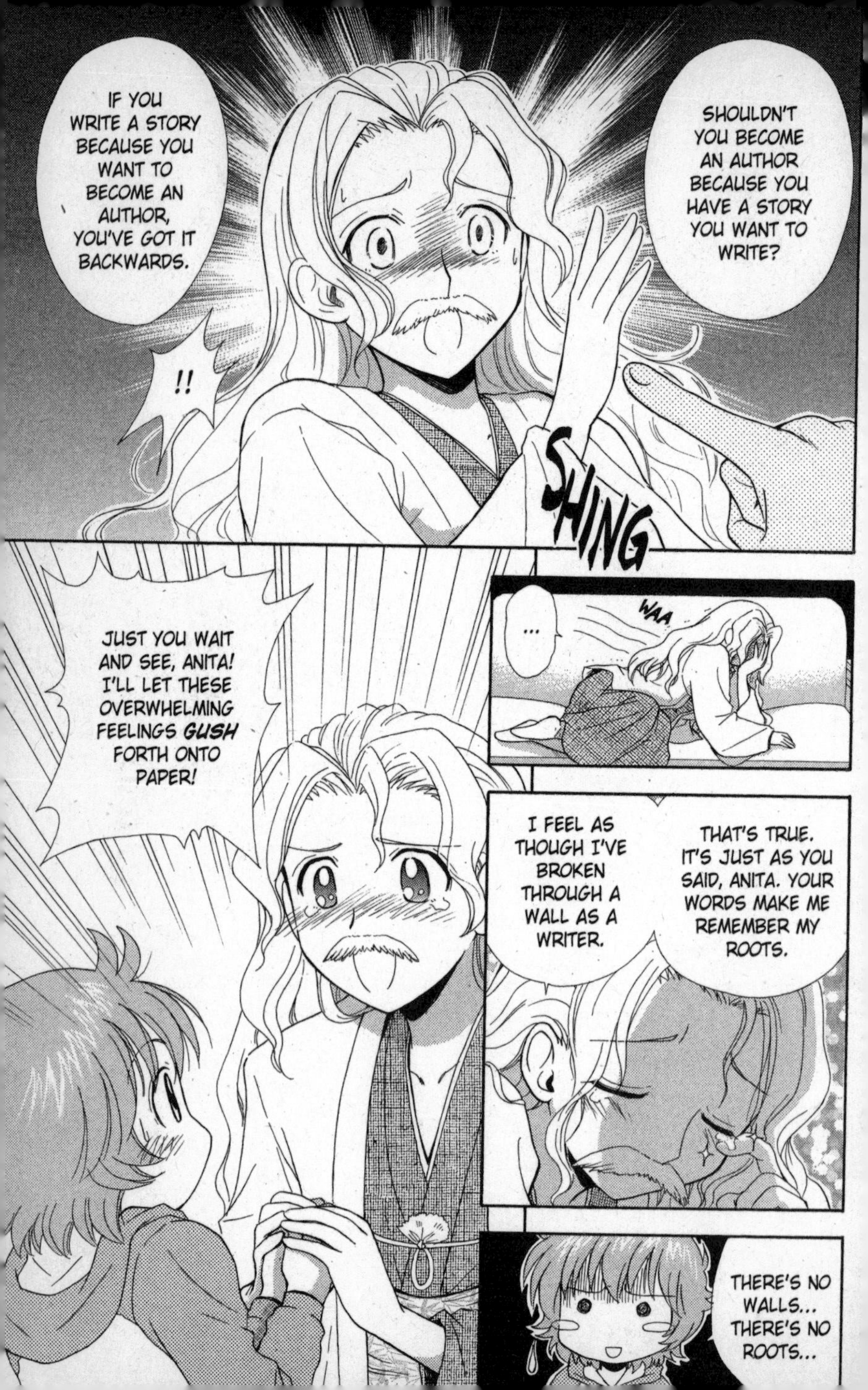
SHOULDN'T YOU BECOME AN AUTHOR BECAUSE YOU HAVE A STORY YOU WANT TO WRITE?
IF YOU WRITE A STORY BECAUSE YOU WANT TO BECOME AN AUTHOR, YOU'VE GOT IT BACKWARDS.
!!
SHING
WAA
...
THAT'S TRUE. IT'S JUST AS YOU SAID, ANITA. YOUR WORDS MAKE ME REMEMBER MY ROOTS.
I FEEL AS THOUGH I'VE BROKEN THROUGH A WALL AS A WRITER.
THERE'S NO WALLS... THERE'S NO ROOTS...
JUST YOU WAIT AND SEE, ANITA! I'LL LET THESE OVERWHELMING FEELINGS GUSH FORTH ONTO PAPER!

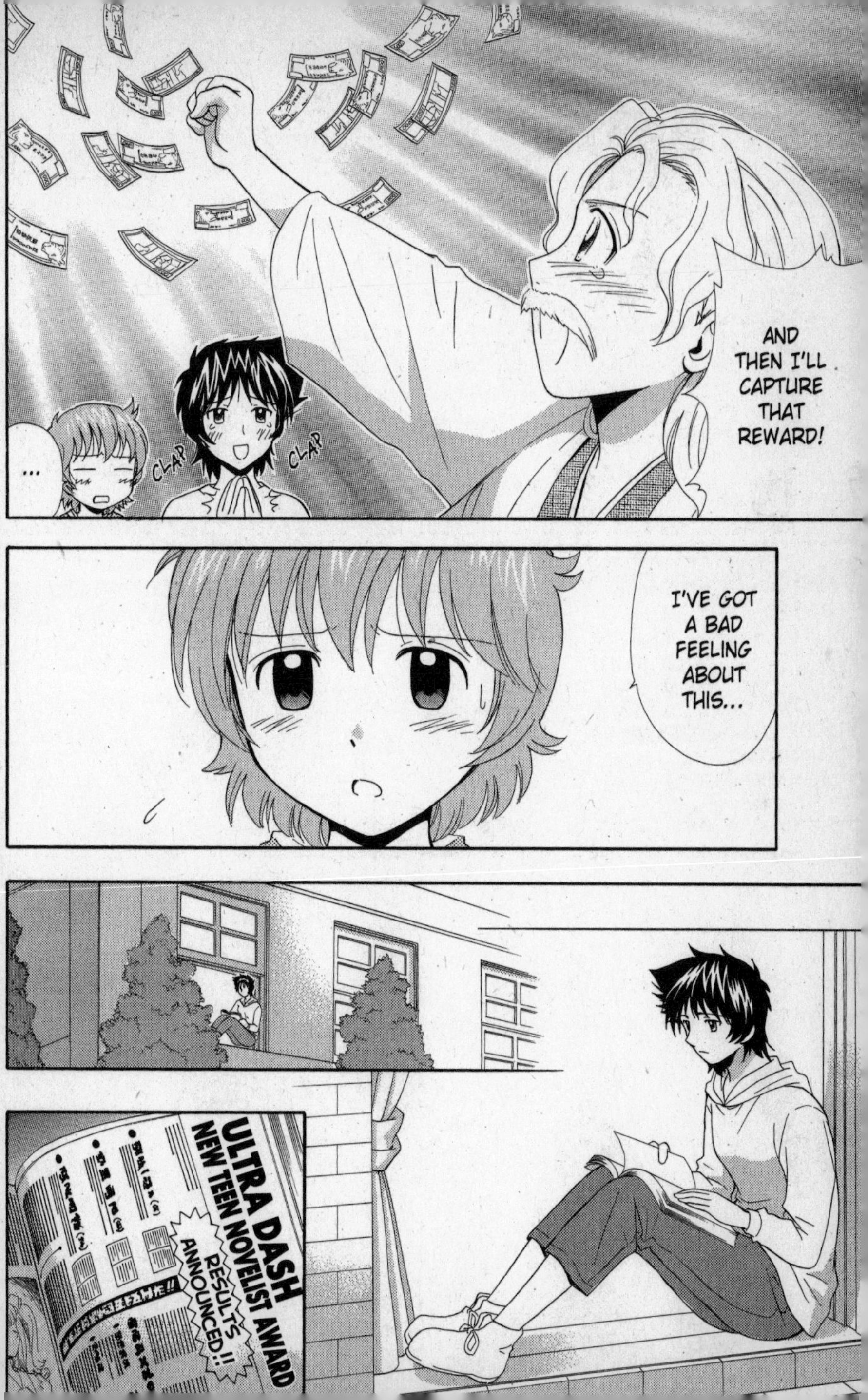
AND THEN I'LL CAPTURE THAT REWARD!
CLAP
CLAP
...
I'VE GOT A BAD FEELING ABOUT THIS...
ULTRA DASH NEW TEEN NOVELIST AWARD
RESULTS ANNOUNCED!!

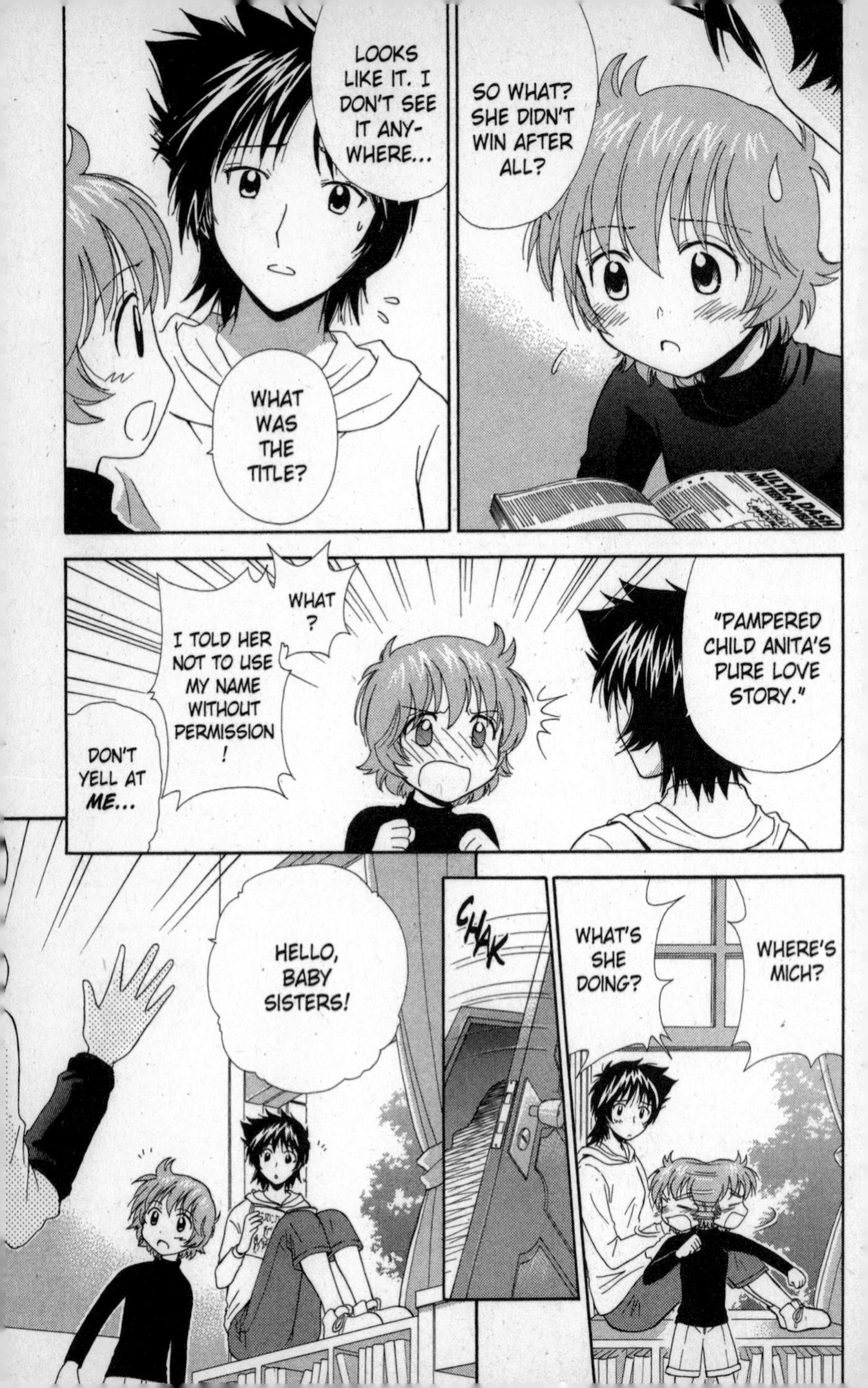
SO WHAT? SHE DIDN'T WIN AFTER ALL?
LOOKS LIKE IT. I DON'T SEE IT ANY-WHERE...
WHAT WAS THE TITLE?
"PAMPERED CHILD ANITA'S PURE LOVE STORY."
WHAT?
I TOLD HER NOT TO USE MY NAME WITHOUT PERMISSION!
DON'T YELL AT ME...
WHERE'S MICH?
WHAT'S SHE DOING?
CHAK
HELLO, BABY SISTERS!

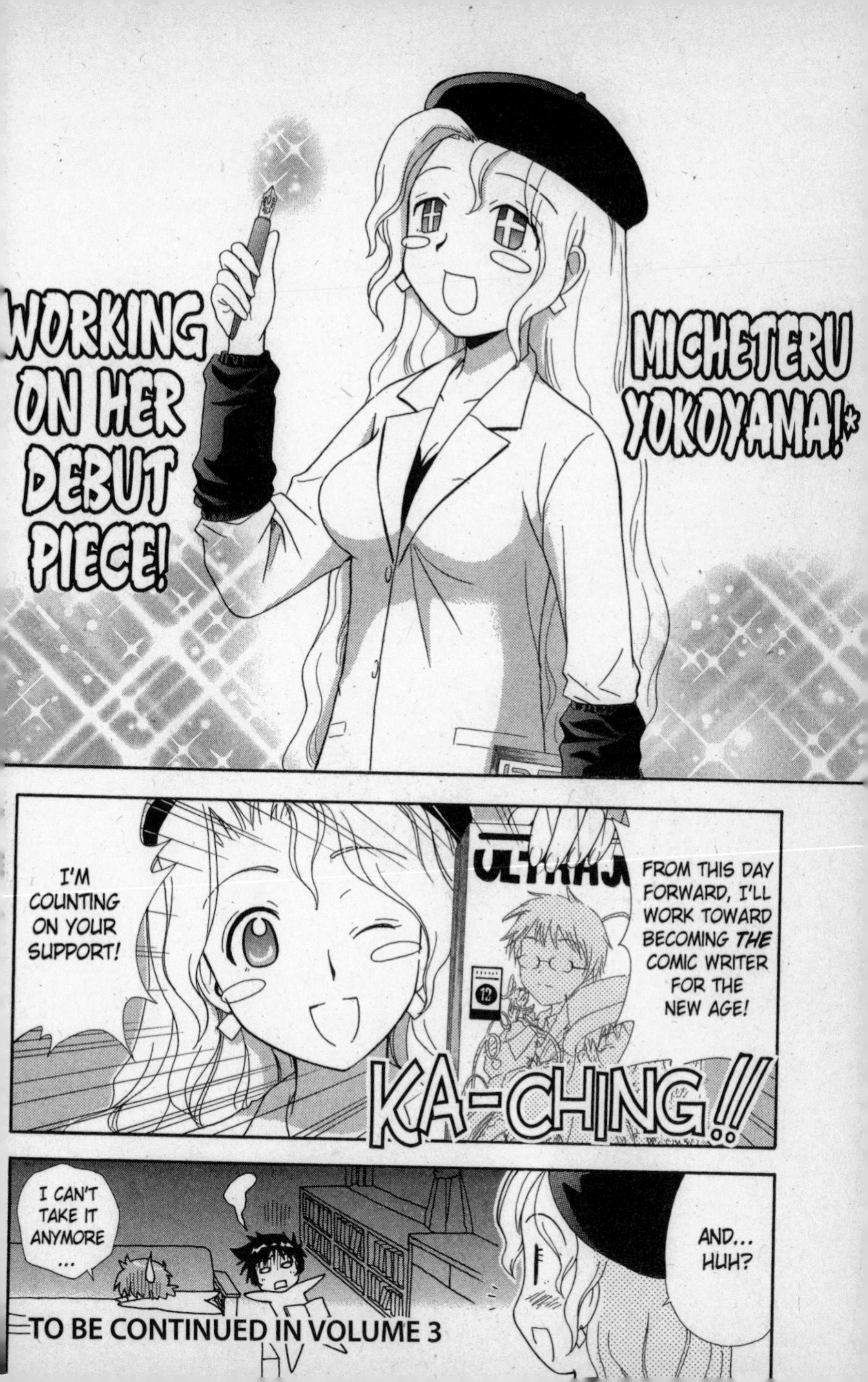
MICHETERU YOKOYAMA!*
WORKING ON HER DEBUT PIECE!
FROM THIS DAY FORWARD, I'LL WORK TOWARD BECOMING *THE* COMIC WRITER FOR THE NEW AGE!
I'M COUNTING ON YOUR SUPPORT!
KA-CHING!!
AND... HUH?
I CAN'T TAKE IT ANYMORE ...
TO BE CONTINUED IN VOLUME 3

STAFF

Yasuyo Hirokane
Ai Udagawa
Taichi Sotoyama

EDITOR
Kunio Kondo

SPECIAL THANKS
Akihiro Yamada
MAGI

(Acknowledgements deleted...)

Ran Ayanaga

http://members.jcom.home.ne.jp/0724236901/

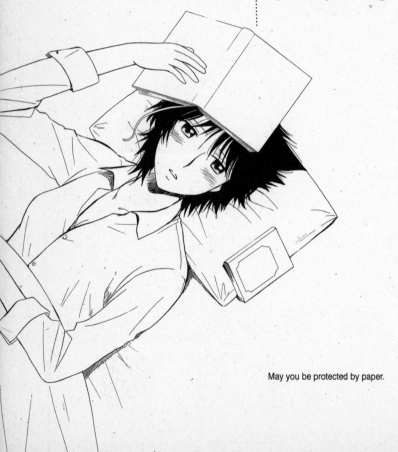

May you be protected by paper.

R.O.D -THE TV-

•AYANAGA WORKS•

THESE ARE THE ORIGINAL DESIGNS BY MS. AYANAGA USED IN THE CREATION OF THE R.O.D. TV SERIES!

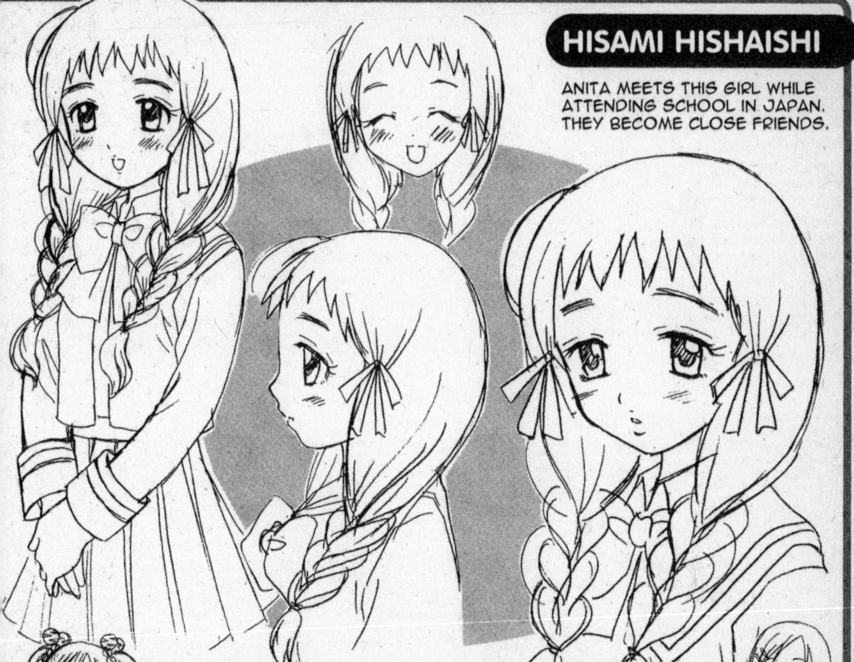

HISAMI HISHAISHI

ANITA MEETS THIS GIRL WHILE ATTENDING SCHOOL IN JAPAN. THEY BECOME CLOSE FRIENDS.

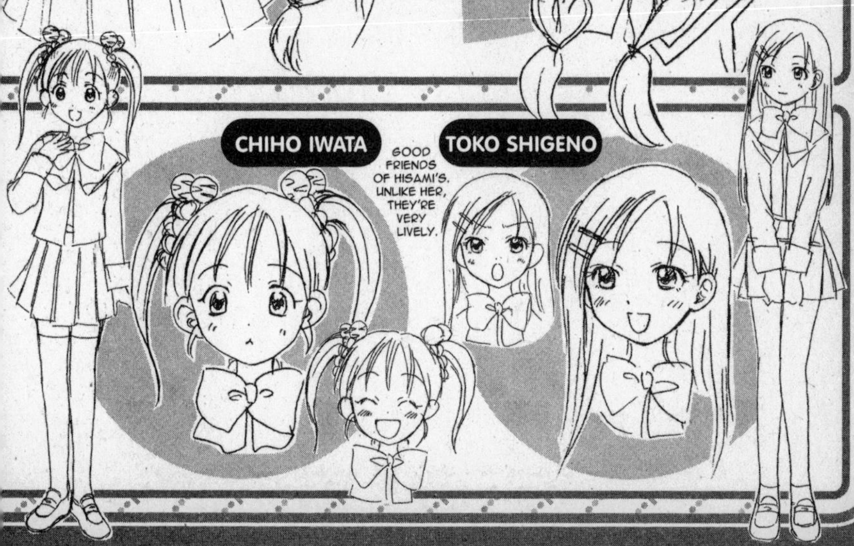

CHIHO IWATA

TOKO SHIGENO

GOOD FRIENDS OF HISAMI'S. UNLIKE HER, THEY'RE VERY LIVELY.

TORU OKAHARA

HE'S ALWAYS PICKING ON HISAMI. HE SEEMS TO HAVE A CRUSH ON HER.

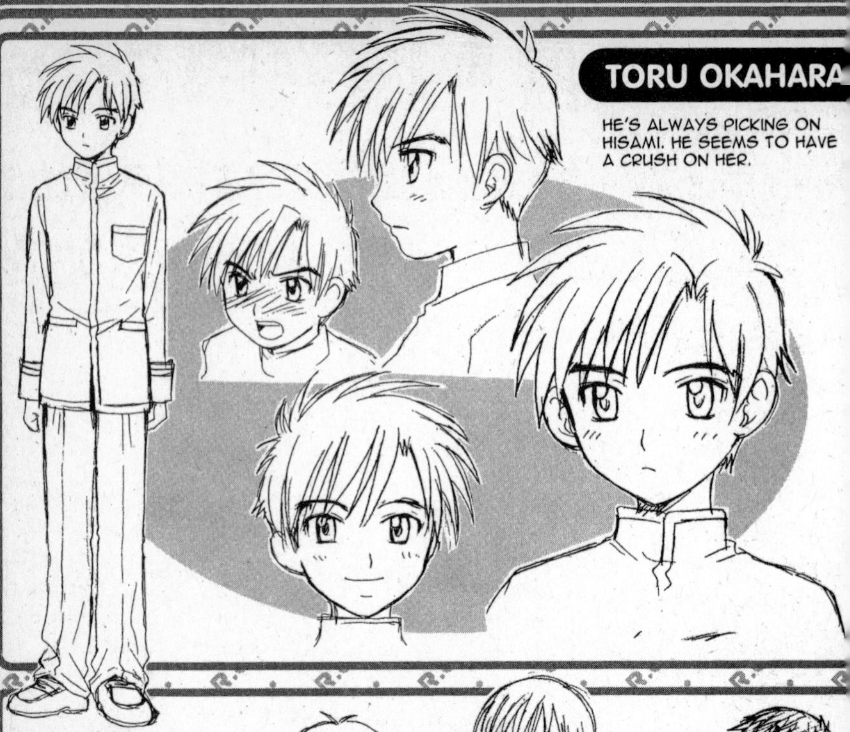

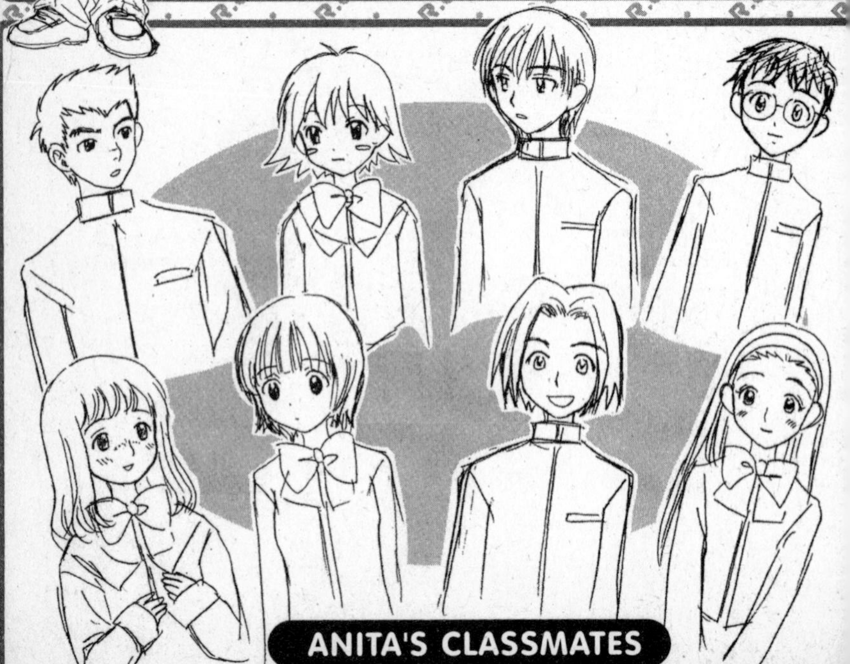

ANITA'S CLASSMATES

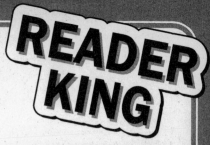

READER KING

ɔr these bonus pages, we kidnapped Director Masunari, ʼho's in a mad rush to finish the anime version of R.O.D, from ıe recording studio, along with Producer Ochikoshi, whose eart is filled with thoughts of production, and writer Kurata, ho has a deadline in just three days. There were smiles on ıeir faces, but in their hearts, they were surely annoyed. Like ıe adults they are, they acted polite.**

ditor: Oh, you must all be exhausted.
irector: I **am** tired right now.
urata: Absolutely.
chikoshi: Ha ha ha. What shall we order?
ditor: I'll have the curried fried rice and iced coffee that's listed ɔ on that wall.
irector: I'll have the same.
urata: Me, too.
chikoshi: Listen, everybody...at least open up the menu. Let's ɔt have four of the same.
ll: You, too?

ʼhat's become of Aya Ueto[1]?

ditor: Well, shall we begin? How's the anime series coming ong?
urata: What can I say? We're still working on it.
irector: We're now at the best part. (This is February 2004 and ıe anime is heading toward the final episode.)
chikoshi: We're getting good comments about it.
irector: About **Fullmetal**[2]?
chikoshi: How could you mention that here?
urata: Well, when the TV verson of **R.O.D** came out, there was big hullabaloo just before it aired. "Why aren't you using ɔmiko?"[3] Of course, we were.
ditor: Yomiko's popularity is deep-rooted. Come to think of it, hen we did a magazine poll, there was someone who sent in) postcards with her name on it.
urata: Really? That's gratifying to hear.
irector: I haven't sent a fan letter since the days of Midori nouchi.[4]
urata: You wrote to her? But why Midori Kinouchi?
irector: Lately, I like Kodaka Kei. But it seems like whenever I ecome a fan of someone, their popularity begins to wane.
chikoshi: Does that mean that Aya Ueto is in danger?
ditor: Aya Ueto and Midori Kinouchi...You like **anybody**, don't ɔu?

ıe story of the three sisters started with a possible story ɔout Tibet.

ditor: By the way, how did you decide on the personalities of ıe three sisters?
urata: I guess through discussions. They took shape as the ory went along.
irector: We took hints from Hane's illustrations to flesh out the ıaracters.
urata: Yes. Something like that...I wanted to use the phrase ʼaper Sisters," so I decided to create three sisters. At that time, asunari was working on **Heart Library**, so we had to make sure ıe characters' personalities didn't overlap.

R.O.D THE ANIMATION AND R.O.D THE GRAPHIC NOVEL... ARE THEY YIN AND YANG? POLAR OPPOSITES?

PROFILES

KOJI MASUNARI
HE IS OBVIOUSLY THE **R.O.D** DIRECTOR. HIS ANIME WORK INCLUDES **RISKY SAFETY** AND **HEART LIBRARY.** HE HAS THE SUPERHUMAN ABILITY MAKE HIS ACTORS PERFORM SUPERBLY ENOUGH TO MAKE FANS WRITHE IN ECSTASY.

HIDEYUKI KURATA
AUTHOR AND SCREENWRITER. BESIDES **R.O.D,** HIS WORKS INCLUDE **BATTLE ATHLETES VICTORY, TRAIN + TRAIN, CLOTH ROAD,** AND MANY OTHERS. FIND OUT MORE IN **ULTRA JUMP** MAGAZINE.

TOMONORI OCHIKOSHI
A VERY CAPABLE PRODUCER FROM ANIPLEX, INC. HE'S A BUSINESSMAN WHO HAS BEEN WORKING TO BUILD SOMETHING GREAT FROM **R.O.D** ALTHOUGH HE'S THE YOUNGEST OF THIS GROUP, HE APPEARS TO BE THE ELDEST.

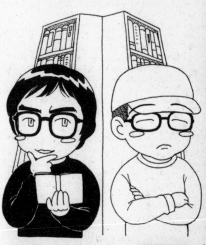

Director: That story about the space alien? I wondered what in the world you were doing. (Laughter)

Kurata: Space aliens are a specialty I often fall back upon. (Laughter)

Editor: Now that you mention it, Ms. Ayanaga said that when she first saw the animation, she was cowed by the movements of the three sisters. But it looks like she knows what she's doing now.

Kurata: Is that so?

Director: It's a learning experience for me, too.

Kurata: As the writer of the original story, having everyone influencing each other in a positive way is more than I can ask for.

Ochikoshi: In the anime version, Ms. Ayanaga has helped us out by creating the original character designs. Please buy the DVD and check them out.

Will demons laugh? [5]

Editor: And do you have any plans for the sequel that everyone's wondering about?

Director: Well, we're still in the middle of production, so…

Kurata: We'll think about it after this one is done. What we do know at this point is that R.O.D still worked even when we switched the main characters from Yomiko to the three sisters, so I think there's room for change in the next version. But, actually, it all depends on what Aniplex decides to do. (Laughter)

Ochikoshi: By all means, do that. And in order to make this a great work, we would like everyone to please buy the DVD. (Laughter)

All: Enough, already… (Laughter)

Well, it's almost time to go…

Editor: Then shall we wrap things up?

Kurata: The novel and manga versions of R.O.D are still continuing,[6] so I hope you will all keep supporting us.

Ochikoshi: Whatever you do, please buy our DVD.

Director: By the way just how much money did Aniplex make on ▓▓▓▓▓▓▓, anyway?

Ochikoshi: Well…ha ha ha…

Editor: Whatever you do…

All: …please continue to support us.

---

1. A popular actress.

2. The immensely successful **Fullmetal Alchemist** anime series came out at about the same time as the **R.O.D** anime series.

3. There are two **R.O.D** anime. The first was a three-episode OVA (original video animation) featuring Yomiko Readman, who also appears as the main character in the **Read or Die** manga. Later, Aniplex produced a television anime series based loosely on the **Read or Dream** manga. The TV series is the main topic of discussion in this interview.

4. Another popular actress.

5. An old Japanese adage says, "If you talk about next year, demons will laugh." It's similar to the English saying, "Don't count your chickens before they're hatched."

6. R.O.D started as a series of novels published by Super Dash, the prose imprint of manga publisher Shueisha (which also publishes the R.O.D manga). "Ultra Dash," the publisher to which Michelle sends her novel in Chapter 15, is a reference to Super Dash.

(Laughter)

Director: In the end, almost everything we decided on at our overnighters got changed, even the Tibetan story.

Kurata: Oh, yes…There was a story set in Tibet, wasn't there?

Director: We ended up using the TV show **I Love Cats, After All** for ideas, as Kurata had asked us to, and came up with three sisters with rather unusual personalities.

Ochikoshi: Did you all notice that the placement of the furnitur▓ in Nenene's living room is the same as that in **I Love Cats, After All**? Please buy the DVD and check it out.

Kurata: Who are you talking to?

Director: That's a capable producer for you…

Do we have any "bonds"?

Editor: Because it was designed after **I Love Cats, After All**, this work seems to have a very different tone from the previous **R.O.** stories with Yomiko.

Director: Well, it would've been impossible to do 26 episodes of that OVA version on television (laughter), so we created a more dialogue-based story, with action woven in.

Kurata: If we'd had only dialogue, there would've been a lot of blank spaces. Those three spend all their time reading, you know (Laughter)

Director: The main motif--or theme, rather--was "bonds." In the previous work, we dug deep into the bonds of friendship between Yomiko and Nancy, but this time, we made the theme "family bonds." That's probably the reason it feels so different.

Editor: Why did you decide to stick to "bonds"?

Kurata: In the case of familial love, even if there's resentment or hatred, things can be settled with love, wouldn't you say? I wanted to take something more cut and dried--bonds between two individuals.

Editor: Was there anything you had to watch out for when writing on such a theme?

Kurata: Within family units, there aren't any major crises aside from births, deaths and marriages. Even if something major happens, you can forgive and forget…I'd like people to watch t▓ bonds deepen as they go about their ordinary lives.

Editor: As to that, Masunari has a magical touch when it comes getting the characters to bring out the little nuances in their everyday lives. Take the scene where Yomiko returns…

Director: Well, I have trouble with action scenes…actually, I car do them at all. (Laughter)

Kurata: I'd say he's unsurpassed in portraying reality. I would lik▓ the viewers to look for that as well.

Ochikoshi: The scene where Yomiko and Nenene reunite is a moving one, and it does a wonderful job of depicting the hopelessness of bookworms who aren't able to even run up a flight of stairs. Please look for it on your DVD.

It's not easy to speak when the subject isn't here.

Editor: Director, what do you think of the manga version?

Director: In one word, "cute." At first, I thought the sisters were like spoiled brats, but their personalities evolved very nicely.

Kurata: This was the first project I'd done with Ran Ayanaga, so▓ the beginning, there was a little hesitancy between us. It wasn'▓ until Chapter 7 that I think we began to understand each other (Laughter)

BONUS STORY:
CLEANING UP DEMONS
WITH ANITA THE CLEANER

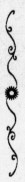

"HA HA HA...I AM THE EVIL MAGIC MAGGIE!"

IN THE MANSION, A FIGURE COVERED IN BLACK WAS LAUGHING. IT WAS MAGGIE. SHE HAD BEEN POSSESSED BY A DEMON THAT JUMPED OUT OF A BOX THAT HER GRANDFATHER HAD LEFT FOR HER.

"HA HA HA...IT'S TOO LATE TODAY, BUT TOMORROW I'LL BUY UP ALL THE SWEETS IN THIS TOWN!"

OH, NO! IF THAT HAPPENED, WHAT WOULD THE CHILDREN HAVE FOR THEIR SNACKS?

"HELLO THERE!" ANITA CAME FLYING INTO THE MANSION ON HER SPARKLING BROOM. BEHIND HER WAS MICHELLE THE FAIRY.

"YIKES!" SAID ANITA. "SHE'S BLACK ALL OVER!"

"BE CAREFUL, ANITA!" SAID MICHELLE.

MAGGIE WAS STARTLED TO SEE ANITA AND MICHELLE SUDDENLY APPEAR. "HMPH! WHO ARE YOU TWO?"

"I'M ANITA THE CHIMNEYSWEEP," ANITA ANSWERED, HOVERING IN MIDAIR. BECAUSE SHE ALWAYS WORKED ON ROOFTOPS, HER SENSE OF BALANCE WAS HIGHLY DEVELOPED. "I'M HERE AT MICHELLE'S REQUEST, TO CLEAN OUT YOUR HEART, MAGGIE."

"HEH HEH...RIDICULOUS. DO YOU REALLY THINK YOU CAN CLEAN OUT MY HEART WITH THAT RAGGED BROOM?"

"WHAT DID YOU SAY? MY BROOM IS THE BEST IN TOWN! THERE'S NOTHING IT CAN'T CLEAN!"

BUT TO USE THAT BROOM, ANITA REALIZED, SHE WOULD HAVE TO LAND. IF SHE DID THAT, LITTLE ANITA WOULD QUICKLY BE CAUGHT BY BIG MAGGIE.

"OH, NO!" SAID ANITA. "WHAT SHOULD I DO?"

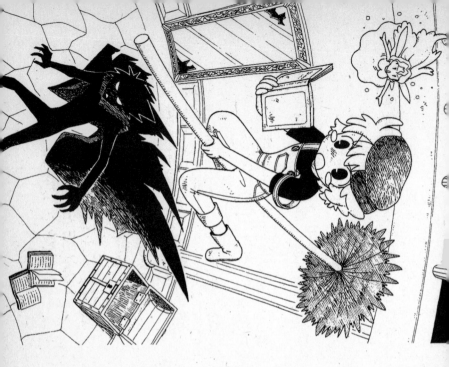

"DON'T WORRY, ANITA. IN THE BOX HER GRANDFATHER LEFT HER, THERE IS AN INCANTATION THAT WILL MAKE MAGGIE UNABLE TO MOVE. IT CAN BE READ ONLY BY SOMEONE WITH A PURE HEART. THAT IS WHY I BROUGHT YOU HERE."

APPARENTLY, THOUGHT ANITA, MICHELLE'S HEART WASN'T VERY PURE. "OKAY. JUST LEAVE IT TO ME."

ANITA DESCENDED ON HER BROOM AND HEADED FOR THE BOX.

"I WON'T LET YOU DO IT!" CRIED MAGGIE, LEAPING TOWARD ANITA. MICHELLE SWEPT DOWN AND FLUTTERED HER WINGS IN FRONT OF THE POSSESSED GIRL.

"OH!" CRIED MAGGIE. "YOU'RE BLINDING ME!"

WITH MAGGIE DISTRACTED, ANITA PICKED UP THE BOOK. BALANCING ON HER BROOM, SHE OPENED THE BOOK AND BEGAN TO READ THE INCANTATION.

"BLACK SHADOW, EVIL HEART, BE GLUED TO THE FLOOR!"

"UGH...I CAN'T MOVE!" MAGGIE CAME TO A STANDSTILL.

TO BE CONTINUED...

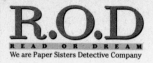

R.O.D

READ OR DREAM

We are Paper Sisters Detective Company

VIZ Media Edition
Vol. 2

STORY BY HIDEYUKI KURATA
ART BY RAN AYANAGA

Translation/JN Productions
Touch-up Art & Lettering/Mark McMurray
Design/Amy Martin
Editor/Shaenon K. Garrity

Managing Editor/Annette Roman
Editorial Director/Elizabeth Kawasaki
Editor in Chief/Alvin Lu
Sr. Director of Acquisitions/Rika Inouye
Sr. VP of Marketing/Liza Coppola
Exec. VP of Sales & Marketing/John Easum
Publisher/Hyoe Narita

Printed in the U.S.A.

Published by VIZ Media, LLC
P.O. Box 77010
San Francisco, CA 94107

10 9 8 7 6 5 4 3 2 1
First printing, January 2007

www.viz.com   store.viz.com

Not Your Run-of-the-Mill Bookworm

Yomiko has a supernatural ability to manipulate paper—she can turn scraps into daggers or make a single sheet hard enough to block bullets! But can her power protect legendary books with secret information before they fall into dangerously wrong hands?

Curl up with *Read or Die* manga—buy yours today at **store.viz.com!**

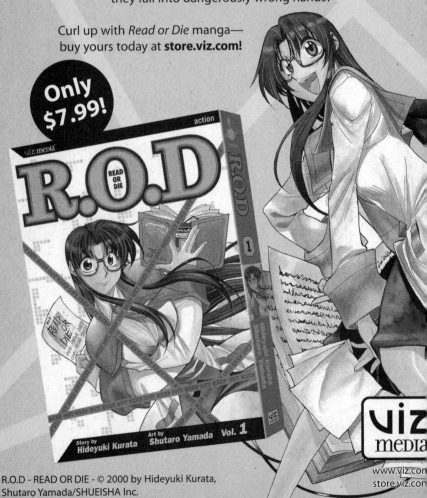

GA?
YOU THINK!

OUR MANGA SURVEY IS NOW AVAILABLE ONLINE. PLEASE VISIT: VIZ.COM/MANGASURVEY

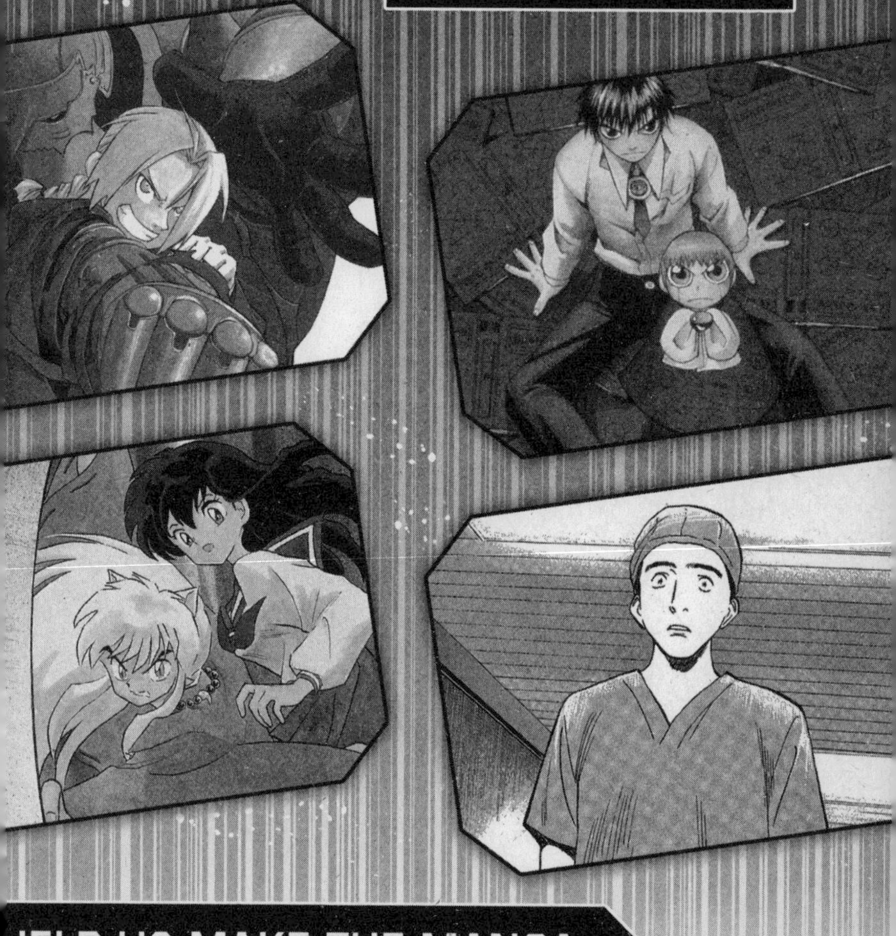

HELP US MAKE THE MANGA YOU LOVE BETTER!

VIZ media

R.O.D
READ OR DREAM
We are Paper Sisters Detective Company

2

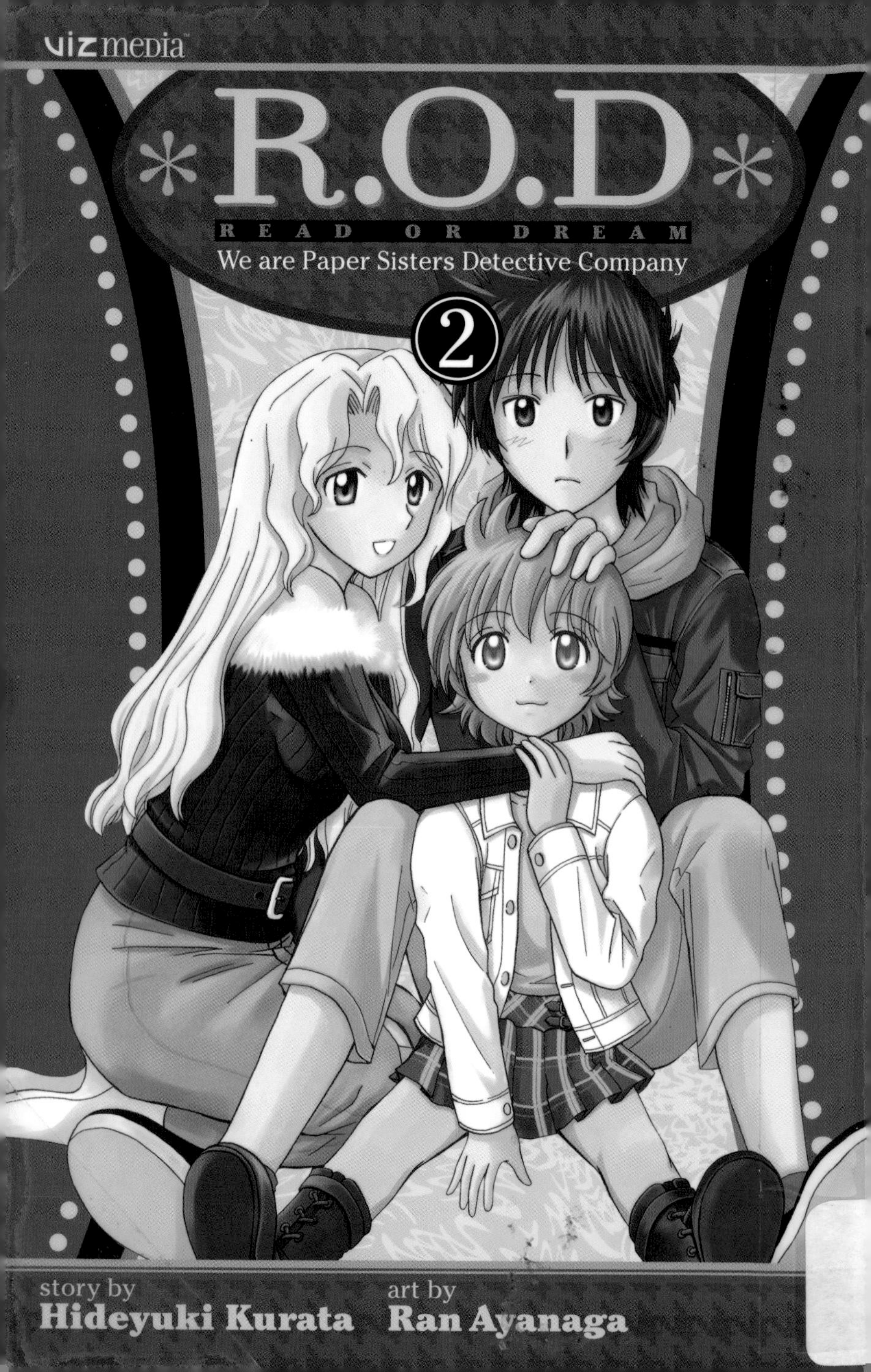

story by
Hideyuki Kurata

art by
Ran Ayanaga

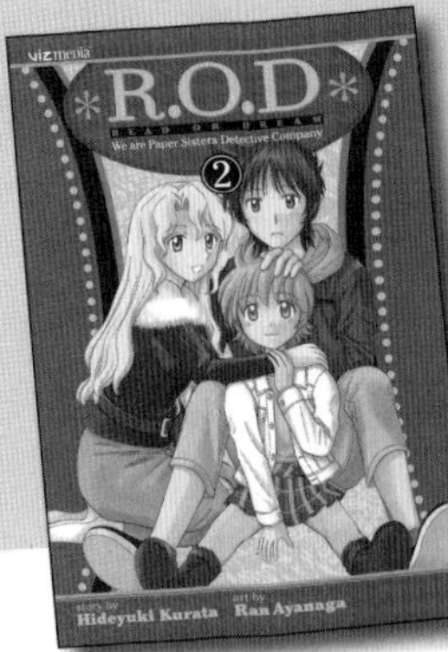
viz media
R.O.D
We are Paper Sisters Detective Company
2
story by Hideyuki Kurata art by Ran Ayanaga

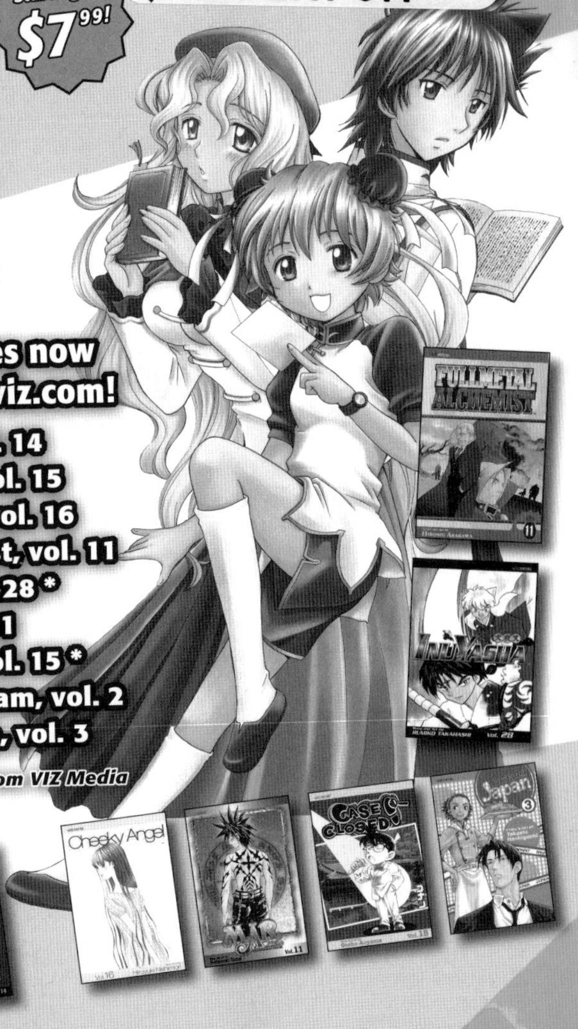
FULLMETAL ALCHEMIST
INUYASHA
Cheeky Angel
CASE CLOSED
Japan
PROJECT ARMS
BASTARD!!